LONG-TERM CARE:
ECONOMIC ISSUES AND POLICY SOLUTIONS

Developments in Health Economics and Public Policy

VOLUME 5

Series Editors
Peter Zweifel, *University of Zürich, Switzerland*
H.E. Frech III, *University of California, Santa Barbara, U.S.A.*

The titles published in this series are listed at the end of this volume.

LONG-TERM CARE: ECONOMIC ISSUES AND POLICY SOLUTIONS

Edited by

Roland Eisen
Johann Wolfgang Goethe-Universität,
Frankfurt am Main

Frank A. Sloan
Duke University
Durham, North Carolina

KLUWER ACADEMIC PUBLISHERS
Boston / Dordrecht / London

Distributors for North America:
Kluwer Academic Publishers
101 Philip Drive
Assinippi Park
Norwell, Massachusetts 02061 USA

Distributors for all other countries:
Kluwer Academic Publishers Group
Distribution Centre
Post Office Box 322
3300 AH Dordrecht, THE NETHERLANDS

Library of Congress Cataloging-in-Publication Data

A C.I.P. Catalogue record for this book is available from
the Library of Congress.

Copyright © 1996 by Kluwer Academic Publishers

All rights reserved. No part of this publication may be reproduced, stored in a retrieval system or transmitted in any form or by any means, mechanical, photo-copying, recording, or otherwise, without the prior written permission of the publisher, Kluwer Academic Publishers, 101 Philip Drive, Assinippi Park, Norwell, Massachusetts 02061.

Printed on acid-free paper

Printed in the United States of America

Contents

Contributing Authors and Participants vii

Introduction
Roland Eisen and Frank A. Sloan 1

Part One: International Comparisons

1. An International Comparison of Trends in Disability-Free
   Life Expectancy
   Emmanuelle Cambois and Jean-Marie Robine 11

2. Possibilities and Problems in a Cross-Country Comparative Analysis
   of Long-Term Care Systems
   Trond O. Edvartsen 25

Part Two: Empirical Research into the Demand and Provision of Long-Term Care Services

3. Effects of Strategic Behavior and Public Subsidies on Families' Savings
   and Long-Term Care Decisions
   Frank A. Sloan, Thomas J. Hoerger and Gabriel Picone 45

4. Women's Role in the Provision of Long-Term Care, Financial Incentives,
   and the Future Financing of Long-Term Care
   Sandra Nocera and Peter Zweifel 79

5. Determinants of Institutionalization in Old Age
   Thomas Klein 103

6. The Impact of the Community Long-Term Care Insurance Law
   on Services for the Elderly in Israel
   Denise Naon 115

7. The Effect of Public Provision of Home Care on Living and Care
   Arrangements: Evidence from the Channeling Experiment
   Peter Kemper and Liliana E. Pezzin 125

Part Three: Germany - A Model for Dealing with the Problems of Long-Term Care?

8. Social Protection for Dependence in Old Age: The Case of Germany
   Bernd Schulte 149

9. Determining the Long-Term Care Needs of Individuals Living in Private Households: Results from a Survey
   Ulrich Schneekloth 171

10. The Long-Term Costs of Public Long-Term Care Insurance in Germany. Some Guesstimates
    Winfried Schmähl and Heinz Rothgang 181

Part Four: Theoretical Issues and Policy Recommendations

11. Long-Term Care Insurance and Trust Saving in a Two-Generation Model
    Peter Zweifel and Wolfram Strüwe 225

12. Long-Term Care - An Inter- and Intragenerational Decision Model
    Roland Eisen and Hans-Christian Mager 251

13. The Assessment and the Regulation of Quality in Long-Term Care
    Gabriele Johne 285

14. Almost Optimal Social Insurance for Long-Term Care
    Mark V. Pauly 307

Subject Index 331

Contributing Authors and Participants

Prof. Dr. Norbert Andel
Johann Wolfgang Goethe-Universität
Frankfurt am Main
Institut für öffentliche Wirtschaft, Geld
und Währung
Professur für Finanzwissenschaft
D-60054 Frankfurt am Main

Andreas Besche
Verband der privaten
Krankenversicherung e.V.
Bayenthalgürtel 26
D-50968 Köln

Prof. Dr. Friedrich Breyer
Fakultät für Wirtschaftswissenschaften
und Statistik
Universitätsstraße 10
D-78434 Konstanz

Emmanuelle Cambois
Equipe INSERM Démographie et Santé
Centre Val d'Aurelle
Parc Euromédicine
F-34094 Montpellier Cedex 5

Prof. Dr. Diether Döring
Akademie der Arbeit in der Universität
Frankfurt am Main
Mertonstr. 30
D-60054 Frankfurt am Main

Trond O. Edvartsen
Johann Wolfgang Goethe-Universität
Frankfurt am Main
PflEG-Projekt
D-60054 Frankfurt am Main

Prof. Dr. Roland Eisen
Johann Wolfgang Goethe-Universität
Frankfurt am Main
Institut für Konjunktur, Wachstum und
Verteilung
Professur für Wirtschafts- und
Sozialpolitik
D-60054 Frankfurt am Main

Eckhard Häßler
Allianz Lebensversicherungs AG
Reinsburgerstraße 19
D-70178 Stuttgart

Prof. Dr. Richard Hauser
Johann Wolfgang Goethe-Universität
Frankfurt am Main
Institut für Konjunktur, Wachstum und
Verteilung
Professur für Sozialpolitik
D-60054 Frankfurt am Main

Thomas J. Hoerger
Center for Health Policy Research and
Education
125 Old Chemistry Building
Durham NC 277 08

Gabriele Johne
Universität Trier
Zentrum für Arbeit und Soziales
D-54286 Trier

Ph. D. Peter Kemper
Department of Health & Human
Services
Agency for Health Care Policy and
Research
2101 East Jefferson Street
Rockville MD 20852

Prof. Dr. Thomas Klein
Universität Heidelberg
Institut für Soziologie
Sandgasse 9
D-69117 Heidelberg

Tom J. Laetz
US General Accounting Office
Ernst Schwendler Straße 5
D-60320 Frankfurt am Main

Prof. Dr. Leonard Männer
Universität Göttingen
Abteilung für
Versicherungswissenschaft
Platz der Göttinger Sieben 3
D-37073 Göttingen

Hans-Christian Mager
Johann Wolfgang Goethe-Universität
Frankfurt am Main
PflEG-Projekt
D-60054 Frankfurt am Main

Denise Naon
Brookdale Institute of Gerontology
and Adult Human Development in
Israel
J.D.C. Hill
IL-Jerusalem 91130

Sandra Nocera
Universität Zürich
Institut für Empirische
Wirtschaftsforschung
Blümlisalpstraße 10
CH-8006 Zürich

Prof. Dr. Mark V. Pauly
The Wharton School of the University
of Pennsylvania
Health Care Systems Department
3641 Locust Walk
Philadelphia PA 19104-6218

Liliana E. Pezzin
Department of Health & Human
Services
Agency for Health Care Policy and
Research
2101 East Jefferson Street
Rockville MD 20852

Gabriel Picone
Center for Health Policy Research and
Education
125 Old Chemistry Building
Durham NC 277 08

Prof. Jean Marie Robine
Equipe INSERM Démographie et Santé
Centre Val d´Aurelle
Parc Euromédicine
F-34094 Montpellier Cedex 5

Dr. Heinz Rothgang
Universität Bremen
Zentrum für Sozialpolitik
Parkallee 39
D-28209 Bremen

Prof. Dr. Winfried Schmähl
Universität Bremen
Zentrum für Sozialpolitik
Parkallee 39
D-28209 Bremen

Ulrich Schneekloth
Infratest Sozialforschung
Landsberger Straße 338
D-80687 München

Dr. Bernd Schulte
Max-Planck Institut für ausländisches
und interantionales Sozialrecht
Leopoldstraße 24
D-80802 München

CONTRIBUTING AUTHORS AND PARTICIPANTS

Prof. Dr. Frank A. Sloan
Duke University
Center for Health Policy Research and
Education
125 Old Chemistry Building
Durham NC 277 08

Wolfram Strüwe
Universität Zürich
Institut für Empirische
Wirtschaftsforschung
Blümlisalpstraße 10
CH-8006 Zürich

Dr. Karl-Heinz Wunner
Stürzelhofer Weg 1
D-90518 Altdorf

Prof. Dr. Gert Wagner
Ruhr-Universität Bochum
Lehrstuhl für Sozialpolitik und
öffentliche Wirtschaft
D-44780 Bochum

Prof. Dr. Peter Zweifel
Universität Zürich
Institut für Empirische
Wirtschaftsforschung
Blümlisalpstraße 10
CH-8006 Zürich

INTRODUCTION

In the long run, demographic trends and developments in family structure are expected to lead to a higher proportion of old and very old people in the population. These trends will likely cause an increased proportion of the national income being devoted to long-term care (LTC) services.

In May 1994 both the German Bundestag (House of Representatives) and Bundesrat (Senate) passed the Bill on social LTC insurance. Taking into account almost 25 years of profound discussion, the solution adopted was astonishing for most of the interested community. The bill is limited in the main to issues of short-run financing; the material issues relating to the infrastructure of community services, their quality, and regarding nursing homes, were postponed. However, the debate was not closed, and has been revolving around future problems.

Given this background, the International Workshop "Alternatives for Ensuring Long-Term Care", held from August 28, to September 1, 1994 in Frankfurt (Main) was devoted to the following objectives:

- to provide a detailed analysis of the arrangements and institutions designed to protect the disabled and dependent elderly people in various countries, and to try to evaluate their respective merits, e.g. in coping with the trends mentioned above.

- to discuss the projections of future costs of protection called forth in favor of dependent elderly, to assess the impact of improvements in disability-free life expectancy on the future cost of care and choices between informal and formal care.

- to present empirical research on these decisions, with special consideration of primary caregivers, and on the substitution between in kind and cash benefits as well as between institutional (or formal) care and home (or informal) care.
- to analyze different theoretical approaches in modeling decisions referring to LTC services to be provided both within and between generations.

This volume is structured along these issues. In this Introduction, we intend to provide an overview of the papers and the discussion delivered at the workshop. **Part One** starts with a paper by *Emmanuelle Cambois* and *Jean-Marie Robine* which addresses the issue of whether an increase in overall life expectancy is accompanied by an increase in disability-free life expectancy. While there has been a decline in mortality rates, health status need not to have improved in step. Three different hypotheses are discussed in the paper. However, lack of comparable data permits preliminary conclusions only. On balance, the study tends to confirm the "dynamic equilibrium hypotheses" (which predicts a short-run decline in the ratio of disability free life expectancy to life expectancy) for most of the developed countries.

One of the aims of the International Workshop was to evaluate the merits and shortcomings of different solutions for protecting disabled and dependent elderly people in various countries. In keeping with this aim, the paper by *Trond O. Edvartsen* gives a brief overview of some problems and possibilities in a cross-country comparison of national LTC systems in European countries. Rather than comparing national systems by using performance indicators, it suggests other approaches to achieve more policy relevance. Defining LTC objectives and using micro data to identify variables determining LTC risk may be two interesting approaches in a cross-national comparison. Another approach could be to specify a standardized disabled elderly with respect to characteristics such as degree of disability, income, age, sex, and family situation and then determine the amount of benefits and services that can be provided to the standardized disabled elderly in each survey country. The various levels of services and benefits could then be compared internationally.

Part Two of the volume is devoted to empirical issues. The paper by *Frank A. Sloan, Thomas J. Hoerger* and *Gabriel Picone* leads the way. The authors examine determinants of LTC decisions and savings behavior within families, using information from the 1984 and 1989 waves of the National Long-Term Care Survey (NLTCS). The NLTCS is a national survey of disabled elderly persons in the US. The authors develop a two-period model. In the first period, a cognitively aware elderly person decides how much to save, recognizing that in the second period, the amount saved will affect her eligibility for Medicaid. In

INTRODUCTION 3

the second period, the elderly person is either (1) dead, (2) alive and cognitively aware and thus able to make decisions for herself, or (3) alive and cognitively impaired in which case the child makes LTC decisions on behalf of the parent. The second period's decisions are (1) whether to enter a nursing home or to be cared for in the community, and (2), if community care is chosen, how many hours of formal and informal care the elderly person shall receive.

In contrast to the Kemper and Pezzin chapter in this volume, the authors find no evidence that public subsidies have crowded out private effort as measured by the amount of informal care subsidies. However, these subsidies have been quite limited compared to those under the Channeling experiment. Medicaid subsidies of nursing home care, operating through the amount of wealth elderly families can retain after paying for nursing home care, do affect the decision to place a disabled elderly person in a nursing home (versus remaining in the community). The authors find no indication that availability of Medicaid has displaced private savings of elderly persons.

Starting from a simple household production model in line with Gary Becker, *Sandra Nocera* and *Peter Zweifel* relate the reservation wage for care to intrinsic preferences for caregiving, productivity in non-market work, and wages in labor markets. To test the hypothesis that reservation wages asked for caregiving to a disabled family member are gender-specific, the authors use three samples of the adult Swiss population. Two of the data sets come from social health insurers ("sickness funds"), one largely rural, the other doing business in the urbanized canton of Zurich. The third sample was provided by a private health insurer.

In order to test their central hypothesis, the authors form six subsamples, for the three data sources combined with the two genders. A first set of estimations result in a lack of significance of the wage rate attainable on the labor market in five of the six regression equations. A second regression based on the larger number of observations available from the pooling of subsamples was therefore performed. The wage rate continues to be irrelevant for women, who seem to pay more attention to their health status and whether or not they live alone. For men, however, the wage rate becomes a significant explanatory variable. In addition, men with only limited education appear to ask for a lower reservation wage for care, especially if combined with high productivity in providing LTC.

In the final section, Nocera and Zweifel plead for a voucher system that would allow recipients to choose the source of care. They also calculate the value of such a voucher.

Thomas Klein analyzes the determinants of institutionalization in old age, based on longitudinal data from the German Socio-Economic Panel (1984-1991). Using event history analysis, he studies the impact of age, sex, chronic diseases, marital status and housing conditions on the risk of institutionalization. His findings are in line with other studies in that (1) women do not appear to have a higher risk of institutionalization than men once age and marital status are controlled for, (2) age and living conditions have a major impact, and (3) the age effect mainly reflects poor health.

As described by *Denise Naon*, Israel's Community Long-Term Care Insurance Law (CLTCI) specifically seeks to enable frail people to stay at home as long as possible. Public provisions of special services (such as personal care, day-care, and housekeeping), are designed to alleviate the burden falling on family caregivers. The situation in Israel is especially interesting because the CLTCI law (implemented in 1988) pursues the same goals as the German statutory LTC insurance law, motivating the crucial question, whether the CLTCI law does fulfill its objectives. This question cannot be answered affirmatively because of the contemporaray lack of available observations.

Peter Kemper and *Liliane E. Pezzin* use in their study data from the Channeling experiment, a national study of expanded public financed case management and subsidies of home care conducted in the United States from 1982 to 1985. The "basic" intervention offered little financial support of additional home care services, being intended to merely fill in gaps in existing home care coverage. By contrast, the "financial" intervention expanded home care coverage appreciably, regardless of eligibility under existing public programs.

The first objective of their analysis is to assess impacts of subsidies of home care on living arrangement transitions. Persons who need LTC may live alone, with others, or live in a nursing home. Individuals presumably choose the living arrangement that yields the most efficient mix of care, given preferences and constraints. The second objective is to measure the extent to which formal care displaces informal care.

The "basic" intervention had a small effect on living arrangements of unmarried persons, increasing by only 2.8 percentage points the probability that persons who lived with others initially would live alone 12 months later. The "financial" intervention had substantially larger effects, significantly shifting living arrangements of unmarried persons toward greater independence. These latter results imply that generous formal home care may allow unmarried elderly persons with disabilities to live more independently, while a small subsidy is not sufficient to change existing living arrangements. Channeling resulted in increased hours of formal visiting care but had no effect on hours of informal care provided by visiting caregivers. With regard to resident informal care, results are different. For unmarried persons, the Channeling interventions did not displace such care. But for married persons, there was a considerable decrease in resident informal care hours. Thus, some "crowding out" of private effort may occur, presumably effort of the spouse in care giving. To the extent that spouses are overburdened with care, as when caring for a severely cognitively impaired spouse, such crowding out may well be desirable. Public policy must be guided by both equity and efficiency.

Part Three of the volume deals with the German solution to the LTC problem and its long-run financial consequences. *Bernd Schulte* develops a broad picture of the German system of protection for the dependent elderly prior to the enactment of the new law on social LTC insurance of 1994: (1) LTC insurance will be administered by the statutory sickness funds; (2) the provision of benefits is governed by different "principles", specifically "informal care comes before formal care"; (3) there is a choice between cash benefits and benefits in kind (depending on three "degrees of dependency"); (4) time spent on non-professional nursing activity (within the family or the "neighborhood") is credited the same as times of gainful employment towards provision for old age in social security.

Ulrich Schneekloth was one of the individuals in charge of the large German survey on "Possibilities of and Limits to an Independent Conduct of Life". He presents the main facts about frail people living in private households. The survey shows that the family (still) assumes responsibility in the main; the primary caregiver is most often a female relative, i.e. the wife, daughter, daughter-in-law, and mother. Every other frail person lives in a household comprising of three or more members while only every fifth person lives alone.

Winfried Schmähl and *Heinz Rothgang* present a simulation model of expenditure under the statutory public LTC insurance law in Germany. By varying its parameters, they are able to identify the most important determinants of cost development. Their results show that - quite contrary to the developments in other branches of German social insurance and the Dutch experience - (1) demographic developments will result in a moderate rise in costs only; more important than demography are (2) patterns of utilization (cash benefits vs. in-kind benefits), and (3) the politically determined levels of benefits.

Part Four of the volume presents theoretical papers and some policy recommendations. *Peter Zweifel* and *Wolfram Strüwe* develop a model depicting the relationship between parent and child as a principal-agent problem. The conceptual framework is the same as that presented earlier in the book by Sloan and co-authors. When an elderly person is disabled, she may not be able to make decisions on her own, but must rely on the decisions of her children. Thus, when she is healthy and able to make financial decisions, she takes into account how children are likely to act, conditional on resources available if and when she is unable to act on her won. In contrast to earlier contributions to the subject, however, Zweifel and Strüwe not only assess the incentive effects of LTC insurance, but also the incentive effects of trust savings in the form of a reverse mortgage.

The authors find that when the child's wage is low, it is not in the parent's interest to buy LTC coverage, a point made earlier by Mark V. Pauly (1990). Such coverage would only displace care that the child would otherwise provide. However, trust saving for LTC is less affected by such moral hazard problems because it creates less of an incentive to caregivers to diminish the amount of informal care they supply.

As in earlier chapters of this volume and in other research on LTC, *Roland Eisen* and *Hans-Christian Mager* analyze LTC decision making in a two-stage model. First, as in the other studies, the parent (or parents) decide on wealth and amount of LTC insurance to purchase. In the second stage, when the person is unable to act on her own, the care decision is made by the children (rather than a single child), depending on the price of care and the market wage. In contrast to most other studies on this topic, Eisen and Mager add realism by allowing for several children, addressing the question of how members of a family decide about caregiving. To this end, they model a cooperative game which permits children to specialize in caregiving depending on their market versus LTC productivities. Higher parent wealth is predicted to boost her bargaining power and encourage use of formal care. Conversely, an increase in the wage rate raises the bargaining power of every child, resulting in less informal care for the parent. Increased LTC insurance coverage also gives the parent added bargaining power while encouraging use of formal care. However, the impact of such coverage on the amount of informal caregiving cannot be deduced because of offsetting effects.

As described by Bernd Schulte, the present German statutory LTC insurance law is very vague with regard to the question of ensuring sufficient infrastructure and quality of LTC. Evaluation of LTC services is therefore of great importance. *Gabriele Johne*, critically deals with the issues involved, such as the quality assessment process to be used, the trade-off between micro and macro quality levels, and the incentives emanating from reimbursement mechanisms under third-party payment.

While her emphasis on the possibilities of competitive mechanisms in ensuring quality may appear a bit enthusiastic to some readers, her paper convincingly argues that the main policy task at hand is the implementation of an incentive compatible reimbursement system to eliminate inefficiencies, which has to be based on outcome to reflect changes in functional status of patients.

In the final paper of this volume, *Mark V. Pauly* puts forward a provocative argument: LTC insurance largely protects bequests for non-poor, non-needy heirs, while Medicaid in the United States is a social program covering LTC, with a deductible set at a value slightly less than the individual's wealth. Therefore, coverage in excess of that provided by Medicaid largely serves to protect bequests. However, existing Medicaid policy needs to be improved in terms of (1) coverage of persons with needy dependents, (2) coverage of the small minority of LTC users who do return to normal health, and (3) coverage of non-institutional formal care.

Acknowledgment

The editors wish to thank Volkswagen-Stiftung, Förderkreis für die Versicherungslehre an der Johann Wolfgang Goethe-Universität, Allianz Lebensversicherungs AG, Landeszentralbank Hessen, Hessisches Ministerium für Wissenschaft und Kunst, and the President of the University of Frankfurt for their financial contribution to this International Workshop on Long-Term Care. Without their support, an instructive and lively exchange of ideas would not have taken place, and this volume would never have been written. But of course, funds are not the only success factor, much if not most hinges on the people involved and their motivations to work. Thanks to all.

    Roland Eisen   Frank A. Sloan

PART ONE:
INTERNATIONAL COMPARISONS

1 AN INTERNATIONAL COMPARISON OF TRENDS IN DISABILITY-FREE LIFE EXPECTANCY

Emmanuelle Cambois and Jean-Marie Robine

1 Introduction

Given the decline in mortality experienced by most developed countries for several decades, principally at very high ages, the population structure is undergoing massive modifications. Among other things, this has a specific impact on the average state of health of the population. This point has led to the development of a new type of indicator, close to life expectancy: health expectancy. Life expectancy assesses the level of mortality by the number of years lived by the population; it gives quantitative information about the expected average length of life. Similarly, health expectancy assesses the level of health of the population, by the number of years lived in good and bad health; it combines both, quantitative information indicated through mortality and more qualitative information about health expressed by morbidity.

2 The concept of "health expectancy"

2.1 Theories of the evolution of health status

The lengthening of life was not expected and this development is disturbing; current debatte focuses on whether people survive diseases only to live on poor health. During the first half of the 1980s, researchers have discussed the relationship between the evolution of mortality and the evolution of morbidity which has gradually centred around three theories [Robine/Brouard/Colvez (1987), Crimmins (1990)]. A general decline in health can be forecasted using the first [Gruenberg (1977), Kramer (1980)], an improvement in health by the second [Fries (1980), (1989)], while no change will be expected following the third [Manton (1982)].

1) According to Gruenberg and Kramer, the postponement of death will result in a worsening of the severity of chronic diseases [Gruenberg (1977), Kramer (1980)]. This is what Kramer (1980) called the *"pandemic of mental disorders, chronic diseases and disabilities"*. In 1991, Olshansky et al. (1991) have further refined this theory, which they have called an *"expansion of morbidity hypothesis"*.

2) The theory of the compression of morbidity was first proposed by Fries (1980). "The compression of morbidity thesis postulates that (a) if the morbid period is defined from the onset of chronic infirmity until death, and (b) if the time occurrence of such morbid events can be postponed, and (c) if adult life expectancy is relatively constant, then (d) morbidity will be compressed into a shorter period of time" [Fries (1989)].

3) Manton (1982) is responsible for the concept of "dynamic equilibrium". According to this concept, the decline in mortality leads to an increase in the prevalence of chronic diseases. These diseases will in general be milder in character.

It is important to note that all these theories concerning the present evolution of the health status of populations may be expressed as the relationship between health expectancy and life expectancy. Using disability as an example, the *"pandemic"* theory may be expressed as a decline in the ratio of disability-free life expectancy to life expectancy, *"compression of morbidity"* as an increase in the ratio of disability-free life expectancy to life expectancy (compression of morbidity may be unrelated to the rectangularisation of the survival curve). Taking into account levels of severity, the theory of *"dynamic equilibrium"* means a decline in the ratio of total disability-free life expectancy to life expectancy and a levelling off or an increase in the ratio of severe disability-free life expectancy to life expectancy (see Table 1).

Table 1: Relationship between theories and health expectancies

Pandemic of disability	(Disability-free life expect./ Life expect.) ↘
Compression of morbidity	(Disability-free life expect./ Life expect.) ↗
Dynamic equilibrium	
all levels of disability :	(Disability-free life expect./ Life expect.) ↘
severe disability :	(Severe disab.-free life expect. /Life expect.) →

2.2 The methods of calculation

There are essentially three different methods of calculating health expectancies: (i) the "observed prevalence table method" or Sullivan's method; (ii) the double decrement life table method; (iii) and the multi-state life table method. All three methods are based on life table process; they all consist in estimating probabilities of being in a specific state and in building a life table in which the usual person-years become specific person-years lived in the state under consideration. The cumulation of specific person-years leads to "specific health expectancies", applied to various states. The choice of the method depends on the type of data used; transition probabilities, required to obtain specific person-years, are estimated by different processes, according to the nature of these data.

(i) The principle of the calculation of disability-free life expectancy was postulated as early as 1964 [see Sanders (1964)] and a first method of calculation was proposed later by Sullivan (1971). It constitutes the simplest method: in the standard life table, the "person years" are multiplied by the probability of being disabled, estimated by age-specific observed rates of disability. These data are collected by cross-sectional surveys on health which are often regularly run. Once the table is modified, the specific health expectancy is calculated in the traditional manner, according to various states of functional disability under consideration. Thus, one can get, among others, the value of *disability-free life expectancy*.

(ii) Katz et al. (1983) proposed an indicator, computed with the multiple decrement life table, previously used during the 50's in the field of insurances, for the calculation of benefits [see Jordan (1952) and Spiegelman (1957)]. This method is based on a life table which considers a multiple attrition phenomenon. Death is no longer the only absorbing state: any event that provokes the loss of the original characteristic known by the initial cohort, is considered as a decrementing event. In this model, the attrition phenomenum is constituted by both mortality and disability, represented here by loss of independence in "activities of daily living" [Katz et al. (1983)] and institutionalization. A sample of healthy individuals is studied twice (two waves longitudinal survey); Katz et al. (1983) estimate the probability of remaining in the initial cohort (being independant in daily life) rather than the probability of separating from it (dying or entering disability). The "disability-free person years" are directly obtained by applying probabilities of remaining healthy to an hypothetical cohort of new-borns. The resultant indicator gives an estimation of the average period of life lived in good health, before dying or becoming disabled. This method does not give an opportunity for recovering from the disabling event. Thus, it constitutes a perfect model, for example, for calculating financed and financing periods of life, for insured states (good and bad health), but it becomes a little bit limited when computing a general healthy life expectancy which should consider potential recoveries, in order to take into account all periods of time spent in good and bad health, either if they are continuous or discontinuous.

(iii) The third method of calculation is based on the so-called increment-decrement life table: the model does not only consider several events that decrease the initial cohort, as in the previous model, but also events that increase the cohort from age to age, principally represented by recoveries. In the field of public health, the first application of such a model has been presented in 1989 (Rogers et al.), with the intention of improving Katz et al.'s method, as recoveries from disabling diseases were revealed not to be negligible [Rogers/Rogers/Belanger (1989)]. Data from longitudinal surveys are required in order to calculate probabilities of transitions between all states under consideration. When probabilities of becoming disabled and of recovering are available, the disability-free person-years, can be calculated: a fictitious cohort of initially healthy individuals is developed, from the starting age of the simulation to the extinction of the cohort, according to age-specific probabilities of becoming disabled and of recovering. The simulation can also be done to obtain the disability-free person-years, for a cohort of initially disabled individuals.

Both latter methods lead to precise indicators but require data collected by longitudinal surveys. Indeed the resultant flow data are necessary for estimating the probabilities of transition between states. Such data are not regularly available, and result from expensive and laborious surveys specifically run for this kind of studies. On the opposite, the observed prevalence of table method is based on the separate collection of mortality and disability data and in the availability of the data that are necessary for the calculation. Basic cross-sectional surveys are sufficient to collect the data of observed prevalence of disability within the population (stock data). However the indicator obtained is not really a period indicator. The problem with this method lies in approximating the period prevalence by the observed prevalence of disability: the *period value* is under- or over-estimated by *"Sullivan's value"* according to the bias carried by the observed prevalence, but the *trend* in the period values is properly represented by the *trend* in "Sullivan's values" [Cambois/Robine (1994)].

The choice of the method depends essentially on the availability of data and on the objectives of the study. The general goal associated with health expectancies is to confirm or invalidate the mentioned theories debating on the modification of the average health level of ageing populations. For this purpose repeated and international studies must be carried out in order to produce homogeneous indicators meant to be compared and studied over large periods. Thus, as flow data are accessible regularly for most countries, the "observed prevalence tables" method seems to be the most appropriate for international trends studies.

3   International review

3.1   The place of health expectancy in the world

Today, a first calculation of health expectancy has been carried out for more than 30 countries [REVES (1993)], principally using the "observed prevalence tables" method. The limits of this method are increasingly well understood. Simulations provide a better means of assessing its imprecision [see Robine/ Mathers (1993)]. Beside methodological choices and despite increasing efforts to standardize health surveys at an international level, direct geographic comparisons are impossible as wide differences still persist.

Differences in study protocols and definitions of disability could alone explain the differences in estimates presented in Table 2 [see United Nations, Chamie (1990b), (1990a), and (1989)].

In the case of Germany, indicators have been produced twice for international reports; as those studies were based on different data collected by different surveys, no conclusion can be drawn in terms of trend. In 1990, Brown gave an estimation of the German active life expectancy at birth for 1983 [Brown (1990)]; also in 1990 Egedi computed a life expectancy in good health at birth, for 1986 [Egedi (1990)] (see Table 3).

Table 2: Disability-free life expectancy at age 65, in developed countries

	Males			Females		
Pays	LE*	DFLE**	DFLE/LE in %	LE*	DFLE**	DFLE/LE in %
United States, 1985	14.6	10.5	71.9	18.6	13.4	72.0
Japan, 1985	15.5	14.1	91.0	18.9	17.1	90.5
Spain, 1986	15.0	6.8	45.3	18.4	6.5	35.3
United Kingdom, 1988	13.7	7.6	55.5	17.6	8.8	50.0
Switzerland, 1988-1989	15.4	12.2	79.2	19.6	14.9	76.0
Netherlands, 1990	14.0	9.0	64.3	19.0	8.0	42.1
France, 1991	15.7	10.1	64.3	20.1	12.1	60.2
Canada, 1991	15.6	8.3	53.2	19.7	9.2	46.7
Australia, 1992	15.4	6.4	41.6	19.2	10.2	53.1
Austria, 1992	14.9	11.5	77.3	18.3	12.2	67.0

*LE: Life Expectancy; **DFLE: Disability Free Life Expectancy.

Sources: Statistical Yearbook – REVES (1993); except for Japan [Chamie, 1990a], France [Robine/Mormiche (1993)], Australia [Mathers (1995)], Austria [Kytir (1994)].

Table 3: Health Expectancy for ex-West Germany

Brown (1990)*: for 1983	for males	for females
Active life expectancy at birth	61.5 years	69.9 years
Life expectancy at birth	70.8 years	77.4 years
Egedi (1990)**: for 1986		
Life expectancy in good health at birth	63.4 years	68.4 years
Life expectancy at birth	71.8 years	78.4 years

* Brown (1990); ** Egedi (1990).

3.2 Trends studies in the world

For other countries, time series of disability-free life expectancies have already been produced (table 4). Chronological series consist of at least two cross-sectional health surveys using the same measures and comparable samples. When these series are juxtaposed, they cover a period that extends for some 30 years. While the use of comparable samples and repeated use of the same measures of disability permit comparisons over time for any study, the strongly different measures of disability used, and differences in the sampling frames, do not allow comparisons between countries, not even to align the American studies one after the other in order to observe a longer time interval [see Robine/ Bucquet/Ritchie (1991)].

Table 4: Countries for which chronological series are available

Countries	Reference	Available years
United States	U.S. Dep. of HEW (1969)	1958 to 1966
	McKinlay et al. (1989)	1964, 1974, 1985
	Dillard (1983)	1962 to 1976
	Crimmins et al. (1989)	1970, 1980
New York State	Tu (1990)	1980, 1986
Japan	OECD (1976)*	1966 to 1970
	Koizumi (1985)*	1965 to 1979
	Nanjo et al. (1987)	1975, 1980, 1985
City of Sendai	Tsuji (1993)	1970, 1990
Norway	Grotvedt et al. (1994)	1975, 1985
United Kingdom	Bebbington (1991), (1994)	1976, 1981, 1985, 1988, 1991
France	Robine et al. (1993)	1981, 1991
Australia	Mathers. (1995)	1981, 1988, 1993
Canada	Wilkins et al. (1995)	1986, 1991
Taiwan	Tu (1992), (1994)	1986 to 1988, 1991
Austria	Kytir (1994)	1992
Netherlands	Perenboom et al., (1992)	1983 to 1990

* Published data are not detailed enough to be discussed in comparison studies.

Source: "Contribution of the network on "Health Expectancy and the Disability Process" to the World Health Report ", by World Health Organization (WHO).

In a first attempt to assess the health status of populations in 1991 American, English and Australian studies have been divided into four levels according to severity of disability: very severe disability, severe to very severe, moderate to very severe, mild to very severe disability. This classification permits to distinguish more carefully the trend in disability according to the degree of severity through the computation of the corresponding indicators. Most authors now distinguish life expectancy without severe disability and life expectancy without disability, all levels combined. Most of the time, a disability free life expectancy means all levels of disability combined.

We are able to describe and compare overall trends in the United States [Mc Kinlay/Mc Kinlay/Beaglehole (1998), Dillard (1983), Crimmins/Saito/Ingegneri (1989)], England [Mathers (1995), Bebbington (1991)], Australia [Mathers, (1995), (1991)], the Netherlands [Perenboom/Boshuizen/van de Water (1993)], Japan [Chaime (1990b)], Taiwan [Tu/Chen (1992)], Canada [Wilkins/Chen (1995)] and France [Robine/Mormiche (1993)] (see Figure 1).

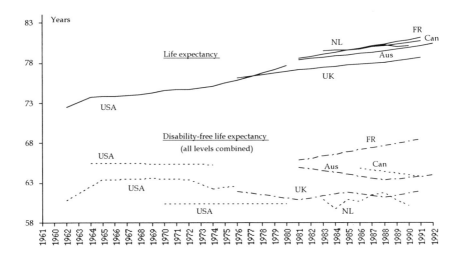

Figure 1: Disability-free life expectancy (all levels combined), for females at birth, international comparison from 1962 to 1991

Over a period of 30 years, there has been a 7 year increase in life expectancy at birth among females from the most developed countries. By contrast, there has been a stagnation at about 63 years in disability-free life expectancy, all levels combined: thus the 7 years of life expectancy gained seem to be almost equivalent to an extra 7 years of disability. The Dutch series is difficult to interpret as it is based on self-rated perceived health [Perenboom/Boshuizen/van de Water (1993)]. Only the Canadian study 1986-1991 seems to indicate a clear decrease in disability-free life expectancy [Wilkins/Chen (1995)], and the French study

1981-1991 a marked increase [Robine/Mormiche (1993)]. In these ten years, disability free life expectancy in France has increased by 3 years for men, reaching 63.8 years, and by 2.6 years for women reaching 68.5 years; meanwhile for both sexes total life expectancy only increased by 2.5 years reaching 72.9 years for males and 81.1 years for females. Gains in disability-free life expectancy are half due to decreases in mortality and half to the decrease in disability at each age. Thus, in France, the increase in disability free life expectancy exceeds the increase in life expectancy: increase in life expectancy and decrease in the prevalence of disabilities (all levels combined) are associated.

In fact most of the new series are only formed with two points whereas the shape of the British series, already covering five points, leads to more careful interpretation. Thus, the last indicator produced for the United Kingdom (1991) [see Bebbington (1994)] and for Australia (1993) [Mathers (1991)], modifies the 1981-1988 conclusions, giving a newly upward trend to the disability-free life expectancy.

Studying health expectancy considering severe and very severe disabilities for all countries yields results, that indicate a significant difference in trends: indeed, as shown in Figure 2, life expectancies without severe and very severe disabilities are on a parallel course to total life expectancy.

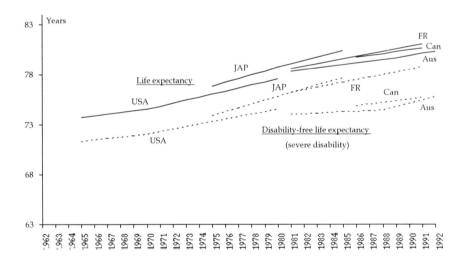

Figure 2: Disability-free life expectancy (severe disability) for females at birth, international comparison from 1965 to 1991

3.3 Conclusion of the trends studies

As already noticed, the lack of harmonization hinders proper international comparisons and conclusion should be given very carefully and provisionally: chronological series are too short to give any definitive interpretation and to valid one of the theories on changes in the health level of population. Anyway, it seems that trends are similar for most of the studied countries and an important information is given by these figures.

In fact, this two-level study shows that, at the worst, the population is undergoing a *pandemic* of *light and moderate* disabilities, *but not of severe* disabilities. It tends to confirm, for the latter, the theory of *"dynamic equilibrium"*. According to Manton (1982), the increase in life expectancy is partly explained by a slow down in the rate of progression of chronic diseases. Thus, although the decline in mortality leads to an increase in the prevalence of disabilities, these disabilities are less severe. The results discussed here are essentially the same for males and females at birth and at age 65.

For the specific French case, the results are even more optimistic as they seem to illustrate the theory of compression of morbidity for disabilities all levels combined. Identical results about the diminishing of the prevalence of disabilities, have also been observed in the United States of America recently [see Crimmins/Ingegneri (1991), Manton/Corder/Stallard (1993), National Research Council (1994)]. The French results, in favour of a compression of morbidity, confirmed by some isolated studies, should be verified in other countries, before concluding that, of late years, increases in life expectancy are really accompanied by a rise in disability-free life expectancy, thus leading to a compression of morbidity.

At least, by reference to the existing series, it is possible to conclude that the increase in life expectancy does not lead to a pandemic of (very) severe disabilities in the most developed countries.

Work On Harmonization In Calculations

An international harmonization in protocols, surveys and definition of concepts is urgently needed in order to carry on the development of such indicators; international organizations are working on this. For this purpose, the aims of REVES [see Bone, 1992], the international Network on Health Expectancy and Disability Process, are **1.** to consider the necessary conditions for a comparison of several calculations of health expectancy, with a particular view to international geographical comparisons; **2.** to reflect on how to interprete chronological series of health expectancy; **3.** to examine the possible uses of health expectancy for socio-medical planning and programs; **4.** to look at the possibilities of procedural standardization of data collection and health expectancy calculation procedures.

In 1993, the European Community has decided to support the creation of EURO REVES [see Robine (1995)], in order to produce homogeneous indicators for the member countries.

References

Bebbington, A. (1994): *Oral communication to the 7th meeting of the International Network on Health Expectancy (REVES)*, Canberra, February 1994.

Bebbington, A.C. (1988): The expectation of life without disability in England and Wales: 1976-1988, in *Population Trends 66*, 26-29.

Bone, R.M. (1992): International efforts to measure health expectancy, in *Journal of Epidemiology and Community Health 46*, 555-558.

Brown, S.C. (1990): *Aging and disability trends in the Third World*. Unpublished Working Paper presented at the Population Association of America Annual Meeting, May 1990 in Toronto.

Cambois, E./Robine, J.M. (1994): *Use of demographic tools in the assessment of health level of populations*. Proceedings of workshop 'Life table in Europe: data, methods and models'. Louvain-la-Neuve, April 1994 (to be published).

Chamie, M. (1989): Survey Design Strategies for the study of Disability, in *World Health Statistics Quarterly 42*, 122-140.

Chamie, M. (1990a): *Data collection Standards for Disability: Implications to the Study of Disability-Free Life Expectancy*, in 2nd Work-group meeting REVES, Network on Health Expectancy and the disability process / Réseau Espérance de vie en Santé, Geneva, March 1990 (Principal Working Paper, REVES Paper No. 28).

Chamie, M. (1990b): *Report of the Committee on the Conceptual Harmonization of statistics for the study of Disability-Free Life Expectancy*. Reves Paper N° 41, Strasbourg, November 1990.

Crimmins E.M./Saito Y./Ingegneri, D. (1989): Changes in life expectancy and disability-free life expectancy in the United States, in *Population Development Review 15*, 235-267.

Crimmins, E.M. (1990): Are Americans healthier as well as longer-lived?, in *Journal Insurance and Medicine 22*, 89-92.

Crimmins, E.M./Ingegneri, D.G. (1991): Trends in health among the American population, in A. Rappaport/S. J. Schieber (eds.): *Demography and Retirement: the 21st Century*, Wesport/London: Praeger, 225-242.

Dillard, S. (1983): Durée ou qualité de la vie ?, in *Les Publications du Québec 70*. (Conseil Affaires Sociales et de la Famille; collection: La santé des Québécois). Montréal.

Egedi, V. (1990): Population ageing and changing lifestyles in Europe, in *Fourth Meeting of the seminar on present demographic trends and lifestyle in Europe*. Strasbourg, 18-20 September.

Fries, J.F. (1980): Aging, natural death, and the compression of morbidity, in *New England Journal of Medicine 303*, 130-135.

Fries, J.F. (1989): The compression of morbidity: near or far?, in *Milbank Memorial Fundation Quarterly / Health and Society 67*, 208-232.

Gruenberg, E.M. (1977): The failures of success, in *Milbank Memorial Fundation Quarterly / Health and Society 55*, 3-24.

Jordan, C.W. (1952): *Society of Actuarie's textbook on life contingencies*. Chicago: The Society of Actuaries.

Jordan, C.W. (1975): *Society of Actuarie's textbook on life contingencies*. Second edition. Chicago: The Society of Actuaries.

Katz, S./Branch, L.G./Branson, M.H./Papsidero, J.A./Beck, J.C./Greer, D.S. (1983): Active life expectancy, in *New England Journal of Medicine 309*, 1218-1224.

Kramer, M. (1980): The rising pandemic of mental disorders and associated chronic diseases and disabilities, in *Acta Psychiatrica Scandinavica 62*, 282-297.

Kytir, J. (1994): Lebenserwartung frei von Behinderung, in *Statistische Nachrichten 8*, 650-657.

Manton, K.G./Corder, L.S./Stallard, E. (1993): Estimates of change in chronic disability and institutional incidence and prevalence rates in the U.S. elderly population from the 1982, 1984, and 1989 National Long Term Care Survey, in *Journal of Gerontological Nursing 48*, 153-166.

Manton, K.G. (1982): Changing concepts of morbidity and mortality in the elderly population, in *Milbank Memorial Fundation Quarterly / Health and Society 60*, 183-244.

Mathers, C.D. (1991): *Health expectancies in Australia 1981 and 1988*. Canberra: Australian Institute of Health; AGPS, 117.

Mathers, D.C. (1995): Health expectancy in Australia 1993: premilinary results, in D.C. Mathers, J. McCallum, J.M. Robine (eds.): *Advances in health expectancies:* Canberra: Australian Institute of Health, 198-212.

McKinlay, J.B./McKinlay, S.M./Beaglehole, R. (1989): A review of the evidence concerning the impact of medical measures on recent mortality and morbidity in the United States, in *International Journal of Health Services 19*, 181-208.

Nanjo, Z. Shigematsu (1987). *Construction of Health Life Tables*. Paper presented at the 27th Meeting of Kyùshù Region (Population Association of Japan), August 22, 1987.

National Research Council, Commitee on National Statistics. *Trends in disability at older ages; summary of a Workshop*. 1994, V.A. Freedman/B.J. Soldo (eds.): Washington DC: National Academy Press.

Olshansky, S.J./Rudberg, M.A./Carnes, B.A./Cassel, C.K./Brody, J.A. (1991): Trading off longer life for worsening health: the expansion of morbidity hypothesis, in *Journal of Aging and Health 3*, 194-216.

Perenboom, R.J.M./Boshuizen, H. C./van de Water, H.P.A. (1993): Trends in health expectancies in the Netherlands, 1981-1990, in *Calculation of health expectancies: harmonization, consensus achieved and future perpectives.* John Libbey Eurotext.

REVES (1993): *Statistical World Yearbook 'Health expectancy'.* Paris, Les Editions INSERM.

Robine, J.M./Brouard, N./Colvez, A (1987): Les indicateurs d'espérance de vie sans incapacité (EVSI) : des indicateurs globaux de l'état de santé des populations, in *Revue Epidemiologie Sante Publique 35,* 206-224.

Robine, J.M./Bucquet, D./Ritchie, K. (1991): L'espérance de vie sans incapacité, un indicateur de l'évolution des conditions de santé au cours du temps: 20 ans de calcul, in *Cah Quebecois Demographie 20,* 205-235.

Robine, J.M./Mathers, C. (1993): Measuring the compression or expansion of morbidity through changes in health expectancy, in *Calculation of health expectancies: harmonization, consensus achieved and future perpectives.* Montrouge: John Libbey Eurotext, 269-286.

Robine, J.M./Mormiche P. (1993): L'espérance de vie sans incapacité augmente, in *INSEE Première 281,* 1-4.

Robine, J.M. (1995): Presentation and work program of EURO-REVES, a European concerted action for harmonisation of health expectancy in Europe, in D.C. Mathers/ J. McCallum /J.M. Robine (eds.): *Advances in health expectancies.* Canberra: Australian Institute of Health and Welfare, 295-308.

Rogers, R.G./Rogers A./Belanger, A. (1989): Active life among the elderly in the United States: multistate life-table estimates and population projections, in *Milbank Memorial Fundation Quarterly 67,* 370-411.

Sanders, B.S. (1964): Measuring community health levels, in *American Journal of Public Health 54,* 1063-1070.

Spiegelman, M. (1957): The versatility of the life table, in *American Journal of Public Health 47,* 297-304.

Sullivan, D.F. (1971): A single index of mortality and morbidity, in *HSMHA Health Report 86,* 347-354.

Tu, E.J.-C./Chen, K. (1992): *Changes in active life expextancy in Taiwan: compression or expansion?* in 5th International Workshop of REVES, Ottawa, February 1992, (Reves paper No. 104).

United Nations Statistical Office (1990): *Disability Statistics Compendium.* New York: United Nations (Statistics on Special Population Groups, Series Y, No. 4).

Wilkins, R/Chen, J./Ng, E. (1995): Changes in health expectancy in Canada from 1986 to 1991, in D.C. Mathers/J. McCallum/J.M. Robine (eds.): *Advances in health expectancies.* Canberra: Australian Institute of Health and Welfare, 115-132.

2 POSSIBILITIES AND PROBLEMS IN A CROSS-COUNTRY COMPARATIVE ANALYSIS OF LONG-TERM CARE SYSTEMS

Trond O. Edvartsen

1 Introduction

Within the framework of the global subject "European social policy" the Volkswagen-Stiftung is financing the research project "Long-Term Care in the EU – An Institutional and Empirical Comparative Survey with Respect to Possibilities and Problems of Convergence" (PflEG-Project). One of the aims of the PflEG-Project is to give a cross-national comparative analysis of the national long-term care programmes in the European Union and Scandinavia. A comparison of national long-term care systems will have to start with an identification of all relevant parts of each national system that provide care benefits and services. For this purpose we are producing reports on each national system, which are made by post-graduate students and will be brought into a comparative synopsis at the end of the project.

In our survey we focus on the disabled elderly, i.e. disabled people aged 60 and over. We choose to disregard those parts of the national long-term care systems that provide care benefits and services for children and adults under the age of 60. The reason for this is that long-term care has become a political problem primarily because of demographic changes: A decreasing number of potential workers in the labour force will have to provide an increasing number of people aged 60 and over – who also live longer ("double ageing society") – with long-term care benefits and services.

The aim of this paper is to outline some of the possibilities and problems in cross-country analysis of long-term care systems in Europe. Section 2 of this paper outlines some possible approaches to define disability using activities of daily living and instrumental activities of daily living. Section 3 discusses the difficulties and possibilities of a classification of the national long-term care systems. Section 4 through 7 outline possibilities and shortcomings of performance indicators, intra-national comparisons, standardised model cases, and micro data. Finally, section 8 draws some conclusions.

2 Definition of Disability

The starting point in a cross-national comparison of long-term care systems will have to be a definition of disability. A disabled elderly may be defined as a person not being able to perform one or more (a) "activities of daily living" (ADLs) or (b) "instrumental activities of daily living" (IADLs). Table 1 shows two possible indexes based on Katz et al. (1963) and Lawton/Brody (1969) containing 10 ADLs and 10 IADLs respectively.[1]

Using ADL and IADL indexes, it is then possible to express various degrees of disability by the number of ADLs or IADLs, that the disabled elderly cannot perform without assistance. However, there are no standard lists of ADLs or IADLs. The two lists shown in Table 1 could be extended to include further activities or be shortened by some activities. Further, rather than just to ask whether the elderly is able to perform a particular activity or not, one could ask to what degree he is able to perform it. The answer categories could then include:[2]

- no need for help;
- some need for help;
- distinct need for help.

Setting "no need for help" equal to zero, "some need for help" equal to one, and "distinct need for help" equal to two,[3] one may compute a total degree of disability for an elderly by adding the scores of all activities together. Using the total of 20 ADLs and IADLs in Table 1, the score would then range from 0 through 40. Various degrees of disability may then be classified by defining categories according to the ADL and IADL score. Table 2 shows one possible arbitrary categorisation:

Table 1: Activities of Daily Living and Instrumental Activities of Daily Living

ADLs	IADLs
Move outdoors	Make phone calls
Walk between rooms	Handle money
Use stairs	Do shopping
Continence	Get to distant public offices and facilities
Toileting	Use public transport
Wash and bathe oneself	Walk or go by public transport to a medical doctor
Dress and undress	Take medicine
Get in and out of bed	Complete forms and applications
Eating	Preparing meals
Cut toe-nails	Do housework

Source: Based on Katz et al. (1963) and Lawton/Brody (1969), quoted in Dieck/Garms-Homolová (1991), 133 and 325.

Table 2: Possible Categorization of Different Levels of Disability

Score	Level of disability
1 - 3	low
4 - 8	medium
9+	high

In addition, one may define the degree of disability by the frequency in which help is needed in performing the ADLs and IADLs. For example, the German Long-Term Care Social Insurance Act implemented in 1995 defines three levels of disability based on a) the frequency in which help is needed to perform ADLs and b) the frequency in which help is needed to perform IADLs. The various ADLs and IADLs are shown in table 3.

Table 3: ADLs and IADLs used in the German LTC Insurance

ADLs	IADLs
Washing	Shopping
Bathing	Preparing meals
Brushing the teeth	Cleaning
Combing	Washing up the dishes
Shaving	Laundering
Toileting	Heating the apartment
Eating	
Getting in and out of bed	
Dressing	
Walking	
Standing	
Using stairs	
Walking outdoors	

The three levels of disability are defined as follows:

Low level of disability: The disabled is a) in need of help in performing at least two ADLs once daily, and b) in need of help in performing IADLs several times a week.

Medium level of disability: The disabled is a) in need of help in performing ADLs at least three times a day, and b) in need of help in performing IADLs several times a week.

High level of disability: The disabled is a) in need of help 24 hours a day in performing ADLs, and b) in need of help in performing IADLs several times a week.

Table 4: Levels of Disability According to the German Long-Term Care Social Insurance Act

Degree of disability	Frequency in which help is needed to perform ADLs		Frequency in which help is needed to perform IADLs
low	at least once a day concerning two or more activities	and	several times a week.
medium	at least three times a day	and	several times a week.
high	24 hours a day	and	several times a week.

To define various levels of disability by the frequency in which help is needed to perform ADLs and IADLs seems more appropriate than simply counting the number of ADLs and IADLs, which the disabled elderly cannot perform without any help: The frequency in which help is needed is a better indicator of the elderly's dependency level (see table 4).

3 Description and Classification of the National Long-Term Care Systems

The national long-term care systems can be analysed by looking at the institutions that organise, finance, and provide long-term care benefits and services. However, an institutional approach may be insufficient when one wants to ensure that all adequate aspects of the national systems are taken into account. For example, institutions providing long-term care benefits and services may in some survey countries be institutionally identical, however, functionally, they may diverge considerably. We therefore extend the institutional approach functionally. All benefits and services that functionally affect the situation of the disabled elderly are considered to be part of the national long-term care system.[4]

In addition to the formal care providers, one will also have to consider the informal care suppliers, such as family members, neighbours and friends of the disabled elderly (so called Small Social Networks). The importance of informal care varies from country to country. Traditionally, it has been suggested that informal care is more common in the South of Europe than in the North. However, examining Germany reveals that even in central or northern Europe, informal care plays a considerable role in ensuring long-term care for the disabled elderly.

A description of the national long-term care systems should include a classification of each system into pre-defined categories. These categories may be public insurance versus social insurance or private insurance systems, universal versus categorical systems, tax financed versus contribution financed systems, formal versus informal care systems, home care versus nursing home care, services in kind versus cash benefits, etc.. Deciding which national system belongs to the one or the other category may be difficult – even if all benefits and services were organised, financed and provided for by a single institution. The Long-Term Care Social Insurance Act found in the Netherlands is rather an exception among the European long-term care systems. Commonly, the long-term care risk is not ensured by a single institution, but is usually covered by the benefits and services of several institutions such as the national health system, the national pension system, the social assistance system, private organisations, charity societies, etc.. Hence, the national long-term care systems seem to be mixed systems rather than pure systems, and therefore do not just fit into one of the available categories. Purely tax financed systems are just as rare as systems financed by contributions only; social insurance systems are usually complemented by private insurers or publicly managed services; some services and benefits may be universal while other are categorical etc.. Nevertheless, describing a national system by pre-defined common categories is a necessary condition that makes it possible to compare national long-term care systems and to clarify differences and common features.[5] Hence, we may categorise the European long-term care systems as shown in Table 5.

Table 5: Classification of National Long-Term Care Systems in Europe

	Public Insurance Systems	Mixed Systems	Bismarckian Social Insurance Systems
Eligible persons	Residents		Employees
Financing	General Budget		Contributions
Organisation	Public		Semi-public
Countries	B DK GB GR I IRL L N P S SF	E(?) F	D (?) NL

Source: Based on a similar classification of pension systems in OECD countries made by Holzman (1988).

Of course, this classification scheme simply suggests the main characteristics of the national long-term care systems. One could just as well argue, that many of the systems would also fit well into the category of mixed systems. For example, in spite of the implementation of the Long-Term Care Social Insurance Act in Germany in 1995/6, the German system will still not be a pure social insurance system. E.g. the benefits and services amounting to about 3,500 DM per person for highly disabled elderly are likely to be insufficient with respect to those having the highest level of care needs. Hence, the social assistance system will probably still play a considerable role in ensuring Long-Term Care in Germany.

4   Comparison by Performance Indicators

One of the objectives of a cross-national comparative study may include measuring the performance of the national long-term care systems. This can be executed by using a number of performance indicators, such as expenditure for long-term care as a proportion of GNP, expenditure per disabled elderly, proportion of expenditure financed by taxes, proportion of disabled elderly living in nursing homes, number of non-institutionalised disabled elderly receiving cash benefits or services in kind, proportion of the disabled elderly receiving informal care only, number of persons employed in home care services/nursing homes per 100 disabled elderly, number of disabled elderly as a proportion of the total number of elderly, number of the elderly as a proportion of persons in employable age and average income of the disabled elderly as a proportion of average working income etc..

Since the figures needed to compute many of the performance indicators are often not based on equivalent definitions or compiling methods, any comparison using performance indicators must be examined critically. Due to diverging national definitions or compiling methods the use of national accounts will prove to be very difficult. The comparability of international accounts as OECD or ILO may – as far as they are available on long-term care topics – be better.[6]

In this regard, the GNP seems to be one of the more comparable figures, although its shortcomings and limitations as a measure of a country's welfare or overall production of goods and services are well known.[7] The problem of incomparable or unavailable data on many of the indicators mentioned above in national or international statistics could be solved by using survey sample data. Unfortunately, comprehensive sample surveys on a national or international level, which include all the countries and variables requested for a cross-national comparison of European LTC systems, are hardly available. To solve this problem by carrying out an own sample survey is likely to exceed the financial and organisational capacities of a single project.[8] The pooling of several independent national sample surveys may be a way to overcome this obstacle. Yet, the sample survey approaches used in each study are likely to be quite different. The comparability of such studies may then be even more questionable than that of national and international statistics. In addition, sample survey data available on LTC aspects in European countries often suffer from a rather small number of observations and is often restricted to a small geographical area of any country.[9] This, of course, makes such data less reliable and representative.

The number of disabled elderly is one good example, where inequivalent national definitions make it difficult to provide comparable performance indicators across nations. There are at least two obvious limitations with respect to the comparability of the number of disabled elderly: The heterogeneous definitions of "disability" and the diverging definitions of "the elderly" in the survey countries.

To account for the latter is easy, if statistics are available making it possible to adjust the figures according to the survey definition of "the elderly". The heterogeneous definitions of "disability", however, are much harder to account for when making sure that national figures on disabled elderly are comparable. The access criteria concerning long-term care benefits and services may in some countries be set very high, while other countries have less restrictive legal definitions of disability. This, of course, will have a strong influence on the officially compiled number of disabled elderly and makes a cross-national comparison based on performance indicators very difficult. A group of elderly, which by definition is accounted for as disabled in one country may not be disabled according to the legal definitions of another country. Due to varying legal definitions of disability, it appears to be rather difficult to ensure, that, in cross-national studies, the groups of disabled elderly analysed are equivalent. Consequently, any performance indicator based on inequivalent defined groups of disabled elderly will suffer under the lack of comparability.

Table 6 shows the disability ratio for various age groups in Germany based on three data sets during the 1980s.

The three surveys show some major differences in the disability ratios. The overall disability ratio varies from 2.1 to 2.9 percent of the population. In the age group 65 and over the Socialdata survey finds a disability ratio of 11.1 whereas Thiede (1990) computes a disability ratio of 8.8 using the data from the Socio-Economic Panel. The differences in the disability ratio may be due to diverging definitions of disability and compiling methods. In this respect, the data on disabled persons in the Socio-Economic Panel is not based on any categorical definition of disability. Rather, the head of the household is asked if there is any person living in his household being in need of long term care. Given the two answer categories, Yes and No, it is the subjective decision of the head of household to decide if any member of the household is disabled and in need of LTC services. Another critical aspect of the Socio-Economic Panel data is the

Table 6: Disability Ratios in Germany

Socialdata		Socio-Economic Panel		Ministry of Social Affairs (BMAS)	
Age Group	Disability Ratios	Age Group	Disability Ratios	Age Group	Disability Ratios
7 - 17	0.6	17 - 29	0.2		
18 - 64	1.4	30 - 49	0.5	- 40	0.7
		50 - 59	0.9	40 - 60	0.5
60 - 64	1.7	60 - 64	1.9		
65 - 79	8.0	65 - 74	3.8	60 - 80	5.0
		75 - 84	11.4		
80+	28.4	85+	31.4	80+	20.0
65+	11.1	65+	8.8		
Overall	2.9	Overall	2.3	Overall	2.1

Source: Socialdata (1980), Thiede (1990), BMAS (1991).

small number of observations in each wave, varying between 126 and 176 disabled persons in all age groups for the years 1985-1991. The total number of persons in the panel declines from about 12,000 in 1985 to about 9,500 in 1991.[10] Despite of the limitations of the Socio-Economic Panel, especially on long-term care items, this is the only available panel data survey for Germany. In the Socialdata survey, where an overall number of 75,000 persons were interviewed in 1978, the number of disabled persons is compiled by assessing the degree of disability using a catalogue of ADLs and IADLs. The degree of disability is further specified by giving each ADL and IADL a score ranging from 0 to 4, whereas 0 means "no need" and 4 "very high needs". In this respect, the Socialdata survey seems much more convincing than the Socio-Economic Panel data. Concerning the figures offered by the German Ministry of Social Affairs, it is not clear how these figure are computed or which survey they are based on, as the Ministry does not release any information on this.

Even if the various national legal definitions of disability were similar, the compiled figures on the number of disabled elderly may still be incomparable. Due to the diverging interpretations and handling of the "obvious identical legal definitions" in practice, the access to long-term care benefits and services can vary considerably between the countries.

Concerning the number of disabled elderly receiving institutional care, it is often difficult to ensure that the observed institutions are functionally equivalent. This problem often occurs when distinguishing between nursing homes and other old age residential dwellings. The dwellings may be institutionally equivalent, while functionally inequivalent and vice versa. Drawing a clear borderline between institutions that provide long-term care services and others that only provide housing is often problematic. The problem of equivalence is accompanied by an identification problem concerning mixed institutions, i.e. institutions that by definition and/or factually offer housing and care services to groups other than disabled elderly. For example, it is quite common for a nursing home to house non disabled too. This may be due to the lack of other appropriate dwellings for the elderly or to the fact that there are clear economic incentives for the elderly choosing to live in a nursing home rather than in other dwellings. Maydell (1992) argues that in the Netherlands there have been clear monetary incentives, which make it more advantageous for elderly people to live in a nursing home rather than in other dwellings.[11] A similar situation has also been observed in German hospitals. While medical care is covered by the Social Health Insurance long-term care is not. Consequently, there were clearly economic incentives staying in a hospital even if nursing home care were needed rather than medical care. Kehr (1988) and Klar et al. (1989) estimate the number of hospital beds that are inappropriately occupied by patients aged 60 and over at 35,000. This equals approximately 10.5 million patient days a year.[12]

Another figure that is difficult to compile, is the overall number of beneficiaries of formal home care (home nursing, home help or cash benefits). Official statistics are usually available on the number of beneficiaries receiving a single service or benefit. Because of to the fact that some disabled elderly receive more than one service or benefit (e.g. home help as well as home care), a simple aggregation of the recipients of each type of service or benefit is not appropriate because double counting occurs. Controlling for this duplication of benefits or services in national accounts may often be very difficult.[13]

In addition to the problem of duplication of benefits and services, there may also exist an identification problem with respect to the beneficiaries. If the institutions delivering home care benefits and services provide the same or similar kinds of benefits or services not only to disabled elderly but also to other groups, it will be difficult to identify the disabled elderly among all these beneficiaries. This may be the case if e.g. care services and benefits are integrated into a common health and social assistance system, as for example the home care services in Denmark and Norway.

5 Defining National Long-Term Care Objectives

An alternative approach to a cross-national study of long-term care systems could be to use an intra-national comparison method defining national long-term care objectives. Rather than to compare the performance of the long-term care systems across the survey countries using indicators based on national accounts, the relevant question in this approach is, to what extent do the survey countries achieve their own national long-term care aims? Hence, in an intra-national approach it may be possible to avoid some of the difficulties that appear in cross-national comparisons using performance indicators, e.g. inequivalence of national definitions and compiling methods.

A cross-national comparison could then be carried out by comparing the national degrees of goal accomplishment. However, a problem arises due to the fact that some countries set the goals for their long-term care system rather high, whereas other countries are less ambitious. In this case, a cross-national comparison of the degrees of goal accomplishment may not be meaningful. One possibility, to solve this problem, could be to construct common aims for all survey countries. For example, prevention of poverty (e.g. by defining a poverty line) and prevention of institutionalisation (e.g. degree of institutionalisation). Yet, to define equivalent goals for all survey countries is difficult. The acceptance of various goals depends on cross-cultural differences, even if restricted to some "minimum acceptable level". There may be agreement on some goals, such as improving functional status, disability-free life expectancy, and the efficiency services and benefits are provided to the disabled elderly, whereas there will probably be disagreement on how the LTC burden should be distributed among families, other elderly, and the population in general.

Even when a pure intra-national comparative method is chosen, at least three major problems still remain. First, who is to define the aims of the national long-term care systems: the government, the responsible ministry (or ministries), the political parties, the labour unions, the interest groups of the disabled? Second, if several definitions for the aims of the national long-term care system exist, which definition should be chosen? Third, in some countries the goals of the national long-term care systems may be vaguely expressed and hence not be operational for an intra-national comparison.

6 Standardised Model Cases

Perhaps a more interesting method of comparing national long-term care systems is to use standardised model cases. In this approach, the cross-national comparison is carried out by defining various cases of a standardised disabled elderly (e.g., the "labour equivalent average production worker"), and looking at the type and the level of benefits and services that can be provided to the various standardised disabled elderly.

Figure 1 shows some possible cases of a standardised disabled elderly. First, the degree of disability has to be defined for the standardised elderly. This can be accomplished by using ADLs and IADLs as shown in section 2. The degree of disability can then be set by defining a number of ADLs and IADLs that the standardised elderly is unable to perform on his or her own without assistance, or by defining how often the standard disabled elderly is in need of help to perform the ADLs and IADLs. However, many countries taken into account in our survey on LTC in Europe (e.g. Denmark, Great Britain, Ireland, Norway and Sweden) do not use clearly specified ADLs or IADLs schemes in their assessment for care services and benefits. Rather, in these countries each local authority decides the assessment for care services on its own in a rather subjective manner, often not using any predefined assess criteria at all. This means that no general criteria to assess the individual care needs of and the services to be provided for an disabled elderly can be generated for the country as a hole. One possibility to account for these countries in an analysis based on standardised model cases could be to define an "average disabled elderly", and hence compute the average amount of benefits and services provided to this elderly. However, for the comparison across the countries this is still not a very satisfactory solution.

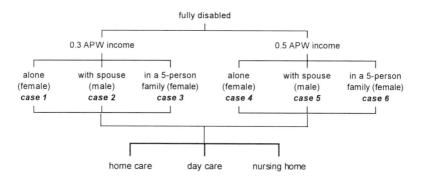

Figure 1: Standardised Model Cases

Second, in view of the fact that some services may be means-tested, the income (and the wealth) positions of the standardised disabled elderly have to be specified. However, due to the different welfare levels in the survey countries, this cannot be accomplished by expressing the income and wealth in nominal amounts of any currency. Rather, the income and wealth positions of the standardised elderly should be expressed as proportions of an average production worker's (APW) income in each country. In this respect, the income of other household members, such as spouse and children, should be taken into account. This can e.g. be done by defining a "household equivalent APW income", using the OECD equivalent scale, where the first adult person in a household is given the weight 1.0, any further adult person 0.7 and any children 0.5. Concerning the income, it would be interesting to define a poverty line, and then ask, to what extent a "wealthy" disabled elderly (or its household) will become "poor" due to payments for care.

Finally, one has to specify age and sex of the standardised disabled elderly, as some benefits and services, e.g. pensions, are likely to diverge with respect to these characteristics too.

Having defined the various cases of a standardised disabled elderly, one is confronted with the problem to specify the kind and the amount of benefits and services that can be provided to the standardised disabled elderly. This must be executed by studying national acts and legislative guidelines. Cash benefits to the standardised disabled elderly should be expressed as a proportion of an average production worker's income. The amount of services in kind is to be accounted for as hours or visits a day, week, month or year. However, it must be kept in mind that the levels of benefits and services provided, in practice, may diverge considerably from those according to law. For instance, the delivery of benefits and services may in practice be more generous than specified in national acts and legislative guidelines, or the provision of benefits and services may – e.g. due to insufficient supply capacities – in practice not reach the level specified in national acts and legislative guidelines.

E.g. in case 3 in figure 1 the disabled elderly is set to be a female person living in a 5-person family (e.g. the disabled elderly woman is living together with her daughter, her son in law and her two grand children). The household equivalent APW income is set to 0.3. The objective of the standardised model cases is then to specify the amount and the kind of services and benefits, i.e. "home care", "day care", and "nursing home", that can be provided to this standardised disabled elderly woman.

7 Micro Data

A final approach to cross-national comparisons may be based on micro data compiled in sample surveys. With the use of micro data, it may be possible to identify the variables determining the risk of being disabled during old age or the variables determining the choice between home care and nursing home care, etc..

Theoretically, it can be suggested that the risk of becoming disabled during old age depends on variables such as:

- White collar versus blue collar employment, where, due to physically harder working conditions, blue collar workers are expected to have a higher long-term care risk than white collar workers.
- Income and wealth, where a negative correlation should be expected (e.g. due to better nutrition and better housing conditions).
- Housing conditions, where the long-term care risk should be positively correlated to housing not being suitable for elderly frail people.
- Sex, where women are supposed to have a higher long-term care risk than men due to the fact that (1) their life expectancy is higher, and (2) they are younger than and hence survive their spouses, which often implies that they are living alone.
- Level of education, where a negative correlation should be expected.

The choice between home care and nursing home care may depend on variables such as:

- Age, where a positive correlation between the choice of institutional care and age should be expected.
- Income and wealth, where a negative correlation between the choice of institutional care and income and wealth should be expected.
- Housing conditions, where housing conditions not being suitable for elderly frail people should be positively correlated with the choice of institutional care.
- Number of children, where a negative correlation between the number of children and the choice of institutional care should be expected (higher potential of informal care providers).
- Distance between the elderly's home and that of the children, where a positive correlation between the distance and the choice of institutional care should be expected.

(For some empirical evidence for the U.S. and Germany see e.g. Kemper/Pezzin, Klein, and Sloan et al. all in this volume.)

The lists of determinants suggested above might be extended by further factors that may have an influence on the risk of disability or the choice between home care and nursing home care. For example, people living in rural areas may have a smaller risk of disability and institutionalisation than people living in urban areas, e.g. due to housing condition (detached housing with only one or two floors versus high-rise buildings) or family size, which may tend to be larger in rural areas than in urban areas (higher potential of informal care providers).

Further, one should keep in mind that several determinants are correlated with each other. For example, income and wealth are likely to be determined by the status of being a white collar or blue collar employee and by the level of education. Yet, income and wealth will probably correlate with better housing conditions.

Finally, micro data analysis will have to be based on panel data or sample survey data. However, it appears to be very difficult to find adequate and reliable micro data on long-term care in European countries. This is especially a problem in cross-national comparisons where representative and comparable data based on equivalent national definitions and compiling methods must be available for several countries. Taking Germany as an example, it appears to be very difficult to get access to reliable micro data even for one single country. The Socio-Economic Panel (SOEP) seems to provide the most adequate data for Germany concerning a micro data analysis on long-term care. Yet, one of the main limitations of the SOEP data is the small number of observations available for disabled elderly. For the years 1985-1991 the maximum available number of observations on disabled persons varies between 126 and 176 in each census. These observations also include disabled aged 60 and under. When distinguishing the disabled according to variables such as age and sex, the number of observations decrease considerably, increasing the problem of insignificant results.[14]
In addition, as mentioned in chapter 4, the decision whether a household member is accounted for as disabled or not is a rather subjective judgement of the head of the household, making the compiled data less reliable.

8 Conclusions

The use of intra-national comparisons, standardised model cases, and micro data in a cross-national comparison of long-term care systems may in some cases provide more interesting and more reliable results than comparisons based on performance indicators. In addition, some of the shortcomings and difficulties encountered when using performance indicators based on national accounts – such as inequivalence of national definitions and compiling methods – may be avoided. Still, the problems of intra-national comparisons, standardised model cases, and the use of micro data are also apparent. The decision, as to which approach appears to be the most appropriate, will depend heavily on the available data of each survey country.

In the European context, an improvement of national and international statistics appears to be necessary in order to make cross-national analysis of long-term care systems more reliable or even possible. In this respect, there is a special need for micro data on long-term care, which is hardly available at all in any European national or international panel data survey. As we have seen in the papers by Kemper/Pezzin and Sloan et al. in this volume the availability of data concerning long-term care seems to be much better in the U.S..

Acknowledgment

The author wishes to thank Roland Eisen and Frank A. Sloan for helpful comments and advice on earlier versions of this paper. He also gratefully acknowledges the financial support of the Volkswagen-Foundation.

Notes

[1] Quoted in Dieck/Garms-Homolová (1991), 133 and 325.
[2] See Dieck/Garms-Homolová (1991), 135.
[3] See Platz (1989), 48.
[4] See Hauser (1991), 198, who discusses the problems in an international comparison of pension systems.
[5] See Ritter (1992), 6-7.
[6] See Kaim-Caudle (1973), 48, and Ritter (1992), 179.
[7] See e.g. Tobin/Nordhaus (1972).
[8] See e.g. Ritter (1992), 221.
[9] See e.g. the studies by Lundh (1991), Christensen/Hansen (1993), and Gundtvedt/Beverfelt (1989).
[10] See Hanf (1993), 7-15.
[11] See Maydell (1992), 31-32.
[12] See Kehr (1988), 407 and Klar et al. (1989), 141.
[13] Daatland (1990), 106 states this problem using official statistics of Norway to compute the overall number of beneficiaries of long-term benefits and services.
[14] See Hanf (1993), 15.

References

BMAS, Bundesministerium für Arbeit und Soziales (Ministry of Social Affairs) (1991): *Sicherung bei Pflegebedürftigkeit – Fakten und Argumente*. Bonn.
Christensen, I. M./Hansen, E. B. (1993): *Offentlige udgifter til pleje af ældre*. AKF rapport. Copenhagen: Amternes og Kommunernes Forskningsinstitut.
Daatland, S. O. (1990): *Ressurser og ressursbruk i eldresektoren, Dagens mønster og utviklingen over tid*. Report No. 5-1990. Oslo: Norsk gerontologisk institutt.
Dieck, M./Garms-Homolová, V. (1991): Home-care Services in the Federal Republic of Germany, in A. Jamieson (ed.): *Home Care for Older People in Europe – A Comparison of Policies and Practices*. Oxford et al.: University Press, 118-130.
Gundtvedt, O. H./Beverfelt, E. (1989): *Dagsentre for eldre – mer enn et sted å være?* Report No. 2-1989. Oslo: Norsk gerontologisk institutt.
Hanf, V. (1993): *Die Situation Pflegebedürftiger in der Bundesrepublik und der Einfluß möglicher Absicherungsmaßnahmen*. Thesis at the University of Frankfurt/Germany.
Hauser, R. (1991): Probleme der vergleichenden Analyse von Systemen sozialer Sicherung – Drei Beispiele aus dem Bereich der Alterssicherung, in Th. Thiemeyer (ed.): *Theoretische Grundlagen der Sozialpolitik II*. Schriften des Vereins für Sozialpolitik 205. Berlin: Duncker & Humblot, 195-223.
Holzman, R. (1988): *Reforming Public Pensions*. OECD Social Policy Studies No. 5. Paris.
Kaim-Caudle, P. R. (1973): *Comparative Social Policy and Social Security, A Ten-Country Study*. London: Robertson.
Katz, S./Ford, A.B./Moskowitz, R.W./Jackson, B.A./Jaffe, M.W. (1963): Studies of Illness in the Aged: The Index of ADL – A Standardized Measure of Biological and Psychosocial Function, in *Journal of Medical Association 185*, 914-919, quoted in Dieck/Garms-Homolová (1991), 133 and 325.
Kehr, H. (1988): Krankenhaus-Fehlbelegung – Gründe, Hintergründe und Ausmaß von Fehlbelegung in bundesdeutschen Krankenhäusern, in *Die Ortskrankenkasse 13*, 404-408.
Klar, R./Müller, U./Schulte-Mönting, J. (1989): Eine repräsentative Studie zu Umfang und Struktur von Fehlbelegungen bei über 60jährigen Akutkrankenhauspatienten, in *Öffentliches Gesundheitswesen 51*, 139-142.
Lawton, M. P./Brody, E. M. (1969): Assessment of Older People: Selfmaintaining and Instrumental Activities of Daily Living, in *The Gerontologist 9*, 176-186, quoted in Dieck/Garms-Homolová (1991), 133 and 325.
Lundh, U. (1991): *Vård och omsorg i eget boende på äldre dar*. Linköping Studies in Arts and Science No. 73, Linköping.
Maydell, B. v. (1992): *Die Pflegefallversicherung im europäischen Vergleich*. Manuskript. Bonn.
Platz, M. (1989): *Gamle i eget hjem, Vol. 1*. Rapport 89-12, Copenhagen: Socialforskningsinstituttet.
Ritter, U. P. (1992): *Vergleichende Volkswirtschaftslehre*. München et al.: Oldenburg.

Socialdata (1980): *Anzahl und Situation zu Hause lebender Pflegebedürftiger*, Schriftenreihe des Bundesministers für Jugend, Familie und Gesundheit 80, Stuttgart et al.: Kohlhammer.

Thiede, R. (1990): *Die gestaffelte Pflegeversicherung. Sozialpolitische und Ökonomische Aspekte eines neuen Modells.* Frankfurt a. M./New York: Campus.

Tobin, J./Nordhaus, W. D. (1972): *Economic Growth*, in National Bureau of Economic Research (NBER), Fiftieth Anniversary Colloguium V 52, New York/London.

PART TWO:
EMPIRICAL RESEARCH INTO THE DEMAND AND PROVISION OF LONG-TERM CARE SERVICES

3 EFFECTS OF STRATEGIC BEHAVIOR AND PUBLIC SUBSIDIES ON FAMILIES' SAVINGS AND LONG-TERM CARE DECISIONS

Frank A. Sloan, Thomas J. Hoerger and Gabriel Picone

1 Introduction

Inspired by Becker (1974), (1981), economists have returned to the classic idea that intrafamily decisions lie at the heart of many important aspects of economic behavior. Models of the family generally emphasize either altruism or strategic exchange as the major motivation for behavior. Models of altruism assume that family members provide services or transfers to one another because they care about each other. By contrast, strategic exchange models emphasize that family members exchange services for cash or in-kind transfers. For example, a child may provide attention to a parent in exchange for bequests. The strategic exchange models generally allow for altruistic behavior; strategic effects arise when one family member can induce another to exchange more services or transfers than the second member prefers to provide.[1] Both types of models have been used to analyze how public policies affect family decisions.

Few areas offer greater potential for interaction between family decisions and public policy than long-term care for the elderly. Because their health deteriorates gradually or because of sudden health shocks, the elderly face an appreciable probability of not being able to care for themselves [Kemper et al. (1991)]. Care to enable disabled persons to function may be provided in a nursing home, or alternatively in the community with paid help, and/or unpaid help obtained from relatives and friends.

There is little private insurance against such risk [Pauly (1990)]. Rather, such care is primarily paid from savings of the elderly and their children, in-kind transfers in the form of informal care, and from public sources of which Medicaid is by far the most important one. Savings and obtaining a subsidy from Medicaid are closely related in that an individual's income and wealth determine a person's eligibility for Medicaid and the amount of the subsidy if the person is determined to be eligible. Availability of Medicaid subsidies for long-term care (LTC) services may have decreased demand for private long-term care insurance, caused some elderly parents to make *inter vivos* transfers to their children and others, decreased elderly families' savings, decreased the time relatives and friends spend in caring for the disabled elderly ("informal care") and increased their use of purchased long-term care services ("formal care") in the community.

The purpose of this study is to investigate the effects of Medicaid and strategic behavior on (1) the probability of entering a nursing home, (2) amounts of formal and informal care provided elderly persons in the community, and (3) asset accumulation. To provide a conceptual framework for studying the interaction between Medicaid subsidies, strategic behavior, and family decisions, we present a two-period model motivated in part by Bernheim et al's (1985) strategic bequest model. Bernheim et al. argue that, by threatening disinheritance, parents can extract more attention from their children than the children would like to provide. Empirically, they find that the number of children's telephone calls and visits to their parents rises with parents' wealth. Testing for strategic effects is an important part of our empirical work. We measure childrens' attention by informal care provided to disabled parents, which plausibly has more value to parents than telephone calls or visits.

We present our basic model in Section 2. Extensions of the model are discussed in Section 3. Section 4 describes our primary data source, the National Long-Term Care Survey (NLTCS), and other data sources, and how we have adapted the data to our two-period model, followed by more detailed empirical specification in Section 5. In Section 6, we present our empirical results. We find that Medicaid subsidies increase the probability of entry in the nursing home and use of formal care of elderly who remain in the community. However,

Medicaid subsidies have not "crowded out" informal care provided by relatives and friends of the elderly. Nor has Medicaid reduced wealth accumulation by the elderly. Overall, we find little empirical support for the hypothesis that caregiving by children is motivated by the prospect of receiving bequests from their parents. We discuss our evidence on the strategic bequest motive in Section 7 and present conclusions in Section 8.

2 Conceptual Model

2.1 Outline of the Model

In the sequential two-period model, there are two actors: a widowed parent and the parent's grown child. In period 1, the parent is healthy and chooses consumption and savings to maximize expected utility. Three states can occur in period 2. First, with probability β, the parent will die (d). Second, with probability ρ, the parent will become cognitively unaware (u) in period 2. Because the parent is incapable of making decisions, the child will decide whether to place the parent in the nursing home or leave her in the community. The child also decides optimal levels of formal and informal care in the community. To capture the asymmetry in preferences between parent and child, we assume that in the community the parent receives greater utility from informal care than formal care, whereas the child only worries about the total care received by the parent.

In the third state, the parent will be cognitively aware (a), but with worse health than in period 1. Because she is aware, the parent will decide whether to enter the nursing home or not, and, in the latter case, how much formal and informal care to purchase. A key question is how much informal care the parent will be able to receive; in general, the amount will depend on both the parent's demand for informal care and the child's supply. If the parent can credibly threaten to disinherit her child, she may be able to extract more informal care than the child would like to supply.

At the end of period 2, the parent dies. Any remaining assets are inherited by the child; such bequests give the parent utility.

The parent solves her problem rationally through the use of backwards induction. The parent first determines optimal choices of nursing home, formal, and informal care in period 2, taking period 1's saving as exogenous. This produces optimal response functions that depend on savings and other variables. Given these functions, the parent chooses period 1 consumption and savings to maximize expected utility from both periods.

One of the reasons Pauly (1990) gives for the nonpurchase of long-term care insurance is that parents fear that if they have such insurance, their children will be too quick to place them in a nursing home when they are no longer able to resist. If parents eschew such coverage, the children will face the full price of nursing home which will cause corresponding reductions in their bequest. Consequently, they will be more reluctant to place the parent in the nursing home. In this study, we formalize Pauly's idea, but here, instead of not purchasing private health insurance, the parent can make herself ineligible for a Medicaid subsidy for nursing home care by saving more. Consequently, she will be less likely to be institutionalized when and if she becomes cognitively impaired.

2.2 Second-Period Decisions: Choices of Formal and Informal Care in the Community and Choice of Nursing Home Care

In the second period, the decision is made whether the parent lives in a nursing home or in the community. If in the latter, a decision must be made about use of informal and formal care.

2.2.1 The Parent is Cognitively Unaware

We distinguish between cases in which the parent is cognitively unaware and aware. In the first case, because the parent is unable to make decisions, the child decides whether to institutionalize the parent or leave her in the community and, if the latter, how much formal and informal care to purchase. To decide, the child compares his utility in the alternative locations.

a. Community Location. Although the optimal choice of formal and informal care in the community at this stage is made by the child, the parent has different preferences than the child, and this difference may affect the parent's first period decision. If the parent remains in the community, her utility is given by

$$U_u^Q(Q) + U_u^I(I) + V_u^C(C^K) \tag{1}$$

where Q, total care in the community, is the sum of informal care (I) and formal care (F), C^K is the child's consumption, U refers to utility from the parent's consumption and V is the utility from the child's consumption; the subscript u indicates the parent is cognitively unaware.

In contrast, the child's utility is given by

$$U_u^Q(Q) + V_u^C(C^K) \tag{2}$$

Although the child still receives utility from the total care received by the parent, the child receives no additional utility from informal care.[2]

The child spends the parent's savings (S) and the child's income (Y), which depends on his wage rate (w) and the amount of informal care (I) he provides, on formal care and consumption according to

$$S + Y(w, I) - p^F F - C^K = 0, \quad (3)$$

where p^F is the price of formal care.

Providing informal care reduces the child's income, with $Y_I < 0$ and $Y_{II} < 0$. Substituting (3) into (2), maximizing over F and I, and suppressing obvious subscripts and superscripts, yields

$$\frac{\partial U}{\partial Q} - p^F \frac{\partial V}{\partial C^K} = 0 \quad (4a)$$

and

$$\frac{\partial U}{\partial Q} + Y_I \frac{\partial V}{\partial C^K} = 0, \quad (4b)$$

respectively. If both first-order conditions are satisfied, $p^F = -Y_I$. Because the child views formal and informal care as perfect substitutes, the child provides informal care as long as its shadow price is less than the price of formal care. The child will purchase care until the parent's marginal utility from consumption equals the marginal utility of the child's foregone consumption.

Effects of Public Subsidies. Two types of public subsidies may affect the mix of care in the community. First, a low income parent may receive a cash supplement equal to M, thereby shifting out the child's budget constraint. The increase in the budget constraint increases total care (Q). Because there is no change in the relative prices of formal and informal care ($p^F, -Y_I$), the amount of informal care does not change. Therefore, only F rises as the cash transfer rises. The second subsidy consists of an in-kind transfer by Medicaid to the recipient of $\overline{Q}$ units of formal care. The usual result for an in-kind transfer holds: the parent will consume at least as much formal care as before, although the child will purchase less formal care privately. The amount of informal care provided will not change.

Other comparative statics. With an increase in p^F, formal care falls, informal care rises, and total care falls. If the parent's savings (S) do not affect Medicaid eligibility, an increase in S shifts the child's budget constraint out.[3] As with M, this increases formal care and has no effect on informal care.

Medicaid eligibility standards for community care subsidies consist of savings thresholds.[4] Parents with savings below the thresholds are eligible for subsidies, while parents with higher savings are not. Consequently, formal care falls discontinuously when savings reach the threshold level. Above the threshold, savings have their usual positive effect on formal care. Since in-kind transfers and cash subsidies do not affect I, the amount of informal care will not change as S crosses the savings threshold.

b. Nursing Home Care. The child's utility from placing the parent in the nursing home is

$$U_u^N(\overline{N}) + V_u^N(C^K), \tag{5}$$

where $C^K = S + Y(w) - p^N \overline{N}$ and $Y(w)$ is the child's income when he provides no informal care. We assume that only a fixed quantity of nursing home care $\overline{N}$ can be purchased for the out-of-pocket expenditure p^N.[5] As a result, there are no choice variables to be selected in the equation, but changes in exogenous variables affect the child's utility, conditional on selecting nursing home care.

Increases in the child's income increase the child's utility if the nursing home is selected, while increases in price lowers utility. If Medicaid changes eligibility requirements, the amount of money the child can keep after paying for nursing home care changes. This amount, which we call residual wealth in the nursing home, equals $S - p^N \overline{N}$. The effect of savings on utility depends on whether the parent is eligible for Medicaid. To be eligible, the parent's savings must lie below the state's savings threshold, T. If the parent is on Medicaid, she pays her entire savings (minus a small allowance for personal consumption) for nursing home care; Medicaid pays the remainder. In a sense, Medicaid coverage has a variable deductible equal to the parent's savings.

c. Community Care vs. Nursing Home Care. To choose between sites for the parent, the child simply compares the maximum utilities calculated above. Consequently, a probit equation estimating the probability of entering a nursing home should include any variable which affects utility in one or both states. Variables only affecting utility in one of the states have definite signs in the equations, whereas variables affecting both utilities in the same direction have indeterminate signs, since it is impossible to tell which marginal effect is larger without placing further structure on the problem. Therefore, we predict that more liberal Medicaid eligibility for nursing home care, lower nursing home prices, and higher prices or lower subsidies for formal care in the community will increase the probability of nursing home placement. Variables affecting both utilities and having indeterminate effects are child's income and parent's savings.

STRATEGIC BEHAVIOR AND PUBLIC SUBSIDIES

In one case, savings clearly reduces the probability of institutionalization, however. If savings are below the Medicaid threshold for nursing home care and above the threshold for community subsidies, increasing S only increases utility in the community, since higher savings in the nursing home simply translate into a higher deductible. We exploit this exception empirically by including separate terms for residual wealth in the nursing home and community in our equation estimating the probability of nursing home entry.

2.2.2 The Parent is Cognitively Aware

If cognitively aware (a), the parent decides about her care.

a. Community Location. When the parent selects formal and informal care in the community, she must consider how much informal care the child will supply. This issue was easily resolved in the cognitively unaware case since the child chose his utility-maximizing level of informal care. Now, because of the asymmetries in preferences (see (1) and (2)), parent and child will prefer different levels of formal and informal care. Can the parent induce the child to provide more informal care than the child prefers? Or if the child provides his optimal level of informal care, can the child prevent the parent from buying too much formal care, thereby "squandering" the child's inheritance?

To resolve these questions, we first examine extreme solutions which alternatively give each participant the full gains from trade. At the one extreme, the child provides his or her optimal level of formal and informal care. This outcome is supported as a Nash equilibrium by the child's threat to withhold informal care if the parent purchases any level of formal care different than the child's optimal level.[6] This outcome is identical to that in the unaware state and the same comparative statics apply.

At the other extreme, the parent possesses superior bargaining power and captures all the gains from trade.[7] In this outcome, the parent achieves her optimal levels of formal and informal care by threatening to disinherit the child if the child does not provide the parent's optimal level of informal care.[8]

In the optimal outcome for the parent, she receives more informal care and less formal care than when she is cognitively unaware. The first order conditions maximizing the parent's utility (1) differs from the first-order conditions that maximize the child's utility. The first-order conditions for the parent are:

$$\frac{\partial U^\eta}{\partial Q} - p^F \frac{\partial V}{\partial C^K} = 0 \qquad (6a)$$

and

$$\frac{\partial U^Q}{\partial Q} + \frac{\partial U^I}{\partial I} + Y_I \frac{\partial V}{\partial C^K} = 0 \tag{6b}$$

The first-order conditions for the child are (4a) and (4b); (4a) and (6a) are identical. Totally differentiating either equation shows that the locus of I and F satisfying the equation is negatively-sloped. At the values of F and I which maximize the child's utility, equation (6b) will be greater than zero, implying that the locus of points satisfying (6b) lies above those satisfying (4b). Therefore, the parent will prefer more informal care and less formal care than the child prefers.

To go beyond the extremes, we treat the problem as a simultaneous move, strategic bargaining problem. A natural way to introduce the bargaining process is to assume that the bargaining solution maximizes a weighted sum of the parent's and the child's utilities, where the weight on the parent's utility is

$$\theta = \frac{S}{S + Y(O, W)} \tag{7a}$$

and the weight on the child's utility is

$$(1 - \theta) = \frac{Y(O, W)}{S + Y(O, W)} \tag{7b}.$$

If neither party has complete bargaining power, the parent and child will choose points formal and informal care solutions for parent and child along the locus of points satisfying (4a).[9] Thus, the parent will do at least as well in the community when aware as when unaware. The parent's bargaining power should increase with her savings level, since the threat of disinheritance becomes more distasteful to the child. Consequently, savings should have a larger effect on the informal care the parent receives than when she is unaware.

b. *The Nursing Home Decision.* We assume that the parent has the same preferences over nursing home care as the child.[10] Therefore, the parent receives the same utility from nursing care when aware as when unaware.

c. *Community Care vs. Nursing Home Care.* Because she receives more utility in the community and the same amount of utility in the nursing home, the parent is less likely to enter the nursing home when aware than when unaware. Similarly, an aware parent in the community should consume more informal care and less formal care than an unaware parent. By strengthening the parent's bargaining power, the parent's saving should have a negative effect on the probability of nursing home entry, relative to its effect in the unaware state. Looking only at aware parents, explanatory variables such as prices and Medicaid policies which have unambiguous signs on the probability of entering a nursing home in the unaware state should have the same sign, but not necessarily the same magnitude, as in the aware state.

2.2.3 Summary of Comparative Statics

Results from the comparative statics analysis for period 2 decisions are summarized in Table 1.

2.2.4 The Parent Dies

If the parent dies (d) before the second period, her savings pass to the child.

2.3 First-Period Decisions

In period 1, the parent chooses saving (S) and consumption (C_1) to maximize expected utility, subject to the constraint that the parent's wealth, Λ, equals $S + C_1$. Substituting for C_1, the first-order condition for saving is

$$-\frac{\partial U_1}{\partial C_1} + \rho \frac{\partial (\psi_u)}{\partial S} + (1-\beta-\rho) \frac{\partial (\psi_a)}{\partial S} + \beta \frac{\partial V_d}{\partial S} = 0$$

where

$$\psi_i = \max[U_i^Q(I_i(S) + F_i(S)) + U_i^I(I_i(S)) + V_i^C(Y(w, I_i(S)) + S - p^F F_i(S)) +$$

$$+ U_i^N(\overline{N}) + V_i^N(S + Y(w) - p^N \overline{N})]. \qquad (8)$$

This condition has the usual interpretation in a saving model: the parent equates the marginal utility of foregone consumption in period 1 with the expected marginal utility of savings in period 2.

An important policy question is whether Medicaid subsidies increase or decrease savings. Unfortunately, comparative statics on S yield generally ambiguous predictions because (1) S has zero or positive effects on residual wealth in the nursing home, depending on whether the parent is eligible or ineligible for Medicaid; (2) the parent may be placed in the nursing home if unaware but remain in the community if aware; the two locations have different marginal utilities; and (3) derivatives of $\partial \Psi_i / \partial S$ with respect to the exogenous variables are not easily signed because the second-period optimal response functions ($I_u(S)$, $F_u(S)$, etc.) implicitly include such variables. Nevertheless, the model clearly indicates that variables which influence second period decisions will also affect the first-period savings decision.

3 Extensions Of The Model

3.1 Multiple Children

The model can easily be modified to include the case of multiple children. Bernheim et al. (1985) argue that children will provide more informal care in the presence of siblings since the parent's threat of disinheritance is more credible. This argument suggests that more children increase informal care to aware parents, but, except for the effect of more children on the time price of care, more children should have no effect on care provided unaware parents.

3.2 A Living Spouse

The presence of a living spouse will affect the model in several ways. Presumably, the spouse, not the child, will decide whether to admit a cognitively unaware parent to the nursing home. The spouse will probably place greater weight on the parent's preference for informal care than the child places, and therefore more willingly provide such care. Consequently, the probability of nursing home entry should fall. Second, because most persons in our sample are 75 or older, most spouses will be retired and have no children at home. Thus, the spouse's cost of providing informal care may be less than the child's, thereby increasing provision of informal care and lowering the probability of entering the nursing home. Indeed, the cost of providing informal care may be so low that $-Y_1 < p^F$ for relevant levels of informal care; if so, no formal care will be purchased. Finally, the spouse may fear impoverishing himself by admitting his wife to a nursing home.

3.3 Severity of Illness

As the parent becomes more severely disabled, the marginal benefits of both community care and nursing home care probably increase. Benefits from nursing home care plausibly rise more rapidly than benefits from community care as severity rises, increasing the probability of nursing home entry.

3.4 Nursing Home Care is Rationed

Our model implicitly assumes that the parent can enter the nursing home if that gives her (or her child) greater utility than care in the community. In fact, nursing home markets may not be in equilibrium. Overall admissions into nursing homes may be supply-constrained when certificate of need laws limit construction of nursing homes and prices cannot adjust to equate demand with limited supply. Even if private-pay patients face no constraint on admissions, Medicaid-subsidized patients may have difficulties gaining admittance because Medicaid generally pays much less than a nursing home regular prices [Ettner (1993); Nyman (1985); Nyman (1988); U.S. General Accounting Office (1990)]. We found that 66 percent of the 1989 NLTCS sample would have qualified financially for Medicaid at entry to a nursing home, but only 37 percent of nursing home residents in our sample were actually subsidized by Medicaid in the first month following entry. Thus, many persons who were in the community may have wanted to be institutionalized. Consequently, the probability of entering a nursing home will be less in states where nursing home markets are supply constrained. The constraints may also affect formal and informal care in the community through a selection effect.

4 Data Sources

The U.S. Census Bureau conducted the NLTCS in 1982, 1984, and 1989. Criteria for inclusion in the sample were that the respondent be at least age 65 and need help in one or more Activities of Daily Living (ADL) or Instrumental Activities of Daily Living (IADL) for a period of at least three months. ADLs are limitations requiring help with basic personal activities, such as eating and bathing. IADLs are limitations in other, less personal activities, such as shopping and doing the laundry. The 1989 survey contains 5,708 respondents, with 1,354 residing in nursing homes.

Data on state Medicaid program characteristics – eligibility standards and Medicaid reimbursement rates – came from several published [U.S. Department of Health and Human Services (1984), (1985), (1987); Budish (1989); Commerce Clearinghouse (various years)] and unpublished sources [Harrington et al. (1990); Neuschler (1987)]. Information on the probability of receipt of Medicaid home health benefits and per capita Medicaid home health expenditures came from unpublished Medicaid program data (Health Care Financing Administration Form 2082.) Discounts relative to private pay were derived by taking the difference of the private pay nursing home price and a weighted average of skilled nursing facility and intermediate care facility Medicaid reimbursement rates. State-specific estimates of the private pay nursing home price came from the 1985 National Nursing Home Survey (NNHS) of individual nursing homes. We updated values to 1989 using the medical service component of the Consumer Price Index. Medicaid price data for 1989 came from a telephone survey described in Swan et al. (1993). We obtained nursing home bed data from Harrington et al. (1990). Gross hourly price of home health services came from an unpublished survey conducted for the American Health Care Association.

Our model makes an important distinction between cognitively aware and unaware elderly persons. We defined cognitively impaired persons as (1) those who answered fewer than seven out of 10 questions on a cognitive functioning test administered during the NLTCS to sample persons, both in the community and in nursing homes, correctly, and (2) persons who could not respond to the questionnaire and required a proxy respondent. Questions on the cognitive functioning test ranged from questions about today's date and the person's age to "who is the President of the United States now" and "subtract 3 from 20 and keep subtracting from new number you get, all the way down."

5 Empirical Specification

5.1 Probability of Being in a Nursing Home in 1989

The dependent variable was one if the person was in a nursing home in 1989 and was zero other wise. We divided our sample into persons with cognitive impairments and others in 1989. We dropped all persons who had been in the nursing home for less than three and more than 60 months at the time of the survey or with stays primarily subsidized by Medicare.

To distinguish between determinants of demand for nursing home care and of nursing home willingness to accept a patient who wants to enter, we included measures of nonprice rationing by nursing homes in the analysis. The data did not allow one to distinguish cases in which nursing home care was not demanded from those in which such care was demanded but the person was refused entry. Thus, we estimated a bivariate probit model with partial observability [Poirier (1980); Abowd and Farber (1982)] as well as a univariate probit model with nonprice rationing variables included.

5.1.1 Demand

a. Residual Wealth in the Nursing Home. Our model predicts that increased levels of residual wealth in a nursing home raise the probability of being institutionalized. Residual wealth in the nursing home was defined as the difference between wealth – the sum of the value of nonhousing assets and the present value of nonbequeathable income accruing to the parent – and the present value of payments from the parent to the nursing home, using a (real) discount rate of three percent. Residual wealth is the potential bequest (or the amount available for consumption and bequests when there is a spouse). Nonhousing wealth came directly from the survey. The present values reflect the probabilities of living each of 30 years from 1989. To compute survival probabilities, we estimated a hazard model with data from the 1982 NLTCS sample and dates of death on these persons extending through 1991 from Medicare records.

To compute each year's net price of nursing home care to the parent, we started with the 1989 gross price of nursing home care.[11] We subtracted the subsidy that the person could anticipate from Medicaid if she entered a nursing home on the survey date, but added back the cash transfer from public sources that the person might lose if she became institutionalized.

Medicaid generally excludes housing wealth for purposes of determining eligibility. Thus, we excluded housing wealth from our measure of residual wealth in the community.[12]

Nursing home care is sold as a fixed bundle of services. Thus, the decision is to buy the total bundle or none at all. By contrast, in the community, the parent may use different quantities of formal care and informal care depending on their prices. Therefore, we did not subtract expenditures on formal and informal care when we defined residual wealth in the community. Instead, residual wealth in the community was simply the sum of nonhousing assets and the present value of nonbequeathable income accruing to the parent. Terms for the prices of formal and informal care were also included in the equation.

b. Residual Wealth in the Community. Conceptually, as residual wealth in the community rises, the parent is more likely to remain there, both because her utility is relatively high and because the rise in wealth increases her bargaining power. Although utility of living in the community decreases as prices of formal and informal care increase, thereby increasing the probability of institutionalization, unlike N, amounts of F and I are not fixed. Therefore, separate variables for nonhousing wealth and price of informal and formal care were included to represent residual wealth in the community.

c. Prices of Formal and Informal Care. We included two measures of the price of formal care: the hourly wage paid aides in nursing homes in 1989 by state, and the expected weekly per capita home health subsidy by Medicaid in 1989. The latter variable was defined as the product of a binary variable for Medicaid eligibility, the probability of receiving any home health benefit from Medicaid if a recipient, and the Medicaid subsidy for home health care per recipient and per week. Unlike the nursing home, recipients could purchase some formal care and receive other formal care services from Medicaid.

The price of informal care in the community was measured by numbers of the children (1) living within 30 minutes of the parent, (2) 30 minutes to an hour away, and (3) more than an hour away and (4) a binary if the patient was married. Unfortunately, the NLTCS only obtained wage rates of potential caregivers for one actual provider of informal care to persons living in the community.[13]

d. Housing Assets and Spouse's Nonbequeathable Income. Both housing assets and the spouse's nonbequeathable income typically are not affected by whether or not the "parent" is admitted to a nursing home. Yet such wealth and income may affect the admission decision.[14] The NLTCS did not ask respondents in nursing homes about the value of the house. We imputed a measure of housing assets at entry for institutionalized persons, using data from the community sample.[15] The spouse's nonbequeathable income is for the survey month. Higher housing wealth and spouse's nonbequeathable income should reduce the probability of institutionalization.

e. Other Variables. We also included: number of ADLs and a binary variable for being cognitively unaware in 1989 to measure functional states; gender; and age.

5.1.2 Supply

a. Discount Medicaid Obtains. To account for rationing of Medicaid patients by nursing homes on account of the discount Medicaid obtains, we calculated how much the nursing home could expect to receive if the patient never qualified for Medicaid. We then calculated the nursing home's projected revenues taking into account when the patient would become eligible for Medicaid and the Medicaid payment levels to nursing homes in the state. The difference between the first and second measures is the Medicaid discount. Our hazard model estimated the probability that the person is alive during each period.

b. Other Supply Variables. We include several other supply variables: number of nursing home beds per 1,000 state population for bed availability; binaries for blacks and Hispanics to measure possible discrimination; and number of ADLs and a binary for unaware persons to measure homes' willingness to accept functionally impaired patients. More beds should improve Medicaid recipients' access to nursing homes; *cet. par.*, being black, unaware and having more ADLs should decrease nursing home willingness to accept an elderly person for admission.

5.2 Hours of Formal and Informal Care Provided to Elderly in the Community

The dependent variables for our empirical analysis of formal and informal care are hours of help for ADLs and IADLs provided to the elderly person during the week before the survey. We defined two alternative measures of informal care: hours of help provided by anyone, including spouses and unpaid volunteers, and hours of help provided by children or children-in-law. For formal care, we used hours of care paid by someone.

The sample includes all persons in the community in 1989 stratified on the basis of cognitive impairment. Alternatively, we used a binary variable for impaired persons when we analyzed the two samples together. The specification of the formal and informal care equations was the same as the equation for the probability of entry into the nursing home with these differences. First, residual wealth in the nursing home and nursing bed ratio variables were excluded. Second, we combined housing and nonhousing wealth into a single variable. Third, we included the number of IADLs the person had at the survey date and a binary variable for persons who lived in communities with more than 50,000 population (urban).

We used a two-stage procedure to estimate the formal and informal care equations. In the first, a bivariate probit was estimated for the decision to live in the community versus a nursing home and to use any informal or formal care. With consistent estimates of the parameters of the two selection processes and the correlation of their error terms, we calculated a Mills ratio which was used to estimate informal and formal care equations in the second stage with the Mills ratio as a regressor [see, e.g., Connelly (1992)]. As discussed below, results using this procedure were often not robust. Alternatively, we estimated equations of I and F with Tobit analysis without taking sample selection into the community into account.

5.3 Nonhousing Assets

The dependent variable for our empirical analysis of savings was the family's nonhousing assets in 1989. We limited the analysis to nonhousing assets because housing assets are illiquid and comparatively difficult to adjust to optimal values. Also, Medicaid excludes the home as a countable resource under several circumstances. The sample for our analysis of savings behavior was limited to persons who were not cognitively impaired in 1984 and were in the sample in both 1984 and 1989.

Although the comparative statics analysis did not yield unambiguous hypotheses, conceptually, all exogenous variables from period 2 should appear in this equation for the period 1 decision. The explanatory variables, defined for 1984, were: predicted probability of being dead by 1989; predicted probability of being cognitively impaired in 1989; black; nonbequeathable income of sample person and spouse; housing assets; nonhousing assets; composition of nonhousing assets (savings accounts, bonds, stocks, etc.), measured by binary variables indicating whether or not such assets were in the portfolio; binary variables identifying persons who would have been immediately eligible for Medicaid in 1984 if they entered a nursing home, persons who would never be eligible for Medicaid in a nursing home, again using 1984 standards, because their nonbequeathable income was too high, and persons who would be immediately eligible for Medicaid-subsidized formal care in the community. Families immediately eligible could look forward to paying zero net prices for care. Those never eligible would know that they would have to pay for much or most of their care out-of-pocket. We included other exogenous variables defined for 1989: married; number of children; private nursing home price; and nursing home beds per 1,000 state population. To account for the impact of unanticipated health shocks on wealth, we included variables for the number of admissions to nursing homes that occurred between 1984 and 1989 and the number of admissions to hospitals during 1988-9. The NLTCS did not obtain hospitalizations for earlier years.

To estimate the probability of dying between 1984 and 1989 or being cognitively impaired in 1989, we estimated a probability function with probit, conditional on levels of variables defined for 1984. The dependent variables were one if the person died before the 1989 survey and one if the person was cognitively impaired in 1989.

6 Results

6.1 Levels of Nursing Home, Formal and Informal Care

Cognitively unaware persons were four times more likely to be in a nursing home than the cognitively aware (Table 2). In fact, cognitively aware persons

STRATEGIC BEHAVIOR AND PUBLIC SUBSIDIES 61

had a low probability of being institutionalized, 0.06. Cognitively unaware persons received six hours of formal care weekly while cognitively aware persons received two hours of such care. Cognitively unaware persons received three times as much informal care from all sources than did cognitively aware. Children were twice as likely to provide informal care when the parent was cognitively unaware, and when they did, they provided more of it.

6.2 Nursing Home Choice Regressions

Our model predicts that the probability of choosing to enter a nursing home rises as residual wealth in the nursing home increases and falls as the parent's residual wealth in the community increases. The first prediction is strongly supported in both univariate and bivariate probit regressions (Table 3). Residual wealth in nursing home coefficients are statistically significant at the one percent level in the regressions based on the entire sample, and at least at the five percent level in the two subsamples. Admission elasticities, evaluated at the observational means, are -0.2 at the highest and in the univariate regression for the entire sample, about one fourth of this. A $10,000 increase in residual wealth in the nursing home raises the probability that a cognitively aware person would be admitted by 0.01. The corresponding increase in the probability for cognitively unaware is 0.02. Effects are small, but residual wealth has a greater effect for the cognitively unaware than for the cognitively aware. In our model, the child makes the choice when the parent is cognitively unaware. In the bivariate probit regression, residual wealth has a larger effect – a change in 0.03 in the probability for a $10,000 increase in residual wealth.

Coefficients on residual wealth in the community, measured by nonhousing wealth, have anticipated negative signs, but they are statistically insignificant. We attribute lack of significance to multicollinearity. When the sample is limited to persons who would qualify for Medicaid immediately on entry to the nursing home, more precise results on the coefficient on the wealth variable were obtained.

The price of formal care in the community has the anticipated positive effect on the decision to enter a nursing home, and the coefficient is statistically significant at the 10 percent level or better in both the univariate and bivariate regression with the aware and unaware samples pooled. More generous Medicaid subsidies for home health care in the community have no statistically significant effect on nursing home entry. The effects may be insignificant because the subsidies are small; the mean expected subsidy per week for our 1989 sample was only $1.41, with a range from zero to over $40.

We measured the price of informal care by the number of children of the elderly person, categorized by distance from the parent. As anticipated, availability of nearby children clearly lowers the probability of institutionalizing parents, much more so for cognitively unaware than aware parents.

As expected, higher amounts of spouse's nonbequeathable income decrease the probability of institutionalization. Likewise, coefficients on housing assets are negative. Housing assets may capture omitted heterogeneity in unmeasured preferences for house ownership.

Our model predicts that a low price of informal care leads to a lower probability of being in a nursing home. Our measure of this price, number of children by travel time from parent, in fact exerts a negative impact on this probability. But if less informal care were provided to unaware parents on average, one would expect the effect of nearby children to be greater for such parents. In fact, unaware elderly receive more such care (Tables 2 and 3), and the coefficient on the number of children within 30 minutes of the parent is larger for the unaware than for this aware. A plausible interpretation is that when children live near the parent, the effect of the productivity increase of informal care dominates any strategic effects associated with being unaware. We entered "cognitively unaware" on both demand and supply sides of the bivariate model. The coefficient on cognitively unaware is significant on both sides. We anticipated that the coefficient would be positive on the demand but negative on the supply side.

Overall, the findings on the supply variables indicate supply-side limitations to entry. Of greatest interest are the roles of the supply of nursing home beds and the discounts that Medicaid obtains from nursing homes. In states with more nursing home beds per person over age 75, the elderly were more likely to enter, suggesting important supply constraints. Surprisingly, however, the Medicaid discount does not have significant negative effects on entry. In fact, the coefficient is positive and significant in the bivariate probit analysis. The results on number of ADLs and the cognitively aware binary variable imply that nursing homes are more willing to accept functionally impaired persons.

6.3 Formal and Informal Care Regressions

Estimated equations for formal and total informal care and for informal care provided by children are shown for the total community sample (Table 4) and separately for cognitively aware and unaware elderly (Table 5). We initially estimated these equations with the two-stage sample selection procedure mentioned in Section 5 and alternatively with Tobit not correcting for sample selec-

STRATEGIC BEHAVIOR AND PUBLIC SUBSIDIES 63

tion. Results from the two-stage procedure sometimes were implausible (e.g., standard errors were implausibly low) and were not robust to changes in equation specification. We therefore present estimates based on both approaches in Table 4 when we were able to obtain plausible estimates with the sample selection procedure. In Table 5, only conditional Tobit estimates are presented.

6.3.1 Informal Care

The price of formal care has no effect either on the total amount of informal care the respondent received or on informal care provided by the elderly person's children (Table 4). The coefficients are negative, the opposite of what our model predicts. These results, viewed in combination with those for formal care, where the price has an unexpected positive and insignificant effect, do not necessarily mean that these choices are not influenced by price. First, if the price of informal care is below the price for formal care within the relevant range of hours, the gross price would have no effect. Unfortunately, the NLTCS did not provide sufficient information on the wage of potential care givers (with the exception of the primary caregiver) to allow one to make inferences about the price of informal care. Second, we have used the wage of aides employed by nursing homes for the gross price of formal care. Many households may face a far different price, even if they use personnel in this skill category.

Our model predicts that the Medicaid subsidy $\overline{Q}$ should affect formal but not informal care if the parent is unaware. The subsidy's effect is positive and almost statistically significant at conventional levels (12 percent) in the formal care equation, but the subsidy has a negative impact on informal care and in one regression, the effect is almost significant. These results suggest, if anything, some crowding out of private effort as a consequence of this public subsidy which, considering the substantial differences among states, is meaningful.

Bernheim and coauthors (1985) hypothesized that wealthy parents receive more attention from their children because the payoff in terms of a subsequent bequest is higher. Also, parents with more children should receive more attention because the threat of disinheritance is more credible. Using data on numbers of visits and telephone calls by children to their parents, they found empirical evidence in support of their theoretical framework.[16] Our results on informal care, another measure of attention, are relevant to their work in two respects. First, the pattern of decreasing attention with distance of children from parents suggests that some of the effect of children can be attributable to time prices. Second, wealthier parents get less informal care from the children than poorer parents, a result clearly inconsistent with the strategic bequests model. The strongly significant negative effect for informal care provided by children when the parent is cognitively aware (column 1 of Table 5) is particularly telling, because it provides the best opportunity for children to impress their parents.

Having a spouse reduces informal care provided by children much more when the elderly person is unaware. Again, time price is much more influential when a higher quantity of care is provided to the recipient, as in the unaware case.

6.3.2 Formal Care

The number of children living within 30 minutes of the parent has an important negative impact on formal care hours. Other children do not make a difference. Married elderly demand much less formal care.

Having children nearby lowers demand for formal care by both aware and unaware. The effect is stronger for the unaware. From our model, one would have expected use of formal care by the unaware to be particularly sensitive to relative factor prices, and, more importantly, to the Medicaid subsidy (Table 1). But our results do not show this. The negative effect of marital status is appreciably greater for the aware than the unaware, but the exchange relationship hypothesized to exist between parents and children does not plausibly extend to spouses. The Medicaid subsidy has a positive effect on formal care levels, although the effect is never significant. The price of formal care only has the anticipated effect on the cognitively aware's formal care, but the coefficient is not statistically significant. Assets do not affect use of formal care by either the aware or the unaware.

6.4 *Nonhousing Assets*

Three issues are particularly important in our analysis of nonhousing assets. First, how does the probability of being in each of the three states – dead, cognitively aware, cognitively unaware – affect savings? Second, does the prospect of receiving a Medicaid subsidy in the event of a catastrophic expense affect savings? Third, to what extent do health shocks affect wealth of the elderly? Three Tobit regressions are shown, two based on the entire sample of persons who reported the levels of financial assets in both 1984 and 1989 and were cognitively aware in 1984 and a third limited to persons who were in the community in 1989 (Table 6).

Cognitively aware elderly with at least one ADL/IADL impairment face substantial probabilities of an adverse outcome within a five year period. In our sample, 33 percent of the cognitively aware respondents to the 1984 survey died before 1989. Another 18 percent were cognitively impaired by 1989. Although statistical significance is lacking, the signs on the coefficients for both adverse outcomes are consistently negative, implying that the marginal utility of wealth is lower for persons in poor health, a result in agreement with other empirical evidence [Viscusi and Evans (1990)]. The coefficient on the probability of being unaware implies that a .01 increase in the probability leads to a $607 or $546 decrease in nonhousing assets on average, conditional on positive nonhousing assets.

The answer to the second question is that Medicaid does not crowd out savings, at least as measured by nonhousing assets. Persons who would have satisfied the state Medicaid program's income and asset standards immediately on entry in 1984 saved less, but those who would never have qualified in 1984 because their nonbequeathable income exceeded the state's income ceiling for Medicaid eligibility saved even less on average. We included several exogenous determinants of use of care in the second regression. The theory does not yield unambiguous predictions about these variables' direction of effect on savings. None of these variables have statistically significant impacts on nonhousing assets' accumulation in either direction.

To the extent that the bequest motive is an important determinant of savings by the elderly, one would expect that the number of potential heirs, measured here by the number of children, would affect wealth. We find no effect. In regressions not reported, we split the number of children into the distance groups used in other parts of our analysis. No effect of the number of children was detected in that analysis either.

The answer to the third question is that health shocks, at least those associated with admissions to a nursing home, do have appreciable impacts on wealth. Judging from the coefficients on the number of nursing home stays during 1984-89, each stay decreases nonhousing assets by about $20,000 on average. With persons who were in the nursing home in 1989 excluded (column 3), the estimated effect falls substantially and loses statistical significance. Admissions to a hospital do not affect savings, but, unfortunately, the NLTCS only recorded hospital admissions for the year before the interviews.

7   Are Strategic Effects Important?

Our empirical analysis provides three major tests of the types of strategic effects described by Bernheim and coauthors (1985). First, our strategic model suggests that having more children leads to a lower probability of entering the nursing home, less formal care, and more informal care. The empirical results are consistent with these hypotheses. However, the results may be confounded by the childrens' locations, which will affect their supply of care. This appears to be the case, as nearby children have much larger marginal effects on nursing home entry and care in the community. Moreover, the number of children (and their locations) also has significant effects in the equations for the unaware only. The strategic model predicts that, *cet. par.*, the number of children will not affect the amounts of care provided since an unaware parent cannot disinherit her children. Thus, the observed significant effects again suggest that the number of children affects the supply of care independently of any strategic effects.

The second strategic test comes from the coefficients on unaware in the pooled equations. The strategic model suggests that unaware parents will be more likely to be placed in the nursing home and receive less informal care and more formal care in the community than aware parents. While unaware parents are more likely to be placed in nursing homes as expected, they actually receive more informal care and less formal care than aware parents. We noted above that being unaware might increase the marginal productivity of all types of care. While it is not possible theoretically to say how the relative productivities change across settings and between formal and informal care, it seems plausible that there would be a larger increase in productivity in nursing homes. Thus, a change in productivity associated with being unaware in consistent with both the observed increase in the probability of entering the nursing home and the greater use of informal care.[17] This is not to say that strategic effects are necessarily nonexistent: had the unaware parents become aware for an instant, they might have been disappointed in the amount of informal care they had been getting. However, the positive productivity effect on informal care appears to far outweigh any negative strategic effect.

Perhaps our cleanest test of strategic effects is the coefficient on total wealth in the informal care equation for cognitively aware parents. The strategic model predicts that children will provide more informal care to rich parents because they have more to lose through disinheritance. Our result shows that richer parents actually receive less informal care than poorer parents.

Because this result directly contradicts Bernheim et al.'s finding that rich (but not necessarily disabled) parents receive more telephone calls and visits, we examined our estimate in greater detail. A potential criticism of our specification is that we have not fully controlled for the supply of care from children, so that a parent's wealth may be correlated with omitted variables. For example, a parent who knows her child is unusually reluctant to provide informal care may need to hold larger stores of wealth to induce him to provide any care at all.[18] To correct for this endogeneity, we used a two-stage approach. We first estimated wealth as a function of education and other exogenous variables in the model and then reestimated the informal care equation with the fitted value of wealth. Education was included because it is correlated with wealth, but logically independent of the childrens' supply function.[19] The coefficient on the fitted wealth variable appears in column 2 of Table 6; for comparison, the coefficient on wealth, treated exogenously, from Table 4 appears in column 1. Wealth has an even stronger negative effect in column 2.[20] Bernheim and coauthors distinguish between bequeathable and nonbequeathable wealth under the presumption that children only respond strategically to bequeathable wealth. In column 3, we divide wealth into its bequeathable and nonbequeathable components and estimate the Tobit equation assuming bequeathable wealth is exogenous. Column 4 repeats the analysis under the assumption that bequeathable wealth is endogenous. In both equations, both types of wealth have negative effects on informal care; the coefficient on bequeathable wealth is appreciably more negative when this variable is considered to be endogenous. Thus, our finding that informal care falls as the parent's wealth rises is quite robust.

Do our results rule out the strategic bequest motive? Perhaps strategic effects do not become important until a parent amasses a sizable fortune. Most of the elderly in our sample were quite poor, but this is the lot of most disabled elderly persons.[21] Because a relatively few large estates will naturally account for a disproportionate share of all bequests, the strategic bequest motive could still be an important determinant of overall bequests, despite our results, but not of the informal care children provide elderly parents. It is perhaps reassuring that children are willing to provide substantial amounts of informal care to even poor, unaware parents, probably out of a sense of altruism.

8   Conclusion

This study has presented and tested a model which analyzes the effects of family behavior and government policy on long-term care for the elderly. Some Medicaid subsidies, such as those reflected in the present value of the amount of non-housing wealth elderly can retain if they enter the nursing home, affect choice of living in a nursing home versus in the community. Also, greater availability of Medicaid subsidies of care in the home increases the amount of formal care the elderly receive. However, we find no indication that these public subsidies have decreased relatives' and friends' willingness to provide informal care to the elderly. This result is consistent with past research [see, e.g., Tennstedt et al. (1993), and Wiener and Hanley (1992)].

Strategic effects arise in the model because children make long-term care decisions when a parent is cognitively unaware, whereas the parent makes decisions when she is aware. However, the empirical results indicate that strategic effects are not an important determinant of long-term care decisions. Family members are an important source of long-term care. This result suggests that altruism motivates much of informal care and points the way to future research studying variation in altruistic attitudes amongst potential caregivers.

Appendix

Table 1: Comparative Statics Results: Period 2

Part A: Formal and Informal Care in the Community

	Parent Is Unaware		Parent Is Aware	
	F	I	F	I
p^F	−	+	−	+*
S	+	0	Ambig.	+
W	+	−	+	Ambig.
M	+	0	+	+
$\overline{Q}$ ***	−	0	−	+
θ**	n.a.	n.a.	−	+ −

Part B: Probability of Parent Being in a Nursing Home

	Parent Is Unaware	Parent Is Aware
p^F	+	+
$S-p^N \overline{N}$	+	+
W	+	+
M	−	−
$\overline{Q}$	−	−
θ	n.a.	−

* Assumes that the substitution effect dominates the income effect associated with the price change.
** θ includes children's and parent's wealth. See eq. 7a in text.
n.a. = not applicable.
*** Result for formal care represents the amount of formal care purchased from family funds. Total formal care consumption, $F + \overline{Q}$ rises.

Table 2: Means of Dependent Variables

	Cognitively Aware		Cognitively Unaware		Total
Probability of entry into nursing home	0.06		.0.27		0.14
Formal care*	2.26	(0.21)	5.98	(0.25)	3.53
Informal care*					
Total	10.40	(0.51)	30.68	(0.78)	17.32
Kids only	3.68	(0.28)	17.96	(0.56)	8.60

* Hours per week in the community sample. Numbers in parentheses are fraction of non-censored values.

Table 3: Nursing Home Choice

Explanatory Variables	Univariate Probit		Bivariate Probit	
	All	Cognitively Aware	Cognitively Unaware	All
Demand				
Intercept	-2.78^a	-3.36^a	-2.04^a	-3.45^a
	(0.60)	(0.96)	(0.78)	(0.53)
Residual wealth in	0.066^a	0.060^b	0.069^b	0.18^a
nursing home ('0000$)	(0.021)	(0.030)	(0.033)	(0.030)
Residual wealth in	-0.028	-0.025	-0.023	-0.0090
community ('0000$)	(0.028)	(0.023)	(0.027)	(0.021)
Price of formal care	0.06^c	0.058	0.062	0.13^a
($ per hour)	(0.032)	(0.049)	(0.042)	(0.039)
Expected Medicaid subsidy for	-0.00025	0.013	-0.0082	0.005
home health ($ per week)	(0.0054)	(0.0084)	(0.0072)	(0.0087)
No. of children w/in	-0.28^a	-0.17^a	-0.33^a	-0.30^a
30 minutes away	(0.029)	(0.051)	(0.037)	(0.031)
No. of children 31 to	-0.015	-0.075	0.036	-0.009
60 minutes away	(0.058)	(0.072)	(0.079)	(0.069)
No. of children more	-0.048^c	-0.073^c	-0.037	-0.042
than 60 minutes away	(0.025)	(0.042)	(0.032)	(0.031)
Married	-0.24^c	-0.41^c	-0.18	-0.30^b
	(0.12)	(0.22)	(0.15)	(0.13)
Housing assets	-0.19^a	-0.18^a	-0.21^a	-0.26^a
('0000$)	(0.021)	(0.034)	(0.028)	(0.028)
Spouse's nonbequeathable	-0.21^a	-0.17^a	-0.22^a	-0.21^a
income ('00$ per month)	(0.029)	(0.058)	(0.034)	(0.029)
No. of ADLs	0.33^a	0.29^a	0.34^a	0.33^a
	(0.018)	(0.030)	(0.024)	(0.022)
Cognitively unaware	0.45^a	---	---	0.42^a
	(0.079)	(---)	(---)	(0.10)

Table 3 (cont.)

Explanatory Variables	Univariate Probit			Bivariate Probit	
	All	Cognitively Aware	Cognitively Unaware	All	
Age	0.0070	0.016^c	0.0026	0.017^a	
	(0.0055)	(0.0090)	(0.0073)	(0.0057)	
Male	0.080	0.32^b	-0.060	0.22^b	
	(0.089)	(0.14)	(0.11)	(0.094)	
Supply					
Intercept	---	---	---	-1.69^a	
	(---)	(---)	(---)	(0.46)	
Discount ('0000s)	0.044	-0.0003	-0.089	1.05^a	
	(0.040)	(0.053)	(0.063)	(0.23)	
Nursing home beds per	0.010^a	0.0063^c	0.013^a	0.012^c	
1,000 persons ≥ age 75	(0.0023)	(0.0036)	(0.0031)	(0.0067)	
Black	-0.91^a	-1.16^a	-0.80^a	-2.06^a	
	(0.11)	(0.22)	(0.13)	(0.30)	
Hispanic	0.41	---	---	-0.024	
	(0.30)	(---)	(---)	(1.21)	
No. of ADLs	---	---	---	0.28^a	
	(---)	(---)	(---)	(0.059)	
Cognitively unaware	---	---	---	0.75^a	
	(---)	(---)	(---)	(0.25)	
log-likelihood	-853.58	-341.4	-501.59	-858.32	
N	4,235	2,549	1,686	4,235	

^{a} Statistically significant at the one percent level, two-tail test.
^{b} Statistically significant at the five percent level, two-tail test.
^{c} Statistically significant at the ten percent level, two-tail test.
* Wealth other than housing and spouse's nonbequeathable income. See text for discussion.

Table 4: Informal and Formal Care

	Informal Care – Tobits		Informal Care with Selection		Formal
Explanatory Variables	Total	Kids Only	Total	Kids Only	Care Tobit
Intercept	-37.69^a	-76.05^a	-30.99^a	-88.66^a	-90.32^a
	(7.27)	(9.58)	(8.67)	(17.97)	(10.27)
Price of formal care	-0.81	-0.85	-0.61	-0.69	0.65
($ per hour)	(0.51)	(0.68)	(0.53)	(0.72)	(0.69)
Expected Medicaid subsidy	-0.17	-0.017	-0.13	-0.099	0.22
for home health ($ per week)	(0.12)	(0.16)	(0.13)	(0.16)	(0.15)
No. of children within	2.87^a	5.56^a	1.98^a	5.08^a	-4.01^a
30 minutes away	(0.36)	(0.46)	(0.38)	(0.84)	(0.60)

Table 4 (cont.)

Explanatory Variables	Informal Care – Tobits		Informal Care with Selection		Formal Care Tobit
	Total	Kids Only	Total	Kids Only	
No. of children 31 to 60 minutes away	0.76 (0.85)	0.8 (1.01)	0.41 (0.86)	0.84 (1.04)	0.38 (1.31)
No. of children more than 60 minutes away	-0.28 (0.38)	-1.22^a (0.50)	-0.31 (0.38)	-1.16^b (0.57)	0.30 (0.54)
Married	9.52^a (1.59)	-24.10^a (2.21)	7.84^a (1.68)	-27.61^a (3.76)	-8.87^a (2.38)
Total assets ('0000$)	-0.066 (0.059)	-0.15^c (0.087)	-0.08 (0.069)	-0.26^b (0.11)	0.014 (0.079)
Spouse's nonbequeathable income ('00$)	0.90^a (0.17)	0.36 (0.25)	0.71^a (0.17)	0.53^c (0.29)	-0.39 (0.26)
No. of ADLs	4.19^a (0.36)	2.14^a (0.46)	5.59^a (0.38)	4.03^a (0.47)	4.81^a (0.51)
No. of IADLs	6.95^a (0.32)	5.85^a (0.43)	5.92^a (0.55)	6.95^a (0.97)	3.42^a (0.46)
Cognitively unaware	7.46^a (1.29)	9.68^a (1.67)	9.08^a (1.34)	13.07^a (1.87)	-5.90^a (1.90)
Age	0.066 (0.085)	0.54^a (0.11)	0.055 (0.087)	0.52^a (0.14)	0.58^a (0.12)
Male	2.92^b (1.38)	-7.20^a (1.91)	4.35^a (1.46)	-7.91^a (2.29)	-4.47^b (2.03)
Black	-0.43 (1.27)	0.83 (1.70)	-2.34^c (1.34)	-2.70 (1.80)	1.60 (1.79)
Hispanic	0.96 (4.59)	-6.63 (6.06)	3.83 (4.72)	-3.45 (6.44)	-8.67 (7.93)
Urban	-2.32^c (1.18)	-1.82 (1.56)	-2.43^b (1.22)	-2.17 (1.63)	0.74 (1.64)
σ	30.15^a (0.46)	31.24^a (0.68)	--- (---)	--- (---)	33.16^a (0.89)
λ	--- (---)	--- (---)	20.97^a (3.65)	35.66^a (3.65)	--- (---)
log likelihood	-11275.0	-6113.4	---	---	-4848.2
R^2	---	---	0.35	0.30	---
$\bar{R}^2$	---	---	0.34	0.29	---
F	---	---	68.82	29.00	---
d.f.	---	---	17,2172	17,1108	---
N	3,611	2,971	2,190*	1,126*	3,611

^{a} Statistically significant at the one percent level, two-tail test.
^{b} Statistically significant at the five percent level, two-tail test.
^{c} Statistically significant at the ten percent level, two-tail test.
* Number with positive values.

Table 5: Informal and Formal Care: Cognitively Aware and Unaware (Tobit)

Explanatory Variables	Informal Care: Kids Only		Formal Kids Only	
	Cognitively Aware	Cognitively Unaware	Cognitively Aware	Cognitively Unaware
Intercept	-46.35^a	-74.97^a	-54.98^a	-155.39^a
	(8.69)	(17.47)	(8.57)	(23.94)
Price of formal care	-0.83	-0.38	-0.076	2.27
($ per hour)	(0.59)	(1.27)	(0.56)	(1.60)
Expected Medicaid subsidy for	-0.18	-0.015	0.17	0.19
home health ($ per week)	(0.21)	(0.24)	(0.15)	(0.29)
No. of children w/in	4.19^a	5.78^a	-2.68^a	-5.20^a
30 minutes away	(0.44)	(0.78)	(0.55)	(1.22)
No. of children 31 to	0.41	1.71	-0.47	2.45
60 minutes away	(0.87)	(1.89)	(1.10)	(2.98)
No. of children more	-0.48	-1.81^b	0.37	0.24
than 60 minutes away	(0.43)	(0.91)	(0.45)	(1.22)
Married	-15.50^a	-31.36^a	-10.24^a	-2.42
	(2.13)	(3.83)	(2.09)	(5.12)
Total Assets	-0.22^a	0.073	0.056	-0.27
('0000$)	(0.080)	(0.16)	(0.060)	(0.22)
Spouse's nonbequeathable	0.39	0.087	0.084	-0.87
income ('00$)	(0.26)	(0.41)	(0.23)	(0.54)
No. of ADLs	0.63	3.53^a	2.44^a	7.82^a
	(0.45)	(0.76)	(0.46)	(1.01)
No. of IADLs	5.17^a	5.33^a	3.45^a	2.50^a
	(0.41)	(0.72)	(0.41)	(0.95)
Age	0.32^a	0.59^a	0.36^a	1.04^a
	(0.10)	(0.194)	(0.090)	(0.26)
Male	-2.77	-11.04^a	-1.61	-7.91^c
	(1.71)	(3.41)	(1.69)	(4.56)
Black	1.56	-1.89	0.17	5.99
	(1.44)	(3.26)	(1.43)	(4.31)
Hispanic	-6.5	-5.87	-2.69	-19.64
	(5.65)	(10.54)	(6.83)	(16.72)
Urban	-2.90^b	0.013	-0.48	5.43
	(1.36)	(2.89)	(1.33)	(3.84)
σ	20.38^a	38.11^a	21.42^a	46.19^a
	(0.65)	(1.16)	(0.73)	(2.01)
log likelihood	-2877.8	-3123.0	-2788.7	-1943.8
N	1,948	1,023	2,383	1,228

[a] Statistically significant at the one percent level, two-tail test.
[b] Statistically significant at the five percent level, two-tail test.
[c] Statistically significant at the ten percent level, two-tail test.

Table 6: Nonhousing Wealth

	All		Community
	1.	2.	3.
Intercept	-78.8^a	-118.5^a	-87.5^a
	(17.7)	(36.2)	(18.8)
Probability of dying	-18.4	-18.7	-40.8
	(27.5)	(28.0)	(62.4)
Probability of being unaware	-60.7	-54.6	-23.2
	(58.2)	(59.6)	(29.8)
Nonhousing wealth, 1984	1.47^a	1.47^a	1.45^a
	(0.14)	(0.15)	(0.15)
Housing wealth, 1984	0.55^a	0.57^a	0.58^a
	(0.10)	(0.11)	(0.11)
Savings accts., money market funds,	40.4^a	40.1^a	49.3^a
CDs had in 1984	(9.4)	(9.7)	(10.0)
Bonds had in 1984	11.1	9.3	10.2
	(18.3)	(18.9)	(19.4)
Stock had in 1984	26.7^c	26.6^c	26.8^c
	(14.5)	(15.1)	(15.2)
No. of nursing home stays, 1984-89	-19.1^a	-20.6^a	-9.1
	(6.7)	(7.0)	(12.1)
No. of hospital stays, 1988-89	-2.6	7.1	0.35
	(4.3)	(43.5)	(4.82)
Medicaid-eligible at entry	-4.8	-5.9	-4.7
to nursing home, 1984	(10.0)	(10.4)	(10.6)
Not Medicaid-eligible within	-30.9^b	-33.6^b	-34.6^b
10 years of entry, 1984	(13.1)	(13.9)	(13.8)
Immediately eligible for	-15.5	-14.6	-15.7
Medicaid formal care, 1984	(10.2)	(10.4)	(11.0)
Married	-3.9	-3.1	-2.4
	(9.1)	(9.5)	(9.6)
Spouse died, 1984-89	-5.7	-6.8	-5.3
	(12.3)	(12.7)	(12.9)
Price of formal care ($ per hour)	---	4.5	---
	(---)	(7.3)	(---)
Private nursing home price	---	0.42	---
	(---)	(2.02)	(---)
Dif. private and Medicaid	---	2.50	---
price ('000s): year 1, 1989	(---)	(2.66)	(---)
No. of children	---	-0.25	---
	(---)	(1.56)	(---)
Nursing home beds per 1,000	---	0.018	---
persons $\geq$ age 75, 1989	(---)	(0.27)	(---)
Black	---	-31.6	---
	(---)	(57.7)	(---)

Table 6 (cont.)

	All		Community
	1.	2.	3.
Total nonbequeathable income	0.032[a]	0.032[a]	0.031[a]
($ per year)	(0.010)	(0.010)	(0.010)
σ	92.2[a]	92.8[a]	93.5[a]
	(3.0)	(3.2)	(3.3)
log likelihood	-5,955.0	-5,825.3	-5,590.3
N	1,008	989	876

[a] Statistically significant at the one percent level, two-tail test.
[b] Statistically significant at the five percent level, two-tail test.
[c] Statistically significant at the ten percent level, two-tail test.

Table 7: Informal Care: Cognitively Aware (Tobit)

	Exogenous Total Assets	Endogenous Total Assets	Exogenous Beq., Nonbeq. Assets	Endogenous Beq., Exogenous Nonbeq. Assets
Total assets	-0.22[a]	-0.82[a]	---	---
('0000$)	(0.078)	(0.20)	(---)	(---)
Total bequeathable	---	---	-0.13	-0.94[a]
assets ('0000$)	(---)	(---)	(0.089)	(0.26)
Total nonbequeathable	---	---	-0.63[a]	-0.11
assets ('0000$)	(---)	(---)	(0.23)	(0.27)

[a] Statistically significant at the one percent level, two-tail test.
[b] Statistically significant at the five percent level, two-tail test.
[c] Statistically significant at the ten percent level, two-tail test.

Acknowledgment

Partial support for this study comes from a grant from the National Institute of Aging, "Effects of Public Subsidies on Use of Long-Term Care" (#R01 AG09468). We benefitted from helpful comments from participants at the Third Annual Health Economics Workshop at Johns Hopkins University and the National Bureau of Economic Research Summer Institute. We wish to thank Christoph Schenzler, David Van Dalfsen, and Teresa Waters for computational assistance; May Shayne and Jim Kinser for assembling information on state Medicaid policies; Friedrich Breyer, J.S. Butler, Peter Kemper, Liliana Pezzin, Willard Manning, and Joseph Newhouse for advice and comments on earlier versions; and Charlene Harrington, James Swan, Alvin Headen, Baldwin Kloer, Larry Corder, and Francis Pendergrass for providing unpublished data used in this study.

Notes

[1] See, for example, Becker (1974), Becker (1981), Kotlikoff and Spivak (1981), Cox (1987), Bernheim and Stark (1988), Bernheim et al. (1985), Pollak (1988), Becker and Murphy (1988), and Bruce and Waldman (1990).

[2] Several points about these utility functions also apply to the other states. First, the utility functions are separable both between the two individuals' consumptions and between the two components of the parent's utility. The primary justification for this specification is tractability. As usual, assuming separability may affect the comparative statics in an important way. Second, the individuals are altruistic in that each cares about components of the other's utility. It is necessary for the child to care about the parent in order for an unaware parent to receive care because providing either formal or informal care will cost the child. Third, the assumption of separability imposes a special kind of altruism. By assuming that each individual cares about the other's utility from specific components of consumption rather than the other's total utility, we avoid the type of infinite regress that occurs when I care about your utility and you care about my utility.

[3] To simplify the theoretical analysis, we collapse parent's wealth and income. In fact, both income and wealth standards are applied for purposes of determining eligibility for Medicaid. We consider both standards in our empirical analysis.

[4] There are also income thresholds which are considered in our empirical analysis.

[5] Our data set contains no measures of the quantities of formal and informal care received by residents in nursing homes.

[6] We assume that the parent does better with the child's optimal levels of care than she does spending all of her savings on formal care. This is not a very restrictive assumption.

[7] This is the outcome Bernheim et al. (1985) have in mind in their model of strategic bequests. They assume, however, that the parent must have more than one child for the threat of disinheritance to be credible. More realistically, even with one child, the parent's threat is credible since she can give to charity, another relative, or a formal caregiver. Although our model has only one child, we assume disinheritance is credible in order to incorporate the strategic bequest motive; as an extension, we discuss the case of more than one child.

[8] This time we assume that the child is better off at the parent's optimal level of formal and informal care than he or she is when providing no informal care and being disinherited.

[9] The parent and child's indifference curves will be tangent at such points.

[10] An assumption more consistent with Pauly's (1990) analysis of strategic nursing home decisions is that the parent receives less utility than the child from being in a nursing home. This assumption would strengthen our conclusion below that cognitively aware parents are less likely to enter nursing homes than cognitively unaware parents.

[11] For a detailed description of our price variable, see Sloan and Shayne (1993).

[12] In principle, the household could hasten Medicaid eligibility by purchasing a more luxurious house or paying off the mortgage, as Budish (1989) suggests. In practice, this seems unlikely to

happen very often. In our community sample, only 13 percent of households had mortgages in 1989. Some states impose limits on the value of income-producing property that can be excluded for purposes of determining eligibility for Medicaid [Neuschler (1987)]. Only six percent of the 1989 respondents in the community had such assets. We did not account for such limits in our calculations.

[13] We analyze elderly person-caregiver behavior in Sloan et al. (1995).

[14] Some state Medicaid programs require that the house be sold if, a few months following admission, it appears that the person will not leave the nursing home. Also, admission to the nursing home may affect the cash subsidy the spouse receives. See Sloan and Shayne (1993). These possible sources of endogeneity are ignored here.

[15] Some of the sample persons who were institutionalized in 1989 responded to the 1984 community survey. We could have used the housing wealth on those persons available for 1984. But since there were so many replacements in 1989, we would have lost quite a number of observations.

[16] Using the same data source and additional years of data, Hurd and Wang (1991) found little evidence of strategic bequest motives. Also, see Hurd (1989), (1990). Cox (1987) found that patterns of intervivos' transfers are consistent with the hypothesis that children exchange services for transfers from their parents. This hypothesis is closely related to the strategic bequest. However, Cox only observed transfers to recipients; he did not observe services provided by the recipient.

[17] The negative effect for formal care is still somewhat of a puzzle. The same productivity argument applies to ADLs and IADLs; like unaware, these variables increase the probability of entering a nursing home and informal care, but they also increase formal care.

[18] As our discussion of comparative statics on the savings decision indicates, having such a child will produce ambiguous effects on savings. Also note that the number of children has no effect on savings in our wealth equation.

[19] Bernheim and coauthors used lifetime income as an instrument for wealth. This instrument is not on the NLTCS.

[20] Other coefficients (not shown) are virtually unchanged from Table 4.

[21] We compared estimated wealth from the 1989 NLTCS with wealth from other samples. Adjusting for inflation, the NLTCS wealth estimates are similar to those from the National Channelling Demonstration data, also a survey of the disabled elderly [Garber and MaCurdy (1990), p. 180]. Disabled elderly in both the NLTCS and Channelling data bases tend to be poorer than elderly without functional impairments.

References

Abowd, J. M./Farber, H. S. (1982): Job Queues and the Union Status of Workers, in *Industrial and Labor Relations Review 35*, 354-67.

Becker, G. S. (1974): A Theory of Social Interactions, in *Journal of Political Economy 82*, 1063-93.

Becker, G. S. (1981): *A Treatise on the Family*. Cambridge/MA: Harvard University Press.

Becker, G. S./Murphy, K. M. (1988) The Family and the State, in *Journal of Law and Economics 31*, 1-18.

Bernheim, B. D./Stark, O. (1988): Altruism Within the Family Reconsidered: Do Nice Guys Finish Last?, in *American Economic Review 78*, 1034-45.

Bernheim, B. D./Shleifer, A./Summers, L. (1985): The Strategic Bequest Motive, in *Journal of Political Economy 93*, 1138-59.

Bruce, N./Waldman, M. (1990): The Rotten-Child Theorem Meets the Samaritan's Dilemma, in *Quarterly Journal of Economics 105*, 155-65.

Budish, A. (1989): *Avoiding the Medicaid Trap*. New York/NY: Henry Holt and Co., Inc.

Commerce Clearing House, Inc. (1984-1990): *Medicare and Medicaid Guide*. Chicago/IL.

Connelly, R. (1992): The Effect of Child Care Costs on Married Women's Labor Force Participation, in *Review of Economics and Statistics 14*, 83-90.

Cox, D. (1987): Motives for Private Income Transfers, in *Journal of Political Economy 95*, 508-46.

Ettner, S. L. (1993): Do Elderly Medicaid Patients Experience Reduced Access to Nursing Home Care, in *Journal of Health Economics 12*, 259-80.

Garber, A. M./MaCurdy, T. (1990): Predicting Nursing Home Utilization among the High-Risk Elderly, in D. A. Wise (ed.): *Issues in the Economics of Aging*. Chicago/IL: University of Chicago Press, 173-204.

Harrington, C./Preston, S./Grant, L/Swan, J. H. (1990): *Trends in Nursing Home Bed Capacity in the States*. Paper presented at the American Public Health Association Annual Meeting, New York.

Hurd, M. D. (1990): Mortality Risk and Bequests, in *Econometrica 57*, 779-813.

Hurd, M. D. (1990): Research on the Elderly: Economic Status, Retirement and Consumption and Saving, in *Journal of Economic Literature 28*, 565-637.

Hurd, M. D./Du Wang (1991): *Some Doubts about the Empirical Relevance of the Strategic Bequest Motive*. Working Paper.

Kemper, P./Spillman, B. C./Murtaugh, C. M. (1991): A Lifetime Perspective on Proposals for Financing Nursing Home Care, in *Inquiry 28*, 333-44.

Kotlikoff, L. J./Spivak, A. (1981): The Family as an Incomplete Annuities Market, in *Journal of Political Economy 89*, 372-91.

Neuschler, E. (1987): *Medical Eligibility for the Elderly in Need of Long Term Care*. Washington/D.C.: Congressional Research Service for Congress.

Nyman, J. A. (1988): Excess Demand, the Percentage of Medicaid Patients, and the Quality of Nursing Home Care, in *Journal of Human Resources 23*, 76-92.

Nyman, J. A. (1985): Prospective and 'Cost-Plus' Medicaid Reimbursement, Excess Medicaid Demand, and the Quality of Nursing Home Care, in *Journal of Health Economics 4*, 237-59.

Pauly, M. V. (1990): The Rational Non-Purchase of Long-Term Care Insurance, in *Journal of Political Economy 98*, 153-68.

Poirier, D. J. (1980): Partial Observability in Bivariate Probit Models, in *Journal of Econometrics 12*, 209-18.

Pollak, R. A. (1988): Tied Transfers and Paternalistic Preferences, in *AEA Papers and Proceedings 78*, 240-44.

Sloan, F. A./Picone, G./Hoerger, T. J. (1995): *The Supply of Children's Time to Disabled Elderly Parents*. Unpublished.

Sloan, F. A./Shayne, M. W. (1993): Long-Term Care, Medicaid, and Impoverish ment of the Elderly, in *The Milbank Quarterly 71*, 575-99.

Swan, J. H./Harrington, C. H./Grant, L./Luehrs, J./Preston, S. (1993): Trends in Medicaid Nursing Home Reimbursement, 1978-89, in *Health Care Financing Review 14*, 111-132.

Tennstedt, S. L./Crawford, S. L./McKinley, J. B. (1993): Is Family Care on the Decline? A Longitudinal Investigation of the Substitution of Formal Long-Term Care for Informal Care, in *The Milbank Quarterly 71*, 601-24.

U.S. Department of Health and Human Services, Social Security Administration (1987): *The Supplemental Security Income Program for the Aged, Blind, and Disabled: Characteristics of State Assistance Programs for SSI Recipients*. Washington/D.C.: U.S. Government Printing Office.

U.S. Department of Health and Human Services, Social Security Administration (1985): *The Supplemental Security Income Program for the Aged, Blind, and Disabled*. Baltimore/MD: U.S. Government Printing Office.

U.S. Department of Health and Human Services, Social Security Administration (1984): *The Supplemental Security Income Program for the Aged, Blind, and Disabled: Selected Characteristics of State Supplementation Programs as of January 1984*. Washington/D.C.: U.S. Government Printing Office.

U.S. General Accounting Office (1990): *Nursing Homes: Admission Problems for Medicaid Recipients and Attempts to Solve Them*. Washington/D.C.: U.S. Government Printing Office, GAO/HRD-90-135.

Viscusi, W. K./Evans, W. N. (1990): Utility Functions That Depend On Health Status: Estimates and Economic Implications, in *American Economic Review 80*, 353-74.

Wiener, J. M./Hanley, R. J. (1992): Care for the Disabled Elderly: There's No Place Like Home, in S. M. Shortell/U. E. Reinhardt (eds.): *Improving Health Policy and Management: Nine Critical Research Issues for the 1990s*. Ann Arbor/MI: Health Administration Press, 75-110.

4 WOMEN'S ROLE IN THE PROVISION OF LONG-TERM CARE, FINANCIAL INCENTIVES, AND THE FUTURE FINANCING OF LONG-TERM CARE

Sandra Nocera and Peter Zweifel

1 Introduction

Policy makers in industrialized countries fear a cost explosion in the provision of institutional long-term care (LTC) reminiscent of the one these countries have experienced in their health care sectors. However, at present the majority of persons in need of LTC live in their homes, with a daughter typically providing care to a parent or a wife to her husband [Kendig et al. (1992), Abelin/Schlettwein-Gsell (1986); for additional references, see Höpflinger (1994)]. Therefore, an important policy issue is the extent to which the future increase in the demand for LTC will continue to be met by these informal caregivers, who have to bear considerable opportunity costs in terms of leisure and wage income foregone. A measure of these opportunity costs is provided by the reservation wage for care, i.e. the quantity of money that is sufficient to compensate a respondent to provide one hour's worth of LTC. Thus, gender-specific differences could be reflected in women's lower reservation wage for care compared to men. Even if a gender-specific difference should not be observed, there may still be hidden differences in determinants that may become more marked in the future. In that event, a policy designed to encourage the provision of informal LTC through financial incentives directed at the caregiver, tailoring the amount of subsidy in such a way as to match her reservation wage for care, will meet with considerable problems. As an alternative, a voucher solution may be envisaged, giving the beneficiary the choice of source of care. In return, the beneficiary would have to search out caregivers whose reservation wage for care is covered by the value of the voucher or pay the difference himself.

The plan of this contribution is as follows. The next section contains a simple microeconomic model serving to identify the determinants of the reservation wage for care, among them factors such as intrinsic preference for caring, productivity in nonmarket work, and wages in the labor market.

The third part of the paper is devoted to an empirical test of these predicted influences. The data base is provided by three samples of the adult Swiss population. Sample A consists of members of a social health insurer whose enrolment is largely rural. Sample B comes from another social health insurer, with sampling limited to members living in the canton of Zurich, an urbanized area. Sample C was provided by a private insurer with activities nationwide. Insurance-related information is available for nonrespondents, complemented by socio-economic characteristics and reservation wages for respondents. The survey also indicates whether the respondent has a relative in need of LTC and the setting in which care is provided to him. The purpose of the empirical work will be to find out whether reservation wages asked for giving care to a disabled family member and their determinants are indeed gender-specific. Sample selection processes operating at different levels will be given particular attention.

The fourth part of the paper discusses the financial incentives necessary for inducing different types of individuals to provide informal LTC. In view of the emerging problems with a targeted subsidy, an attempt will be made to calculate the value of a voucher designed to cover the opportunity cost of informal LTC.

The final part will present a summary and conclusion.

2 Theoretical Framework

In this section, a very simple representation of an individual who considers providing LTC is developed in the aim of deriving a few testable implications concerning her reservation wage for caregiving. Following the tradition of household production modelling initiated by Becker (1965), let the individual be interested in consumption services (C) and leisure (L). The basic attitude towards providing LTC services to a family member (Z) may be positive ($U_Z > 0$ in equation (1) below) for some but negative ($U_Z < 0$) for others. All remaining partial derivatives are positive. The indifference curve of such an individual is given by

$$dU = U_C dC + U_L dL + U_Z dZ = 0. \qquad (1)$$

The production of consumable services requires leisure time and consumption goods (X) as inputs:

$$C = C(L, X). \qquad (2)$$

As regards the production of LTC, it is assumed that consumption goods are provided and paid for by the recipient of care. Thus, the caregiver is only expected to spend time (A) but no money, resulting in the simple LTC production function,

$$Z = Z(A). \qquad (3)$$

The next equation describes the generation of income. Labor income is given by $W \cdot w$, with W denoting working time and w the attainable nominal wage rate. If total time available is symbolized by T and the compensation for caregiving at issue by M, one has, using $W = T - L - A$,

$$Y = (T - L - A) w + M. \qquad (4)$$

This income may be spent on consumption only, savings being of little relevance in the present context. If consumer goods cost p per unit, one has

$$Y = p X. \qquad (5)$$

These building blocks are now used to determine the individual's reservation wage for caregiving, dM/dA (holding U constant, i.e. given dU = 0).

Total differentiation of equation (2) yields

$$dC = C_L dL + C_X dX. \qquad (6)$$

Total differentiation of equation (3) gives

$$dZ = Z_A dA. \qquad (7)$$

Finally, substitution of (5) into (4) and total differentiation with T held constant results in

$$p \cdot dX = -wdL - wdA + dM, \qquad (8)$$

which may be solved for dX to read

$$dX = -\frac{w}{p}dL - \frac{w}{p}dA + \frac{dM}{p}. \qquad (9)$$

Equations (6), (7), and (9) may now be substituted into (1), giving an expression for the indifference curve incorporating production functions and financial constraints:

$$U_C \left\{ C_L \, dL + C_X \left(-\frac{w}{p}dL - \frac{w}{p}dA + \frac{dM}{p} \right) \right\} + U_L \, dL + U_Z \, (Z_A \, dA) = 0. \qquad (10)$$

Collecting terms in dM, dA and dL, one obtains,

$$dM \left\{ \frac{U_C C_X}{p} \right\} = dA \left\{ U_C C_X \cdot \frac{w}{p} - U_Z Z_A \right\} -$$

$$-dL \left\{ U_C C_L - U_C C_X \cdot \frac{w}{p} + U_L \right\}. \qquad (11)$$

This may be solved for the reservation wage for caregiving,

$$\frac{dM}{dA} = w \cdot \left\{ 1 - \frac{U_Z / U_C}{(C_X / Z_A) \cdot w / p} - \frac{dL}{dA} \left(\frac{C_L / C_X}{w / p} - 1 + \frac{U_L / U_C}{C_X \cdot w / p} \right) \right\}. \qquad (12)$$

This expression may be simplified as follows. First, dL/dA, denoting the (optimal) adjustment of leisure given that a change in time devoted to care occurred, would in principle have to be determined by comparative static methods. This analysis will not be performed here because the time constraint says dL/dA = −1 for a given amount of working time W. As long as compensation M is small relative to income, its income effect will cause small reductions of W only. Moreover, large changes of W would entail considerable transaction costs for most dependent workers. Thus, setting dL/dA = −1 − ε (ε small) may constitute an acceptable approximation. Second, if the individual were to act as a cost-

WOMEN'S ROLE IN THE PROVISION OF LTC

minimizing productive unit as far as consumption is concerned, her allocation would have to satisfy the condition,

$$\frac{C_L}{C_X} = \frac{w}{p} \quad \text{or} \quad \frac{C_L/C_X}{w/p} = 1, \tag{13}$$

stating that the ratio of marginal productivities of factors L and X equals the ratio of their prices w and p, with the wage rate w denoting the shadow price of leisure time used for consumption. Under this assumption, the two terms in the parenthesis following dL/dA add to zero. Thus, equation (12) reduces to

$$\frac{dM}{dA} = w \left\{ 1 - \frac{U_Z/U_C}{(C_X/Z_A) \cdot w/p} + (1+\varepsilon)\frac{U_L/U_C}{C_X \cdot w/p} \right\}. \tag{14}$$

Preliminary statistical analysis of the variable on the left-hand side revealed positive skewness in its distribution, which could be remedied by a log transformation. On the assumption that equation (14) describes small deviations of dM/dA around the wage rate w, the approximation $\ln(1 - a + b) \approx -a + b$ is used to obtain,

$$\ln\frac{dM}{dA} = \ln w - \frac{(U_Z/U_C) \cdot Z_A}{C_X \cdot w/p} + (1+\varepsilon)\frac{U_L/U_C}{C_X \cdot w/p} + \mu, \tag{15}$$

with μ symbolizing a stochastic error term whose properties will be discussed in section 3.1 below.

Conclusion 1: Based on a microeconomic model of household production, the reservation wage asked for caregiving is predicted to have an elasticity of one w.r.t. the wage rate (w) the individual can expect to earn on the labor market. However, discrepancies between this reservation wage and w will occur depending on the marginal rate of substitution (MRS) between consumption and caregiving (U_Z/U_C), the productivity of goods in consumption (C_X), the productivity of the individual's time in caregiving (Z_A), the (real) wage (w/p), and the MRS between consumption and leisure (U_L/U_C)

The following specific statements may be made with regard to equation (15).

1. Most individuals will ask for a positive reservation wage for caregiving, implying that they must be compensated (dM > 0) for a sacrifice of their

available time (dA > 0). A sufficient condition for this is $U_Z \leq 0$, indicating an indifferent or negative attitude toward caregiving. If caregiving is valued positively ($U_Z > 0$), then equation (15) is still positive as long as the MRS between consumption and caregiving (U_Z / U_C) is not large compared to the MRS between consumption and leisure (U_L / U_C).

2. Individuals who are very productive in providing LTC (Z_A large relative to the real wage w/p) should ask for a lower reservation wage for LTC than others unless they dislike caregiving. The partial derivative of (15) w.r.t. $Z_A / (w/p)$, holding w and hence w/p constant, amounts to $-(U_Z / U_C) / C_X$, which is negative unless $U_Z < 0$.

3. Individuals who are productive in their use of consumption goods (C_X large relative to the relative price p/w of goods, i.e. $C_X \cdot w / p$ large) should ask for a lower reservation wage for LTC than others. Partial differentiation of equation (15) w.r.t. $C_X \cdot w / p$, holding w and hence w/p constant, yields an expression proportional to $\{U_Z / U_C \cdot Z_A - (1 + \varepsilon) U_L / U_C\}$, which is negative unless $U_Z > 0$.

4. Individuals who have a high stated reservation wage for work should have a high reservation wage for care. The term (U_L / U_C) denotes the reservation wage for (additional) work in a pure leisure-consumption situation, and the derivative of equation (15) w.r.t. (U_L / U_C) / (w / p) can be shown to be positive.

Conclusion 2: The reservation wage for caregiving is expected to be positive even for individuals who like caregiving, to depend negatively on productivity in providing LTC and the productivity of goods in consumption, and positively on the reservation wage for work.

3 Empirical Results

3.1 Data sources and research strategy

The data pertain to members of three Swiss health insurers: A is a sick fund, B is also a sick fund whose members were only sampled in the urbanized Zurich area, while C is a private insurer. Samples were drawn randomly within broad age categories; in the case of insurers B and C, members below age 40 were not contacted at all because it had been decided to focus on LTC issues, in contradistinction to a broader interest in the process of ageing in the case of insurer A. Between March and June 1993, approximately 6,000 mailed questionnaires were sent to members of A and 8,000 each to members of B and C, of which a minimum of 19 percent and a maximum of 27 percent were returned; however, the share of respondents providing all the information necessary for this investigation is much lower, see variable PART40R in table 1, where six subsamples are distinguished in order to also document gender differences.

In view of the differences surfacing in table 1, a cautious maintained hypothesis is to admit six different sample selection mechanisms that should be estimated prior to analyzing equation (15), the behavioral relationship of primary interest. Moreover, selection mechanisms may be operative not only with regard to participation in the field study, but also with regard to the reservation wages for care and for work (either of which may be infinite rather than finite), and with regard to labor force participation. In principle, each of these three selection mechanisms has the potential of introducing correlation between the explanatory variables appearing on the right-hand side of equation (15) and the error term μ. For example, a marked preference for caregiving (U_Z / U_C large) may make participation in the field study more likely, which has an impact on the value of μ under general conditions [Heckman (1979), Greene (1993, section 22.4.2)]. However, any correlation between U_Z / U_C and μ causes the parameter estimates pertaining to equation (15) to be biased.

In theory, these sample selection equations should be estimated simultaneously with equation (15) for efficiency. Yet, actual experience suggests that there is a considerable risk of numerically ill-conditional data sets, resulting in very unstable joint parameter estimates [Amemiya (1981)]. In addition, full information estimation procedures have the drawback of contaminating the structural equation of primary interest with specification errors prevalent in the sample selection equation. Since knowledge of nonparticipants is limited to a few insurance-based characteristics, it was deemed safer to give preference to Heckman's two-step estimator using the inverse of Mill's ratio over full information estimation.

Likewise, the structural equation (15) will be estimated separately for each of the six subsamples and a merging performed only after having carried out a series of Chow tests for homogeneity. After this step, the full regression specification will be reduced in an attempt to bring out the crucial factors determining the reservation wage for care.

3.2 Three sample selection mechanisms

Mechanism No. 1: Participation in field study. Since only members beyond age 40 were contacted in the case of insurers B and C, it was decided to exclude respondents below age 40 from the database of insurer A as well for this investigation. Apart from purely statistical considerations, it may be argued that questions concerning LTC and the provision of care tend to be taken more seriously by members of an age group having parents typically at retirement age and beyond. Accordingly, age of the respondent is one of the common explanatory variables appearing in all of the six sample selection mechanisms specified. Indeed, age turned out significant at the 0.05 significance level or better in five out of six cases.

As to insurer A, there were four additional pieces of information available (e.g. number of visits and total benefits paid between 1990 and 1992); however, no common specification for men and women could be found. In the case of insurer B, five characteristics were known besides age, among them premiums paid (1990 through 1992), which turned out to have a highly significant positive impact on the probability of participation in the field study, independent of gender. Finally, pretty much the same information had been made available by insurer C about their nonrespondents. Again, however, it proved impossible to identify a common sample selection mechanism for both sexes.

On the basis of this scanty information, only a mediocre statistical fit could be expected in the six probit analyses, and the calculated values of the inverse of Mill's ratio (λ_P) cannot be claimed to amount to more than very rough approximations. Moreover, these estimates never attain statistical significance at the 0.1 level of significance in subsequent analyses of selection mechanism resulting in finite reservation wages for care or work (FINITE, see table 1) and labor force participation (PARTLAB). Entering λ_P into the equation explaining the (finite) reservation wages for care (LNCARE) does not seem to make a statistically recognizable difference either (see table 1 again).

Mechanism No. 2: Finite reservation wage for care and for work. Respondents may decide to state an infinite reservation wage for care or for work, causing them to drop out of the usable sample. Basically, two different sample selection mechanisms may be imagined for generating finite rather than infinite reservation wages for care and for work, respectively. However, in view of the scanty information available and the lack of fit of the probit models estimated for λ_P (see previous paragraph), the two mechanisms were combined into one, using a common simple specification.

Among the female members of insurer A, the presence of children strongly increased respondents' probability of stating finite reservation wages. Among its male members, no significant predictor of this probability could be identified. For this reason, tests for significance with regard to λ_F could not be carried out in the case of insurer A (M), as evidenced in table 1. Among members of insurers B and C, the common factor contributing to finite values of the reservation wages for care and work is the propensity to provide care to a lightly disabled member of the family (PROPCL, see table 2 below for a short definition and descriptive statistics). Beyond this single common factor, sample selection mechanisms appeared to differ between the sexes.

Estimates of λ_F failed to display significant coefficients in the six equations designed to model labor force participation. However, they were highly significant in two of the six equations for LNCARE (i.e. the log of the reservation wage for care, given that it is finite).

Mechanism No. 3: Labor force participation. Attempts to determine the factors responsible for the decision to participate in the labor market proved to be completely unsuccessful. This failure does not really come as a surprise in view of the very low number of respondents reporting no earnings in the labor market. Accordingly, it was not possible to model this particular sample selection process.

Conclusion 3: In principle, sample selection mechanisms may be operative at three levels, (1) participation in the field study, (2) asking for a finite rather than an infinite reservation wage for care or for work, and (3) labor force participation. Whereas mechanisms No. 1 and 2 can be roughly modelled on the basis of available information, this is not possible for No. 3 since almost all retained respondents happen to be in the labor force. There is no evidence to the effect that mechanism No. 2 depends on mechanism No. 1, while mechanism No. 2 has a recognizable influence on LNCARE in two subsamples of men only.

3.3 Description of variables used in the estimation of the structural equation

With the exception of the reservation wage for care (RCARE and LNCARE, respectively) the variables used for estimating equation (15) appear in alphabetic order in table 2.

The variable RCARE derives from the response to the question, "Imagine that you were to be paid a fixed amount of 1,000 Swiss francs (700 US$ at 1993 exchange rates) for providing care to a disabled family member. How many hours of care would you be willing to provide for this amount of money?"

Assume that a respondent marked 47 hours on the pertaining visual analog scale. Her reservation wage for care would then amount to some 21 Swiss francs (15 US$), corresponding to the average value for female members of insurer A (see first entry of first column of table 2). It must be admitted that the framing of the question fails to secure the indifference condition $dU = 0$ of equation (1). However, a detailed circumscription of this condition in a mailed questionnaire would have proved impractical, causing the number of completed questionnaires to be reduced even more. RCARE thus contains a (positive) measurement error, which does not bias estimation results as long as it is uncorrelated with explanatory variables.

Finally, it may be noted that the means of RCARE differ importantly across health insurers but not much between female and male members of a given insurer. While this appears to contradict our maintained hypothesis, which emphasizes the particularly important role of women in providing care to family members, it still remains to be seen whether gender-specific partial effects exist. In particular, certain factors may be relevant for one sex but irrelevant for the other, offsetting these partial effects.

As to the explanatory variables, their relationships with the postulated theoretical quantities is given in the second column of table 3 below. In an earlier version of the paper, an attempt was made to define these indicators as closely to their appearance in equation (15) as possible. However, multiplication and division of most explanatory variables by the wage rate w was found to introduce severe multicollinearity. Therefore, the indicator variables are now left in their original form. In order to account for the nonlinearity of equation (15) w.r.t. the wage rate, regressions containing $1/w$ and $(\ln w)^2$ were also estimated. However, these additional regressors did not add to the explanatory power of the equation.

First, the presence of children is indicated by CHILD=1, whose partial effect on LNCARE would have to be negative if it unambiguously signalled superior nonmarket productivity, in keeping with Conclusion 2. It must be admitted however that the presence of children might also depress nonmarket productivity, causing the predicted sign of the regression coefficient pertaining to CHILD to be undetermined (see table 3).

In other instances, the relationship between the indicator and the theoretical quantity is unambiguous. For example, a respondent reporting good health (HLTHY=1) should profit from good nonmarket productivity C_X. Based on

Conclusion 2 once more, the partial relationship between LNCARE and HLTHY should be negative. Among the remaining indicators of C_X, SCHOOL1 and SCHOOL2, representing individuals having limited formal education, are predicted to be associated with high values of LNCARE, whereas SCHOOL4 up to SCHOOL8 are predicted to go along with low values of LNCARE.

A strict implementation of equation (15) would call for all indicators of the productivity in caregiving Z_A being multiplied by all indicators of the preference for caregiving U_Z / U_C and divided by all indicators of C_X (as well as w/p). Since this procedure again risks to introduce a great deal of multicollinearity, the product $(U_Z / U_C) \cdot Z_A$ is approximated by the sum, $(U_Z / U_C) + Z_A$. It may be assumed that a respondent caring for a family member at home (HOUSE=1) has a particularly high productivity Z_A, which unambiguously should lower LNCARE according to Conclusion 2. Conversely, a respondent having a disabled family member cared for in an institution (INST=1) probably has a below average productivity in caring activities, calling for a high value of LNCARE.

An explanatory variable of particular importance should be the stated propensity to give care to a lightly disabled family member (PROPCL=1) and a severely disabled family member (PROPCS=1), respectively. Presumably both variables indicate a high rate of substitution between consumption and caregiving U_Z / U_C, causing LNCARE to be lower than otherwise.

Finally, the subjective trade-off between consumption and leisure, U_L / U_C, appearing in the third term of equation (15), is reflected by the reservation wage for additional work (RWORK). RWORK was calculated from the response to the survey question, "Imagine that you were paid a fixed amount of 1,000 Swiss francs (700 US$ at 1993 exchange rates) for (additional) work. How many hours would you be willing to work for this amount of money?" A strong preference for leisure is predicted to result in a high reservation wage for care according to Conclusion 2.

3.4 Estimation of the structural equation

A first set of OLS estimations, performed separately for each of the six subsamples, is displayed in table 3. The most important result to be noted is the significance of LNWAGE in only two of the six regression equations, with its coefficient in the male subsample of insurer C even being significantly negative rather than positive. This constitutes a rather strong rejection of equation (15) and the microeconomic model specified in equations (1) through (5). In addition, the coefficient of PROPCL, while being negative as predicted in five out of six cases, lacks significance. It is significantly positive, contrary to prediction, once more in the male subsample of insurer C.

Other elements of the model receive a measure of statistical confirmation, however. In particular, PROPCS has a consistently negative coefficient which is significant in three of the six regressions. And while the battery of indicators referring to C_X, the nonmarket productivity in the use of consumer goods (CHILD, ... SCHOOL8), contributes to statistical explanation only in some cases, the indicator of preference for leisure (RWORK) has the predicted positive coefficient in all six regressions, with statistical significance in five of six. Finally, sample selection effects appear to be relevant in two regressions only, both based on subsamples of men. Coefficients of determination range between 0.16 and 0.38, which may be deemed satisfactory in view of the rather limited sample sizes in the important rule of unmeasured personal characteristics.

Conclusion 4: Separate regressions of the reservation wage for care (LNCARE) based on six subsamples contradict the hypothesis that LNCARE depends positively on the wage rate attainable on the labor market (lnw) in four out of six cases and by implication Conclusion 1.

In order to obtain more clear-cut results, it is of interest to see whether some or all of these subsample regressions may be pooled. Since sample selection effects with regard to finite reservation wages for care and work were present among men (see row labelled λ_P, λ_F of table 3), they were reintroduced into the regressions for women to admit the possibility of gender-specific sample selection mechanisms. The outcomes of the pertinent Chow tests for homogeneity are displayed in table 4.

First, F-tests were performed to find out whether the regression equations explaining the reservation wage of women differ significantly between the three insurers. The hypothesis that women of subsamples A and B are characterized by the same structure must be rejected at the 0.05 level of significance, while for the other two subsamples (B+C, A+C) it may be accepted (see panel I of table 4). Finally, there are three ways to test for full homogeneity across the three subsamples, (A+B)+C, (B+C)+A, (A+C)+B. The calculated F-values amount to 1.03, 1.79, 1.07 respectively, exceeding the critical value of 1.57 in one instance only.

Turning to the male respondents (panel II of table 4), all three subsamples pass the homogeneity test. When it comes to a comprehensive pooling of the three subsamples, adding C to the combination (A+B) is rejected, while the other two possibilities may be accepted.

Evidently, the statistical evidence does not speak so strongly against pooling across insurers as to obviate the issue of whether women differ significantly from men with regard to their reservation wage for care and the relative importance of its determinants. The pertinent test statistic is displayed in panel III of table 4, indicating unambiguous rejection of homogeneity.

Conclusion 5: While pooling respondents of a given sex across the three insurers is only weakly rejected, pooling the two sexes is clearly rejected at the 0.05 significance level.

The first part of Conclusion 5 notwithstanding, it may still be worthwhile to explore the properties of gender-specific regression equations based on the larger number of observations available from a pooling of subsamples. The results of this exercise appear in table 5. The first and second columns repeat the full specification of table 3 for women and men, respectively, while columns three and four contain reduced specifications emphasizing factors of statistical significance.

Starting with columns one and three, the first thing to note is that coefficients and t-ratios are reasonably stable when compared with columns one, three and five of table 3. But there is a major surprise in that the wage rate becomes a significant exlanatory variable in both regressions, although its coefficient clearly differs from +1, the value predicted in Conclusion 1. In addition, women of only limited education (SCHOOL1) appear to ask for a lower rather than higher reservation wage for care, contrary to Conclusion 2.

In the case of men (columns two and four of table 5), the wage rate seems to become irrelevant when the subsamples are pooled. In addition, men of only limited education (SCHOOL2) appear to ask for a lower rather than higher reservation wage for care, whereas men having a university education (SCHOOL8) seem to ask for a higher rather than a lower reservation wage for care, contrary to Conclusion 2. However, men's productivity in providing care (indicated by HOUSE for high productivity and INST for low productivity) has an important and statistically recognizable effect on their reservation wage for care, as predicted by Conclusion 2.

In conclusion, what are the similarities and differences between the two sexes with regard to the compensation required for inducing them to provide LTC to a family member? The common determinants appear to be:

- the stated propensity to provide care to a severely disabled family member (PROPCS), with a lightly stronger partial effect in the case of women;

- the stated reservation wage for work (RWORK), a high value of which causes the reservation wage for care to be adjusted upwards much more among women, however.

With regard to gender-specific differences, the following items merit emphasis:
- while an increased wage in the labor market (LNWAGE) serves to drive up women's reservation wage for care, this relationship is conspicuously absent among men;
- while the stated propensity to provide care to a lightly disabled family member (PROPCL) lowers the reservation wage for care among women, such an effect cannot be discerned among men;
- whereas the presence of a child (CHILD) causes men to ask for a lower reservation wage for care, this does not seem to affect women;
- whereas productivity differences with respect to caregiving (HOUSE, INST) do not seem to have an impact on the reservation wage for care among women, they are quite important among men;
- whereas having completed only a primary school (SCHOOL1) serves to lower the reservation wage for care asked by women, such an effect can be seen among men having completed a basic school (SCHOOL2), with a stronger partial effect in the case of women;
- whereas having a university education (SCHOOL8) serves to drive up the reservation wage for care of men, this seems not to affect women.

Conclusion 6: There are gender-specific determinants of the reservation wage for care (LNCARE) in that women ask for a higher LNCARE if their wage on the labor market is high (somewhat as predicted in Conclusion 1), while men do not. In addition, women adjust LNCARE more strongly upwards when their reservation wage for work is high.

4 Implications for the future financing of LTC

If present trends continue, the cost of institutional LTC is expected to rise in the future [Groenenboom et al. (1994)]. One policy alternative designed to cope with this surge is to substitute informal care, typically provided by relatives and family members, for institutional LTC. From the point of view of these family members, providing LTC is not without its own opportunity cost, as is evidenced by the theoretical analysis provided in the second section of this paper. A measure of this opportunity cost is the reservation wage asked for giving care to a disabled member of the family, indicating the amount of resistance to be expected against any attempt to substitute informal care for institutional LTC.

To overcome this resistance, policy makers may consider paying a subsidy to informal caregivers or distributing vouchers to individuals in need of LTC. Although the two alternatives look equivalent from a financial point of view, the voucher solution has the important advantage of giving the recipient a choice. In fact, he is free to redeem his voucher with an informal caregiver outside the family or use it towards covering the cost of accommodation in a home if he so prefers [Felder/Zweifel (1994)]. Therefore the remainder of this section is devoted to calculating the value of such a voucher.

According to expert estimates, about 100 hours per month suffice to take care of a lightly disabled elderly person. Judging from the values of RCARE appearing in the first row of table 2, the value of a voucher inducing a Swiss individual to provide this amount of care may range anywhere between 2,100 Swiss francs (1,500 US$ at 1993 exchange rates) and 5,100 Swiss francs (3,640 US$), with the lower bound representative of the rural parts of the country. However, such an extrapolation is frought with considerable uncertainty. Above all, the amount of compensation stated in the survey is much lower, viz. 1,000 Swiss francs (700 US$). Extrapolation by a factor of three or even five is always risky, for the reservation wage for LTC may well vary for LTC services in excess of the stated amount.

Table 2 shows that while women's wage rate in the labor market is lower than that of men, they ask for almost the same value of the reservation wage for care. Since women's future wage rates may be expected to increase as their education improves, the value of the voucher will have to be adjusted upwards in the course of time.

The present study is based on information that an administrative body implementing a subsidy will not have at its disposal. Specifically, it will not know who is inclined to provide care to a disabled family member and who is not, and who would ask for a high reservation wage for (additional) work and who would not. Information about both quantities would have to be gathered in field studies. This consideration again militates against a subsidy (and any attempt to grade it according to observed characteristics of informal caregivers) while lending support to a voucher solution where it is up to the recipient of the voucher to spend it on LTC services giving him the best value for money.

Conclusion 7: For a policy designed to encourage the substitution of institional LTC by informal LTC, a voucher has important advantages over a subsidy paid to caregivers, which would have to depend on characteristics not easily observed by administrators. The value of a voucher sufficient to induce a Swiss individual to provide LTC to a lightly disabled family member may be calculated to range between 2,100 Swiss francs (1,500 US$ at 1993 exchange rates) and 5,100 Swiss francs (3,600 US$).

5 Summary and Conclusion

The objective of this contribution is to find out about the scope of substitution of institutional long-term care (LTC) by informal care, taking into account that informal care is dominantly provided by women. For this purpose, the so-called reservation wage for care and its possibly gender-specific determinants are of particular interest. A simple microeconomic model of household production was developed in order to formulate a few predictions about the value of the reservation wage for care. According to this theory, the elasticity of this reservation wage with respect to the wage attainable on the labor market should be unity (Conclusion 1). In addition, it should depend negatively on the individual's productivity in providing LTC and positively on her stated reservation wage for work (Conclusion 2). Empirical work to test these predictions was based on a total of 1,200 respondents to a mailed questionnaire who were contacted in 1993 through three Swiss health insurers. Considerable amount of attention was given to sample selection mechanisms, which however prove irrelevant with few exceptions (Conclusion 3). Regressions of the reservation wage for care were fitted to six subsamples (female/male, three insurers), which contradicted the elasticity prediction of Conclusion 1 (Conclusion 4). The hypothesis that respondents of a given sex are characterized by the same structural relationship across the three insurers was only weakly rejected. However, there was clear evidence suggesting that the two sexes should not be pooled (Conclusion 5). Accordingly, gender-specific pooled regressions were performed in an attempt to identify differences in the determinants of the reservation wage for care between women and men. Here, the reservation wage of women was found to react positively to the wage on the labor market, albeit with an elasticity of less than +1. No such effect seemed to be at work among men. In addition, women adjust their reservation wage for care more strongly upwards when their reservation wage for market work is high (Conclusion 6). These findings are of relevance for a policy aiming at encouraging the substitution of institutional by informal LTC. Because a subsidy paid to informal caregivers would have to be gauged to caregiver attitudes about which administrators have no information, a voucher solution is suggested. The empirical results of this investigation may be used to roughly determine the value of such a voucher in Switzerland (Conclusion 7).

Appendix

Table 1: Descriptive statistics and outcomes of tests for three sample selection mechanisms[a]

	Sample A		Sample B		Sample C	
	F	M	F	M	F	M
PART40R [=1 if individual participated in field study and is between 40 and retirement age (=62 F, =65 M)] → λ_P	$\frac{75}{3,335}=$ 0.022 (0.147)	$\frac{100}{2,745}=$ 0.036 (0.186)	$\frac{95}{4,180}=$ 0.023 (0.150)	$\frac{246}{3,068}=$ 0.080 (0.271)	$\frac{115}{2,013}=$ 0.057 (0.232)	$\frac{757}{6,154}=$ 0.123 (0.328)
FINITE (=1 if individual asks for a finite reservation wage for care or for work) → λ_F	$\frac{64}{75}=$ 0.853 (0.354)	$\frac{89}{100}=$ 0.890 (0.313)	$\frac{80}{95}=$ 0.842 (0.365)	$\frac{214}{246}=$ 0.870 (0.336)	$\frac{95}{115}=$ 0.826 (0.379)	$\frac{646}{757}=$ 0.853 (0.375)
PARTLAB (=1 if individual has positive earnings)	$\frac{59}{64}=$ 0.922 (0.268)	$\frac{89}{89}=$ 1.000 (0.000)	$\frac{75}{80}=$ 0.938 (0.243)	$\frac{211}{214}=$ 0.986 (0.117)	$\frac{94}{95}=$ 0.989 (0.104)	$\frac{643}{646}=$ 0.995 (0.032)
H_0: Inverse of Mill's ratio $\lambda_P = 0$ [b]:						
in equation for FINITE	n.s.	n.s.	n.s.	n.s.	n.s.	n.s.
in equation for PARTLAB = 0	n.s.	–	n.s.	n.s.	n.s.	n.s.
in equation for LNCARE	n.s.	n.s.	n.s.	n.s.	n.s.	n.s.
H_0: Inverse of Mill's ratio $\lambda_F = 0$ [b]:						
in equation for PARTLAB = 0	n.s.	–	n.s.	n.s.	n.s.	n.s.
in equation for LNCARE	n.s.	–	n.s.	***	n.s.	***

[a] standard errors in parentheses.
[b] *, **, ***: significantly different from zero at the 90%, 95%, 99% confidence level; n.s. = not significant; –: not applicable.

Table 2: Description of variables[a]

	Sample					
	A		B		C	
Variable	F (1)	M (2)	F (3)	M (4)	F (5)	M (6)
RCARE (Reservation wage for care)[b]	21.30 (11.76)	24.63 (15.67)	40.96 (58.44)	40.48 (34.93)	51.09 (68.18)	47.83 (54.07)
LNCARE (log of RCARE)	2.93 (0.51)	3.07 (0.51)	3.41 (0.66)	3.47 (0.65)	3.56 (0.76)	3.56 (0.72)
CHILD (= 1 if individual has children, = 0 otherwise)	0.88 (0.33)	0.89 (0.32)	0.68 (0.47)	0.84 (0.37)	0.59 (0.50)	0.77 (0.42)
HLTHY (= 1 if HEALTH > 2, = 0 otherwise)[c]	0.95 (0.22)	0.90 (0.30)	0.88 (0.33)	0.91 (0.29)	0.96 (0.20)	0.96 (0.20)
HOME1 (= 1 if living together with spouse but without children, = 0 otherwise)[d]	0.15 (0.36)	0.12 (0.33)	0.27 (0.45)	0.31 (0.46)	0.31 (0.46)	0.37 (0.48)
HOME4 (= 1 if living without a spouse but with children, = 0 otherwise)[d]	0.03 (0.18)	0.01 (0.11)	0.20 (0.40)	0.03 (0.17)	0.15 (0.36)	0.02 (0.14)
HOME6 (= 1 if living alone, no children/parents in the neighborhood, = 0 otherwise)[d]	0.05 (0.22)	0.02 (0.15)	0.15 (0.36)	0.04 (0.20)	0.23 (0.43)	0.07 (0.25)
HOME7 (= 1 if living alone, children/parents in the neighborhood, = 0 otherwise)[d]	0.07 (0.25)	0.02 (0.15)	0.11 (0.31)	0.02 (0.15)	0.12 (0.32)	0.04 (0.19)
HOUSE (= 1 if a disabled family member receives care at home, = 0 otherwise)	0.10 (0.30)	0.10 (0.30)	0.07 (0.25)	0.05 (0.21)	0.07 (0.26)	0.07 (0.25)
INST (= 1, if a disabled family member receives care in an institution, = 0 otherwise)	0.03 (0.18)	0.01 (0.11)	0.07 (0.25)	0.08 (0.01)	0.04 (0.20)	0.08 (0.27)
PROPCL (= 1 if willing to give care to a lightly disabled family member, = 0 else)	0.75 (0.44)	0.75 (0.43)	0.73 (0.45)	0.79 (0.41)	0.77 (0.43)	0.73 (0.44)
PROPCS (= 1 if willing to give care to a severely disabled family member, = 0 else)	0.34 (0.48)	0.26 (0.44)	0.35 (0.48)	0.29 (0.45)	0.30 (0.46)	0.26 (0.44)
RWORK (Reservation wage for work)[b]	37.14 (43.58)	43.05 (37.03)	60.09 (64.35)	87.78 (110.17)	79.45 (69.79)	90.93 (80.02)
SCHOOL1 (= 1 if completed a primary school, = 0 otherwise)[e]	0.08 (0.28)	0.08 (0.27)	0.01 (0.12)	0.01 (0.10)	0.04 (0.20)	0.02 (0.16)

Table 2 (cont.)

Variable	Sample A		Sample B		Sample C	
	F (1)	M (2)	F (3)	M (4)	F (5)	M (6)
SCHOOL2 (= 1 if completed basic school, = 0 otherwise)[e]	0.07 (0.25)	0.04 (0.21)	0.09 (0.29)	0.06 (0.23)	0.05 (0.23)	0.03 (0.18)
SCHOOL4 (= 1 if completed a vocational school, = 0 otherwise)[e]	0.14 (0.35)	0.10 (0.30)	0.16 (0.37)	0.11 (0.32)	0.11 (0.31)	0.08 (0.28)
SCHOOL6 (= 1 if completed a higher vocational school, = 0 otherwise)[e]	0.05 (0.22)	0.21 (0.41)	0.17 (0.38)	0.12 (0.32)	0.19 (0.40)	0.21 (0.41)
SCHOOL7 (= 1 if completed a college, = 0 otherwise)[e]	0.19 (0.39)	0.17 (0.38)	0.08 (0.27)	0.17 (0.37)	0.06 (0.25)	0.11 (0.32)
SCHOOL8 (= 1 if completed a university, = 0 otherwise)[e]	0.03 (0.18)	0.11 (0.32)	0.07 (0.25)	0.17 (0.38)	0.10 (0.30)	0.22 (0.41)
WAGE (monthly earnings/monthly working hours)[b]	37.07 (28.19)	37.29 (16.39)	36.26 (19.29)	48.51 (56.02)	36.51 (27.55)	48.30 (20.87)
LNWAGE (log of WAGE)	3.37 (0.79)	3.49 (0.59)	3.45 (0.55)	3.73 (0.50)	3.44 (0.53)	3.79 (0.44)
N	59	89	75	211	94	643

[a] standard deviations in parentheses.
[b] in Swiss francs, 1 Swiss franc = 0.7 US$ at 1993 exchange rates.
[c] HEALTH is a visual analog scale ranging from 0 (=very bad subjective health) to 4 (=excellent subjective health).
[d] benchmark category is HOME2 (=1 if living together with spouse and children).
[e] benchmark category is SCHOOL3 (=1 if completed apprenticeship plus vocational school).

Table 3: Full OLS regression estimates for LNCARE[a]

Variable (Predicted sign)	Theoretical Variable, see equation (15)	Sample A		Sample B		Sample C	
		F (1)	M (2)	F (3)	M (4)	F (5)	M (6)
CONSTANT		3.281*** (0.495)	2.123*** (0.470)	3.002*** (0.646)	3.576*** (0.407)	2.592*** (0.658)	3.006*** (0.276)
LNWAGE (+)	w	0.075 (0.084)	0.301*** (0.094)	0.029 (0.159)	-0.081 (0.120)	0.194 (0.136)	-0.224** (0.104)
PROPCL (-)	U_Z / U_C	-0.233 (0.162)	-0.156 (0.125)	-0.169 (0.177)	-0.030 (0.169)	-0.215 (0.170)	0.372** (0.162)

Table 3 (cont.)

		Sample					
	Theoretical	A		B		C	
Variable (Pred. sign)	Var., see equ. (15)	F (1)	M (2)	F (3)	M (4)	F (5)	M (6)
PROPCS (-)	U_Z / U_C	-0.092 (0.130)	-0.177 (0.124)	-0.262* (0.152)	-0.217** (0.100)	-0.260 (0.160)	-0.159*** (0.061)
CHILD (+/-)	C_X	0.266 (0.287)	-0.088 (0.236)	0.012 (0.214)	-0.170 (0.137)	-0.152 (0.180)	-0.136* (0.075)
HLTHY (-)	C_X	-0.645** (0.291)	-0.333* (0.175)	0.170 (0.236)	0.083 (0.149)	0.330 (0.347)	0.045 (0.128)
HOME1 (+/-)	C_X	0.101 (0.185)	0.047 (0.187)	-0.034 (0.207)	-0.076 (0.102)	-0.079 (0.218)	-0.032 (0.063)
HOME4 (+/-)	C_X	0.385 (0.313)	0.581 (0.463)	0.214 (0.217)	0.285 (0.258)	-0.143 (0.239)	0.042 (0.193)
HOME6 (+/-)	C_X	0.155 (0.393)	0.700* (0.411)	0.198 (0.230)	0.270 (0.234)	0.131 (0.262)	-0.056 (0.122)
HOME7 (+/-)	C_X	-0.346 (0.227)	0.679** (0.330)	0.583** (0.272)	0.164 (0.289)	0.150 (0.266)	0.051 (0.144)
SCHOOL1 (+)	C_X	-0.725*** (0.233)	-0.276 (0.215)	0.351 (0.702)	-0.513 (0.452)	-0.432 (0.363)	0.062 (0.172)
SCHOOL2 (+)	C_X	0.154 (0.247)	-0.063 (0.268)	0.308 (0.264)	-0.696*** (0.252)	-0.216 (0.322)	-0.068 (0.148)
SCHOOL4 (-)	C_X	-0.409** (0.178)	-0.005 (0.179)	0.121 (0.203)	0.076 (0.142)	-0.098 (0.237)	0.165 (0.101)
SCHOOL6 (-)	C_X	0.240 (0.279)	-0.041 (0.140)	-0.320 (0.195)	-0.265 (0.219)	-0.409* (0.209)	0.065 (0.074)
SCHOOL7 (-)	C_X	-0.114 (0.186)	-0.285* (0.156)	0.057 (0.278)	-0.021 (0.124)	-0.282 (0.321)	0.052 (0.090)
SCHOOL8 (-)	C_X	-0.318 (0.323)	-0.066 (0.174)	0.043 (0.317)	0.201 (0.131)	0.235 (0.255)	0.146* (0.078)
HOUSE (-)	Z_A	0.052 (0.277)	-0.283* (0.158)	-0.078 (0.343)	-0.156 (0.206)	0.356 (0.271)	-0.243** (0.105)
INST (+)	Z_A	-0.552 (0.416)	0.681 (0.457)	0.618** (0.275)	0.162 (0.164)	-0.129 (0.349)	0.125 (0.098)
RWORK (+)	U_L / U_C	0.003* (0.001)	0.002* (0.001)	0.003*** (0.001)	0.001 (0.0004)	0.005*** (0.001)	0.002*** (0.0003)
λ_P, λ_F [b]		n.s.	4.392 (3.119)	n.s.	1.430** (0.635)	n.s.	3.902*** (0.922)
$\overline{R}^2$		0.38	0.29	0.29	0.16	0.29	0.17
N		59	89	75	211	94	643

[a] standard errors in parentheses.
[b] λ_P for sample A (M); λ_F for samples B (M) and C (M).
*, **, ***: significantly different from zero at the 90%, 95%, 99% confidence level; n.s. = not significant.

Table 4: Outcomes of Chow tests for homogeneity[a]

I. Female respondents, homogeneity across three insurers

Women	Error sum of squares	N, M	Calculated F-value	Critical F-value (p = 0.05)
A	6.46521	59		
B	17.19387	75		
C	29.91524	94		
A+B	33.59580	134	$F(20, 94)=1.97$	1.69
B+C	52.73773	169	$F(20, 129)=0.77$	1.65
A+C	46.05910	153	$F(20, 113)=1.50$	1.66
(A+B)+C;(B+C)+A;(A+C)+B	70.45759	228	$F(20, 188)=1.03;1.79;1.07$	1.57

II. Male respondents, homogeneity across three insurers

Men	Error sum of squares	N, M	Calculated F-value	Critical F-value (p = 0.05)
A	12.69577	89		
B	68.89855	211		
C	265.95751	643		
A+B	88.36623	300	$F(20, 260)=1.08$	1.57
B+C	347.49094	854	$F(20, 814)=1.54$	1.57
A+C	288.06686	732	$F(20, 692)=1.17$	1.57
(A+B)+C;(B+C)+A;(A+C)+B	368.28941	943	$F(20, 903)=1.78;1.02;1.43$	1.57

III. Female and male respondents

A+B+C	Error sum of squares	N, M	Calculated F-value	Critical F-value (p = 0.05)
Women+Men	463.93327	1,171	$F(20, 1,131)=3.25$	1.57

[a] The Chow test is a F-test indicating, whether the data can be pooled or if separate regressions must be run [Pindyck and Rubinfeld (1991, 116)]. The appropriate F statistic is:

$$F_{k, N+M-2k} = \frac{(ESS_R - ESS_{UR})/k}{ESS_{UR}/(N+M-2k)}, \text{ with}$$

ESS_R restricted error sum of squares
ESS_{UR} unrestricted error sum of squares
N, M number of observations of the two regressions
k number of restrictions.

Table 5: Full and reduced OLS regression estimates for LNCARE[a)]

Variable (Predicted sign)	Theoretical Variable, see equation (15)	Full regression estimate F (1)	Full regression estimate M (2)	Reduced regression estimate F (3)	Reduced regression estimate M (4)
CONSTANT		2.781*** (0.325)	3.063*** (0.198)	2.882*** (0.233)	3.129*** (0.067)
LNWAGE (+)	w	0.128* (0.070)	0.047 (0.054)	0.128** (0.064)	
PROPCL (-)	U_Z / U_C	-0.268*** (0.098)	-0.086 (0.067)	-0.273*** (0.094)	
PROPCS (-)	U_Z / U_C	-0.190** (0.089)	-0.169*** (0.049)	-0.200** (0.087)	-0.183*** (0.047)
CHILD (+/-)	C_X	-0.031 (0.114)	-0.112* (0.061)		-0.120** (0.052)
HLTHY (-)	C_X	0.083 (0.161)	0.010 (0.088)		
HOME1 (+/-)	C_X	0.018 (0.111)	-0.001 (0.051)		
HOME4 (+/-)	C_X	0.128 (0.127)	0.141 (0.148)		
HOME6 (+/-)	C_X	0.212 (0.152)	0.050 (0.103)		
HOME7 (+/-)	C_X	0.196 (0.142)	0.167 (0.121)		
SCHOOL1 (+)	C_X	-0.468** (0.200)	-0.124 (0.133)	-0.427** (0.191)	
SCHOOL2 (+)	C_X	0.011 (0.164)	-0.238** (0.112)		-0.280*** (0.106)
SCHOOL4 (-)	C_X	-0.086 (0.125)	0.121 (0.077)		
SCHOOL6 (-)	C_X	-0.195 (0.124)	0.004 (0.062)		
SCHOOL7 (-)	C_X	-0.224 (0.144)	0.015 (0.068)		
SCHOOL8 (-)	C_X	0.173 (0.168)	0.165*** (0.062)		0.153*** (0.054)
HOUSE (-)	Z_A	0.106 (0.152)	-0.211** (0.084)		-0.211** (0.084)

Table 5 (cont.)

		Full regression estimate		Reduced regression estimate	
Variable (Pre-dicted sign)	Theoretical Variable, see equation (15)	F (1)	M (2)	F (3)	M (4)
INST (+)	Z_A	0.179 (0.184)	0.155* (0.081)		0.155* (0.080)
RWORK (+)	U_L / U_C	0.005*** (0.001)	0.002*** (0.0003)	0.005*** (0.001)	0.002*** (0.0003)
λ_P, λ_F b)		n.s.	1.212*** (0.290)	n.s.	1.518*** (0.195)
$\bar{R}^2$		0.33	0.19	0.33	0.19
N		228	943	228	943

a) standard errors in parentheses.
b) λ_P for sample A (M), λ_F for samples B (M) and C (M).
*, **, ***: significantly different from zero at the 90%, 95%, 99% confidence level; n.s. = not significant.

Acknowledgment

The authors wish to thank Mark V. Pauly (University of Philadelphia) as well as Stefan Felder and Markus Meier (University of Zurich) for valuable comments and criticisms.

References

Abelin, Th./Schlettwein-Gsell, D. (1986): Behinderungen und Bedürfnisse Betagter. Eine multifaktorielle epidemiologische Studie unter städtischen Bedingungen (Impairements and Needs of the Aged. A Multifactorial Epidemiological Study of Urbanized Areas), in *Schweizerische Medizinische Wochenschrift 116*, 1524-1542.

Amemiya, T. (1981): Qualitative Response Models: A Survey, in *Journal of Economic Literature 14*, 1483-1536.

Becker, G.S. (1965): A Theory of the Allocation of Time, in *The Economic Journal 75*, 103-27.

Felder, S./Zweifel. P. (1994): *The Role of Government in the Provision and Financing of Long-term Care: an Overview*, in J. C. Rey/C. Tilquin (eds.): SYSTED 94, Proceedings of the 5th International Conference on Systems Sciences in Health-social Services for the Elderly and Disabled, Lausanne: Institut suisse de la santé publique, 505-509.

Greene, W.H. (1993): *Econometric Analysis*. 2nd ed.. New York: MacMillan.

Groenenboom, G.K.C./de Klerc, M.M.Y./Huijsman, R. (1994): *Estimating Cost of Care for the Elderly*, in J.-C. Rey/C. Tilquin (eds.): SYSTED 94, Proceedings of the 5th International Conference on Systems Sciences in Health-social Services for the Elderly and Disabled, Lausanne: Institut suisse de la santé publique, 490-494.

Heckman, J.J. (1979): Sample Selection Bias as a Specification Error, in *Econometrica* 47, 153-161.

Höpflinger, F. (1994): *Frauen im Alter – Alter der Frauen. Ein Forschungsdossier.* (Aged Women – Ageing of Women. A Research Documentation). Zürich: Seismo.

Kendig, H.L./Hashimoto, A./Coppard, L.C. (1992) (eds.): *Family Support for the Elderly. The International Experience*. Oxford: Oxford University Press.

Pindyck, R.S./Rubinfeld, D.L. (1991): *Econometric Models and Economic Forecasts*. New York: McGraw-Hill.

5 DETERMINANTS OF INSTITUTIONALIZATION IN OLD AGE

Thomas Klein

1 Introduction

Institutionalization in old age is expensive and most elderly prefer to stay independent and live at home as long as possible. Therefore, a vital interest exists for the individual as well as for the society to learn about the risks of institutionalization and about the determinants which either cause or avoid institutionalization. On the one hand, knowledge on the determinants of institutionalization in old age is valuable to detect people most at risk, and, on the other hand, to forecast future demands for care.

In the context of aging populations in western industrialized countries, institutionalization in old age increasingly has attracted research in the past two decades [Branch (1984), Kastenbaum/Candy (1973), Palmore (1976), Shapiro/Tate (1985), (1988), Vicente/Wiley/Carrington (1979)]. Nevertheless, empirical results still differ considerably as to the ratio of institutionalization the individual experiences throughout life. While cross-section analysis counts about 4-5% of the population aged 65 and over being institutionalized [referred to as the "4% Fallacy"; Kastenbaum/Candy (1973)], longitudinal studies find up to 50% of the population reaching the age of 65 who become institutionalized before death.

Besides differing results on the overall ratio of lifetime institutionalization, uncertainty also exists on the determinants of the risk of institutionalization. Essentially, this lack of knowledge is due to a lack of longitudinal data on the national level over a period of at least 20 or 30 years.

This paper reports on an analysis of longitudinal panel data on a new approach to assess overall involvement of individuals in institutionalization, and on the determinants that govern the process of institutionalization. Among the main results, *women* appear to have *no* higher *risk* of institutionalization than men if other variables are controlled for, but women nevertheless experience *institutionalization more often* and at younger ages. Furthermore, life expectancy and mortality are of major significance for institutionalization.

2 Data and Methods

The analysis is based on the German Socio-Economic Panel Survey [Hanefeld (1987), Wagner/Burkhauser/Behringer (1993)] which started in 1984, and has been carried out annually since then. The survey is representative on the national level for the population living in private households. With reference to former West-Germany, the data set includes about 12,000 persons. Referring solely to Germans aged 65 and over in 1984 or have reached that age until 1991, and taking missing values for various variables into account, a final number of 1,230 cases is analyzed (see Table 1). Among the persons formerly living in private households, a relatively low number of 55 institutionalizations is observed.[1]

Because of the large number of persons not institutionalized within the relatively short period of 7 years from 1984-91 (end-of-study censoring) and because of the considerable number of deaths before institutionalization (follow-up censoring), the data were analyzed by means of event history analysis [for details compare Blossfeld/Hamerle/Mayer (1989)]. In this context, the rate of institutionalization r(t) at age t is defined by

$$r(t) = \lim_{\Delta t \to 0} (P(t, t+\Delta t) / \Delta t) \qquad (1)$$

where t refers to age minus 65 years.[2] The impact of various variables x_i (including age) on the institutionalization rate was determined by the log-linear regression model

$$r(t) = \exp(\beta_0 + \beta_1 x_1 + \beta_2 x_2 + \ldots + \beta_n x_n). \qquad (2)$$

Relying on the equation $c_i = (\exp(\beta_i) - 1) * 100$, the impact of single variables on the rate of institutionalization can be given as %-effect.

A major problem was that a considerable number of 907 persons (Table 1) had already been older than 65 years of age in 1984 (left censoring). It is well-known by their age how long they have already lived without institutionalization, as the original sample in 1984 was restricted to private households. Despite this fact, this group is selected in favor of a relatively low rate of institutionalization, and is therefore not representative for the population reaching the age of 65. Especially, the older the persons when they were drawn into the sample in 1984, the more they are selected by a low rate of institutionalization, and, for this reason, the selection is supposed to cause an under-estimation of any age effect. In order to cope with the problem, the number of years above the age of 65, the person already had reached when being drawn into the sample in 1984, was taken as a measure of selection and was controlled for by inclusion into the regression model (2).

Table 1: Data Description and Case Numbers

Age in 1984	Cases of Institutionalizations
58-65 years	274
65 years	49
above 65 years	907
together	1230

Source: Socio-Economic Panel Survey 1984-91, own computation.

Based on the estimation of institutionalization rates described so far, the probability of institutionalization during an individuals' lifetime is derived by

$$F(t) = 1 - \exp(-\int_0^t r(u)\,du). \qquad (3)$$

and the age distribution of institutionalizations is

$$f(t) = dF(t)/dt. \qquad (4)$$

However, equations (3) and (4) are based on the assumption that nobody dies before institutionalization. A more realistic approach in the presence of mortality is to reduce all age-specific institutionalization probabilities f(t) by the probability to survive from age 65 until the respective age.[3] Given this survival probability called $S_m(t)$, the true age distribution of institutionalization is derived by

$$f_{true}(t) = f(t) * S_m(t), \qquad (5)$$

and the true probability an individual is likely to get institutionalized until age t equals

$$F_{true}(t) = \int_0^t f_{true}(u) \, d(u). \qquad (6)$$

For the results given below, the survival values $S_m(t)$ rely on the F.R.G. life table of the years 1986/88.

3 Results

Table 2 reports on the %-impacts of the different variables on the rate of institutionalization. In the various columns of Table 2 different variables were integrated in the regression model. In the first column, model 1 solely refers to the age impact, with the result that every additional year of age seems to increase the risk of institutionalization by 22%. Yet, as outlined above, the older persons are selected in favor of a relatively low rate of institutionalization, because the original sample was restricted to private households. Controlling for selection by the number of years above the age of 65 (see model 2 of Table 2) the person had already reached when drawn into the sample in 1984, the age impact increases to almost 45%. Therefore, the increase of the institutionalization rate caused by every additional year of age is noticeable. However, the question arises whether or not a considerable amount of the "age-effect" is due to other variables such as an increasing surplus of women, a declining health condition, or an increasing number of widowhoods.

It is obvious from model 3 of Table 2 that the age-specific institutionalization rate of women is more than 100% above the rate of men, while the age effect is almost unchanged if sex is controlled for. Therefore, the surplus of women in institutions for the aged cannot be ascribed solely to their higher life expectancy: neither their surplus numbers among the aged nor the age increase of institutionalization rates is enough to explain the sex difference.

In model 4 chronic diseases and recent stays in hospital are added to the variables discussed so far, but none has a statistically significant impact. The effect of age is slightly reduced, meaning that only a minor part of the increasing rate of institutionalization by age is due to declining health. The sex difference, however, increases considerably if health is controlled for. Obviously, the excess life expectancy of women is accompanied by better health in old ages, i.e. because

Table 2: Determinants of Institutionalization Risk (%-Effects)

Variable	Model (1)	(2)	(3)	(4)	(5)	(6)
Age (minus 65)	22.4**	44.9**	45.8**	41.3**	41.2**	49.7**
Age when drawn into Sample (minus 65)[1]		-20.4**	-21.3**	-21.1**	-21.3**	-27.9**
Sex (women = 1)			115.0**	177.5**	19.7	12.2
Chronic disease (=1)[2)5)]				61.0	76.7	-42.7
Recent stay in hospital (=1)[1)5)]				-19.9	-23.0	-22.8
Single[2]					596.9**	805.1**
Divorced[2]					498.8**	481.5**
Widowed[2]					172.5*	162.8+
Age * Chronic disease						7.7+
Housing without WC or central heating (=1)[5]						-37.4
Distance to public transport[3)5)]						102.3**
Distance to shops[3)5)]						-45.3+
Distance to bank[3)5)]						11.7
Distance to doctor[3)5)]						-3.0
Distance to park[3)5)]						-6.8
Distance to next center[4)5)]						-11.5
10-years scooling (Mittlere Reife) (=1)						11.1
High School (Abitur) (=1)						-20.6
Other/no schooling (=1)						-21.2
Living on social assistance benefits (=1)[2]						-25.8
Intercept	-99.97**	-99.96**	-99.97**	-99.98**	-99.98**	-99.98**
Number of persons	1230	1230	1230	1230	1230	1230
Number of events	55	55	55	55	55	55
Number of episodes	8134	8134	8134	8134	8134	8134
Log-likelihood	-306.8	-290.8	-287.0	-277.2	-271.0	-251.2

** $p < 0.01$; * $p < 0.05$; + $p < 0.10$.

[1] number of years above the age of 65, the person already had reached when drawn into the sample in 1984.
[2] time-dependent.
[3] less than 10 minutes on foot = 1, 10-20 min. = 2, more than 20 min. = 3, not within walking distance = 4.
[4] less than 10 km = 1, 10-25 km = 2, 25-40 km = 3, 40-60 km = 4, 60 km and more = 5.
[5] Missing values were treated as separately dummy variables, whose coefficients are omitted from the table.

Source: Socio-Economic Panel Survey 1984-91, own computation.

women less often suffer from chronic diseases, the sex difference increases if health is kept constant.

In addition to age, sex, and health, marital status is attached to the next model of Table 2. With reference to married persons, the institutionalization rate of singles is almost 600% higher, while the rate of divorced is almost 500% above the rate of married, and widowhood increases the institutionalization rate by about 170%. Despite the impact of widowhood on the rate of institutionalization, the age impact keeps unchanged, i.e. the increase of institutionalization rates by age cannot be ascribed to changes in marital status. But, an interesting result of model 5 is that the sex difference almost disappears if (in addition to age) marital status is kept constant statistically. This means that the observed sex difference is to a considerable extent due to the fact that women experience widowhood much more often than men. Therefore, with reference to women becoming older, the excess life expectancy of women is important for institutionalization rates in two ways: besides a higher rate on the basis of higher ages, their life expectancy is responsible for a higher rate of institutionalization in the sense that widowhood usually is experienced by women. Furthermore, as a consequence of World War II, within the elderly population in the 1980's in Germany single women with a high institutionalization rate are relatively frequent.

The final model in Table 2 considers a variety of further variables, concerning housing conditions and social status. Among them, only the distance to public transport affects significantly the institutionalization rate. Furthermore, chronic diseases become important in interaction with age, i.e. the higher the age, the stronger the effect of chronic diseases on the rate of institutionalization.

According to equations (3) and (4), the impact of the various variables on the institutionalization rate allows for deducing the age distribution of institutionalizations in different groups, and, on these grounds, their lifetime ratio of institutionalization as well as their average age of institutionalization are obtained. The procedure is illustrated by Figure 1 (see appendix), together with some preliminary results for men. The curve ascending up to the level of 100% gives the accumulated institutionalizations, and the upper uni-modal curve represents the age distribution of institutionalizations, both in the absence of mortality, corresponding to equations (3) and (4). Due to the monotonic age increase of the institutionalization rate (as obvious from Table 2), the population institutionalized would reach 100% sooner or later. It is limited to a lower level only because deaths occur before the risk of institutionalization has been realized. Yet, the uninterrupted lines in Figure 1 report on the true ratio of institutionalization until the respective age (see equation (6)), and on the true age distribution of institutionalizations (equation (5)). The true lines are below the lines derived solely from the rate of institutionalization analyzed before, because a decreasing part of the population reaches the age under consideration. Obviously, institutionalization is experienced by more than 40% of the male population reaching the age of 65. Analogously, the sex difference is reported on by Figure 2 (see appendix). Due to the higher life expectancy of women, the probability of women to experience institutionalization is even higher than for men.

Concerning other determinants of institutionalization, the ratios of experiencing institutionalization individually are given by Table 3. Additionally, Table 3 reports on the average age of institutionalization in different groups. According to Table 3, chronic diseases count for almost 6 %-points of institutionalization, and for almost 1 year of acceleration that institutionalizations take place on average. Interestingly, the impact of social factors like marital status and distance to public transport is even larger than the impact of chronic diseases.

Table 3: The Impact of Selected Determinants of the Institutionalization Rate on Life Time Probability and Average Age of the Institutionalization of Men

	Life time ratio of institutionalization (%)	Average age of institutionalization (%)
Men together	42.3	79.7
Health Status:		
without chronic diseases	39.5	80.1
with chronic diseases	45.3	79.2
Marital status:		
married	40.0	80.2
single	61.8	75.6
divorced	57.5	76.5
widowed	49.7	78.2
Distance to public transport:		
less than 10 minutes	36.7	80.9
10-20 minutes	43.6	79.4
more than 20 minutes	50.6	78.0
not within walking distance	57.6	76.5

For the variables not taken into consideration mean values were assumed.

Source: Computations on the basis of Table 2, model 6.

4 Discussion

Although the Socio-Economic Panel Survey analyzed in this paper was not designed to evaluate old age institutionalization, and the data tend to be less valid for the elderly than for the rest of the population, the general amount of lifetime institutionalization is within the order of magnitude of U.S. longitudinal studies [Vicente et al. (1979), Shapiro/Tate (1988)]. In fact, according to the findings presented in this report, and in line with U.S. studies, the ratio of institutionalization experienced by the elderly during the rest of their life might on average exceed 50%. In any case, lifetime figures are far above the 4-5% of the elderly institutionalized at any point in time.

In addition, with reference to the impact of marital status, the results of a variety of other studies are confirmed. Furthermore, walking distance to public transport has a considerable impact on the rate of institutionalization, while the distance to single facilities is of minor importance. With reference to health, chronic diseases do also increase the rate of institutionalization, though recent hospitalization seems to be relatively unimportant. Yet, the effect of chronic diseases is reinforced by age, i.e. among the oldest the rate of institutionalization is most often increased by chronic diseases. In general, in the case of less intensive care, the results provide evidence for the speculation that the impact of social variables might exceed the impact of health conditions.

Interestingly enough, the sex difference of institutionalization rates observed widely is almost entirely due to women reaching higher ages, and to the fact that women experience widowhood more often than men. In other words, the sex difference almost vanishes if age and marital status are kept constant. Therefore, the higher institutionalization rate of women is linked to their higher life expectancy, whereby the higher life expectancy operates via older ages of the female population as well as via frequent widowhoods of women.

Finally, the impact of age on the risk of institutionalization is of special interest. As opposed to sex, the impact of age could not be ascribed to other variables. Even if declining health and an increasing number of widowhoods are controlled for, the institutionalization rate increases by at least 40% with every additional year of age. Therefore, in consideration of the significant age effect, a monotonic age increase of the institutionalization rate can be taken for sure, even if part of it is still due to variables not analyzed here. Perhaps the most important conclusion is that only mortality prevents single individuals from institutionalization. In other words, the probability of an individual to experience institutionalization is dominated by mortality. In this context, one could argue that an increasing life expectancy of future generations will contribute to an increase in institutionalizations. However, life expectancy at the age of 65 has by far not increased as much as life expectancy at birth. Moreover, it is still undecided whether or not disability life expectancy also increases. Finally, the data analyzed in this paper do not allow to distinguish between the impact of age and of cohort on the rate of institutionalization. Further research is necessary.

Appendix

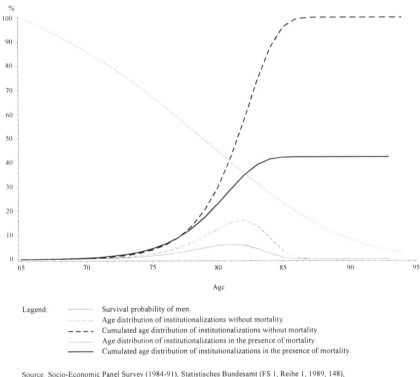

Legend:
- .... Survival probability of men.
- – – – Age distribution of institutionalizations without mortality.
- – – – – Cumulated age distribution of institutionalizations without mortality.
- ——— Age distribution of institutionalizations in the presence of mortality.
- ——— Cumulated age distribution of institutionalizations in the presence of mortality.

Source: Socio-Economic Panel Survey (1984-91), Statistisches Bundesamt (FS 1, Reihe 1, 1989, 148), own computation on basis of Table 2 (Model 6)

Figure 1: Institutionalization by Age

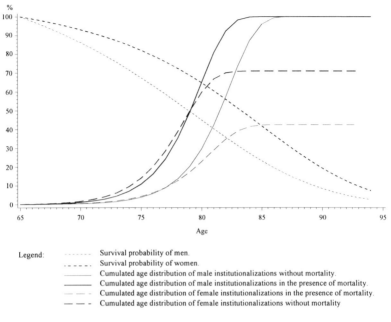

Figure 2: Institutionalization by Age and Sex

Notes

[1] The data tend to be less valid for the elderly than for the rest of the population. In this context, institutionalization primarily refers to sheltered housing (Altenwohnheime) and to homes for the aged (Altenheime), while nursing homes (Altenpflegeheime) are under-represented. Nevertheless, the Socio-Economic Panel Survey is one of the first to give panel information on institutionalizations representative on the national level.

[2] In the F.R.G. there is no lower age limit for admission in homes for the aged. Yet, from an empirical point of view, the process of institutionalization seems to start around the age of retirement. Nonetheless, our results proved to be almost uneffected by the exact zero-point chosen, because very few institutionalizations occur before the age of 70.

[3] This implies that mortality before institutionalization is taken as a competing risk. For the assumptions of competing risk analysis compare Klein (1988).

References

Blossfeld, H./Hamerle, A./Mayer, K.U. (1986): *Ereignisanalyse. Statistische Theorie und Anwendung in den Wirtschafts- und Sozialwissenschaften.* Frankfurt/New York: Campus.

Branch, L.G. (1984): Relative risk rates of nonmedical predictors of institutional care among elderly persons, in *Comprehensive Therapy 10*, 33-40.

Hanefeld, U. (1987): *Das Sozio-ökonomische Panel. Grundlagen und Konzeption.* Frankfurt/New York: Campus.

Kastenbaum, R./Candy, S. (1973): The 4% fallacy: a methodolical and empirical critique of extended care facility population statistics, in *International Journal of Aging and Human Development 4*, 15-22.

Klein, T. (1988). Zur Abhängigkeit zwischen konkurrierenden Mortalitätsrisiken, in *Allgemeines Statistisches Archiv 72*, 248-258.

Palmore, E.B. (1976): Total chance of institutionalization among the aged, in *The Gerontologist 16*, 504-507.

Shapiro E./Tate R. (1985): Predictors of long-term care facility use among the elderly, in *Canadian Journal on Aging 4*, 11-19.

Shapiro E./Tate R. (1988): Who is really at risk of institutionalization?, in *The Gerontologist 28*, 237-245.

Vicente L./Wiley J./Carrington, A. (1979): The risk of institutionalization before death, in *The Gerontologist 19*, 361-367.

Wagner G./Burkhauser, R.V./Behringer, F. (1993): The English language public use file of the German Socio-Economic Panel, in *The Journal of Human Ressources 28*, 429-433.

6 THE IMPACT OF THE COMMUNITY LONG-TERM CARE INSURANCE LAW ON SERVICES FOR THE ELDERLY IN ISRAEL

Denise Naon

1 Background

In this paper, I will discuss Israel's long-term care system, and what we can learn from the recent implementation of long-term care insurance. I will report on research findings regarding its effect on coverage, the provision of informal care, expenditures for long-term care and institutionalization rates.

First, however, I would like to say a few words about our elderly population, whose constitution naturally affects long-term care planning.

Due to its high birth rate, Israel's population is quite young relative to most western populations. Even following the recent mass immigration from the former Soviet Union, which has changed the elderly population by 15% in three years, the elderly comprise only 10% of Israel's total population. Moreover, their percentage in the overall population is expected to remain low in the coming years. However, this low percentage masks the significant growth in the absolute number of elderly in the total population. For example, the number of people aged 75 and over has doubled in the last 20 years.

A significant percentage of the elderly are economically disadvantaged. Due to immigration, about one-third of them have neither savings nor work-related pensions. As a consequence, they depend on a basic income maintenance program, and their ability to buy services is very limited.

The percentage of elderly people with disabilities in activities of daily living (ADL) is about 14%. Most of the disabled elderly live at home; only 20% of them live in institutions. In other words, 2.5% of Israel's elderly live in nursing homes.

2   The Long-Term Care System

The responsibility for financing services of the elderly is shared by government and public agencies. These agencies operate within a complex system based on disability levels and types of services.

Acute care and rehabilitation are the responsibility of non-profit sick funds (see Table 1). Although Israel still does not have compulsory health insurance, the sick funds provide nearly total coverage: 97% of the population have health insurance. Ninety-five percent of the elderly are members of the largest sick fund, which provides care through a network of local clinics.

Community long-term care – personal care, homemaking, and the like – is provided to the more severely disabled elderly by Israel's social security administration (the National Insurance Institute (NII)), based on entitlement; while the same services are provided to the less severely disabled elderly by the Ministry of Labor and Social Affairs, on the basis of income tests and within budgetary constraints. The institutional long-term care provided in sheltered housing and old age homes is financed by the Ministry of Labor and Social Affairs, while that provided in nursing homes is financed by the Ministry of Health. The sick funds are responsible for complex and acute nursing cases.

The Community Long-Term Care Insurance Law

The provision of long-term care services through health and social agencies based on income tests is common in many countries. In Israel, a decision was made to expand the services provided to the most severely disabled elderly through a social security program. The Community Long-Term Care Insurance

(CLTCI) Law, implemented in 1988, formally defined the government's legal obligation to provide a basic level of long-term care services to the severely disabled elderly, on the basis of personal entitlement and clearly-defined eligibility criteria. Consequently, the program operates according to insurance principles, and is paid for by contributions from the working population (0.2% of wages), and not by a budget that relies on general taxes. I would note that the entire elderly population – even new immigrants who have not paid contributions to social security – is insured under the law.

The aim of the CLTCI law is to enable dependent persons to stay at home as long as possible and, by providing services, to reduce the burden on family caregivers. The emphasis of the law is on providing home and community care, not institutional care. Nevertheless, families still bear primary responsibility for the care of their relatives, as benefits cover only some of the elderly person's basic needs.

The following are some of the basic principles of the CLTCI law:

1. Eligibility for benefits under the law is extended to men over age 65 and women over age 60 who are severely functionally disabled in ADL, or who require constant supervision as a result of cognitive disabilities. Younger disabled people are eligible for cash benefits in the framework of a different program, which was implemented 12 years ago.
Less disabled people (those disabled in only one ADL) and elderly people who live in nursing homes are not eligible for benefits under the law. However, people who live in sheltered housing or old age homes that are *not* publicly subsidized *may* apply for benefits. At present, there is a legal debate over whether to allow people who finance their own care in nursing homes to apply for benefits.

2. In contrast with other social security benefits, those provided under the DLTCI law are income-tested, though the test is very liberal: Only people with an income three times greater than the average wage cannot receive the full benefit. In fact, only 3% of applicants are refused because their income is too high.

3. Eligibility is for in-kind services, not cash benefits. Cash benefits are almost nonexistent, and are provided when services are not available. Services may be requested from among a prescribed basket of services, which includes personal care at home, day care, housekeeping, supervision, laundry, meal preparation, undergarments for the incontinent, and an alarm system. Medical, paramedical and social support services are not covered under this law;

they are still the responsibility of the Ministry of Health, the sick funds and the Ministry of Labor and Social Affairs.

4. There are two levels of eligibility, according to the degree of dependency. The amount of services provided is equivalent to 25% or 37% of an average wage – that is, $300 or $450 – according to the level of eligibility. To give an example of how much care the benefits afford, "personal care" usually amounts to between two and three hours per day of care in the home, or to six hours at a day care center. The benefits are linked to average wages in order to maintain their purchasing power of time.

5. The services themselves are provided by certified for-profit and non-profit agencies. The social security administration pays these agencies for the services they provide; it will not pay private individuals providing care.

6. The social security administration has overall responsibility for operating and monitoring this system of benefits, and for determining eligibility. A nurse visits the elderly person in his home, and makes an assessment using a uniform tool for measuring ADL. However, the development of the care plan is delegated to local committees, comprising a social worker from the Ministry of Labor and Social Affairs and a nurse from the elderly person's sick fund. Together with an elderly person's family, these committees decide on care plans, contract with service providers, and monitor changes.

Three features characterize this insurance program. The first is its combination of a broad, universal approach to the determination of eligibility with a differential approach to the provision of services.

The second feature is its combination of a centralized system of eligibility assessment with a decentralized system for the development of care plans. Centralized assessment by a few trained public health nurses assures maximum equity under the law and maximum control over targeting and costs. Decentralized care plan development through local social workers and primary care nurses assures that family needs and choices are respected.

The third feature is the division of responsibility for the financing of long-term care provided in the *community* and that provided in *institutions*. As noted, the sources of financing for these two types of care are basically and essentially different: community care is mostly an insurance program, while institutional care is budgeted from general taxes.

The following is a discussion of research findings on the impact of the CLTCI law on coverage, informal care, institutionalization and expenditures.

3   The Impact of the CLTCI Law

The Impact on Coverage

The law has had a dramatic impact on the coverage of disabled elderly people. The number of elderly people receiving home care increased from 7.000 to 20.000 during the first year of the law's implementation, and to 49.000 at present, five years hence: that is, from 2% to nearly 10% of the elderly population. Of those receiving care, nearly 80% are receiving the basic benefits, and 20% are receiving basic and supplemental benefits. The increase in the number of those receiving care reflected, in the main, the very dramatic increase in the number of moderately disabled elderly people who began receiving services. In the past, this group had "fallen through the cracks", due to economic constraints and the division of provision between the health and social services. In contrast, the percentage of severely disabled elderly receiving care under the law increased only slightly, as a high percentage of them were already receiving services. However, there was an increase in the number of hours of care they received.

Table 1:   The Extent of Personal Care Services in Israel Before and After Implementation of the Community Long-Term Care Insurance Law, by Source of Financing, 1984-1994

	Before		After	
	1984	1988	1991	1994
Total	4,900	7,500	33,000	52,000
Social Security Administration			33,000	49,000
Other Sources (Ministry of Labor, sick funds)	4,900	7,500	2,600	3,000
% of general elderly population	1.4	2.0	8.1	10.0

The Impact on the Elderly and Their Families

Clearly, the aim of the law was to make care more appropriate and reduce the burden on family caregivers. As expected, research findings showed that the addition of services has a positive effect on an elderly person's sense of well-being, and reduces his unmet needs. However, it is interesting to note that the provision of additional formal services did not cause a decrease in the amount of informal assistance provided by families. Formal community services supplement – rather than replace – informal care. Moreover, the provision of formal services does not weaken the network of informal support. Families continue to provide an average of 20 hours of care per week. It seems that the provision of some services formally gives family caregivers a sense of being supported, which enables them to maintain high levels of involvement in the care of their elderly relatives.

Following implementation of the law, there was a significant decrease in the number of elderly people buying private services. Services that were once bought privately are now being provided through public funding. The proportion of private financing of personal care services is very low, compared to other countries – only 17% in 1990. Thus, the law may well have had a major effect on the financial status of the disabled elderly.

The Impact on Institutionalization

One of the goals of the CLTCI law was to prevent institutionalization as much as possible. A follow-up study of rates and patterns of institutionalization before and after implementation of the law has generated interesting findings:

1. During the first year of implementation, the number of applications for institutional care increased significantly – by more than 50%. We believe the reason for this is that the law "reached out" to severely disabled elderly in the community: Many of the thousands of elderly people who applied for benefits had had no previous contact with social services. Those who were "suddenly" found to need services in excess of what the law could provide were encouraged to apply for institutional services. In addition, those who began applying for institutional care were far more disabled than those who had applied for such care previously. It seems, therefore, that the law does provide an alternative for the less severely disabled, though this was at first masked by the bulk of applications from the more severely disabled elderly.

2. Four years after the implementation of the law, we found there had been a decrease in the rate of demand for institutionalization – dropping to levels lower than those that had existed before the law. In particular, the decrease in requests for beds for frail elderly was quite significant. In fact, at present it is even difficult to fill all of the institutional beds earmarked for frail elderly.

The Impact on Expenditures

In 1993, the total expenditure for implementation of the law was close to $150 million. In general, the law changed the distribution of resources between community and institutional long-term care. Prior to the law's implementation, 83% of public funds for long-term care were allocated to institutional care. In 1993, four years after the law's implementation, public funds for institutional care represented only about 45% of all public funds for long-term care. Expenditure for community services provided under the law is actually about three times greater than the income from contributions to the relevant section of social security.

4 Issues Arising from Implementation of the CLTCI Law

I would like to conclude with some general issues arising from the follow-up of the implementation of the law.

1. The first issue concerns the integration of the role of personal care aid and homemaker. The law emphasizes personal care, provided at relatively low cost by para-professionals – not nurses, as is the practice in many countries. These so-called "personal care aides" also perform basic house maintenance chores, thus integrating the roles of personal caregiver and homemaker. Obviously, having a single provider for a range of home care services has its advantages. On the other hand, some feel that it becomes more difficult to attract and employ qualified people as personal care aides when they are also required to assume what are considered "lower status" homemaking responsibilities.

2. The second issue concerns the dilemma of cash versus in-kind benefits. As noted, the law provides for in-kind rather than cash benefits – unlike other social security programs. Cash benefits would both compensate family caregivers for services, and enable elderly people to make independent choices in the acquisition of services, according to personal preference. Yet the decision to provide services was based on the assumption that they would be more effective in reducing the burden of care, and that, in the long run, they would stimulate the availability of services – as has in fact occurred. Experience providing cash benefits to younger disabled people has shown that these are usually not utilized to obtain services, but rather to supplement income. Thus cash benefits cannot be expected to significantly reduce the burden of care or

to spur development or services. Moreover, the decision to provide in-kind benefits was also influenced by the assumption that providing such benefits would reduce the amount of demand to only those really in need. Indeed, despite the increase in the number of recipients, there is a significant percentage of severely disabled elderly who have not applied for benefits. When asked why they didn't apply, they responded that they receive enough support from their families and therefore do not want services. We can reasonably assume that if there were cash benefits, these people would apply for them, and that expenditure for this program would consequently increase.

3. The third issue concerns the development of for-profit agencies and the effect of this on quality of care. Despite the law's aim of providing services and not monies, the government did not want to become the direct provider of services, nor to be the employer of thousands of caregivers. Therefore, the law mandated that publicly-funded services be provided by licensed non-profit or for-profit agencies. This led to a dramatic increase in private, for-profit service providers. At present, 50% of recipients get their care form private agencies. According to the law, these agencies may reserve 20% of the monies they receive for their own administrative costs and for profits. This considerable overhead diminishes the number of hours of care provided or the wages paid to personal care aids, and can therefore affect the quality of the providers. Research on the differences in quality of care provided by for-profit and non-profit agencies is now being conducted.

However, in addition to cost considerations, the choice between these two types of benefit depends on how a society believes it can best achieve its social goals, and not whether it values the independence of its citizens. Societies that have well-developed networks of services can realistically adopt programs based primarily on cash benefits, because these can then easily be used to obtain services in the community. Whichever type of benefit is chosen, it must be evaluated according to its outcomes, such as the improvement in the situation of the elderly and their family caregivers, the degree to which disabled elderly people may remain in their homes for as long as possible, and the range of services provided.

4. Another issue concerns cutting off other supplementary programs. As I noted earlier, Israel now has a dual system: universal coverage for the severely disabled, and budgeted, means-tested coverage for the less disabled. However, there was great concern that with the expansion of services for the most disabled, budgets for the less disabled would be cut, causing them to receive fewer services than in the past. Budgets for other programs have indeed been

cut. To counteract this, it seems that some of the professionals making assessments have deemed eligible people who on strict grounds might not have fully met eligibility criteria for disability. Despite efforts to prevent this through the use of standard procedures, the element of subjectivity in assessment remains. In fact, we have found that the situation of the less disabled has not gotten worse – despite cutbacks in budgets for supplementary programs – because many of them are indeed receiving benefits under the law.

5. This brings me to my last point: The number of elderly people receiving benefits five years down the road greatly exceeds the predictions made before implementation of the law. Even taking into account the large number of immigrants from the former Soviet Union, the number of recipients is about twice the number predicted. The majority of this difference may probably be explained by the following:

- First, as I mentioned, assessment of eligibility is more liberal than was planned, ensuring that the less disabled receive care, despite budget cuts.
- Second, the problem of reassessment: the law mandates reassessing eligibility, but does not fix the time between one assessment and the next. In fact, it is now well known that the functional ability of a significant percentage – around 20% to 30% – of the elderly improves over time. Without reassessment, these elderly continue to receive benefits, and as a consequence the system only adds beneficiaries and does not remove those whose functional ability has improved to just above the eligibility level.
- Lastly, a system based on principles of entitlement has a major impact on demand, because it removes the stigma associated with applying for benefits. When it comes to social security, people feel they have "earned" coverage through past contributions. We should keep in mind that the demand for public long-term care systems is affected by the role played by the acute and rehabilitation care system, and by the private sector. In the future, two changes will affect Israel's long-term care system. The first of these is the imminent implementation of a compulsory health insurance law, which will include the provision of institutional care through the sick funds. The second of these is the increase in private insurance programs for community and institutional nursing services, which are becoming more and more popular.

7 THE EFFECT OF PUBLIC PROVISION OF HOME CARE ON LIVING AND CARE ARRANGEMENTS: EVIDENCE FROM THE CHANNELING EXPERIMENT

Peter Kemper and Liliana E. Pezzin

1 Introduction

Public financing of long term care in the United States is limited largely to nursing home care for low income persons through the Medicaid program. The states and federal government have extended some financing to cover paid care provided in the home, but this has remained limited. Because the cost of covering nursing homes has escalated rapidly in recent years and because the elderly voice strong preferences for care at home rather than in institutions, there has been considerable interest in expanding public coverage of home care.

This interest in home care led to a series of social experiments starting in the 1970's to test the effects of public provision of formal home care. The main policy questions of interest concerned two behavioral responses to expanded public financing: First, do persons in need of long term care substitute care at home for nursing home care? If effects on living arrangements are large, then total long term care costs might be reduced to the extent that care provided at home is less costly than care received in nursing homes. Second, does publicly-financed home care replace unpaid care provided informally by family and friends? If paid formal care simply displaces informal family care, then public long term care costs will rise without a corresponding increase in the total care received by the persons with disabilities. In general, these experiments found little evidence of either behavioral response [See Kane/Kane (1987), Kemper et al. (1987), and Weissert et al. (1988) for reviews of these experiments]. The purpose of this paper is to investigate the extent to which public provision of home care affects living arrangement transitions and the provision of formal and informal care using data from the largest of these experiments, known as the "Channeling" experiment.

2 The Channeling Experiment and Data

The Channeling experiment was a national test of expanded public financing of home care conducted from 1982 to 1985. It sought to substitute case-managed care at home for care in nursing homes, thereby reducing long term care costs and improving the quality of life of elderly clients and their families. The target population was disabled elderly persons (age 65 or older) who are at high risk of nursing home placement [see Kemper et al. (1988) for a description of the Channeling demonstration, its evaluation, and findings].

2.1 The Interventions

Two Channeling interventions were tested, each in five communities, or "sites". Both interventions provided case management. Case managers, typically social workers but in some cases nurses, assessed needs and resources available to the client; developed a plan of care which specified the types and amounts of care to be provided; and arranged for services to implement the care plan. Thereafter, case managers monitored the client's needs and care provision, and periodically conducted a formal reassessment of needs and care plan revision. Together these core case management functions were designed to overcome problems of lack of information and ability to manage home and community-based services. Such case management was more comprehensive and provided over a longer period than that of existing providers such as home health agencies or hospital discharge planners. In addition, Channeling was implemented through case management agencies that were separate units of existing nonprofit or government agencies.

The two interventions differed with respect to the extent of funding for home care services. The "basic" intervention had very limited financing for additional home care services intended to fill in the gaps in existing coverage of home care. The "financial" intervention, on the other hand, substantially expanded coverage of home care, regardless of eligibility under existing government programs. Case managers were allowed to authorize payment for the full range of home- and community-based services, including personal care (e.g., help with bathing, toileting, or eating) and supportive services (e.g., help with house cleaning, meal preparation, or shopping) – as well as traditional home health care (nursing, therapy, and home health aide care) and community services (e.g., transportation, home-delivered meals, and adult day care).

Expenditures under the financial intervention were subject to limits on individual and average expenditures and, for high income participants, cost sharing. Individual expenditures were limited to 85% of nursing home costs, and average expenditures for the caseload as a whole were limited to 60% of nursing home costs. Neither limit turned out to be constraining. Participants with income over twice the eligibility level for Supplemental Security Income were required to share in the cost of services. Because the participants were generally poor and because certain services were exempted, only 5% of participants were subject to cost sharing. Thus, the financial intervention was direct provision of home care subject to a case manager's authorization and cost limits rather than an unconstrained insurance program that entitles participants to subsidized home care.

As intended, there was a major difference in the amount of direct services purchased with Channeling funds under the two interventions. In terms of service expenditures directly authorized by Channeling case managers, the basic intervention spent $38 per client-month (varying from $17 to $60 across the five sites), while the financial intervention averaged $471 (varying from $398 to $612 across sites) reflecting the greater expansion of service coverage. Although the amount of funds spent on direct services differed by intervention, they were dominated in both cases by home health personal care and other low-skill in-home care services. Under the financial intervention, such services accounted for 74% of the total spent on direct services; traditional home health care – including skilled nursing and therapy – was the next largest category, accounting for 15% of the direct expenditures; with the remaining 11% spent on home-delivered meals, transportation, adult day care, medical supplies, and other direct services. The corresponding figures for the basic intervention were 78%, 0.2% and 22% [Corson et al. (1988)].

A screening interview with the elderly applicant, family members, or care providers was the basis for determining eligibility. In addition to age, applicants had to meet two main eligibility criteria: disability and unmet need. For disability, one of three specific criteria had to be met: (i) moderate disability in two or more activities of daily living (ADLs–bathing, dressing, toileting, transfer, and eating–plus continence); (ii) three severe impairments in instrumental activities of daily living (IADLs–housekeeping, shopping, meal preparation, taking medicine, transportation, telephoning, and managing finances); or (iii) two severe impairments in IADLs and one severe disability in ADLs. For unmet need, the applicant had to have at least two unmet needs for help with ADLs or IADLs expected to continue for at least six months, or the informal caregiver system had to be sufficiently "fragile," in the sense that the informal network was judged unable to provide needed care.

Applebaum (1988) estimated that about 5% of the elderly population would meet the Channeling eligibility criteria. Channeling served between 4.5 and 31.9% of the estimated eligible population in the experimental sites. Thus the experiment was not (and was not intended to be) a systemwide intervention.

As expected, eligible applicants were old and frail – the average age was 79 years old, and most had multiple functional limitations. Indeed, 19% were so seriously disabled that they needed help with all five of the activities of daily living (ADLs) of bathing, dressing, toileting, transferring, and eating. The sample was also rather poor – average monthly income was just under $530.

2.2 The Evaluation

The experiment was evaluated using a randomized experimental design. After the eligibility screening interview, eligible applicants within sites were randomly assigned to a treatment or control group. An in-person follow-up interview was administered 6, 12, and, for half the sample, 18 months after eligibility screening and randomization. The follow-up interviews obtained extensive information on service use and costs, indicators of quality of life, the person's living arrangement and the hours of care received regularly in the home from formal and informal caregivers who did not live with the disabled elderly person. Reported nursing home use was verified through claims used in reimbursing nursing homes under Medicare and Medicaid (the programs that pay for some nursing home care) as well as extracts of provider records, while death was verified through death records. Separate follow-up interviews were administered to primary informal caregivers but only to a subsample of about 40% of the disabled elderly persons. This interview obtained information on, among other things, the hours spent on care by informal caregivers living in the same household.

The evaluation of the experiment by Kemper et al. (1988) found that Channeling benefitted clients and their informal caregivers in several ways: it reduced unmet needs, increased confidence in receipt of care and satisfaction with arrangements for it, as well as increased overall life satisfaction. However, the costs of the additional home care – provided in most cases to clients who would not have entered nursing homes even without expanded home care – were not offset by reductions in nursing home cost. Hence, total costs increased. The evaluation also found that declines in informal care were generally small and not statistically significant [Christianson (1988)].

Several aspects of the potential effect of public provision of formal care on living and care arrangements, however, were not addressed in the evaluation of the Channeling experiment. In particular, the evaluation did not make separate estimates of the effect on hours of care provided by persons residing in the same household and did not formally recognize the potential effect through living arrangement changes. Indeed, although Wooldridge/Schore (1988) analyzed Channeling's impact on the choice between nursing homes and community living arrangements, the earlier evaluation did not analyze Channeling's effects on living arrangements *within* the community. In addition, when estimating program impacts, the evaluation used regression-adjusted difference in means for the entire sample without recognizing the important differences in endowments of potential informal caregivers between married and unmarried persons.

2.3 Purpose of the Paper

This paper, which builds on our previous work [Pezzin et al. (1994)[1]], addresses these issues and contributes to our understanding of the effects of subsidized home care on living and care arrangements of the elderly by analyzing two potential behavioral responses to a publicly financed home care program. First, we consider Channeling impacts on living arrangement transitions. Persons who need long term care can choose to live alone, relying primarily on help from visiting caregivers; live with others, relying on care from other household members; or live in a nursing or personal care home where they are cared for by the staff of the home. Individuals (and their families) presumably choose the living arrangement that provides the most efficient mix of care, given their preferences and constraints. Over time, the person's ability to remain in the initially chosen (typically more independent) living arrangement may change due to diminished physical or mental functioning possibly combined with insufficient family or financial resources. While Channeling's provision of formal home care at no direct cost to the individual is likely to enhance the elderly person's ability to live independently, this impact may vary depending on the person's prior living arrangement. By extending the analysis to encompass impacts on transitions from initial living arrangements to both institutional and within-community living arrangements, we assess whether public provision of home care affects specific segments of the eligible population differentially depending on their living arrangement prior to the intervention.

Second, we examine the extent to which formal care displaces informal care overall, and extend the analysis to consider effects on visiting and resident care hours separately. In terms of a standard household production theory, long term care can be produced through the use of two, mainly low skilled labor inputs: formal (paid) care and informal (unpaid) care, provided in kind by family members and friends. Publicly provided formal care "displaces" informal care if it leads to an absolute reduction in caregiving efforts. Here we analyze the extent of displacement by estimating Channeling's effect on hours of formal and informal care. A significant reduction in hours of care due to the intervention is evidence of displacement, and the extent of displacement can be assessed by comparing the magnitude of the increase in formal care with the magnitude of any decrease in informal care.

For both living arrangement transitions and hours of care analyses, we examine Channeling's impacts separately for married and unmarried individuals. In choosing living and care arrangements, married and unmarried individuals have substantially different endowments of potential informal care. The presence of a spouse, normally the primary caregiver for married persons, increases the availability of informal care and changes the incentives to move into an institution. Overall, we expect unmarried elderly persons to be more responsive to a home care intervention than married persons. We examine outcomes at 12 months after randomization, which is the longest period of follow-up available for the full sample.

Throughout, our interest is primarily in the effects of the interventions on these outcomes rather than the underlying determinants of living arrangement transitions and provision of formal and informal care. Therefore, we capitalize on the experiment's randomized design, making it unnecessary to specify a structural model to obtain unbiased estimates of program impacts. Instead, we estimate experimental impact models which exploit the orthogonality of the

EVIDENCE FROM THE CHANNELING EXPERIMENT 131

Channeling treatment to pre-program variables to obtain estimates of program effects.

Before proceeding, it is important to note an inherent limitation on inferences based on such a social experiment. Because persons in the sample had applied to a home care program and been determined eligible, they are representative of the eligible applicant population in the 10 experimental sites. Consequently, the results may not be generalizable to other target populations or communities. Despite the inherent limits on generalizability, analysis of these data on eligible applicants randomly assigned to a treatment or control group produces a powerful test of the effects of a targeted home care program.

3 Methods

3.1 Living Arrangement Transitions

Living arrangement transitions in response to Channeling's intervention can be described parametrically by a simple first-order stationary Markov chain, where the behavior of the chain depends only upon the origin state (pre-experimental living arrangement) and not on the amount of time spent in that state. Let LA_0, LA_1 and LA_2 represent the mutually exclusive living arrangement categories defined for unmarried persons as: (i) living alone; (ii) living with others, where the elderly person lives with either relatives or non-relatives, or in congregate housing; and (iii) institutional living, which includes living in a nursing or personal care home. The analogues for these three living arrangement categories for married persons are living: (i) with spouse only, (ii) with spouse and others, and (iii) in a nursing home or personal care home. The set of $\{LA_{ikt}\}$, $S_i = \{LA_0, LA_1, LA_2\}$, referred to as the state space, accounts for the full spectrum of living arrangement options.[2] Because of Channeling's eligibility rules, which required that persons in nursing homes be certified for discharge, only the two community living arrangements – living alone, LA_0 and living with others, LA_1 – are defined as origin states from which individuals make a transition into either one of the destination states in S_i.

Let $P_{ijk}(t-1,t)$ represent the probability that an elderly person i in living arrangement j ($j = LA_0, LA_1$) at time $t-1$ is observed in living arrangement k ($k = LA_0, LA_1, LA_2$) at time t such that

$$P_{ijk}(t-1,t) = \text{Prob}(LA_i(t) = k | LA_i(t-1) = j) \qquad (1)$$

Finally, let us also introduce X, the [1×h] vector of exogenous variables capturing the relevant characteristics that may affect an individuals's propensity to change living arrangements. These independent variables include the program treatment status, TREAT, the primary variable of interest, as well as a set of pre-program variables, all measured at screen, prior to randomization.[3] Assuming a log-linear functional form between transition probabilities and the exogenous variables, the model can be written as:

$$\ln P_{ijk}(t-1,t) = \beta_{k1} TREAT_i + \sum_h \beta'_{kh} X_{ih,t-1} + \varepsilon_{ikt} \quad (2)$$

where i indexes individuals, t refers to the twelve-month follow-up time period, t-1 refers to pre-program time period, and ε_{ikt} captures unobserved randomly distributed errors affecting P_{ijk}.

Assuming an extreme value distribution for the error term, $F(\varepsilon_i) = e^{-e^{\varepsilon_i}}$, the three-destination-state specification yields a multinomial logit model of the form,

$$P[LA_i(t) = k | LA_i(t-1) = j] = \frac{e^{\beta_{k1} TREAT_i + \sum_h \beta'_{kh} X_{ihk}}}{\sum_{k \in S_i}^{K} e^{\beta_{k1} TREAT_i + \sum_h \beta'_{kh} X_{ihk}}} \quad (3)$$

where β_k, k = 0,1,2, are the vectors of coefficients to be estimated, via maximum likelihood. The model is identified by assuming, without loss of generality, that $\beta_2 = 0$. As indicated, the models are estimated separately for each of the two origin states in the community for the married and unmarried subgroups (defined according to the elderly person's marital status at the time of the twelve month follow-up).

3.2 Hours of Formal and Informal Care

Channeling's impacts on hours of formal and informal (visiting and resident) care are estimated using a Tobit model. To make maximum use of available data on hours, separate relationships are estimated for hours provided by resident informal caregivers (obtained only for the caregiver subsample) and hours provided by visiting caregivers (available for the full sample). By doing so, only the analysis of resident informal care hours for persons living with others was restricted to the smaller subsample.

The general formulation for the censored regression model of hours of care can be written as

$$H_{ilt} = 0, \quad \text{if } \gamma_1 TREAT_i + \sum_m \gamma_1' Z_{im,t-1} + \mu_{ilt} \leq 0$$

$$H_{ilt} = H_{ilt}, \quad \text{if } \gamma_1 TREAT_i + \sum_m \gamma_1' Z_{im,t-1} + \mu_{ilt} > 0 \quad (4)$$

where, the dependent variables H_{ilt} are the hours of each type of care l – visiting formal, visiting informal and resident informal – received in an average week. In addition to previously defined notation, Z is a [1×m] vector of pre-program variables that includes X, as well as the individual's living arrangement at screen $LA_{i,t-1}$, and μ_{ilt} are independently and normally distributed residuals capturing unobserved components that affect the amount of care received.[4]

4 Results

4.1 Living Arrangement Transitions

The distribution of initial living arrangements (just prior to the experimental intervention) can be inferred from the sample sizes shown in Table 1. Among unmarried persons, about three-fifths lived alone initially; among married persons, the vast majority were living with only their spouse. Consistent with the experiment's focus on the community population, only 3.5% of the control group were in nursing or personal care homes initially (result not shown).[5]

The transitions from these initial living arrangements that would take place in the absence of any intervention are indicated by the transitions of the control group. While the majority of people remained in the same living arrangement twelve months later, many did change. About a fifth of unmarried persons and a tenth of married persons were in a nursing or personal care home 12 months later. Although these are high one year risks of placement in a nursing or personal care home, especially for unmarried persons, they are relatively low given Channeling's objective of targeting the population at very high risk of entering nursing homes.

Within the community, individuals changed living arrangements at relatively high rates. Of those living alone at screen, about 21% of the control group for the basic intervention and 14% of control group for the financial intervention reported living with others one year later. Not surprisingly, a much smaller proportion of those initially living with others – less than 5% – reported living alone one year later. Among those living with only their spouse initially, 9 and 17 percent reported living with others a year later. (So few married persons lived with someone in addition to their spouse that estimates of control group transitions for that group are not meaningful.)

Table 2 presents the multinomial logit estimates of the coefficients for the experimental treatment variables for unmarried and married persons.[6] These coefficients represent Channeling's impact on the log-odds of moving from each origin state – alone, with others – into either one of the community destination states – alone, with others – rather than moving into a personal care or nursing home. (Recall that, for identification purposes, personal care/nursing home is used as the reference living arrangement category in the estimation of the transition probability models.)

For unmarried persons living alone initially, we find a significant positive coefficient on the financial intervention treatment variable, implying that the intervention makes continuing to live alone more probable relative to the omitted category, a nursing or personal care home. For unmarried persons receiving the basic intervention and married persons in general, none of the coefficients on the treatment variables is statistically significant at the 5% level.

Because the coefficients in Table 2 are expressed in terms of log-odds ratios, these results are somewhat difficult to interpret. Table 3 displays estimates of the differences in predicted transition probabilities (including transitions into nursing and personal care homes, the reference category) in the presence and absence of the interventions. These probabilities are calculated by substituting the values of the independent variables for each observation into the appropriate multinomial logit equation, based on equation (3). The individual predictions are then averaged for the two relevant subpopulations (the basic intervention treatment and control groups and the financial intervention treatment and control groups).

The difference between the predicted probability under the intervention (that is, assuming TREAT = 1) and that in the absence of the intervention (that is, assuming TREAT = 0) is the estimated impact of Channeling on the probability of transition to alternative living arrangements.[7]

The less generous basic intervention had little effect on living arrangement transitions of unmarried persons. It increased the probability that unmarried persons living with others initially live alone 12 months later by 2.8 percentage points,[8] with a corresponding (nonsignificant) decrease in transitions to nursing or personal care homes. No other transitions were significantly affected by the basic intervention.

The financial intervention had substantially larger effects, significantly shifting the living arrangements of unmarried persons toward greater independence. For persons initially living alone, Channeling increased the probability of continuing to live alone a year later by .087 – an increase of 14 percent from the control group mean proportion living alone of .612. The probability of moving into a nursing or personal care home was correspondingly reduced by .077, a decrease of 30 percent from the control group mean. For unmarried persons living with others prior to the experiment, the financial intervention increased the probability of a transition to living alone a year later by .058, with a corresponding (nonsignificant) reduction in the probability of continuing to live with others.

In contrast with these significant results for the unmarried, the lower panel of Table 3 indicates that the differences in transition probabilities between treatments and controls for married persons were small and statistically nonsignificant.

4.2 Displacement of Informal Care

Table 4 displays the Tobit estimates of Channeling's impacts on formal and informal hours of care for both the unmarried and married samples. (Results for the entire set of control variables are available from the authors upon request.) The dependent variables include time spent providing home nursing, therapy, personal care (help with bathing, dressing, toileting, transferring, and eating) and help with household activities such as housework, laundry, and shopping that was required because of disability. Hours of formal care include only hours of care provided in the home by visiting caregivers. Care provided by the staff of nursing and personal care homes or by paid live-in caregivers are omitted from the measure of formal care – both formal and informal hours are assumed to be zero for persons in nursing or personal care homes.

We observe significant positive treatment coefficients in all but one case in the formal care hours equations. None of the coefficients in the visiting informal hours equations was statistically significant. For resident informal care, the treatment coefficients were not significant for the unmarried sample but were significant and opposite in sign for the married sample.

To obtain point estimates of impacts on hours of care, we calculated predicted hours of formal and informal care received in the presence and absence of the intervention. Predicted hours of care, shown in Table 5, are computed for all observations, based on the coefficients and standard error estimates from the Tobit model, according to the conditional mean function

$$E(H_{ilt}) = \Phi_t \hat{\gamma}_1' Z_{it-1} + \hat{\sigma} \phi_t, \qquad (4)$$

where Φ_t and ϕ_t are the standard normal cumulative distribution and probability density functions, respectively, evaluated at $(\hat{\gamma}_1' Z_{it-1})/\hat{\sigma}$. The individual expected values are averaged over the corresponding sample based on basic and financial sites. The resulting treatment-control difference is the estimate of Channeling's overall experimental impact on hours of care.[9]

The most consistent finding is an increase in hours of formal visiting care. The basic intervention's 2.7 hour increase in formal care from 7.8 to 10.5 hours for unmarried persons is statistically significant but the slightly smaller increase for married persons is not significantly different from zero at the .05 level. Consistent with its generous expansion of coverage of home care, the financial intervention increased hours of formal care overall by a rather substantial 5.9 hours for unmarried persons and 5.2 hours for married persons.

Channeling had no effect on hours of informal care provided by visiting caregivers. The treatment-control differences in hours of informal visiting care are consistently very small and nonsignificant.

The results concerning resident informal care are inconsistent. For unmarried persons, the basic intervention did not affect resident care; the treatment-control difference of minus 3 hours under the financial intervention, although reasonably large, is not significantly different from zero at the 0.05 level. For married persons under the basic intervention, resident informal hours are significantly lower by 9.1 hours. We find the magnitude of this estimate implausibly large – it suggests that a (nonsignificant) 1.9 hour increase in formal care is associated with an 8.6 hour decrease in total hours of informal care, for an unexpected reduction in total hours of care of 6.5 hours. The results for the financial intervention are also contrary to expectations: under the financial intervention resident informal hours are 9.9 hours greater for treatments than controls (although this predicted difference is not statistically significant at the 0.05 level). We are cautious in interpreting these results because of the small married sample available for the analysis of resident informal hours ($N = 279$) and because caregiver reports of hours of care provided to persons living in the same household are inevitably subject to reporting error.

These disparate results concerning displacement do not mean that formal and informal care are not substitute inputs in the production of long term care. Substitution can occur in the absence of displacement of informal care. For example, for unmarried persons the basic intervention had virtually no effect on informal caregiving. Despite this absence of displacement, the ratio of formal to informal hours of care increased from .33 in the absence of the intervention to .46 under the basic intervention (computed from Table 5). Thus, the absence of displacement is perfectly consistent with the substitutability of formal and informal care in the production of long term care. Indeed, based on the point estimates, we observe an increase in the relative use of formal care in response to Channeling's expansion of publicly provided home care for both groups and interventions.

5 Conclusions

This paper has analyzed two potential behavioral responses to public provision of home care: shifts to more independent living arrangements and displacement of unpaid family care. We found that the Channeling experiment's more generous financial intervention had sizable, statistically significant effects on living arrangement transitions for unmarried persons. For those who lived alone prior to the experiment, the financial intervention increased the probability of remaining alone a year after enrollment by 8.7 percentage points relative to the control group. This was associated with a corresponding reduction in the probability of moving into a nursing or personal care home during the next year of 7.7 percentage points. For those initially living with others, Channeling induced a 5.8 percentage point increase in the probability of living alone a year later. In contrast, except for a 2.8 percentage point increase in the probability of living alone for those initially living with others, provision of only limited additional home care under the basic intervention did not significantly affect living arrangements of unmarried persons, and neither intervention affected living arrangement transitions of married persons.

With respect to Channeling's effects on hours of care, we found that, as intended, the Channeling interventions, particularly the financial intervention, increased the amount of formal care received. Hours of resident informal care were not significantly affected for unmarried persons, although the point estimates suggest that the financial intervention reduced resident informal care by 3 hours a week. The resident informal care results for married persons were inconsistent, with a large decrease under the basic intervention and a large increase under the financial intervention. Because of their inconsistency, possible measurement error, and the small size of the married sample, definitive conclusions cannot be drawn about the effects on resident informal care and hence displacement for married persons. Finally, we found no evidence that either intervention resulted in displacement of visiting informal care for either married or unmarried persons.

Our findings indicate that publicly provided home care can affect living arrangements. Specifically, the results support the view that a generous formal home care program can allow unmarried elderly persons with disabilities to live more independently.[10]

While these favorable living arrangement findings are important, they are not large enough to alter the original evaluation's basic conclusion about cost: that reductions in the cost of institutional care are too small to offset the increased cost of publicly-financed home care. Analysis of the financial intervention's impact on expenditures (not shown) indicate that the earlier conclusion holds for all subgroups, including those living alone initially for whom the potential for cost savings was the greatest. On average, nursing home expenditures over the year after enrollment were reduced by $400 while formal home care expenditures increased by over $2,000. Furthermore, the limited effect of the basic intervention suggests that it may be difficult for home care programs with limited funding to affect living arrangements in the same way that Channeling's generous financial intervention did.

Some might argue that because providing formal home care increases the likelihood that unmarried persons, particularly those living alone, will live independently, benefits should be targeted at these groups. Given the expenditure estimates just presented, however, such targeting would have to be justified based on increased quality of life resulting from greater independence rather than cost savings. Moreover, limiting eligibility to those who are unmarried or living alone may be ultimately inefficient if it induces changes in living arrangement or marital status that are prompted solely by the potential for receiving public home care benefits. The decision to target public home care at these subgroups depends, in part, on the value placed on the benefits resulting from greater independence and the cost of such unintended effects, and, in part, on value judgments concerning the equity of limiting public benefits based on attributes such as living arrangement and marital status.

Appendix

Table 1: Living Arrangement Transitions for the Control Groups

Initial Living Arrangement	Sample Size	Living Arrangement at 12 Months			
		Unmarried Persons			
		Alone	With Others	Nursing Home	Total
Basic Intervention					
Alone	302	.609	.209	.182	1.00
With Others	221	.054	.742	.204	1.00
All	523	.375	.434	.191	1.00
Financial Intervention					
Alone	304	.612	.135	.253	1.00
With others	185	.027	.800	.173	1.00
All	489	.391	.387	.223	1.00
		Married Persons			
		Spouse Only	Spouse, Others	Nursing Home	Total
Basic Intervention					
Spouse only	154	.727	.169	.104	1.00
Spouse and others	24	.167	.708	.125	1.00
All	178	.652	.242	.107	1.00
Financial Intervention					
Spouse only	153	.778	.098	.124	1.00
Spouse and others	15	.400	.600	.000	1.00
All	168	.744	.143	.113	1.00

Note: Persons in nursing homes initially are classified based on prior living arrangement; the small group in personal care homes are classified as living with others initially and with nursing homes at 12 months.

Table 2: Maximum Likelihood Estimates of Living Arrangement Transitions

Initial Living Arrangement	Living Arrangement at 12 Months			
	Unmarried Persons			
	Alone		With Others	
Alone				
Basic Intervention	.051	(.230)	.121	(.270)
Financial Intervention	.599*	(.203)	.386	(.275)
Log Likelihood		−1196.2		
N		1545		
With Others				
Basic Intervention	.764	(.464)	.230	(.243)
Financial Intervention	1.509*	(.623)	−.131	(.267)
Log Likelihood		−623.3		
N		1086		
	Married Persons			
	Spouse Only		Spouse and Others	
Spouse				
Basic Intervention	−.265	(.362)	−.191	(.425)
Financial Intervention	.038	(.347)	−.035	(.452)
With Others				
Basic Intervention	−.181	(.933)	−.255	(.882)
Financial Intervention	.070	(1.021)	.412	(.970)
Log Likelihood		−644.7		
N		988		

Note: Response functions contrast the log of each living arrangement response probability with the log of the probability for the nursing home category. The lower panel, Table 2b, pools all origin states in order to gain degrees of freedom in estimating the transition probabilities of the married sample. Standard errors are in parentheses.

* Statistically significant at the .05 level (two tail test).

Table 3: Channeling Impacts on Living Arrangement Transition Probabilities

Initial Living Arrangement	Living Arrangement at 12 Months		
	Unmarried Persons		
	Alone	With Others	Nursing Home
Basic Intervention			
Alone	-.003 (.068)	.012 (.047)	-.008 (.032)
With others	.028* (.002)	.007 (.033)	-.036 (.032)
All	.013 (.097)	.006 (.161)	-.018 (.066)
Financial Intervention			
Alone	.087* (.032)	-.010 (.027)	-.077* (.020)
With others	.058* (.016)	-.064 (.040)	-.006 (.039)
All	.072 (.051)	-.028 (.051)	-.044* (.021)
	Married Persons		
	Spouse Only	Spouse and Others	Nursing Home
Basic Intervention			
Spouse only	-.027 (.018)	.005 (.011)	.022 (.012)
Spouse and others	.007 (.005)	-.024 (.028)	.018 (.011)
All	-.025 (.024)	.001 (.052)	.023 (.028)
Financial Intervention			
Spouse only	.008 (.034)	-.006 (.015)	-.003 (.022)
Spouse and others	-.052 (.200)	.076 (.200)	-.024 (.090)
All	.003 (.049)	.002 (.032)	-.005 (.024)

Note: Persons in nursing homes initially are classified based on prior living arrangement; the small group in personal care homes are classified as living with others initially and with nursing homes at 12 months. Standard errors are in parentheses. Predicted probabilities for the "All" rows are based on estimates from models that pool all origin states.

* Statistically significant at the .05 level (two tail test).

Table 4: Maximum Likelihood Estimates of Hours of Care Provision

	Resident Informal Hours		Visiting Informal Hours		Visiting Formal Hours	
	Unmarried Persons					
Basic Intervention	-.95	(5.05)	-.59	(2.43)	5.84*	(1.60)
Financial Intervention	-8.12	(4.98)	.02	(2.40)	11.29*	(1.56)
σ	33.99*	(1.64)	35.10*	(0.81)	24.62*	(0.47)
Log Likelihood	-1442		-6135		-7858	
N	701		2597		2614	
	Married Persons					
Basic Intervention	-12.04*	(6.28)	1.51	(3.15)	3.81	(2.53)
Financial Intervention	12.74*	(6.16)	-.44	(3.07)	8.50*	(2.39)
σ	30.55*	(1.60)	26.08*	(1.05)	23.21*	(0.68)
Log Likelihood	-1064		-1993		-3150	
N	279		978		984	

Note: Resident hours of care are only available for a subsample of elderly persons for whom a caregiver interview is available (see text). Standard errors are in parentheses.

* Statistically significant at the .05 level (two tail test).

Table 5: Treatment-Control Difference in Hours of Formal and Informal Care

	Treatment	Control	Difference
		Unmarried Persons	
Basic Intervention			
Informal Care			
Visiting	8.2	8.3	-0.1 (0.3)
Resident	14.8	15.2	-0.4 (1.6)
Total[a]	23.0	23.5	-0.5
Formal Care	10.5	7.8	2.7* (1.3)
Financial Intervention			
Informal Care			
Visiting	9.3	9.2	0.1 (0.8)
Resident	11.8	14.8	-3.0 (1.7)
Total[a]	21.1	24.0	-2.9
Formal Care	14.2	8.3	5.9* (2.0)
		Married Persons	
Basic Intervention			
Informal Care			
Visiting	6.0	5.5	0.5 (0.4)
Resident	25.3	34.4	-9.1* (4.2)
Total[a]	31.3	39.9	-8.6
Formal Care	10.7	8.8	1.9 (1.4)
Financial Intervention			
Informal Care			
Visiting	6.2	6.3	-0.1 (0.9)
Resident	36.8	26.9	9.9 (5.5)
Total[a]	43.0	33.2	9.8
Formal Care	16.4	11.2	5.2* (1.6)

[a] Total is the sum of the estimates for visiting and resident hours. Because they were estimated for separate samples, standard errors for the difference in predictions could not be computed.

* Statistically significant at the .05 level (two tail test).

Acknowledgment

The authors wish to thank Mark Pauly, Frank Sloan and Jim Reschovsky for helpful comments on an earlier version of this paper, Dawn French for secretarial support, and Margie Odle and Ellen Singer of Social and Scientific Systems, Bethesda, Maryland for programming support. The views expressed in the paper are those of the authors. No official endorsement by either the Department of Health and Human Services or the Agency for Health Care Policy and Research is intended or should be inferred.

Notes

[1] The key feature of our earlier study is to explicitly account for the joint nature of families' living and care arrangement decisions when estimating the potential substitution effects of a formal home care subsidy program. Based on a joint model of choice of living arrangement and hours of informal care, that analysis examined the extent to which public provision of formal care reduces provision of informal care directly, through its effects on hours of care received given living arrangement, and indirectly, through its effects on living arrangement choices. Although recent literature focusing on living arrangement decisions of the elderly has recognized that alternative living arrangements reflect, in part, long term care needs of elderly persons [Bishop (1987) and (1988), Kemper (1990) Börsch-Supan et al. (1992), Stern (1994), Sloan et al., in this volume; Hoerger et al. (1995)], none of these studies focuses on the issue of substitution of paid for unpaid care *per se* or provides the basis for estimating the effect of subsidized home care on living arrangement choices.

[2] Note that we did not include attrition as an absorbing state. Earlier investigations indicated that attrition due to death and non-response had no impact on the assessment of the treatment effects. See Brown (1988) and Pezzin et al. (1994) for technical details and results from such analyses.

[3] These pre-program regressors, which are orthogonal to the treatment variables and are included to control for pre-existing differences across individuals on characteristics that affect the outcomes, include a set of site dummy variables, economic and health status, prior service use, and demographic variables.

[4] In principle, the model would be described by a system of L equations, corresponding to *visiting formal, visiting informal* and *resident informal* care, which ideally would be jointly estimated. The estimation is not done this way for two reasons. First, unlike visiting hours of care which are available for the entire population, resident hours of care are available only for the subsample for whom a caregiver interview was administered. Joint estimation would require estimating all parameters only for this smaller subsample. Second, estimation of systems of equations involving censored variables is far from trivial, and a logically-consistent estimator is yet to be devised. Consequently, single equations were estimated separately for the three types of hours, producing consistent but possibly inefficient impact estimates.

[5] The initial living arrangement of those in nursing homes was defined based on their prior living arrangement; the few persons in personal care homes were classified as living with others initially.

[6] The results on the lower panel are based on a model that pools all origin states in order to gain degrees of freedom in estimating the transition probabilities of the married sample. The reported estimates are based on coefficients of interaction terms between the treatment variables and the origin state (with spouse only, spouse and others). Not shown in Table 2 are the coefficients of the vector of pre-experimental economic, demographic and health status variables, prior service use, and site dummies included in the living arrangement transition models and found to be generally consistent with expectations. The results for the entire set of control variables are available from the authors upon request.

[7] The reported standard errors for the differences in predicted probabilities of living arrangement transitions are based on a linear Taylor series approximation. In particular, let $z(X'\beta) = \text{prob}(LA_{it} = j | TREAT_i = 1) - \text{prob}(LA_{it} = j | TREAT_i = 0)$ be the difference in predicted probabilities for treatments and controls. The variance of $z(X'\beta)$ for each living arrangement choice is then obtained by evaluating $\text{Var}[z(X'\beta)] \approx g\text{Var}[\hat{\beta}]g$ at the estimated parameter vector $\hat{\beta}$, where $g = \partial z / \partial \beta$.

[8] Note that, because the standard errors involve derivatives of nonlinear functions, some predicted differences turn out not to be significant at $p < 0.05$ level even though the parameter estimate itself is significant at that level, and vice versa.

[9] A similar method as the one described in footnote 3 is used to estimate the reported standard errors for the differences in predicted hours of care. In particular, defining $z(Z'\gamma) = E(H_{ilt} | TREAT_i = 1) - E(H_{ilt} | TREAT_i = 0)$ as the difference in predicted hours of care for treatments and controls, we obtain the variance of $z(Z'\gamma)$ for formal and informal hours by evaluating $\text{Var}[z(Z'\gamma)] \approx g'\text{Var}[\hat{\gamma}]g$ at the estimated parameter vector $\hat{\gamma}$, where $g = \partial z / \partial \gamma$.

[10] Other studies report a similar finding using nonexperimental data. Based on estimates from a multinomial probit model of living arrangement decisions applied to a nationally representative sample of American elderly, Hoerger et al. (1995) find that making Medicaid-subsidized home health services more available significantly increases the probability that elderly persons will live independently from their children. Using that same data, Ettner (1994) reports evidence that Medicaid home care benefits significantly lower the probability of nursing home entry. It is also important to point out that the results presented in this study are not inconsistent with the earlier evaluation of the experiment by Wooldridge/Schore (1988). Their analysis of the probability of nursing home use found that the percent in a nursing home after twelve months was lower among the treatment than control groups, but differences were small and statistically nonsignificant. However, they did not analyze living arrangements within the community (that is, living alone versus living with others) nor did they investigate the potential differential impacts of the Channeling intervention on individuals according to their marital status or initial living arrangement. Finally, the original evaluation analyzed impacts on nursing home use, whereas the present study combines both nursing and personal care homes.

References

Applebaum, R. A. (1988): Recruitment and Characteristics of Channeling Clients, in *Health Services Research 23*, 51-66.

Bishop, C. (1987): *Living Arrangement Choice of the Elderly and Demand for Disability-Related Services*, Brandeis University Working Paper. Waltham/MA.

Bishop, C. (1988): *Transitions in the Living Arrangements of the Elderly.* Paper presented at the 1988 Allied Social Sciences Association annual meetings.

Börsch-Supan, A./Hajivassiliou, V./Kotlikoff, L./Morris, J. (1992): Health, Children, and Elderly Living Arrangements: A Multi-Period, Multinomial Probit Model with Unobserved Heterogeneity and Autocorrelated Errors, in D. Wise (ed.): *Topics in the Economics of Aging.* Chicago: University of Chicago Press, 79-108.

Brown, R. (1988): The Evaluation of the National Long Term Care Demonstration: Estimation Methodology, in *Health Services Research 23*, 23-50.

Christianson, J.B. (1988): The Effect of Channeling on Informal Caregiving, in *Health Services Research 23*, 99-118.

Corson, W./Granneman, T./Holden, N. (1988): Formal Community Services Under Channeling, in *Health Services Research 23*, 83-98.

Ettner, S. (1994): The Effect of Medicaid Home Care Benefit on Long Term Care Choices of the Elderly, in *Economic Inquiry XXXII*, 103-127.

Hoerger, T./Picone, G./Sloan, F.A. (1995): Public Subsidies, Private Provision of Care and Living Arrangements of the Elderly, in *Review of Economic Statistics 6*.

Kane, R.A./Kane, R. L. (1987): *Long Term Care: Principles, Programs and Policies*, New York: Springer.

Kemper, P./Applebaum, R.A./Harrigan, M. (1987): Community Care Demonstrations: What Have We Learned?, in *Health Care Financing Review 8*, 87-100.

Kemper, P./Brown, R./Carcagno, G. et al. (1988): The Evaluation of the National Long-Term Care Demonstration, in *Health Services Research 23*, Special Issue.

Kemper, P. (1990): Living Arrangement and the Demand for Home Care: An Illustrative Theoretical Model, in *AHCPR Program Note*, Rockville/MD.

Pezzin, L.E./Kemper, P./Reschovsky, J. (1994): *Does Publicly Provided Home Care Substitute for Family Care?* Experimental Evidence with Endogenous Living Arrangements. Paper presented at the 1994 American Economic Association meetings, Boston/MA.

Sloan, F.A./Hoerger, T./Picone, G. (1996): Effects of Strategic Behavior and Public Subsidies on Families' Savings and Long-Term Care Decisions, in *this volume*.

Stern, S. (1995): *Estimating Family Long Term Care Decisions in the Presence of Endogenous Child Characteristics.* Working Paper University of Virginia.

Weissert, W./Cready, C.M./Pawelak, J. (1988): The Past and Future of Home and Community Based Long Term Care, in *The Milbank Quarterly 66*, 309-388.

Wooldridge, J./Shore, J. (1988): The Effect of Channeling on the Use of Nursing Homes, Hospitals and Other Medical Services, in *Health Services Research 23*, 119-128.

PART THREE:
GERMANY - A MODEL FOR DEALING WITH THE PROBLEMS OF LONG-TERM CARE?

8 SOCIAL PROTECTION FOR DEPENDENCE IN OLD AGE: THE CASE OF GERMANY

Bernd Schulte

1   The Challenge

Demographic development in Germany [See for details Enquete-Kommission (1994)], as in most of the other European Union Member States, is characterized by an ageing of the population due to a prolonged life expectancy and a decline in birth rates. The proportion of persons over 65 rose to about 15 per cent at the beginning of the 1960s and will rise further. While there had still been less than 30 pensioners to 100 contributors in 1991, model calculations have produced a ratio of more than 90 to 100 for the year 2030.

The role of women and family structures are increasingly changing, too. These changes are characterized by a decrease in the number of marriages, rising divorce rates, an increase in extra-marital partnership and cohabitation, a shrinking of the average household size, a rise in the number of one-parent families, and especially in one-person households as well as by a higher rate of women in the work-force and in economic activities, in general. Thus the large family is being increasingly replaced by single-person households and small family units with the result that services which used to be rendered by the family more often require external solutions, such as child-care facilities and nursing services for the aged and the disabled.

Elderly persons experience change in many areas – physical and psychic ageing, loss of spouses and partners, retirement from work, reduction of income, etc. – and ageing entails *specific needs and problems.*[1]

It must be borne in mind in this respect that individuals – and, of course, the elderly, too – differ greatly in respect of their problems and needs. Accordingly the elderly constitute an extremely *heterogeneous group*. On the one hand, there are elderly persons who can still work and perform services for others and who can still live independently, and on the other hand, there are elderly persons who are only partially independent and require the help of others in some areas, while still others have completely – or almost completely – lost their independence and their capacity for self-care due to chronic disease or physical or mental conditions which result in both functional impairment and physical dependence on others.

The *classical life-phase breakdown* into the three phases (a) *education phase* (15-20 years), (b) *working phase* (40 years, but often only 20 years for women because of a break for child-rearing), and (c) *retirement phase* (15-20 years) may be modified with regard to the latter phase into four sub-phases each covering a particular sub-group of old persons:

(i) "young old persons" (55-65 years, still working or no longer working because of early retirement (this sub-phase can go beyond the 65th year and ends only with the loss of the ability to perform services – of whatever kind – for others while maintaining independence.);
(ii) "old persons" (i.e. persons who have lost the capability to perform services for others, but who are still independent and can still care for themselves);
(iii) "old old persons" (i.e. persons whose independence is increasingly limited and who are dependent on the help of others, to a limited extent in the first instance); and
(iv) "old persons in need of care" (i.e. those persons who, because they have lost their independence, require institutional care) [See Buttler et al. (1988)].

Persons who lack the capacity for self-care may need a wide range of medical, economic, social, personal and supportive services. The *"reduced capacity for self-care"* which is characteristic for requiring care can be the result of illness, a complement to invalidity, or simply an accompaniment to old age. The need for care is identified by an inability to fulfill particular social functions. This inability does not constitute a typical social risk as is the case with illness, old age and invalidity, but due to increasing longevity and to medical progress, there are more and more people who are likely to need some level of personal care or support.

A research report, commissioned by the German Federal Minister for Youth, Family and Health and published in 1984, on "Social Security for Long-Term Care in European Neighbouring Countries"[2] identified the *"reduced capacity for self-care"* as the characteristic for requiring care. It is clear from this definition that the social situation of persons in need of care does not constitute a typical or "classical" social risk (as is the case with "sickness", "pregnancy", "motherhood", "invalidity", "industrial accident and occupational disease", "unemployment" and "old age", but it is a social situation which can be considered as an "attendant risk", i.e. a "risk" arising in the context of another risk, e.g. sickness, invalidity or old age. For this reason "need for care" is mostly not clearly dealt with by social legislation or often only indirectly dealt with. The vagueness of the term "long-term need for care" comes in the main from the fact that it delineates a specific social situation that says something about this need of a person, i.e. his or her need for care. The person concerned lacks "the capacity for self-care" and "independence", as is demonstrated by the fact that he or she can no longer carry out all functions necessary for daily life. To counterbalance these deficits aids, e.g. technical devices and household equipment, as well as help from another person in the household can be necessary.

The need for caring or nursing sharply increases with age. In the age group above 80 every third person now needs daily care. Besides, the high prevalence of morbidity among older people translates into an overproportionate need for health services.

2   The Case for Reform

2.1   *General Aspects of Long Term Care*

In Germany, as it is the case in most countries, there is a sharp *institutional and legal division between sickness and dependence upon care*. Since the former is covered by health insurance while the latter continues to be largely a personal, "private" risk for which there are mostly no adequate public provisions, a prolongation of stay in a general hospital is often the only way to prevent older patients from having to foot the bill for delivery into nursing homes. In the case of persons in need of institutional care, the persons concerned can often only afford to pay the bill if they resort to the means-tested public assistance schemes which are often perceived as a source of stigma.

As in most other EU Member States the supply of personnel for *community care services* in Germany cannot be considered adequate. Denmark, the Netherlands, and the United Kingdom being obviously the countries with the most extensive build-up of such services. In addition, all countries report noteworthy *regional disparities* in the provision of services. Thus, even in the – with regard to their spending on overall social protection – "leading" Member States of the EU the build-up of social services does not seem to keep pace with the needs of an ageing society so that frail elderly persons and their family members are often put under a very heavy strain – again with the notable exception of Denmark. Special *nursing homes* for frail people are not only in short supply, but also very expensive. In most countries the available nursing homes are understaffed – again with the notable exception of Denmark which reports over 50 000 people employed in nursing homes equivalent to 63 staff members per 1000 people aged 65 and over.

There is more or less general consensus that all countries need more geriatric research, more community physicians specialized in geriatrics as well as special hospitals for geriatric patients, and social security reforms which provide for a coverage of the risk of long-term care. More specifically, there are five recurring topics, which are discussed in all EU Member States [See EC (1993)]: (i) the lack of integration between health and social services; (ii) the lack of special geriatric hospitals or of special facilities for long-term care; (iii) the inadequacy of coverage of long-term care under social security; (iv) deficits in coordination in community care services; and (v) the need for decentralized services which would integrate public and other forms of help.

In most countries the *financing and operation of health and social services are separated*, with different levels of government and/or different national ministries being in charge of the two kinds of services. Whereas health services are financed from social insurance contributions or from general taxation, social services are usually administered and financed by local governments as well as by various voluntary associations. Thus the functionally necessary integration of services is impeded by a structural differentiation of responsibilities.

Problems of coordination between medical and social services or between hospital and community services are widely reported, too. While community care for persons living in private households often requires the coordination of services provided by various public and voluntary agencies, residential care is provided under one common organizational roof, there continues to be an administrative incentive to admit elderly people to residential care. Since the mid-1970s most Member States have moved to a *policy where institutional care is substituted by community care*. The idea behind this reversal of policy is not only to unburden public budgets but also to develop the potential for self-help and to let older people remain as long as possible in their 'natural' environment

SOCIAL PROTECTION FOR DEPENDENCE IN OLD AGE   153

with its established social network. It must be noted, however, that the care potential within the family system is seriously shrinking, as declining birth rates and the increasing labour force participation of women considerably reduce the number of persons available for help in private households (*see above 1.*). Since community services can only complement but not substitute care rendered in the family system, the twin process of a growing number of elderly people who need support and of a shrinking pool of voluntary, and mostly – to nearly 90 per cent – female – carers, who provided the bulk of support in the past will invariably lead to a growing demand for institutional care in specialized geriatric hospitals and in residential homes for older people. The present shortage of supply of outdoors care facilities does not only overburden the family system but also the general hospitals in the acute sector.[3]

The *financial risk of long-term care* has become a policy issue in several countries. Basically, three alternative models are being discussed which might be labelled the 'market solution', the 'transfer solution' and the 'social insurance solution'.

(i) The *'market solution'* wants to make all citizens beyond a certain age liable to insure themselves and their dependants privately against the new risk (following, for instance, the model of private, but compulsory insurance against car accidents).
(ii) The *'transfer model'* would introduce a tax-financed long-term care allowance following the general model of housing or child benefit schemes.
(iii) The *'social insurance model'* is based on the idea of a contributory benefit scheme and would either be organized by a special scheme or affiliated with an already existing sickness, invalidity or old age insurance scheme.

As the transition from an acute illness to dependence is frequently a gradual process which requires a flexible integration of medical assistance, nursing, rehabilitation measures, and social services. Only an integrated coverage of both risks under the common roof of health insurance or a coordination of health insurance and care insurance guarantees that frail persons in need of care receive continuous services without becoming the victims of lack of coordination and controversies between various financing agencies.

2.2 Social Protection in General

The characteristic features of the German system of social protection are the large range of facilities offered and the large number of agencies involved in providing them. The complexity of the system is due to several factors: (i) federalism, i.e. Germany being a federal state which is composed of sixteen states *("Länder")*; (ii) the constitutional principle of self-government of the communities; (iii) the principle of self-administration which is characteristic of the social security system; (iv) the principle of subsidiarity which is instrumental for the distribution of competences on the federal government (*Bund*), the Länder, the communities, the social security institutions, and voluntary organisations; (v) and – last but not least – the mandate for establishing a welfare state (*Sozialstaat*) which is set out in the constitution (*Grundgesetz*).

Accordingly, the multitude of social problems in society is met by an equally vast array of social activities which are carried out on a (i) federal, (ii) state (iii) local level and (iv) private or voluntary basis.

The system of social protection rests on three pillars: (i) social insurance (*Sozialversicherung*), with the four traditional branches statutory health insurance, statutory accident insurance, statutory pension insurance, statutory unemployment insurance; (ii) social maintenance and social equalisation systems (*soziale Entschädigungs- und Ausgleichssysteme*), i.e. tax-financed schemes of social protection such as public maintenance for war victims, indemnification for victims of violence, compensation for the adverse effects of vaccination, child benefits, housing benefits; (iii) welfare (*Fürsorge*), i.e. youth welfare services and social assistance.

Social insurance gathers the insured persons up in a collective. The members of this collective pay contributions in order to receive insurance benefits for themselves and their dependents on the occurrence of the insured event, e.g. illness, maternity, invalidity, accident at work, occupational disease, reaching retirement age. The major part of social insurance is financed by contributions paid by employees and employers. Maintenance and social equalisation benefits involve no advance payments, but are financed from state tax revenue.

Welfare benefits are provided in cases of individual need. Social assistance is characterized by the application of a means-test and thus by subsidiarity in relation to other benefit commitments. That means welfare benefits range lower on the scale of legal protection as well as in general public esteem than the insurance and maintenance benefits.

The system of social protection is thus conceived as an unbroken social security net with social assistance forming a safety-net at the bottom below the higher social benefit sectors, in particular social insurance.

For contributory benefit schemes or social insurance, two elements are essential: On the one hand, there is the *risk-spreading* which is typical of insurance, and on the other hand there is a specific *social component* added to this mechanism. It is this second element which distinguishes social insurance from private insurance, social insurance being characterized by the fact that, within this system, there is a spreading of risks and a social equalization, independently of individual need, among the insured (for whom insurance is in most cases compulsory). Social insurance may be financed contributions (which may be supplemented by state subsidies). In contrast to private insurance premiums, the contributions are not, or at least not primarily, set according to the typified (average) risk of the individual insured (according to the principle of individual equivalence), but they are rather – and this is the "social" component of social insurance – calculated according to social criteria by means of a redistribution mechanism, i.e. they are set according to the income – in most cases only the income from gainful economic activities (especially wages) – of the insured.

A further distinction must be made between the function of social insurance as a system of provision for the insured persons according to the principles which have been outlined above, and other functions. Here the point at issue is that social insurance is only used instrumentally in the service of a different social task, in particular that to achieve the social integration of persons who, for one reason or another, do not fit into the classical form of social insurance, or to perform tasks in connection with other social objectives (e.g. the equalization of family burdens).

The decision on whether a risk should be included in social insurance or covered by another branch of the system of social protection can only be made if the functions of social insurance are clearly defined. These depend in particular on the objective aims of the other branches of social benefits and services.

For a long time the task of social insurance was recognized – and this is still largely the case today – as being to protect the insured against situations of individual need, e.g. against the consequences of illness, invalidity, or old-age. This was the original point of departure of German social legislation in the 1880s, too. Today, however, the function of social insurance has undergone a fundamental change. First of all, social insurance has the task of guaranteeing a level of protection with regard to the general vicissitudes of life, the goal in general being to maintain the standard of living reached by the individual insured before the insured event occurred. Secondly, with the advent of the moral and – in many countries (also in Germany) – the legal or even constitutional obligation of the state to provide for its citizens in cases of need (and a corresponding legal entitlement of persons in need to sufficient resources and assistance) it is also a question of protecting the state against any liability to grant social benefits simply because the individual has failed to make any appropriate provision against the risk concerned. This protection function against the lack of individual provision by individuals is intimately connected with the principle of equality, because those citizens who make adequate provision by themselves are subjected to a double burden if they have to pay both insurance contributions to support themselves and taxes to support others. The distinguishing features of social insurance are therefore that it is first in most cases *compulsory* in order to keep the number of persons who have to rely on a social minimum (e.g. social assistance), financed from general taxation as small as possible. And second, in order to take into consideration the ability-to-pay of the ensured person with the consequence that the better off pay higher contributions than those who earn less. (If these higher contributions are not matched by higher benefits this way of financing implies redistributive effects.) Compulsion can thus be used to make sure that a risk-sharing and some sort of redistribution for social purposes take place.

Statutory health, invalidity and old-age as well as unemployment insurance provide security against the general risks of life, i.e. sickness, old-age, invalidity, unemployment irrespective of their cause, whereas statutory occupational injury insurance, which is responsible specifically for occupational injuries and industrial diseases, is intended to compensate for negative effects of specific risks which arise from an accident at work or an occupational disease, and are thus linked to a specific cause.

The *personal constituency of social security schemes* refers to the groups of persons who are protected by such schemes. The range of persons covered is one of the principal elements for classifying social protection schemes. The aspects according to which individuals are included in the range of persons covered by a given scheme depend on various fundamental determinants, in particular the maxims governing the state's social policy: The prevailing ideas on the degree to which the state should participate in social protection as well as on the rôle and reasonableness of individual/family protection and/or private provision, the recognition of specific need situations for protection, the objectives and purposes of social protection schemes, the organisation of and/or the methods employed by such schemes, the way social security schemes are financed, and the nature of the different social benefits. All these factors for determining whether individuals should be included in or excluded from social protection schemes are closely connected to one another.

In deciding on the range of persons covered, generally two fundamental approaches are distinguished, namely the universal approach on the one hand, and the categorial approach on the other hand.

(A) Social protection schemes based on the *universal* approach, sometimes called the Beveridge approach, define the group of persons protected primarily by reference to membership of society as a whole. They presuppose

that all individuals are in need of protection and ask about the social problem situations in which protection is to be afforded. This approach is sometimes called Beveridgian modell.
(B) Social protection schemes based on the *categorical* approach take it for granted that there will be certain social problem situations and ask about the need of specific groups of persons for protection. They define the group of persons protected primarily by reference to their status in the working population and are sometimes referred to as the Bismarckian approach.

2.3 The Current Situation of Health Insurance

The *statutory health insurance scheme* forms the cornerstone of the health care system. It encompasses about 90 per cent of the population, only civil servants, highly paid employees and self-employed persons not being subject to compulsory insurance (either being voluntarily insured under the statutory scheme or being member of private health insurance schemes).

Statutory health insurance is normally financed by the contributions of the employees and their employers or – if self employed- by the insured persons. Contributions are levied as percentages of wages and salaries up to a given income limit income threshold, which is adjusted each year accordingly to the developments in average income. There are two kinds of membership in the statutory health insurance scheme: persons may be insured as obligatory members or as voluntary members. Persons become compulsorily insured regardless of their own will or that of their employer, since the compulsory insurance is an automatic legal consequence of employment. This mandated insurance cannot be precluded in any way by the parties concerned, i.e. the employee/insured or his employer. In general, compulsory insured are wage earners, salaried employees, the pensioners of the pensions funds for wage earners and salaried employees, the persons who are paid out a "transition allowance" because of measures relating to vocational promotion in view of a rehabilitation, some self-employed, the students of state and state-recognized universities, the unemployed who receive unemployment benefit, all the self-employed farmers along with their helping family members and retired farmers who are still provided with board and lodging, the employees of miners' establishments, and the handicapped who take a vocational training at vocational training centres.

In contrast to mandatory insurance, the voluntary insurance contract is based on the declaration of consent by the individual. Persons who formerly were compulsorily insured employees and whose membership in a statutory health scheme has ended because their income exceeds the above-mentioned limit, and severely disabled persons (on certain conditions) can obtain voluntary health insurance cover. Spouses and children are insured provided that they do not earn more than DM 530 per month in West Germany or DM 390 in East Germany and that they are not insured on their own (family health insurance).

In the event of sickness and maternity, the sick funds which are organized in accordance with the principle of social self-government and comprise a large variety of individual local funds, provide benefits in kind and in cash. The statutory health insurance is thus carried out by special corporations under public law, i.e. the sick funds. There is accordingly no uniform insurance carrier for the health insurance, but there are various types of sick funds such as Local Sick Funds (*Allgemeine Ortskrankenkassen*), Industrial Funds (*Betriebskrankenkassen*), Crafts Sick Funds (*Innungskrankenkassen*), Substitute Funds (*Ersatzkassen*), the Federal Miners' Sick Fund (*Bundesknappschaft*), the Sailors' Fund (*Seekrankenkasse*) and the Agricultural Sick Fund (*Landwirtschaftliche Krankenkasse*). These various kinds of sick funds form associations of the *Länder* (e.g. the Local Sick Funds Associations of the *Länder*), and the *Länder* associations of the various sick funds form a federal association, e.g. the Federal Association of Local Sick funds (*Bundesverband der Allgemeinen Ortskrankenkassen*).

The statutory health insurance scheme is governed by the so-called "services in kind-principle" of the provision of (*"Sachleistungsprinzip"*), according to which the sick funds are obliged to warrant the necessary medical treatment, hospital treatment, drugs, other therapeutic measures and aids. In order to fulfill their obligations towards the insured, the sick funds have to cooperate with the producers of health services on the background of a highly complex network of legal and contractual regulations.

Standard benefits granted by the sick funds are prevention measures, sick pay, maternity pay, death benefit and family support. Reimbursements for illness cover medical treatment, hospital care, sickness pay, domestic help and nursing.

As a rule, the insured can claim measures for the promotion of health and the prevention of diseases, preventive dental check-ups, medical examinations to detect certain illnesses, health check-ups, medical and dental treatment, drugs, glasses, hearing aids, orthopedic and other remedies, hospital treatment, payment of the costs or subsidies for necessary sanatorium treatments, and sickness benefits. The insured are free to choose among the medical doctors and dentists who are registered with the health insurance scheme.

In recent years, for a wide range of services and benefits such as drugs, bandages and remedies, in-patient care and stays in hospital, costs of dentures and travel expenses there are out-of-pocket-payments.

As no one should be at an excessive financial disadvantage because of these additional payments, certain groups of the population can obtain partial or even complete exemption from these co-payments. Children and young persons under 18 are exempt in the case of dentures and travel expenses. Besides, there is a so-called "social clause" for recipients of aid to subsistence under the Federal Social Assistance Act, assistance under the War Victims' Compensation Scheme (*Kriegsopferfürsorge*), unemployment assistance, payments under the provisions of the Federal Institute of Labour on the individual promotion of vocational training or on the employment and vocational promotion of the disabled, for residents of old age and nursing homes, if the cost of the home is paid by social assistance or the war victims' compensation scheme, as well as for all insured persons if they claim benefits to which fixed amounts apply.

The central idea of these measures was to shift the emphasis of public health protection from minor ailments to major illnesses and to foster a stronger sense of responsibility among the insured. On the other hand, cost-sharing may lead to a decrease in demand for necessary medical treatments by the poorer parts of the population.

The precise benefits and conditions for medical benefits as well as the contribution rates (average: 12.2%) vary greatly for the members of different sick funds. The relationships between the sick funds and the providers of benefits and services are extremely complex, too. Despite its complexities, the German health insurance scheme makes accessible to its members a rather complete range of medical and related services.

Under the Federal Social Assistance Act, non-insured persons who lack the financial means to cover health expenses may claim specific aids. Preventive health measures are granted to persons who, according to medical expertise, are threatened by a specific illness or by a danger to health. This aid includes necessary recuperative treatment as prescribed by physicians, particularly in the case of children, young persons, elderly people, and mothers. It also includes medical examinations for the early detection of illnesses under more or less the same conditions as they can be claimed by members of the statutory health insurance schemes. Sick aid (*Krankenhilfe*) under the Federal Social Assistance Act includes, in conformity with the corresponding regulations of the statutory health insurance law, medical and dental treatment, the provision of drugs, hospital treatment as well as other goods and services which are necessary for recovery from an illness or for the improvement and alleviation of the effects of an illness. The sick person has a free choice among physicians who give treatment at the rates laid down by the local sick funds. In practice, beneficiaries of sick aid get the same medical treatment as the majority of the population which is insured with the local sick funds. Instead of granting sick aid, i.e. paying for the necessary medical treatment in line with statutory health insurance standards and benefit scales, the social assistance authorities can also pay contributions to the local sick funds on behalf of social assistance recipients. In this case, the beneficiaries of sick aid are insured on a voluntary basis with the local sick funds.

2.4 First Steps to Reforms towards Long Term Care Insurance

It is estimated that there are about 1.650.000 *persons*, i.e. nearly 2 per cent of the population, *in need of long-term care* in Germany. Currently, about 1.2 million persons in need of care are looked after at home, whereas about 450.000 are taken care of in institutions. The majority of persons in need of long-term care – more than 1.2 million – are over 60 years, about 650.000 between 60 and 80 years, and nearly 600.000 are over 80 years old. The increasing importance of the need for long-term care is primarily determined by demographic developments. The problem is aggravated further by the trend towards small families and households, especially towards one-person households. It is estimated that up to the year 2010, the number of people of 60 years and older will rise by another 2.8 million. That means that the number of people in need of long-term care may rise by about 1/4 million over the next 20 years, too.

It was in 1988 first steps were undertaken to alleviate the problem of insufficient community services for persons in need of nursing care. The health insurance scheme then covered the expenditure for professional nursing care at home up to a period of four weeks per year and a ceiling of 1800 DM. Since the beginning of 1991 the health insurance scheme also coveed the cost of community nursing services rendered at home up to a limit of 25 visits or a cost of 750 DM per month or a nursing benefit of DM 400 per month.

The statutory accident insurance (*Gesetzliche Unfallversicherung*) provides comprehensive home or institutional care or alternatively a nursing benefit from DM 300/488 to DM 1200/1951 (new Länder/old Länder) – according to the severity of the patient's condition if the need for long-term care of an insured person is caused by an accident at work or by an occupational disease.

Public service laws provide benefits for civil servants, judges and soldiers in the event of long-term care. In the case of home-care either 50 to 80 per cent of the costs for professional nursing care are refunded depending on seniority and marital status, or, alternatively, a nursing benefit of DM 400.- is granted. In the case of institutional care the nursing-related costs and the expenses for accomodation and meals will be refunded to varying degrees.

In so far as the need for long-term care arises on account of events for the occurence of which society takes a particular responsibility (e.g. injuries resulting from wars, military service or civil alternative service, compulsory vaccinations) a supplement of DM 435 to DM 2161 – depending on the severity of the case – is granted. In the case of home-care the appropriate costs for a nurse, in the case of institutional care the nursing-related costs and the costs for accommodation and meals are financed, while the pensions paid on account of the injury are being deducted.

Some states provide for rather small tax-financed (and not means-tested) benefits in the case of long-term care of blind or severely disabled persons (*Pflegegeldgesetze*).

If the need for long-term care leads to financial hardship, income-tested welfare benefits are provided for by social assistance (*Sozialhilfe*). These benefits are means-tested and granted to cover the costs arising in the case of long-term care. In the area of home-care, appropriate costs and expenses for family carers and of visits by professional nursing staff are being refunded. In addition, a nursing benefit has to be granted if the condition of the person in need of long-term care has reached a certain severity. In these cases the nursing benefit may range from DM 255/350 to DM 696/953 (new/old Länder).

Besides, there are tax exemptions for long-term care, and care periods completed by private carers can be credited in the framework of the invalidity and old age pension insurance to a certain extent.

3   The New Statutory Long-Term Care Insurance Law

There is inspite of the above-mentioned legal provisions at present no comprehensive social protection against the risk of need for long-term care. The above-mentioned schemes that provide for comprehensive benefits to persons in need of long-term care such as social compensation legislation and statutory accident insurance legislation only cover a strictly limited and thus rather small group of persons. The statutory health insurance covers almost 90 per cent of the German population, but it only provides for limited benefits in severe cases of long-term care where the person in need is living at home. Therefore there was a case for reform in the German system of social protection as regards the need for long-term care.

From January 1, 1995, the risk of long-term care will be safeguarded within the framework of a statutory social long-term care insurance scheme (*gesetzliche Pflegeversicherung*) which will work as follows:[4]

- Long-term care insurance is a separate branch of the social insurance system. Benefits are provided by the long-term care insurance funds whose functions are performed by the sick funds.
- All persons who live in Germany are legally obliged to enter the statutory long-term care insurance scheme as is the case with regard to statutory health insurance. Persons who are not subject to statutory health insurance may be released from this obligation provided they prove that they are covered by a private long-term care insurance which offers benefits of a nature and extent which are essentially comparable to those of the statutory long-term care insurance scheme.
- The provision of benefits is governed by two main *principles:* (1) *"prevention and rehabilitation come before nursing"*, and (2) *"home-care comes before institutional care"*.
- In order to avoid, overcome or reduce the need for long-term care, increased prevention and rehabilitation measures are required. Only in this way the conditions for a self-determined life style of people in need of care can be maintained or regained.
- Persons entitled to claim benefits are those who require help in performing regular day-to-day activities. The need for long-term care is subdivided into three care categories the degree and frequency of care required in the single case being the primordial criterion for the assignment of a person in need of care to one of these categories.
- For the majority of people in need of long-term care, it is important that they are able to live in a chosen environment, for instance in their family, for as long as possible. Therefore the new law is centered on the improvement of the conditions for home-care.

  Nursing *cash benefits* for home-care are graded in accordance with the severity of the need for long-term care, amounting to (I.) *(Pflegestufe 1)* DM 400, (II.) *(Pflegestufe 2)* 800 or (III.) *(Pflegestufe 3)* 1.200 per month.

  If the nursing benefit is inadequate to ensure an appropriate degree of home-care, basic nursing and domestic care may be provided as *benefits in kind*. The entitlement to such *benefits in kind* encompasses up to 25, 50 or 75 visits by professional nursing staff up to a value of DM I. 750, II. 1800 or III. 2800 and in exceptionally severe cases 3.750 per month.

  In the case of *holidays* or other *absences*, the person providing care is entitled to a relief nurse for a period of up to 4 weeks up to a total value of DM 2250.- per year.

  Entitlement to benefits starts on April 1, 1995.

SOCIAL PROTECTION FOR DEPENDENCE IN OLD AGE 163

If *home-care* cannot be adequately guaranteed, there is a possibility of part-time institutional care by day or night, or of admittance to a short-term nursing institution.
- If *institutional care* is necessary, the long-term care insurance scheme pays up to DM 2800, in exceptional cases 3300 per month towards the nursing-related costs. The costs for accomodation and meals are borne by the insured, as would be the case with home-care.
- Entitlement to benefits starts on July 1, 1996.
- In order to promote the willingness to provide long-term home-care within the family or the neighbourhood and to acknowledge the considerable efforts of the persons providing such care, the social protection of those persons has been improved, too. Periods of non-professional nursing activity are put on the same footing as insured periods of gainful employment for the purposes of *statutory pension insurance*. A person who regularly provides for people in need of care on a voluntary (unpaid) basis for at least 14 hours per week, is now (compulsorily) insured in the statutory pension insurance. Statutory pension insurance contributions during the period of care are borne by the same insurance of the cared person. This provides an incentive for voluntary care work, and as care for frail people is overwhelmingly provided by women, it may also strengthen the position of women in the pension system. The grading of such periods is guaranteed by the severity of the need of long-term care of the patient and the resulting degree of necessary care provided[5].
- During a period providing care, the persons who perform nursing work are covered by the statutory accident insurance (*Gesetzliche Unfallversicherung*) scheme. In the case of unemployment insurance, assistance will be provided to facilitate the return to normal employment.
- *Expenditure* of the new legislation on long-term care is estimated at about DM 26 billion per year. This expenditure will be financed through the contributions of the insured persons and their employers. The contributions are based on the amount of income of the insured liable to contributions.
- In the case of employees, the insured and the employer each bear half of the contribution. Where the insured person is claiming social security benefits, e.g. unemployment benefits or social assistance, the respective provider of these benefits is liable to pay the contributions.
- In the case of pensioners, half of the contribution is paid by the pensioner and half by the pensions' insurance funds [See for details Laufer (1994)].
- The contribution rate is to be 1.7 per cent.

- In order to safeguard the provision of long-term care, the insurance funds will enter into contracts with the carriers of domestic and institutional long-term care facilities and other organizations providing services and benefits. Through so-called supply contracts, these long-term care facilities will be integrated into public benefit systems with legally defined rights and obligations. The carriers of services and institutions will be obliged to provide nursing care for the insured and, in return, will be eligible to remuneration from the long-term care insurance funds.[6]

4 Outlook on further problems

In the years to come, the Statutory Long-Term Care Insurance Act of 1994 will have to be implemented. Special attention must be given in this respect not only to the financing problems which actually predominate the public debate, but on the provision of services, standards for quality of care, the quality control of services and institutions, choice, participation and legal entitlement to benefits etc.

It is typical for the German welfare state, in the case of services and benefits in kind, to separate the two functions of *granting the benefits* and *providing* them. Possible third-party providers of services are (i) other responsible bodies from the field of public administration (e.g. services rendered in state or municipal hospitals and other consultants); (ii) profit-making private individuals, who have already been mentioned (free-lance doctors, psychologists, physiotherapists and members of other therapeutic professions, pharmacists, opticians, etc., and business enterprises as bodies responsible for hospitals, old age or nursing homes, rehabilitation facilities, etc.); and also (iii) non-profit-making, charitable bodies.

The above-mentioned separation between the granting and providing of benefits, with the immanent element of the "separation of powers", not least in the interests of the person entitled to benefits, is particularly important in connection with the procurement of benefits between the beneficiary/client who is in need of and obtains the benefit and the body responsible for providing it. There is a growing tendency for the obligations of the bodies responsible to overcome the distance between the legal standard and its implementation, but nevertheless there is a kind of "natural" tension both between the responsibility for maximum procurement of benefits, on the one hand, and the responsibility for their thrifty and economic use (and in particular for preventing benefits from being claimed by those not entitled to do so) and between the personal interests of the body responsible and its staff, on the other hand.

This tension makes it appear reasonable, too, to provide the beneficiary/client with advisers and representatives who are independent of the body responsible. This question is particularly important in the case of social services, which are frequently dependent upon the cooperation of the beneficiary/client in the provision of the service. Thus decisions on the treatment in care systems are not only made by the body responsible for the service and the provider of the service, but the person entitled to the service, the beneficiary is also involved and is authorized to participate in the decision himself.

In addition, a social service is a "human service", which is not exclusively determined by economic ideas, but also by ethical, political, etc. objectives, the decisive determinant for the supply ultimately consisting not in what the individual can afford and is willing to pay, but what the community can afford and is willing to pay. It follows from this that social services in the sense described above are "public goods", and that the state – at least the welfare state – has to guarantee them for everyone. This presupposes either a corresponding offer on the part of the state itself, or the guarantee that there will be an adequate offer by third parties, and at the same time the possibility for the individual that he will be able to make use of that offer.

The legal difficulties in handling benefits in kind and services[7] consist first of all in the fact that, unlike cash benefits, there are only rarely cases in which benefits in kind and services have been given concrete form in legislation.

As a rule, entitlements to cash benefits – also entitlements to social cash benefits – are laid down precisely according to their levels, so that any third parties – e.g. courts – who know the relevant provisions and actual conditions can check the calculations and verify them. In comparison to that, it is hardly possible to lay down in general terms which benefits and services are required in the form of "nursing care", "rehabilitation", "placement", "legal advice", "home care", "advice in a practical situation", etc. in a specific individual case. This does not just apply to social services, but services in general. In private law too, they have been given far less concrete form than cash benefits, since there is no formulation comparable to that found in the German Civil Code, according to which someone who is liable to provide an item that is only defined according to its type must provide an item of average nature and quality, i.e. possessing merchantable quality according to the accepted view.

In the field of providing medical benefits in kind and services greatest progress has been made in giving specific legal form to the entitlements to benefits and services in kind. The physician responsible for deciding on adequacy, appropriateness and necessity is for his part subject to supervision concerning his decision (by associations of panel physicians, examining and complaints committees, et al.). The decision on the appropriate kind of services is placed in the hands of the person providing the service (physician), who is for his part responsible to the body responsible for the service (sick fund). At the same time, however, it is indispensable that the person entitled to the service/beneficiary (patient) must be able to cooperate and co-determine.

Positioned between the "state" and the "market", charitable social services, self-help, voluntary, non-profit associations, etc. perform specific tasks in securing, rendering and procuring services, thus justifying a separate mention of them as important alternatives and complements to the public ("state") and private, profit-making ("market") provision of services.

The purely informal provision of services in the context of the family and the neighbourhood, and other "small nets" should also be mentioned here for systematic reasons. Great importance is to be attached to it in part – e.g. in connection with help when someone is in need of care, which is in general only inadequately covered by public and private systems of social protection (though with varying weightings).

A willingness to engage in self-help and to play an active rôle in community-orientated initiatives, indeed to act on purely honorary reasons and to do unpaid work in general, is still widespread, even in western countries – though admittedly to varying degrees. Whether in view of the demographic development and social change – e.g. the fact that women are increasingly engaging in gainful employment – the rôle of unpaid work can be increased, as is sometimes hoped for, is very much a matter of doubt.

In addition, there is the question of whether and to what extent voluntary activities are a suitable means of replacing professional social services. After all, an appeal for self-help and voluntary work in times of "empty coffers" can provide an alibi for a restrictive health and social policy. Even where self-help cannot take the place of professional assistance, it can nevertheless effectively complement the latter, so that the promotion of self-help by public and private bodies can serve to preserve, support and complement an existing and important potential for aid. Last but not least, it must be noted that self-help groups which provide voluntary services close to the level of their community and organized by themselves also perform tasks which are explicitly not intended to be the object of professional work and social benefits or services.

In Germany, the voluntary non-profit associations (*freie Wohlfahrtsverbände*) in the form of charitable organizations characterize the system of social protection in such a specific way – which is without equal in any other European country – that these voluntary welfare institutions have been termed "third social partners". "Voluntary welfare institutions" is a term used to cover the totality of social aids and self-help services provided on a free, non-profit basis and in an organized form.

If the transition from "status to contract" (*Maine*) in the sense of an abandonment of particular rights of the different classes of society and a move towards universal rights for all, in other words the implementation of the principle of equality before the law, is one of the characteristics of modern societies, then it is a specific task of "social" law to adapt the granting of social services to the individual circumstances pertaining in each case, in order to prevent economic and social inequalities from undermining the equality of all before the law. Against this background, social law is not restricted to compensating "material" disadvantages by substantive social law, but also includes compensating "formal" disadvantages by formal social law. In so far as social benefits and services are directed at persons who are at a social disadvantage, the effect of this social disadvantage can also make itself felt in that the individuals concerned are not fully informed of their rights and are largely incapable of enforcing their rights. Usually, the legal system assumes that the citizen knows his rights and that, if necessary, he can obtain expert advice, so that he will be in a position to assert his rights, if necessary by legeal proceedings. Granting a subjective legal entitlement and making access to the courts available might therefore appear sufficient to ensure that the guaranteed legal entitlements can be secured. Nevertheless, restrictions to which a citizen is exposed – and the handicapped are a good example here – can mean that the above-described way of perceiving and securing one's interests in conformity with the law, as presupposed by the law, is not possible. Information, consultation, advice, and effective expert assistance are major additional elements against this background which must be provided in addition to formally guaranteed rights if the gap between the norm and reality is not to make it impossible to secure one's interests and enforce one's rights. The point is that substantive social law remains largely ineffective if there is no appropriate implementation in practice and if those concerned do not benefit from the services to which they are entitled.

Consumer interest – consumer knowledge, consumer choice, consumer rights and consumer participation – as the epitome of the citizens' interests in their capacity as recipients of services, contribution payers, patients, clients, etc. – is one way of defining this situation. Knowledge, choice, rights and participation are at the same time criteria for the effectiveness of social benefits and services.

A further point is that the provision of social benefits and services, especially benefits in kind and services, is a largely genuine action, whereas procedural law is organized legalistically, so that it does not completely capture the interface between the provider and the recipient of the service. The consequence of the ineffectiveness of social benefits and services is that social needs are not met, and that in this respect the benefits do not achieve their objective.

The principle of human dignity, has a *material* side, in the sense that it guarantees a certain minimum level of benefits. But also the *way* in which assistance is granted can infringe human dignity as the "guideline" for the design of social benefits and services. This can be the case, for instance when a distinction is made between individual groups of beneficiaries – e.g. between the granting of benefits to the state's own citizens, on the one hand, and foreigners on the other -, or when social benefits are designed in such a way that they appear repressive and deterrent.

"Human dignity" in the way in which benefits are granted also means, by the way, that the recipient of assistance must be guaranteed a minimum of choice. In the context of social security, the need for choice appears in a variety of ways: (i) with regard to the nature, extent and body responsible for social security; (ii) with regard to the choice of the "community of solidarity" within which protection is sought; (iii) with regard to the provider of the service who is approached with a demand for a benefit – especially social benefits in kind and services; (iv) with regard to the nature of the benefits (cash benefits, benefits in kind, services); (v) with regard to the facilities, groups and, where applicable, individuals to whom one turns for the procurement of benefits.

The greater the extent to which uniformity and compulsion appear necessary (e.g. concerning the nature, extent and body responsible for social security), the more public authorities become involved. By way of contrast, whenever the possibility of choice – especially with regard to the provision and procurement of benefits – is given, it is obvious that a broad – public and private – spectrum is appropriate.

The demand for choice for the individual is based on the premise – which is sometimes secured by law – that everyone must have the possibility of looking for the satisfaction of his needs freely, within the framework of the funds available to him. Only this kind of arrangement for the provision of services prevents the individual from becoming the object of state action and thus corresponds to his position as a subject, namely as someone entitled to benefits. In this sense, the right of the person entitled to benefits to express his wishes and exercise a choice serves to give concrete form to his fundamental rights – human dignity, general freedom of activity, freedom of belief and freedom to practice one's religion, freedom of education – in the law relating to social benefits and services. For the field of the provision of health services, the legal guarantee of the freedom to choose the provider of the service is given its clearest manifestation in the form of the free choice of physicians.

At the same time, however, the freedoms to express wishes and exercise a choice share those restrictions which are characteristic of fundamental social rights in so far as they are merely guaranteed within the framework of what is "economically feasible": thus, the right of a free choice of physicians is restricted in the framework of statutory benefits systems to those physicians who are active in those systems (e.g. in the context of the British or the Italian national health services, or the German statutory health insurance funds); in other words the freedom of choice is restricted to the available and registered providers of services. At the same time, such rights are generally subject to the proviso that the body responsible for providing benefits and services must not incur any additional costs as a result of the choice of service provider exercised by the service recipient/person entitled to the service (though the right to exercise a choice can be extended by permitting the person entitled to declare his willingness to bear any additional costs that might be incurred). Depending on the nature of the service requested, the choice exercised by the person entitled to the benefit deserves a greater or lesser extent of legal protection: thus, the choice is all the more important, the more intense the relationship between those providing and those receiving the service is, e.g. because – as in the case of the relationship with a therapist – it presupposes a special relationship of trust or impinges on the personal sphere. Likewise, the degree of necessity for the recipient of the service to participate in the service is a criterion for the importance to be attached to the choice by the recipient of the service concerning the provider of the service.

This all boils down to the fact that, especially with regard to types and forms of benefits and services, the person of the recipient of the service and the one entitled to the service play a decisive rôle, and that, in designing the forms and types of nursing care benefits and services, it is necessary to take into account the fact that social benefits and services are services which serve to implement the rights and satisfy the needs of human beings.

Notes

[1] See for further details Bundesministerium für Familie und Senioren (1993); Baltes/Mittelstraß (1993).
[2] See Großjohann/Zöllner (1984).
[3] For further information see Pacolet/Versieck/Bouten (1994).

[4] See Gesetz zur sozialen Absicherung des Risikos der Pflegebedürftigkeit (Pflege-Versicherungsgesetz – PflegeVG), Bundesgesetzblatt 1994 I S. 1014; for the debate in Parliament see Deutscher Bundestag (1992).
[5] For further details see Petersen (1994).
[6] For further details see Jung (1994) and Bloch (1994).
[7] See for more details Schulte (1994).

References

Baltes, P. B./Mittelstraß, J. (1992) (eds.): *Zukunft des Alterns und gesellschaftliche Entwicklung*. Akademie der Wissenschaften zu Berlin Forschungsbericht 5. Berlin/New York: de Gruyter.

Bloch, E. (1994): Die Struktur der Pflegeversicherung ab 1995, in *Die Angestelltenversicherung 41*, 237-246.

Bundesministerium für Familie und Senioren (1993) (ed.): *Erster Altenbericht der Bundesregierung*. Bundestags-Drucksache 12/5897 v. 28. September 1993.

Buttler, G. et al. (1988): *Die jungen Alten: eine neue Lebensphase als ordnungspolitische Aufgabe*. Baden-Baden: Nomos.

Deutscher Bundestag (1992): *Einführung einer gesetzlichen Pflegeversicherung* – Öffentliche Anhörung des Ausschusses für Arbeit und Sozialordnung des Deutschen Bundestags am 21., 22. Mai und 3. Juni 1992. Bonn: Bundespresseamt.

EC (1993): *First Annual Report of the European Community Observatory on Older People on 'Social and Economic Policies and Older People'*, Brussels.

Gesetz zur sozialen Absicherung des Risikos der Pflegebedürftigkeit (Pflege-Versicherungsgesetz – PflegeVG), Bundesgesetzblatt 1994 I, 1014.

Großjohann, W./Zöllner, D. (1984): *Soziale Sicherheit bei Pflegebedürftigkeit in europäischen Nachbarländern*. Bonn: Gesellschaft für Sozialen Fortschritt.

Jung, K. (1994): Soziale Pflegeversicherung. Durchgesetzt gegen alle Widerstände, in *Bundesarbeitsblatt 45*, 5-16.

Laufer, H. (1994): Die Rentner in der Pflegeversicherung. Das Pflege-Versicherungsgesetz und seine Auswirkungen für Rentner und Rentenversicherungsträger, in *Die Angestelltenversicherung 41*, 247-259.

Pacolet, J./Versieck, K./Bouten, R. (1994) (eds.): *Social Protection for Dependency in Old Age*. Leuven: Hoger Instituut voor de Arbeid.

Petersen, K. (1994): Die soziale Sicherung der Pflegepersonen in der gesetzlichen Rentenversicherung, in *Die Angestelltenversicherung 41*, 260-267.

Schulte, B. (1994): Types of Benefits and Services, in B. von Maydell/E. M. Hohnerlein (eds.): *The Transformation of Social Security Systems in Central and Eastern Europe*. Leuven: Peeters Press.

Enquete-Kommission (1994): *Zwischenbericht der Enquete-Kommission "Demographischer Wandel – Herausforderungen unserer älter werdenden Gesellschaft an den einzelnen und die Politik"*. Bundestags-Drucksache 12/7876 v. 14. Juni 1994.

9 DETERMINING THE LONG-TERM CARE NEEDS OF INDIVIDUALS LIVING IN PRIVATE HOUSEHOLDS: RESULTS FROM A SURVEY

Ulrich Schneekloth

1 Introduction

At the end of 1991 Infratest carried out a representative survey concerning 'possibilities and limits of an independent conduct of life' on behalf of the Federal Ministry for Family Affairs and Elderly People. Actual planning data is available on number and situation of people who are dependent on help and care living in private households [Schneekloth/Potthoff (1993)]. Some selected results of this large population survey will be presented in the following sections.

1.1 Methodical concept

The effective sample of the survey comprised two representative sub-samples of 60,938 respondents of all ages living in 25,736 households in the old and new 'Länder' (federal states). At the end of 1991 a well trained Infratest interviewer staff carried out all interviews face-to-face. Within each household those persons were asked by the interviewer, who had the best information about all household members.

1.2 The differentiation into 'dependence on help' and 'dependence on care'

In Germany the public social and health service is characterized by the conceptual and institutional differentiation into therapy of an illness, rehabilitation and care. The dependence on care occurs as a result of chronic diseases or handicaps when a certain extent of long lasting disabilities is foreseeable and the curative measures are mainly exhausted [Igl (1992)]. People are classified as a 'person with a severe dependence on care' according to the social health insurance law if they by cause of a disease or handicap are so helpless that they need a considerable amount of support in doing all basic and recurring daily household tasks. In Germany the protection against the risk of getting dependent on care will be resolved more comprehensively in a federal law[1]. It was the aim of the population survey to supply a classification and a qualitative overview of the (entitled) group of people.

Especially for the purposes of this survey a standardized ADL/IADL-list was developed which is based on published scales [see Lawton/Brody (1969) or Katz et al. (1976)]. This list includes 24 basal activities out of the following areas of life:

- hygiene,
- preparation of meals/eating,
- motorization and mobility
- housekeeping
- communication and mobility outdoors

and is suitable for self- as well as external assessment.

The degree of disability concerning particular activities was determined. For each person with disabilities in at least one activity the extent was registered to which this person is dependent on help or care. On the basis of these informations Infratest has developed the *Infratest-care-interval-model*. With its help a separation can be made into persons without disabilities, persons who have a need of domestic help and persons who have a regular need of care.

Regular need of care means the need of support for doing daily physical tasks at least one time a day. These are activities in the areas hygiene, mobility/motorization and nutrition or respectively general need of charge. *Domestic need of help* is defined by disabilities in the area of domestic and social communicative tasks without the presence of a need of care.

The group of people who are dependent on care was classified according to the extent of the required basal assistance.

First level: People with a daily need of care

There is a considerable need of help for regular tasks during the day. Assistance is necessary for doing personal hygiene, i.e. bathing. Furthermore the personal mobility is reduced to the own house or apartment or there are lacks in preparing meals, i.e. cutting food (nutrition). Mentally handicapped or psychically ill persons are needing daily instructions.

Second level: People with a need of care for three times a day

There is an extensive need of help for daily tasks, i.e. washing oneself or personal hygiene, as well as a support with eating meals (nutrition). The person who is dependent on care can stay alone for several hours without being able to move continuously inside the house (mobility). Mentally handicapped or psychically ill persons at least are needing instructions for three times a day.

Third level: Persons with a permanent need of care

Extensive care is necessary throughout the whole day and also the night. People who are dependent on care are helpless in performing all elementary physical tasks, i.e. staying continent, using the toilet or eating. Mentally handicapped or psychically ill persons are needing a permanent control and a stimulus for communication.

2 Number and shares of people in private households who are dependent on help and care

2.1 Number and shares

With the help of the *Infratest-care-interval-model* a projection can be made of the number and shares of people in private households who are dependent on help and care (see table 1). Accordingly 1.2 million persons need regular care at the end of 1991. These people are representing 1.5% of the total population. Nearly 200,000 persons have a permanent need, 450,000 a need for three times a day and 550,000 a daily need of care. Furthermore 2.0 million people need help in housekeeping. These are 2.5% of the total population. Altogether around 3.2

million people in private households are dependent on more or less intensive help or care.

Table 1: People who are dependent on help and care living in German private households*

	Federal territory		the West		the East	
	in thousand	in %	in thousand	in %	in thousand	in %
Total population	80,974	100	65,289	100	15,685	100
Total number of people who are dependent on care	1,195	1.5	960	1.5	235	1.5
people with:						
permanent need	191	0.2	162	0.2	29	0.2
need three times a day	461	0.6	372	0.6	89	0.6
daily need	543	0.7	426	0.7	117	0.7
people who are dependent on domestic help	2,035	2.5	1,511	2.3	524	3.3

* People in private households in Germany, projected and in % of the total population (Time of investigation end of 1991, projected on population data at the end of 1992): New projection according to the delimitation of the Long-Term Care Insurance Law.

Source: Care-interval-model: Infratest 1994.

It is known, that the dependence on care occurs especially in one's high old age. Around 850,000 persons (71%) have been 65 years and older at the time of the interview. This is 6,9% of the total age group. Approximately 535,000 persons (46%) have been 80 years and older. This is 16.8% of the age group. Nevertheless it has to be noticed that 29% of those who are dependent on care were younger than 65 years.

There are no real differences between West and East Germany concerning the shares of people who are dependent on care. However in the new 'Länder' relatively more persons need domestic help. This could be caused considerably by the worse environmental conditions (furnishing of the apartment, infrastructure).

2.2 Mobility limitations and the need of care

Different profiles of disabilities can be generalized depending on the level of care (see for the following table 2).

The group of people with *permanent need of care* is widely helpless in all elementary areas of daily activities. In general these persons are immobile, 97% are not able to leave the bed alone and 94% cannot use the toilet without help. 74% need a permanent supervision and can impossibly stay alone at home for several hours. Own activities in housekeeping are not possible any more.

The group with *a need of care* for three times a day is dependent on help especially in the area of the personal hygiene. 67% are not able to take a bath alone, 58% to take a shower or wash themselves. About one third cannot dress or undress themselves or need daily supervision and a stimulus for conversation.

64% of the people with a *daily need of care* need help for bathing, 40% for taking a shower and 49% for climbing stairs. Three thirds cannot clean the apartment, however 49% are still able to prepare meals.

A considerably high limitation of mobility is the universal characteristic. This can have different reasons. Either disabilities result from a physical handicap or respectively a chronic-somatic disease or because of cognitive deficits on the mentally basis. In the end those disabilities cause that daily tasks cannot be undertaken without supervision or help. Assistance as a basic service is indispensable for this group of people. The key question for improving their situation of life is a system of living as much as possible without barriers. The apartment must be reached easily without climbing stairs. Bedroom respectively bathroom or WC must be equipped with installations for handicapped people. Furthermore total support in housekeeping is necessary, if a conduct of life in a private household will be kept.

2.3 Relevant psychiatric aspects

Apart from mobility problems one may not ignore that older people who are dependent on help and care very often have psychiatric or psycho-social symptoms [see for that: Häfner (1992)].

On the basis of the ADL/IADL-information we can draw some conclusions on cognitive functional disorders. In general 63% of the people who are dependent on care cannot handle their financial affairs; 59% have orientation problems outdoors, and 42% cannot use the telephone any more.

A general indicator for cognitive disabilities is the activity 'orientation alone outdoors'. 47% of people dependent on care who have no severe impairment of

Table 2: People who are dependent on help and care in private households according to disabilities in single activities of daily living*

in %**	Permanent need of care	Need of care for three times a day	Daily need of care	Total need of care	Domestic need of care
Activity: 'No, impossible'					
Un-/Dressing	100	30	18	37	2
Combing hair/Shaving	86	32	16	34	1
Taking a shower/Washing	98	58	40	57	4
Bathing	99	67	64	71	17
Using the toilet	94	23	10	29	1
Staying continent	88	8	7	21	2
Going to bed, getting up	97	22	11	31	0
Sitting down	86	16	7	24	0
Walking indoors	83	18	12	26	1
Climbing stairs	89	42	49	53	6
Eating/drinking	66	1	0	12	0
Cutting food	87	34	19	37	14
Preparing meals	97	77	51	69	10
Preparing/taking medicine	86	49	24	44	3
Cleaning rooms	99	86	75	84	33
Heating	97	72	44	64	11
Shopping	97	90	82	88	36
Using public transportation	99	88	79	86	32
Using the telephone	85	49	20	42	9
Making visits	93	73	59	70	17
Orientation outdoors	96	66	40	59	10
Staying alone at home for several hours per day	74	32	0	25	1
Handling financial affairs	95	74	42	63	18

* Multiple responses.
** People who are dependent on help and care in private households = 100.
Source: Care-interval-model: Infratest 1992.

visions or blindness cannot orientate alone outdoors. Additional 12% have difficulties in orientation. Therefore we can say that apart from help with physical tasks at least every second person who needs care (around 550,000 persons in private households) has a disturbance in orientation which perhaps is to be influenced by medical care or rehabilitation. About 450,000 people of this group are elderly with an age of 60 and above. For most of them we assume that the dependence on care is connected with a disease based on dementia of a middle or high degree.

These figures represent the lowest limit of people who are dependent on regular care with cognitive disabilities in private households. They should not qualify other epidemiological estimations (private households and nursing homes) with about 600,000 patients with reasonable or respectively severe dementia and additional 650,000 with light dementia [see also Häfner (1991)].

3   The situation of care provision

3.1   Family assistance

The family (still) carries the main responsibility for taking care. 77% of people who are dependent on care and 57% of them who are dependent on help receive principally support from one main caring person. Other 14% respectively 21% are in the charge of several persons of equal status. The main caring person mostly is a female relative. 34% of people who are dependent on care are in the charge of their husbands or wives, another 26% of their daughter, another 9% of their daughter-in-law and 16% of their mother. Accordingly the crucial factor for the situation of providing care for dependent people is the immediate presence of close relatives.

The household size is of great importance to characterize the situation of providing care. 46%, this is every second person who is dependent on care, live in a household of about three or more members; 34% are living in a two-person-household, in general with the husband or the wife. However, every fifth person who is dependent on care is living alone in an one-person-household and is dependent on help from outside of his or her own household.

Main caring persons have to be present daily or even round the clock. Their tasks are not limited to guarantee a necessary basic care. Help and care in a private household is rather a full-time-job. 91%, this is nearly each main caring person, say that he or she feels a strong or even a very strong burden. Those representative results emphasize the fact that in general an activity as a main caring person requires a high portion of personal engagement and marks the personal conduct of life.

3.2 Enlisting ambulant services

Ambulant social services are enlisted to a smaller degree in contrast to family help. There are 65% of people who are dependent on care and 57% of them who are dependent on help or respectively their relatives who know about relevant offers in their residential area. Nevertheless only 33% of people who are dependent on care and 16% who are dependent on help are enlisting these relevant services. Comparing the offer on one hand and the enlisting on the other hand it has to be emphasized that only each second person dependent on care who knows about offers in his residential area enlists these professional services.

Central task of professional care is the personal hygiene and medical care. To a lower extent there is a support for domestic tasks. Requests for improvements of the care offered by social services are mainly the following topics:

- care more frequently during the week
- prolonged care
- more frequent care at the weekend
- faster availability in case of an emergency.

The request for a prolonged availability of professional care is obvious in those cases where it is enlisted. All in all it has to be emphasized that ambulant social services are not very much accepted from the affected persons in private households. On one hand, those services are understood as 'welfare'. The planned infra-structural consequences which are coming along with the introduction of the LTC-insurance law could take remedial action. On the other hand, families do not see social services as professional support, which is indispensable for securing the quality of care as well as for the relief of caring relatives. The services are seen rather as a last resort or else as a last try when all other resources in the family are exhausted.

3.3 Coverage of the basic need of care

One question of the representative survey was to find out how far the basic need of care and the basic domestic need is fulfilled for the people in private households who are in charge of somebody. ('According to your opinion is the given support of care and domestic help sufficient?') The coverage of need determined only by this quantitative procedure gives no information about the quality of the services as well as the stability of the support with regard to burden involved by the main caring person. Due to this, it is less reassuring that about 10% of the people who are dependent on care in private households only receive inadequate help for the elementary daily basic tasks.

For this reason the exceeding role of a support system within the family has to be shown clearly once again. Differentiated with regard to the household size 22% of those persons dependent on care who live alone complain about an uncovered need in comparison to 8% of those people living in two-person-households and 6% of them living in households with three or more members. More often than proportionally these are single persons (widowed, divorced or unmarried). It is characteristic that in general ambulant services are enlisted. Finally those people who are dependent on care are living significantly often in bad furnished apartments. If there could not be arranged additional relief actions for these people with an uncovered basic need of care, a 'misplacing in a private household' cannot be excluded[2].

4 Conclusion

The request to live as long as possible in the own household is a characteristic for people who are dependent on care. Consequently people with all degrees of severity are in charge of somebody in private households. Apart from specific medical factors which make care in the household impossible at least from time to time the limits of domestic care are based on the existing family support system.

The additional results of this study show that it often brings a large, and sometimes also unreasonable, burden for the caring person of the family. Ambulant social care services are in contrast rarely enlisted. Reasons for this are deficits of information of the affected persons as well as existing gaps in the area of temporal flexibility or availability of the services. Moreover the affected persons show a general deficit in accepting the professional care support.

Measures for securing quality standards have to start in the area of the arrangement of adequate professional help as well as promotion for the acceptance with affected people. Here it will be essential, among other things, to enlarge the spectrum of capacity of ambulant social services. Therefore the functional care support can be extended also to the area of psycho-social care of the dependent people as well as their caring relatives. In this context the promotion of a continuous rehabilitation of the persons who are dependent on care is of great importance not least to maintain the conduct of life in the private household as long as possible.

The qualitative and quantitative enlargement of ambulant help and care offers is finally without an alternative in consideration with the demographic development. The relative increase of the older population results in a continuously increasing share of senior citizens who are living in an one-person-household. Consequently more and more dependent people have family support systems which become smaller and smaller. There will be only the way of relieving the family from the responsibility of charge if it is planned to give priority to the ambulant care instead of stationary care.

Notes

[1] This law (Long-Term Care Insurance Law [Pflegeversicherungsgesetz]) was passed shortly before the conference took place.

2 The perspectives of the provision of care cannot be assessed in detail here. It is possible that some of these people can receive different help for ensuring a maintenance of life in a private household in the future. Moreover one must take into account the fact that also for people with a 'covered need' a misplacing could exist because of the burden of the main caring person.

References

Häfner, H. (1991): Epidemiologie psychischer Störungen im höheren Lebensalter, in G. Haag/J. C. Brengelmann (eds.): *Alte Menschen. Ansätze psychosozialer Hilfen.* München: Röttger, 27-63.

Häfner, H. (1992): Psychiatrie des höheren Lebensalters, in B. P. Baltes/J. Mittelstraß (eds.): *Zukunft des Alterns und gesellschaftliche Entwicklung.* Berlin/New York: de Gruyter, 151-179.

Igl, G. (1992): *Leistungen bei Pflegebedürftigkeit.* München: Beck.

Katz, S./Akpom, C. A. (1976): A measure of primary sociobiological functions, in *International Journal of Health Services 10*, 493-509.

Lawton, M. P./Brody, E. M. (1969): Assessment of older people: Self-maintaining and instrumental activities of daily living, in *Gerontologist 9*, 179-186.

Schneekloth, U./Potthoff, P. (1993): *Hilfe- und Pflegebedürftige in privaten Haushalten.* Schriftenreihe des Bundesministeriums für Familie und Senioren, Bd. 20.2. Stuttgart/Berlin/Köln: Kohlhammer.

10 THE LONG-TERM COSTS OF PUBLIC LONG-TERM CARE INSURANCE IN GERMANY. SOME GUESSTIMATES

Winfried Schmähl and Heinz Rothgang

1   Introduction

After almost twenty years of discussion [see e.g. Götting/Hinrichs (1993); Haug/ Rothgang (1994) or Götting et al. (1995) for an overview of the sequence of events in policy development and Schmähl (1992) for an analysis of the different proposals discussed] in 1994 a Federal Act was passed concerning the introduction of a new public statutory Long-Term Care Insurance (LTCI)[1] effective April 1, 1995.[2] While at least for the last decade the necessity to cover the risk of long-term care comprehensively has been widely acknowledged, the main obstacle against any solution has been the fear of a 'cost explosion' resulting automatically from any newly introduced system of coverage. Particularly, any attempt to include long-term care into the social insurance system was criticised for this reason, not least from business representatives [see e.g. Engels (1991); Felderer (1992); Dinkel (1993); Ruf (1992), or the declaration of the Federation of Employers reprinted in Soziale Selbstverwaltung (1992)]. Concerns pertaining to this still exist. The aim of this paper therefore is to check to what extent such developments are likely to occur and to identify the main determinants of future expenditure developments within the new insurance's framework.

In the next section a simulation model based on a theoretical discussion of determinants of expenditure developments is introduced. The results of some calculations based on this model and some assumptions concerning benefits are presented in section 3 and 4. The paper ends with a general appraisal about the relative importance of the factors considered as determinants of expenditure development in long-term care, and possible effects of different strategies concerning the adjustment rates for LTCI benefits (in section 5).

2 The Simulation Model

Figure 1 contains a simplified model of factors responsible for expenditure development. Obviously, LTCI expenditure can be calculated as a product of the number of frail persons who receive LTCI benefits and the average payments per head to them. Apart from the legal definition of being in need of care the *number* of beneficiaries depends on the age and gender structure of the population based on demographic developments, and the age- and sex-specific probabilities to become frail. *Average per case expenditure* on the other hand is determined by the proportion of frail persons with different degrees of disability, the type of care chosen, and the respective legal obligations of long-term care funds. Particularly the choice of the type of care is influenced by numerous other factors (see Figure 1). Interestingly, family and household structures, which are among these factors, also influence the very probability to be in need of care [Bundesinstitut für Bevölkerungsforschung (1993), 76-82]. Since even the simplified model in Figure 1 is very complex and numerous impacts can not be quantified, it is not possible to include all factors into the simulation model.

Since demography is the basis of all expenditure calculations, our simulation model is based on a *demographic scenario*, namely the "7. koordinierte Bevölkerungsvorausberechnung" of the Federal Statistics Office (Statistisches Bundesamt), which contains a forecast of the German population according to age, sex and regional distribution between East and West Germany up to the year 2030 [compare Sommer (1992) and Bretz (1986) for details].[3] In this paper, we do not discuss effects of alternative demographic projections: for example, either assuming longer life expectancy or higher numbers of immigrants. Due to lack of data, we do also not use different assumptions concerning age- and sex-specific probabilities of different degrees of disability ("care probabilities") for German and foreign residents.

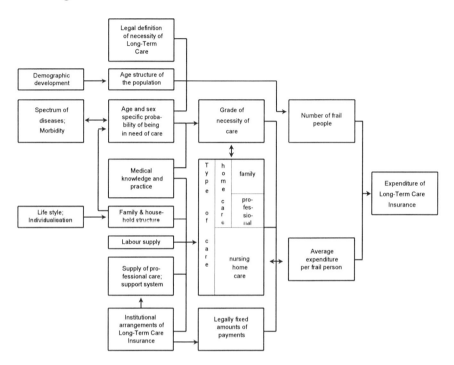

Figure 1: Factors determining LTCI expenditure[4]

The *care probabilities* needed for further calculations are estimated through the relative frequencies of frail people among their age group as identified by Infratest (1992); (1993); and Krug/Reh (1992), 143 (see Appendix). In its study, commissioned by the Federal Ministry of Family and the Elderly (BMFuS), Infratest Sozialforschung dealing with home care only revealed the share of frail people in each age cohort according to dependence grades. However, during the legislative process the legal definitions of the grades of dependence based on the work of Infratest have apparently been narrowed. Pfaff (1995), 724 therefore tries to estimate new probabilities combining the legal definition and Infratest data.[5] Prognos (1995), 172 on the other hand uses the Infratest data unmodified. Since a recoding of the original Infratest data shows differences resulting from the change in definition to be negligible in practice [see also Fachinger et al.

(1995) on this issue], we use the original Infratest frequencies[6]. Krug and Reh on the other hand examined the situation of frail people living in nursing homes. From their data the share of frail people living in nursing homes in each age cohort can be calculated. Thus, both studies together comprise the whole population.[7] Assuming constant age and sex specific probabilities[8] we are able to calculate the likely development of the number of frail people through combining probabilities and demographic scenario.[9] The figures resulting from this exercise relate to the total population. However, only about 90% of them will become members of public insurance.[10] Since in this paper we deal with *public* long-term care insurance only, these figures are multiplied by 0.90 to get the number of frail persons covered by public long-term care insurance.

Turning to the factors determining average expenditure we use the *financial obligations of long-term care funds* as given in the legal framework. The adjustment of these obligations is at the discretion of Federal Government and therefore impossible to predict. In section 3, we therefore assume fixed amounts of benefits[11] while in section 4 different adjustment paths are calculated.

The choice of the *type of care* (family based home care, home care by professionals or nursing home care) is not modelled, i.e. the factors influencing this decision (see Figure 1) are not taken into consideration systematically. We rather use status quo-assumptions. As far as the *choice between transfers in cash and in kind* is concerned, due to the introduction of payments for long-term care into the agenda of health insurance, some observations have been made to base the calculation on. However, variations are calculated to show the sensitivity of expenditure developments with respect to this factor.

Since the establishment of new nursing homes takes considerable time and manpower shortages for nurses are likely to occur, in the short run the number of people living in nursing homes is expected to remain fairly constant. Some authors [Boese/Heuser (1986); Oberender (1986); Wasem (1986)] however have expressed the concern that in the long term a run on nursing homes is to be expected, while others have denied the likelihood of such an effect [Grönert (1981) and (1982); Nöldecke (1985), 9; Schulz-Nieswandt (1989)]. In drafting the bill the legislators took account of such concerns. Therefore, recent analyses based on the institutional arrangements built into the Long-Term Care Insurance Act [see Mager (1995); Schulz-Nieswandt (1995)] support the latter position. Thus, in our simulations the *share of frail persons living in a nursing home* is held constant for each age group. Since the share of frail persons in nursing home care is positively correlated with age, due to demographic development this assumption nevertheless allows for variations in the total share of home and nursing home care over time.[12]

LTC INSURANCE IN GERMANY 185

Varying the share of frail people choosing nursing home care from 27.3% of all beneficiaries to 40% Prognos estimates a considerable increase in spending.[13] The financial consequences of a shift of utilisation patterns towards nursing home care for long-term care funds, however, depend in each case on (1) whether the Medical Service of Health Insurance (MDK) and the concerned LTCI fund judge such a removal necessary, (2) on the grade the concerned person is classified into, and (3) on the type of care chosen previously (see Table 1 for the benefits and Table 2, which set off the additional expenditure for nursing home care against the savings for home care including pension benefits for non-professional caregivers[14]).

Table 1: Monthly payments from LTCI funds according to dependence grade and type of care (in DM)

	in Grade I	in Grade II	in Grade III
Home care:			
cash benefits	400	800	1,300
in kind benefits	750	1,800	2,800[b]
Nursing home care			
if necessary	up to 2,800[a]	up to 2,800[a]	up to 2,800[a]
if unnecessary	750	1,800	up to 2,800

a) For cases of extreme hardship, benefits may reach up to DM 3,300 per month. However, the number of persons receiving such excess payments must not exceed 5% of all frail persons in grade III. On the other hand, average annual spending on all persons in nursing homes must not exceed DM 30,000 which amounts to DM 2,500 per month (§ 43 sec. 2 SGB XI).
b) For cases of extreme hardship, benefits may reach up to DM 3,750 per month. However, the number of persons receiving such excess payments must not exceed 3% of all frail persons in grade III in home care (§ 36 sec. 4 SGB XI).

As table 2 reveals a shift from home to nursing home care may even lead to moderate savings on part of long-term care funds, due to the elimination of pension benefits for non-professional caregivers.[15] In other cases, however, considerable amounts of additional expenditure result from a move into a nursing home. Nursing home care is particularly expensive for long-term care funds if nursing home care is judged as necessary, if the grade of dependence is rather low, and if transfers in cash have been chosen before.

Table 2: Additional LTCI expenditure due to a shift from home to nursing home care (in DM per month)[16]

	in Grade I	in Grade II	in Grade III
necessary			
from family care	+2,300	+1,800	+1,200
from professional care	+1,950	+800	-300
not necessary			
from family care	+250	+800	+1,200
from professional care	–100	–200	–300

'Necessary' moves into nursing homes for persons with low dependence grades, especially with grade I, however, are fairly unlikely. Moreover, it seems plausible that for a high percentage of people concerned, professional home care is tried before such a drastic decision as the removal into a nursing home is taken. First results from a new Infratest study [Schneekloth (1995)] showing that more than half of all frail persons in nursing home care belong to grade III point in the same direction. Hence a simple comparison of average per case expenditure for home and nursing home care, which seems to be the basis of the above mentioned respective Prognos projection, can not be used to estimate the financial consequences of a shift in utilisation towards nursing home care. To the contrary, even a growing share of frail people in nursing homes might not cause dramatic financial consequences for long-term insurance – provided that they belong overwhelmingly to a high dependence grade and have received professional ambulatory care before. Therefore, any future simulation taking into account variations in institutionalisation rates has to make assumptions about these factors.

Finally, further expenditures have to be taken into account. In order of budgetary relevance, these are

- contributions to the pension funds for non-professional caregivers,
- funding for day-, night- or short-term nursing home care,
- payments for substitutes while non-professional carers are on holiday, and
- special aids and teaching arrangements for non-professional caregivers.

Concerning the expenditure of long-term care funds administrative costs must also be added. They are forecasted more or less in proportion to the number of frail persons (see section 3.2.4).

3 The development of LTCI expenditure with constant benefits

In this section we present the results of some projections assuming constant amounts of benefits for all types of care. Alternatively, the results can be interpreted as real expenditure figures deflated by a general price index, given that all benefits are adjusted with the same price index. In order to do so we discuss the changing number of frail persons first (see section 3.1). After that each type of expenditure is analyzed separately (see section 3.2). Finally, all types of expenditure are cumulated. Initial spending figures are compared with the official Federal government figures (see section 3.3.1) and an overview of projected total expenditure until the year of 2030 is given (see section 3.3.2).

3.1 Number of Frail People

Figure 2 shows the number of frail people covered by LTCI resulting from the simulation. It is important to note that distinct developments for ambulatory and stationary care are based solely on demographic development. Since constant age-specific probabilities for home care and nursing home care are used, no change in utilisation patterns is assumed.

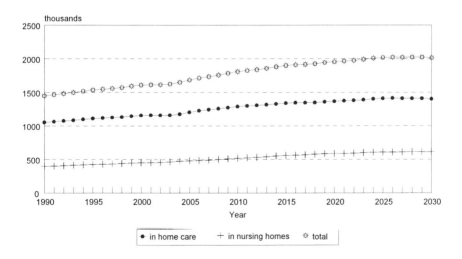

Figure 2: Number of frail people covered by public long-term care insurance

According to the simulation, in 2030 the number of frail people in home care will exceed the respective 1995 figure by 26.4%, whereas the number of frail people in nursing homes will exceed the 1995 figure by 43.92%, leading to an overall increase of 31.14% for the period of time between 1995 and 2030.[17] These rates must be regarded as considerable but not really dramatic.

In the long run the population is expected to decline. Hence, the growth rate is higher if the absolute number of frail people covered by LTCI is put in relation to the (declining) number of all members of public long-term care insurance or to the number of members aged 16 or older (Table 3).[18]

Table 3: LTCI beneficiaries per 100 members of public long-term care insurance

Year	Frail persons who receive LTCI benefits (LTCI beneficiaries)	LTCI beneficiaries per 100 LTCI members	LTCI beneficiaries per 100 LTCI members aged 16 or older
1995	1536360	2.29	2.55
2000	1608806	2.39	2.65
2005	1685482	2.49	2.77
2010	1808824	2.68	2.98
2015	1900304	2.86	3.17
2020	1955517	3.02	3.35
2025	2018006	3.22	3.57
2030	2019733	3.34	3.71

Starting with 2.29 in 1995 the number of LTCI beneficiaries per 100 LTCI members is expected to increase to 3.34 in 2030, thus exceeding the initial figure by 46%. Almost the same rate (45%) results if the number of members of public long-term care insurance aged 16 or older is used as a denominator.

3.2 Components of Expenditure Development

3.2.1 Expenditure on Home Care

For the sake of simplicity for the simulation it is assumed that all kinds of payments will start at the beginning of 1995, i.e. quoted official figures will all be transformed respectively. Since in reality payments will only be made from

April 1995 (home care) and July 1996 (nursing home care), actual expenditure for 1995 and 1996 will be lower than shown here.

Apart from the number of frail persons, expenditure on ambulatory care depends on the grades of dependence mix and the choice frail persons make with respect to transfers in cash and transfers in kind. According to our simulation the number of frail persons in home care in grade I and II are characterised by an almost identical starting point and a very similar development. With respect to grade I or II only half as many persons are in grade III and its increase is considerably lower (21.5% compared to 33.5% in grade I and 38% in grade II, from 1990 to 2030).

To calculate home care expenditure, additional assumptions have to be made with regard to initial choices and likely developments during the next decades. They can be based on experience with care benefits in public health insurance [see von Zameck (1995)]. Since 1991 severely frail members of public health insurance could choose between transfers in cash (DM 400 per month) or in kind (DM 750 per month). Between 80% and 90% of them preferred the cash benefit and only 10% to 20% decided in favour of transfers in kind [Sinha (1994), 345].

As the ratio of amounts between both types of transfers is similar (in grade I it is even equal) to the newly introduced LTCI, this behaviour can be used as an indicator for future decisions. However, this assumption neglects differences between health and long-term care insurance regulations. So, due to a less strict legal definition, the number of claimants of payments for home care in LTCI will be considerably higher than the number of beneficiaries under the regime of health insurance. In addition to the 700,000 beneficiaries of long-term care benefits (funded by statutory health insurance) who will automatically be graded in grade II[19], another 500,000 persons, who did not receive benefits from sick funds are expected to become beneficiaries of LTCI in grade I. Whether the behaviour of 'severely frail persons' also applies to the choice of 'considerably frail people' might be questioned. Furthermore, in health insurance no combination of transfers in cash and in kind was possible, while in LTCI people are encouraged to take parts of their claims in kind and others in cash (§ 38 SGB XI). Nevertheless, the experience of the last three years at least indicates the preference for cash compared to in kind transfers. Moreover, further indicators hint in the same direction. At the moment, only one in three of all frail persons living in private households receives professional care, in most cases additionally to family care [Infratest (1992), 49; Infratest (1993), 180-185]. Hence, the assumption of a 80% share of benefits taken in cash, upon which the Federal Ministry of Labour and Social Affairs (=BMA) has based its expenditure calculation [Jung

(1993b), 621], seems to be quite realistic for the initial phase. Therefore we also use this share as a reference estimate in our simulation.

However, it is highly questionable whether this rate will remain constant over time. In extensive interviews a considerable share of non-professional carers revealed that they are rather under social pressure to do so [Halsig/Zimmermann (1995), 233f.; see also Alber (1990)]. Therefore the willingness to care may drop if social norms weaken. Moreover, growing individualization and changes in lifestyle hint at a diminishing ability and willingness of families to do the bulk of care work. Additionally, the declining ratio of potential caregivers, namely women between 40 and 65, to frail persons indicates a growing demand for professional care simply for demographic reasons [Rückert (1992), 52-56]. The increasing labour force participation of women points in the same direction. Pilot schemes also show that acceptance of professional care can be increased through information and marketing. Finally, since the Long-Term Care Insurance Act opens up the market for commercial organisations, a growing supply is to be expected to meet increasing demand for professional care, particularly in those segments (as weekend and night care) which are in undersupply at the moment [Halsig/Zimmermann (1995), 247]. Thus, all in all, in the long run a shift towards transfers in kind might be expected. Even for the very short period since 1991 such a trend away from transfers in cash can be observed [Sinha (1994), 344].

Though some plausible speculations about the direction of shifts in the takeup of different kinds of benefits seem to be possible, it is almost impossible to quantify the extent of the changes. Therefore, for the calculation of expenditure on home care three scenarios are used to demonstrate the range of possible developments of expenditure: The 'BMA scenario' is based on a constant 80% share of benefits taken in cash, while two other scenarios assume that all benefits are taken in cash or in kind, respectively. They mark the range of developments (Figure 3).

The moderate increase in the number of frail persons (see Figure 2) is reflected in expenditure data. According to this simulation, in the year 2030 expenditure on home care will exceed the 1995 figures by 24.8%.[20] Following the 'BMA' scenario this increase amounts to an additional expenditure of about DM 3 billion. Once again this growth should be considered as moderate.

What is rather striking is the range of expenditure marked by the two extreme scenarios: If all people choose transfers in kind, expenditure will be twice as high as if all people choose transfers in kind. Broadly, each percent of benefits taken in kind rather than in cash leads to an additional expenditure of DM 100 million per year. Since the 'BMA scenario' assumes a high share of transfers in

LTC INSURANCE IN GERMANY

cash, there is considerable potential for expenditure-increasing developments if the mix of transfers shifts. For example, if more people choose transfers in kind than in cash, expenditure figures for 1995 will be higher than the BMA scenario forecasts for 2030. Hence utilisation patterns are at least as important for expenditure development as the demographic effect usually blamed for the expected 'cost explosion'.

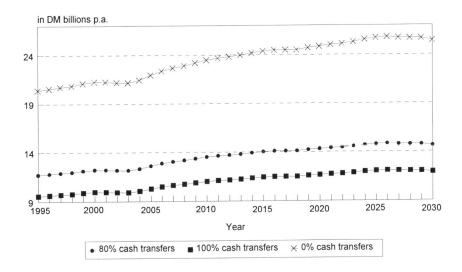

Figure 3: LTCI expenditure on home care

3.2.2 Expenditure on Nursing Home Care

Public long-term care insurance expenditures on nursing home care depend on two factors: the number of frail persons receiving care in nursing homes and the average LTCI payment they receive. Figure 2 contains estimates on the numbers of people who receive nursing home care. The next and final step is to calculate the average expenditure per head and its development.

Apart from cases of extreme hardship the legally fixed maximum payment for nursing home care is DM 2,800 per month (see Table 1). In 1989/90 the average monthly rate for nursing homes was about DM 2,900 per month [Krug/ Reh (1992), 51]. Since then, monthly rates have grown considerably. In Baden-Württemberg in 1993 average monthly rates amounted to DM 4,500 [Sozialpolitische Umschau 290/93 and 291/3], and at the end of that year even the Federal

Ministry of Labour and Social Affairs estimated an average cost of DM 3,600 per month for 1993 [Jung (1993a), 506]. The newest figure available puts forward an average rate of DM 4,154 per month in West Germany for December 1994 [Schneekloth (1995)][21]. Given a constant growth rate, average monthly rates might even reach DM 5,000 by 1996, when nursing home care payments of statutory LTCI funds get started. Subtracting the costs for room and board, which have to be paid by the frail person herself (or by social assistance) and the cost of investment, which should be financed by the states (Länder) the remaining costs are likely to exceed the legally fixed amount of DM 2,800 per month on average.

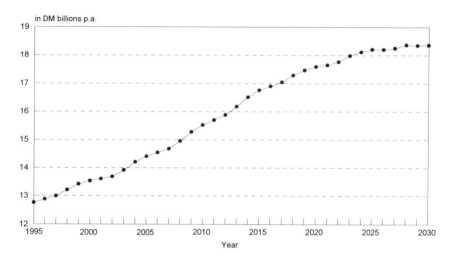

Figure 4: LTCI expenditure on nursing home care

Nevertheless, the average LTCI payments will stay below this amount. First, all persons who do not need nursing home care receive reduced payments (§ 43 sec. 3 SGB XI). Since no experience exists, it is difficult to estimate the effect of this arrangement. Allemeyer (1994), 318f., however, believes that the effect might be considerable. Second, nursing home costs above DM 2,800 will not be covered, while rates below this amount automatically reduce average payments. In this way the existence of a ceiling reduces average payments. Hence, for given average rates, the greater the variance between nursing home rates, the smaller the average payments tend to be. That is why it is difficult to estimate how far average payments will be below the maximum individual benefit of DM 2,800 per month. However, § 43 Abs. 2 SGB XI states that the average yearly expenditure on nursing home care must not exceed DM 30,000 or DM 2,500 per month. Despite average nursing home care costs well above DM 2,800 per month, DM 2,500 therefore seems to be a good estimate of average monthly LTCI expenditure on nursing home care.[22] Hence, Figure 4 is based on the number of frail persons in nursing homes taken from Figure 2 and assumed average expenditures of DM 2,500 per month.

Expenditure on nursing home care is slightly below expenditure on home care based on the 'BMA scenario'. If more transfers in kind are chosen, however, spending on home care may easily exceed the expenditure for nursing home care. Due to different growth rates for the number of persons in ambulatory and nursing home care as identified in Figure 2, expenditure for nursing home care grows more rapidly. Thus, the 2030 figure exceeds the 1995 figure by 43.9% while the respective figure for ambulatory care amounts to just 24.8%.

3.2.3 Expenditure for Contributions to Pension Funds for Non-Professional Caregivers[23]

Statutory LTCI funds are obliged to pay contributions to statutory pension insurance for non-professional caregivers in home care. These contributions are bound to three prerequisites. The caregiver must not be a professional, and neither already receive pensions nor be in full-time employment (i.e. he or she must not work for more than 30 hours a week) [§ 44 SGB XI; compare Krauthausen/ Schmidt (1994)]. According to Infratest (1993)

- 77% of all persons in home care have a non-professional main caregiver [Infratest (1993), 131].
- 68% of those non-professional caregivers are younger than 65 and hence eligible for additional pension benefits [Infratest (1993), 143f.];[24] and
- 90% of all non-professional carers are not in full-time employment [Infratest (1992), 47; Infratest (1993), 143].

Since it can be assumed that all those in full-time employment are non-pensioners, 58% of all non-professional carers can be expected to be given a legal claim to pension contributions.[25] Thus, 44.66% of all persons in ambulatory care can be expected to have a non-professional caregiver with a principle legal claim for pension contributions. This figure is used for the following calculation.[26]

The contribution payment depends on the dependence grade the frail person is classified into and the amount of time the caregiver spends on care work (Table 4). According to these factors a fictitious income is allocated to each caregiver. On this base the monthly contribution to pension insurance is calculated. This income is expressed as a percentage of the average earnings of all members of statutory pension insurance (§ 166 Abs. 2 SGB VI introduced in Art. 5 of the Long-Term Care Insurance Act; see Table 4, column 3). Following the internal calculations of the Federal Ministry for Social Affairs, we used a contribution rate of 19.2% and average yearly earnings of DM 49,190 (West) and DM 35,972 (East) to calculate the contribution payments included in Table 4.

Table 4: Legal obligation of statutory LTCI funds to contribute to pension funds of non-professional caregivers

Grade	Hours of care	Contributions in % of average income	Contributions in DM West Germany	Contributions in DM East Germany
III	28 and more	80	629.63	460.44
	21-27	60	472.22	345.33
	14-20	40	314.82	230.22
II	21 and more	53.3333	419.75	306.96
	14-20	35.5555	279.84	204.64
I	14 and more	26.6666	209.88	153.48

Obviously, the average contribution in each dependence grade depends on the average percentage of average earnings in each grade, which in turn depends on the average weekly hours worked. In our simulation we follow the Federal Ministry of Social Affairs' estimates which assume an average percentage figure of 75% for grade III, 50% for grade II and 25% for grade I.

Furthermore, we base the calculation on figures for West Germany (Table 4, column 4) assuming that the average yearly earnings in East Germany will soon converge to West German annual earnings.[27] The results of the projection are given in Figure 5.

Expenditure on contributions to pension insurance of non-professional caregivers is rather small compared to the ones on home and nursing home care. In 1995, expenditure on contributions to pension insurance of non-professional caregivers amounts to 17.5% of expenditure on home care (BMA scenario) and to 16.3% of expenditure on nursing home care. Moreover, the increase of 25% for the period from 1995 to 2030 is well below the increase for expenditure on home as well as on nursing home care.

LTC INSURANCE IN GERMANY

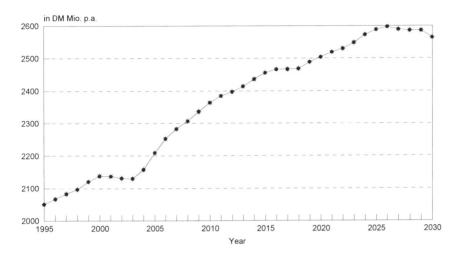

Figure 5: LTCI expenditure on contributions to the pension insurance of non-professional caregivers

3.2.4 Miscellaneous Expenditures

As mentioned before, there are some additional expenditures which should be taken into account.

Day- and night-nursing home care is paid if home care is insufficient (see § 41 SGB XI). Monthly payments are made up to DM 750 (in grade I), DM 1,500 (in grade II), and DM 2,100 (in grade III).

For the frail in grade I this is identical with the limits for home care if transfers in kind are chosen. For people in grade II and III payments differ. However, payments for home care and for day- and night-care together must not exceed the limits for the former. Within these limits any combination is possible. Expenses on day- and night-nursing home care reduce benefits for ambulatory care. Since the simulation assumes maximum benefits on home care (see section 3.2.1.), therefore no further expenditure for part-time nursing home care is considered.

Short-term nursing home care (Kurzzeitpflege) is paid if (particularly subsequent to hospital treatment) home care is temporarily not sufficient (§ 42 SGB XI). Short-term nursing home care is financed for no more than four weeks a year, and respective payments must not exceed DM 2,800 per year. This also applies to *payments for substitutes*, i.e. while non-professional carers are ill or on holiday (§ 39 SGB XI). Thus, depending on the dependence grade and the chosen type of home care (see Table 1), expenditure on short-term nursing home care and payments for substitutes are slightly higher than payments for home care for most people.[28] Hence, any use of these types of benefits cause additional LTCI expenditure.

In its official reasoning added to the bill, government estimates expenditure on day-, night-, and short-term care together to amount to DM 1.8 billion in 1994[29] [Deutscher Bundestag (1993), 175]. However, this is a gross figure. An accurate estimation must subtract DM 1.1 billion for expenditure 'saved' on home care giving a net figure of DM 0.7 billion [Jung (1993b), 622], spent on an estimated 1.089 million publicly insured frail persons in home care (ibid.).[30] Set in relation to each other these BMA figures amount to DM 642.792 per case and year. Multiplied by the respective number of frail persons this figure gives the forecasted additional expenditure on day-, night- and short-term nursing home care in the simulation. The same procedure is applied to the officially estimated expenditure of DM 0.3 billion on payments for substitutes, which leads to 300/1,089 = DM 275.48 per year per frail person in home care.[31]

Special (technical) aids are granted if necessary to render home care possible and not within the agenda of sickness funds (§ 40 SGB XI). This also includes subsidies to changes in housing. Payments for each means are limited, but no overall limit exists.

Official estimates of the expenditure on special aids show a figure of DM 0.1 billion. Once again, this estimate is used to calculate the expenditure per person in home case. The resulting sum of DM 91.83 per year is then multiplied by the respective number of frail persons to produce the estimates used in the simulation.

Furthermore, *teaching arrangements for non-professional caregivers* should be mentioned (§ 45 SGB XI). Long-term care funds may either provide own courses or pay others to teach their caregivers. The respective expenditure, however, is small enough to be neglected. Following this assessment of the BMA we do not include expenditure on teaching arrangements in the simulation.

Finally, *expenditures on administration* are to be considered. Once again we use the official estimate to calculate per person figures which are multiplied by the number of frail people to get the forecasted overall expenditure. This time, however, frail persons in home care and in nursing home care have to be distinguished.

Administrative expenditures were officially estimated at DM 1.5 billion in 1994 [Deutscher Bundestag (1993), 175]: DM 900 million to administer home care and DM 600 million to deal with nursing home care [Jung (1993b), 622].

LTC INSURANCE IN GERMANY   197

Related to the respective numbers used by the BMA, this amounts to DM 826.45 per frail person in home care and DM 1,445.783 in nursing home care per year.

Figure 6 shows the forecasted development for further expenditures. Apart from administrative expenditure all types of expenditure remain well below DM 1 billion per year. However, altogether they have a similar dimension as expenditure on contributions to the pension funds of non-professional caregivers. Due to the construction of the forecast, the overall expenditure increase of 30.3% from 1995 to 2030 reflects the growth of the expected number of frail persons in home care.

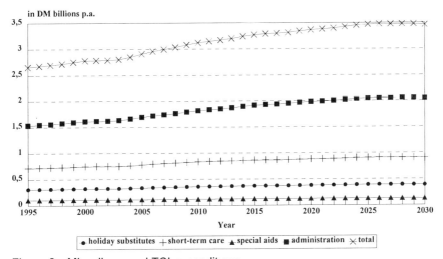

Figure 6:   Miscellaneous LTCI expenditures

3.3 Total Expenditure

Having discussed separately each type of expenditure we now turn to total expenditure, the sum of home care, nursing home care, contributions to pension insurance for non-professional caregivers and other expenditures.

According to respective assumptions concerning ambulatory care a 'BMA', a 'maximal' and a 'minimal' version are distinguished.[32]

3.3.1 Initial Spending

Table 5 shows the projected expenditures for 1995 compared with official government forecasting. Since the latter originally takes into account the real date at which the Long-Term Care Insurance Act comes into effect, the figures published there are much smaller. In order to get comparable figures, they had to be manipulated as if all benefits started on January 1, 1995. Due to changes made during the legislative process, which led to increased benefits, the recent BMA-estimate of expenditure (column 2) is slightly higher than the original one (column 1). Our 'BMA scenario' (column 3) gives an even higher overall expenditure, while the 'minimal' version (column 4) predicts less expenditure. All in all, differences among these scenarios are very small and almost negligible. Since the simulation model is partly based on BMA calculations, this is not very surprising.

Table 5: Expected LTCI expenditure in DM billion per year

Type of benefit	LTCI Bill 1994 expenditure	BMA[a] 1995 expenditure	Simulation: 'BMA scenario' 1995 expenditure	Simulation: 'Minimal scenario' 1995 expenditure	Simulation: 'Maximal scenario' 1995 expenditure
Home Care	9,3 (+ 1,1)	10,79	11,73	9,56	20,40
Holiday substitutes	0,3	0,44	0,31	0,31	0,31
Day-/night- and short- term care	1,8 (-1,1)	0,35	0,71	0,71	0,71
Special aids	0,1	0,11	0,10	0,10	0,10
Subtotal: ambulatory care	11,5	11,81	12,85	10,68	21,52
Contributions to pension insurance for non-professional caregivers	2,9	2,6	2,05	2,05	2,05
Nursing home care	10,7	13,06[b]	12,76	12,76	12,76
Administration	1,5	1,11	1,53	1,53	1,53
Total	26,60	28,58	29,20	27,03	37,87

[a] Expenditure figures are calculated as if all payments would start on 1-1-1995.
[b] 1996 figures.

LTC INSURANCE IN GERMANY

However, a huge difference remains between the 'maximal' version of the simulation model (column 5) and the calculations given in columns one to four. This difference is entirely due to distinct figures for expenditure on home care pointing towards the fiscal importance of the choice between transfers in cash and in kind. Though it seems to be fairly unlikely that a majority of frail persons will immediately choose transfers in kind, the 'maximal expenditure scenario' demonstrates the effect of such a choice, which becomes the likelier the longer the period of time under consideration. Thus, though official calculation is sound for the initial phase, there is no financial reserve that could be used as a buffer against rising expenditure due to increased choices of transfers in kind. Therefore, this can be a considerable danger for future financial development.

3.3.2 Long-Term Developments

More interesting than initial spending is the long-term development of expenditure. Figure 7 shows the projected expenditure of the three scenarios under consideration until 2030.

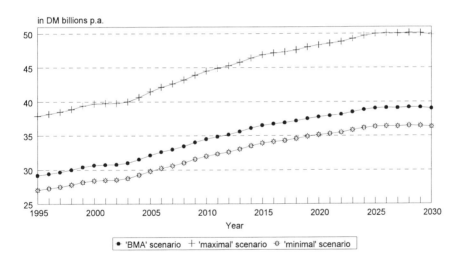

Figure 7: Total expenditure

With 33,7% ('BMA version'), 31,6% ('maximal version') and 34,4% ('minimal version') all scenarios show a similar overall increase. Thus, due to demography LTCI expenditure is expected to increase by one third. Compared with fears of a 'cost explosion' and respective 'nightmare scenarios' produced by opponents of long-term care insurance [see e.g. Engels (1991)] this purely demographically induced overall increase for a 35-year period must still be considered as rather moderate.

However, the striking difference between the 'maximal scenario', on the one hand, and the 'BMA' and the 'minimal scenario', on the other, continues over time emphazising the importance of the choice between professional and familiar types of care in home care. The 1995 expenditure of the maximal scenario exceeds the 2030 expenditure of the minimal scenario and approaches the 2030 spending level of the BMA scenario. Thus, the choice between different types of care is at least as important for long-term expenditure developments as demography.

4 The development of LTCI expenditure and contribution rate with adjusted benefits per case

So far the whole dynamic of the simulation model was based on the demographic development. We now take into account other factors, such as inflation, economic growth and adjustment processes for the legally fixed amount of benefits, and their effect on expenditure and contribution rate.

4.1 Theoretical Considerations

Before any calculation is done it seems to be useful to examine the relationship between the parameters under consideration on a theoretical basis. For all growth processes we assume the exponential model, i.e. if x denotes the parameter under consideration (e.g. income) and n denotes the year[33] it follows that $x_n = x_0 \cdot (1 + g)^n$, with g being the (average) annual growth rate. For n = 1 it follows that $x_1/x_0 = 1 + g$ or $g = x_1/x_0 - 1$.

4.1.1 Expenditure

LTCI expenditure is the product of the number of beneficiaries (N) and the average benefit per beneficiary ($\bar{E}$). The latter depends on the composition of beneficiaries according to dependence grades (G), the type of care chosen (transfers in cash, transfers in kind or nursing home care) (T), and the legally fixed amount of benefit for each grade and type of care (B). If these variables are conceptualised as an index expenditure (E) is

LTC INSURANCE IN GERMANY

$$E = N \cdot \bar{E} = N \cdot G \cdot T \cdot B. \quad (1)$$

Given the status quo assumptions made before (in section 3) N, G and T only depend on demography. Thus they can be summarized as D with $D = N \cdot G \cdot T$. Hence

$$E = D \cdot B. \quad (2)$$

With e, d and b denoting the respective growth rates it follows from the exponential model that[34]

$$e = d + b + d \cdot b. \quad (3)$$

4.1.2 Contributions

The new long-term care insurance is financed almost entirely through contributions of employees, pensioners, and others,[35] which are calculated as a certain percentage of their contributory income ('beitragspflichtiges Einnahmen'). If C denotes the amount of contributions, R the contribution rate, Y the total contributory income ('Gesammtsumme der beitragspflichtigen Einnahmen') and c, r, and y the respective growth rates, equations (4) and (5) follow:

$$C = R \cdot Y. \quad (4)$$

$$c = r + y + r \cdot y.^{36} \quad (5)$$

The total contributory income itself consists of incomes from employees (indexed e), pensioners (indexed p) and others (indexed u)

$$Y = Y_e + Y_u + Y_p. \quad (6)$$

It follows that the overall growth rate of the total contributory income (y) is the weighted mean of the growth rates for each group of contributors (y_e, y_p, y_u) with their share on overall income used as the respective weight:

$$y = a_e \cdot y_e + a_p \cdot y_p + a_u \cdot y_u \quad \text{with } a_i = y_i / (y_e + y_p + y_u)$$
$$\text{for } i = e, p, \text{ and } u. \quad (7)$$

Each y_i depends on the growth rates of the number of the respective contributors (m_i) and their average contributory income per contributor ($\bar{y}_i$)

$$y_i = m_i + \bar{y}_i + m_i \cdot \bar{y}_i ,^{37} \quad (8)$$

Combining equations (7) and (8) it follows that

$$y = a_e(m_e + \bar{y}_e + m_e \cdot \bar{y}_e) + a_p(m_p + \bar{y}_p + m_p \cdot \bar{y}_p) + a_u(m_u + \bar{y}_u + m_u \cdot \bar{y}_u). \quad (9)$$

Substituting y in equation (5) through equation (9) gives the growth rate of the sum of all contributions to the LTCI (c) depending on the growth rates of the number of contributors (employed, pensioners and others) and their respective average contributory income. Hence,

$$c = r + a_e(m_e + \bar{y}_e + m_e \cdot y_e) + a_p(m_p + \bar{y}_p + m_p \cdot y_p) + a_u(m_u + \bar{y}_u + m_u \cdot \bar{y}_u) +$$
$$r \cdot [a_e(m_e + \bar{y}_e + m_e \cdot y_e) + a_p(m_p + \bar{y}_p + m_p \cdot y_p) + a_u(m_u + \bar{y}_u + m_u \cdot \bar{y}_u)]. \quad (10)$$

4.1.3 Contribution Rate

As mentioned earlier parliament has the discretion to adjust the amounts of LTCI benefits. In principle the fixed amount of each type of benefits can be adjusted with a different rate. More likely, however, is an identical adjustment rate for all types of benefits, which keeps relative values constant. For the following calculations we assume such an identical adjustment rate.[38]

For a balanced budget, contributions (C) must be equal to expenditure (E). Using equations (2) and (4) we get

$$R \cdot Y = D \cdot B$$
$$R = D \cdot B / Y. \quad (11)$$

For the growth rates from equation (3) and (5) it follows that

$$c = r + y + r \cdot y \stackrel{!}{=} d + b + d \cdot b = e$$
$$r = (d + b + d \cdot b - y) / (y + 1). \quad (12)$$

4.1.4 Real Purchasing Power

If LTCI benefits are used to buy care services and related goods the real purchasing power (X) is defined as

$$B = P \cdot X$$
$$X = B / P \quad (13)$$

with P denoting the price for those goods and services, X the quantity and B the LTCI benefits. For the respective growth rates (x, b, p) it follows that

$$x = (b - p) / (1 + p).[39] \quad (14)$$

4.1.5 Adjustment Rates

Though benefits are adjusted through parliamentary discretion four 'ideal types' of adjustment paths can be conceptualised:

- In § 30 SGB XI the Government is granted the authority to adjust benefits. However, adjustments are limited to levels which can be financed within the limits of the given contribution rate, i.e. b should be fixed in a way to keep r equal to zero. Using equation (12) the respective adjustment rate b which fulfills this condition can be calculated as

$$r = 0$$
$$(d + b + d \cdot b - y) / (y + 1) = 0$$
$$b = (y - d) / (1 + d). \qquad (15)$$

The adjustment path following this equation is the first scenario we consider.

- However, in the official justification added to the bill the expectation of a growing contribution rate is expressed. Following this reasoning an increasing contribution rate should be permitted as long as it is caused by demographic changes [Deutscher Bundestag (1993)], i.e. r = d. Once again with reference to equation (12), for the respective adjustment rate of this second scenario equation (16) follows:

$$r = d$$
$$(d + b + d \cdot b - y) / (y + 1) = d$$
$$b = y. \qquad (16)$$

- While these scenarios are based on the Long-Term Care Insurance Act or the official justification added to the bill, respectively, the third scenario is just hypothetical. If the real value of the benefits is to be kept constant, b must be equal to the growth of a respective price index for care services and related goods (p).[40] Hence

$$b = p \qquad (17)$$

is the third scenario under consideration.

- Finally, we consider an adjustment rate equal to the general inflation rate (i)

$$b = i. \qquad (18)$$

In this case the real value of benefits (deflated with the general price index) remains constant. This scenario reflects the calculations in section 3 if the respective figures are interpreted as given in real terms.

The effects of these adjustment paths on expenditure, contribution rate and real purchasing power for each beneficiary are shown in Table 6.[41] It shows that the four scenarios described fall into two groups. Scenario 1 and 2 are *budget-related*. The growth rate for benefits is chosen in order to produce a certain growth rate for the contribution rate (either r = 0 or r = d). Hence economic growth reflected by an increase of the total contributory income leads to a high adjustment rate for benefits. Consequently, expenditure is the higher the higher the total contributory income. Whether the real purchasing power grows or declines depends on the relation of y, p and d. Scenario 3 and 4, on the other hand, are *need-related*. Here adjustment rates are chosen, in order to keep real purchasing power constant (scenario 3) or to keep benefits in line with general inflation (scenario 4). Consequently, economic growth is irrelevant for expenditure development, but relevant for the contribution rate. In scenario 3 and 4 the relation of y, d, p (and i) is decisive for the development of the contribution rate.

Table 6: Effects of different adjustment rates on expenditure, contribution rate and real purchasing power

Adjustment rate	Expenditure	Contribution rate	Real purchasing power
General formula	$e = d + b + d \cdot b$	$r = \dfrac{b + d + b \cdot d - y}{1 + y}$	$x = \dfrac{b - p}{1 + p}$
Scenario 1: $b = \dfrac{y - d}{d + 1}$	y	0	$\dfrac{y - d - p - p \cdot d}{(d + 1) \cdot (p + 1)}$
Scenario 2: $b = y$	$d + y + d \cdot y$	d	$\dfrac{y - p}{1 + p}$
Scenario 3: $b = p$	$d + p + d \cdot p$	$\dfrac{d + p + p \cdot d - y}{1 + y}$	0
Scenario 4: $b = i$	$d + i + d \cdot i$	$\dfrac{d + i + i \cdot d - y}{1 + y}$	$\dfrac{i - p}{1 + p}$

Whether expenditure, the contribution rate and real purchasing power grow or decline depends on the numerical relation of the different growth rates mentioned. If all rates are expected to be positive, growth follows directly for seven out of the twelve cells. For the five cells left, whether growth or decline follows depends on the relation of the growth rates under consideration.

The developments of the contribution rate in scenario 3 and of real purchasing power in scenario 1 and scenario 2 depend on the relation of d, p, and y. If $d + p + p \cdot d > y$ declining real purchasing power (as in scenario 1) or a growing contribution rate (as in scenario 3) follows. Given $d + p + p \cdot d > y$ there is a trade off between a constant contribution rate and constant real purchasing power. Scenario 2 marks a kind of middle ground relaxing the demand of a constant contribution rate in order to prevent declining real purchasing power. Nevertheless, if $p > y$ – in spite of a growing contribution rate – declining real purchasing power follows.

4.2 Numerical Calculations

As shown in Table 6, with a given adjustment rule, the development of expenditure, contribution rate and real purchasing power depend on three dynamic processes, the growth of Y, P, and D, which we will try to quantify below.

4.2.1 Specification of Parameters

The annual growth rate d can be drawn from the results of section 3.3.2, which reflect demography only. For simplicity in the following we only use the BMA scenario for further calculation neglecting the maximal and the minimal scenario.

Y and P (and their respective growth rates y and p) are given in monetary terms. For a better interpretation we state them *in real terms*, i.e. in constant money. All nominal figures are therefore deflated by a general price index for private consumption.[42] Since the following data are taken from Prognos (1995) we also use the corresponding price index (Table 7).[43]

Table 7: Deflator of private consumption[44]: Average annual growth rate in %

	1992-2000	2000-10	2010-20	2020-30
Optimistic scenario	2.6413	2.7533	2.7515	3.0951
Pessimistic scenario	2.7215	3.0610	3.1306	3.3601

If all growth rates are given in real terms, obviously $i = 0$ follows. For scenario 1 to 3 the cells in Table 6 remain the same, provided that y and p are interpreted as

given in real terms. Because of i = 0 in scenario 4 a simplification results leading to
- e = d,
- r = (d − y) / (1 + y), and
- x = −p / (1 + p).

Following equation (7) y depends on the growth of the contributory income of the employed (y_e), of pensioners (y_p) and of others (y_u) as wells as of their respective weights (a_e, a_p, a_u). According to Prognos [(1995), 177] in 1995 the employed will have contributed DM 13.2 billion. That is more than 70% of all contributions (i.e. a_e > 0.7). Employed members and pensioners together finance about 90% of the total income of LTCI.[45]

Due to this dominant role of contributions from the employed, Table 8 gives a detailed breakdown of the development of numbers (m_e), their average contributory income ($\bar{y}_e$)[46] and the contributory income (y_e) just for this group. The final row containing the growth rate of the total contributory income (y), however, also includes contributory income from pensioners and others. Since there is no space here to consider the optimistic and the pessimistic scenario we have calculated a "middle ground" growth path, based on growth rates calculated as the arithmetic mean of the respective rates of optimistic and pessimistic scenario. All further calculations are based on this scenario.

Table 8: The development of contributory income:
Average annual growth rates in %

Middle Ground (arithmetic mean)	1992-2000	2000-10	2010-20	2020-30
Number of employed persons (m_e)	0.0905	−0.0107	−0.1909	−0.9105
Average contributory income of employees ($\bar{y}_e$)	1.5149	2.2626	1.8702	2.0754
Contributory income of all employees (y_e)	1.6068	2.2520	1.6762	1.1465
Total contributory income (y)	**1.6076**	**2.1557**	**1.6779**	**1.1257**

Source: Prognos (1995), U-39, U-47, U-83, O-39, O-47, O-83; own calculations.

The final parameter which is to be estimated is p, the growth rate for the price of goods and services used in care. Since long-term care is a labour-intensive service industry with little room for rationalisation, "Baumol's law" applies. It states that prices in labour-intensive industries will rise faster than the general price index if wages keep in line with general wage development, because productivity grows slower (if at all) [Baumol (1967); Baumol/Oates (1972)]. Hence p can be expected to be greater than i, i.e. if stated in real terms p > 0. Given the very high share of labour costs to total costs[47] and assuming that prices follow costs[48], prices for care services and related goods roughly develop in line with the sum of labour costs. If the number of staff used to perform a certain service cannot be reduced, i.e. if no productivity gain is possible,[49] this leads to p being equal to the growth rate of wages for professional carers. Due to an excess demand on the labour market for professional carers (the so-called 'Pflegenotstand'), which – alone for demographic reasons – is to be expected in the near future [Prognos/Dornier (1990), 10-12], wages for professional carers can be expected to grow even faster than average wages [Wasem (1995)]. However, in the following calculations we assume wages of professional carers growing in line with general wage development, and consequently p = $\bar{y}_e$ (see Table 8).[50]

4.2.2 Results

Using the formulae given in Table 6 for scenario 1 to 4 and the parameter values reflected in Figure 7 (for d) as well as Table 8 (for y) and Table 9 (for p) respectively, the simulation gives the results shown in figures 8 to 10.

Figure 8 contains the *development of expenditure* in real terms according to the four scenarios discussed. Obviously there are huge differences between these scenarios. While according to scenario 4 expenditure will rise to DM 39.0 billion by 2030, scenario 3 gives a figure of DM 88.8 billion with scenario 1 (DM 51.7 billion) and scenario 2 (DM 69.1 billion) lying in between. Put in relation to the starting point of DM 29.2 billion this amounts to an overall growth of 33.7% (scenario 4), 77.1% (scenario 1), 136.7% (scenario 2), and 166.4% (scenario 3), respectively.

Scenario 4 is identical with the calculations in section 3. Its dynamics only reflect the demographic development. The other scenarios also take adjustment into consideration. They all lead to much higher expenditures. With an overall growth of 77.1% even an adjustment path chosen in order to keep the contribution rate constant, produces an expenditure increase more than twice as high as for demographic reasons alone. Thus, figure 8 once again emphazises the importance of adjustment relative to the demographic development if expenditure development is to be considered.

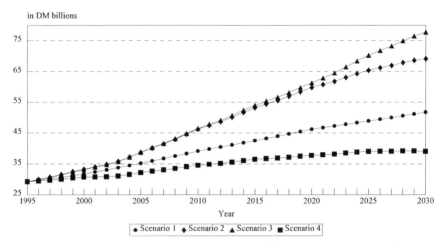

Figure 8: Total LTCI expenditure according to different adjustment rates for benefits

Different adjustment scenarios produce also huge differences in *contribution rates*. According to scenario 4 (inflation-linked adjustments), the contribution rate decreases to 1.283% by 2030, i.e. it falls to 75,5% of its starting value (1.7%). Following scenario 3, on the other hand, it may climb up to 2.557% by 2030 with scenario 1 (constant contribution rate) and scenario 2 (2.272% in 2030) in between. Related to the initial value this amounts to an overall growth of 50.4% (scenario 3), 33.6% (scenario 2), 0% (scenario 1) and −24.5% (scenario 4).

Nevertheless, scenario 3 does not mark the absolute maximum possible. In section 3 we demonstrated that a shift in utilisation patterns produces considerable effects. If e.g. all frail persons in home care apply for in kind transfers, – with an almost identical growth rate – total costs are almost 40% above the reference scenario (BMA scenario, see Figure 7). Applied to the contribution rate, the maximum scenario in Figure 7 and the adjustment in scenario 3 together produce a contribution rate of 3.6% in 2030. Certainly, a 100% choice of in kind transfers marks a very extreme case, a truly worst case. On the other hand, as mentioned above, we might have underestimated price increases for care services and related goods. Higher growth rates would produce even higher contribution rates in scenario 3 while having no influence on this parameter if any of the other adjustment paths is chosen.

LTC INSURANCE IN GERMANY

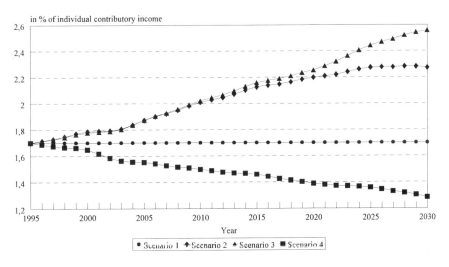

Figure 9: LTCI contribution rate according to different adjustment rates for benefits

The results of our calculation concerning the contribution rate agree more or less with other simulations. Using similar status quo assumptions as far as probabilities and utilisation patterns are concerned, Prognos (1995), O-83; U-83 predicts a contribution rate between 2.2% and 2.4%. This result is based on an adjustment rate equal to the growth rate of the contributory income of employees (ibid., 174). From the wording it is not quite clear whether this refers to the contributory income of *all* employees Y_e or to their *average* contributory income $\overline{Y}_e$. If the former is meant this assumption approaches that of scenario 2^{51}, if it was the latter it is the same as in scenario 3^{52}. However, on the whole, Prognos confirms our findings.[53]

Felderer (1992), 28 projected the development of the contribution rate before the LTCI Act was passed or the bill was made public. Therefore, he had to base his calculations on assumptions, e.g., about the amount of benefits per case. Hence, the absolute amount of expenditure and the absolute contribution rate are of limited interest. The respective growth rates, however, are independent of the initial values and therefore of greater interest. According to his reference model, in 2030 the contribution rate will be about two thirds above its initial value. This figure is even higher than our overall growth rate in scenario 3.

A comparison of the developments of the *expenditure and the contribution rate* demonstrates that both must not be confused. Due to economic growth and hence a growing total contributory income (y), massive expenditure increases can be financed by a constant contribution rate (scenario 1). Scenario 1 produces expenditures rising from DM 29.2 billion in 1995 to DM 51.7 billion in 2030, without touching the contribution rate. Something similar applies to the other scenarios: The growth of the contribution rate is always much below the growth rate of expenditure.

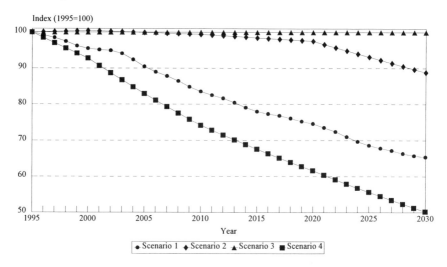

Figure 10: Real purchasing power of LTCI benefits according to different adjustment rates

Finally, *real purchasing power is* considered (Figure 10). Real purchasing power is only constant in scenario 3. In all other scenarios it is diminishing up to 89% (scenario 2), 65% (scenario 1), and 50% (scenario 4), respectively, of its original value by the year 2030.

5 General Conclusion

In this paper we have tried to shed some light onto likely developments of expenditure and contribution rates. Though the simulation suffers from lack of knowledge in certain areas, particularly as far as utilisation is concerned, and estimations of developments (e.g. of economic growth) are always uncertain, our findings have important implications for policy evaluation and future research.

As far as expenditure is concerned the demographic effect is not overwhelming. Due to demography expenditure in 2030 might be about 30-35% higher than it was immediately after the introduction of LTCI (section 3.3.2). Authors who base their argument on demography only [e.g. Dinkel (1993); Felderer (1992)], miss important aspects. Since the elderly – even when receiving long-term care insurance benefits – still contribute to financing, the old age dependence ratio in particular is not a valid indicator of contribution rate development [Schmähl (1989), 287 and (1993b)].

Utilisation is, however, as important as demography. The choices of frail persons between nursing home care and home care and, if the latter is chosen, between informal or professional care are major determinants of expenditure development leading to a considerable range of possible expenditure paths. Any one percentage of the frail in home care choosing in kind benefits rather than cash benefits adds on an additional expenditure of roughly DM 100 million (in constant money). With respect to this choice, official estimates are based on relatively favourable assumptions.[54]

Though these assumptions seem sensible in the short run, in the long run shifts towards professional care are to be expected. Since an initial utilisation ratio of 80% (cash) to 20% (in kind) is assumed in official estimates there is considerable potential for additional expenditure due to changes in behaviour of the frail elderly. Thus, one of the risks for future expenditure developments lies in a shift in utilisation patterns not considered in official calculations.

The results in section 3 are based on LTCI benefits adjusted for inflation. This scenario (4), however, leads to a decreasing contribution rate (which might be welcomed) (see Figure 8), but also to a radical deterioration of real purchasing power (see Figure 9), which will almost certainly not be tolerated by the politicians in charge of adjustment. Therefore scenario 4 must be regarded as unrealistic. If scenarios 1, 2 and 3 are considered, however, it becomes obvious that demography is not the decisive factor influencing expenditure levels. Even scenario 1 (leading to a constant contribution rate) shows an expenditure of DM 51.7 billion in 2030 compared to the DM 39.0 billion in scenario 4, in which only demography is taken into account. Scenario 2 and 3 render even higher figures (DM 69,1 billion and 88.8 billion, respectively). These results point to the relevance of those factors that influence expenditures heavily apart from demography.

Perhaps the most disquieting finding, due to its political implications, is the trade-off between contribution rate and real purchasing power. If the contribution rate is kept constant (scenario 1) – according to the chosen parameters – the real purchasing power of LTCI benefits will have declined to about two thirds of its initial value by the end of the period considered. If to the contrary the real purchasing power is kept constant as in scenario 3, the contribution rate climbs up to 2.6% (see Figures 9 and 10), while scenario 2 produces a deteriorating real purchasing power and at the same time a climbing contribution rate, but to a lesser extent than in scenario 1 and 3, respectively. Thus, there is a dilemma: it is not possible to keep a constant contribution rate and (at least) constant real purchasing power. Hence, in determining the adjustment path politicians have to choose between two evils. Remembering that in these calculations (1) no shift in utilisation behaviour is considered which might reinforce the trade-off between contribution rate and real purchasing power and (2) we chose a rather moderate growth rate of prices for care services and related goods, it becomes clear that the dilemma is serious.

In § 70 SGB XI the legislator is explicitly directed to adjust benefits only insofar as can be financed with a constant contribution rate. Thus adjustments according to scenario 1 follow [see Rothgang (1994) and (1996) for a detailed argument]. A sequence suggesting a growing contribution rate in the official justification added to the bill, however, indicates that the legislators were uncertain about their own decision [compare also Jung (1993b), 622f.]. If the effects on real purchasing power which an adjustment according to scenario 1 will have and the respective problems of legitimacy and acceptancy are taken into consideration, it still seems to be possible that legislators might shift from a budget-related adjustment path to a need-related adjustment path. Only the future will tell whether the legally set adjustment course (scenario 1) will be continued. However, the dilemma between a constant contribution rate and constant real purchasing power seems to be unsoluble. It is impossible to have both at the same time. In this matter politicians face a difficult choice.

As far as further research is concerned these findings stress the importance of factors like (1) utilisation choices, (2) economic growth as reflected in the development of contributory income, (3) the development of prices for care services and related goods, and (4) the chosen adjustment path. Compared to these factors the demographic development is of lesser relevance. Any further research aiming at the projection of the expenditure and the contribution rate should therefore concentrate on these factors rather than putting too much effort into the variation of demographic patterns.

Appendix: Care Probabilities used[55]

in %	Care probabilities for home care in West Germany							
	Age group							
	< 16	16-29	30-64	65-69	70-74	75-79	80-84	> 84
Grade I								
men	0.2	0.1	0.4	1.0	1.5	3.0	3.1	8.1
women	0.3	0.1	0.3	0.3	1.7	2.0	5.6	9.9
total	0.2	0.1	0.3	0.6	1.6	2.3	4.8	9.4
Grade II								
men	(0.0)	0.1	0.4	1.5	1.2	2.9	3.8	10.1
women	0.0	0.2	0.1	0.6	0.8	2.7	3.9	13.5
total	0.0	0.3	0.2	1.0	0.9	2.8	3.8	12.6
Grade III								
men	0.2	0.1	0.1	(0.1)	0.9	1.2	1.6	3.0
women	0.4	0.1	0.1	(0.1)	0.3	0.6	1.3	4.4
total	0.3	0.1	0.1	(0.1)	0.6	0.8	1.4	4.1
Total								
men	0.4	0.3	0.8	2.4	3.6	7.1	8.4	21.2
women	0.7	0.5	0.4	1.0	2.8	5.2	10.8	27.2
total	0.5	0.4	0.6	1.5	3.1	5.8	10.0	26.1

	Care probabilities for home care in East Germany							
	Age group							
in %	< 16	16-29	30-64	65-69	70-74	75-79	80-84	> 84
Grade I								
men	0.2	0.0	0.3	0.8	3.1	5.3	4.9	7.4
women	0.1	0.1	0.4	1.3	2.0	4.6	7.2	9.1
total	0.2	0.0	0.4	1.1	2.4	4.9	6.6	8.6
Grade II								
men	(0.1)	0.2	0.2	1.7	1.6	2.3	5.0	8.7
women	(0.1)	(0.1)	0.3	0.6	1.0	3.2	6.5	15.6
total	(0.1)	0.1	0.2	1.0	1.2	2.9	6.1	13.7
Grade III								
men	0.2	0.1	0.1	0.2	0.5	(0.3)	0.2	4.2
women	0.3	0.1	(0.1)	(0.1)	0.2	0.4	0.6	2.3
total	0.2	0.1	0.1	0.1	0.3	0.3	0.5	4.2
Total								
men	0.4	0.4	0.6	2.8	5.3	7.6	10.0	20.3
women	0.4	0.1	0.7	1.9	3.1	8.2	14.3	29.0
total	0.4	0.2	0.6	2.2	3.9	8.1	13.2	26.5

	Care probabilities for nursing home care in Germany (East and West)						
Age	< 30	30-40	40-50	50-60	60-65	65-70	70-75
in %	0.01	0.04	0.09	0.20	0.38	0.62	0.92
Age	(cont.)	75-80	80-85	85-90	90-95	> 95	Total
in %	(cont.)	2.41	4.77	10.17	16.78	27.83	0.57

Notes

[1] For simplicity in the following only the acronym will be used.

[2] Formally, the act came into force on January 1, 1995, when monthly contributions were collected for the first time. However, payments for home care start April 1, 1995 and funding for nursing home care will not be granted before July 1, 1996. In order to get the insurance started, some minor regulations, concerning the build up of long-term care funds, etc., take effect on June 1, 1994 (Article 68 Pflege-Versicherungsgesetz).

[3] This scenario is also used by Dinkel (1993) while Pfaff (1995) uses its recent update (8. koordinierte Bevölkerungsvorausberechnung). Felderer (1992) and Prognos (1995) use own demographic models.

[4] Figure 1 is a slightly modified version of the figure presented in Schmähl (1992), 21, also used in Bundesinstitut für Bevölkerungsforschung (1993), 75 and the report of the Enquete Commision on Demographic Change.

[5] Since the resulting numbers of frail people receiving benefits from LTCI are far too low Pfaff suspects that these probabilities underestimate the real numbers [Pfaff (1995), 727].

[6] Ulrich Schneekloth of Infratest kindly supplemented the published data through additional frequencies, which thus render more precise calculations possible (see appendix).

[7] A new Infratest study also commissioned by the Federal Ministry examines nursing home care. Detailed results of the representative survey, which took place at the end of 1994, however, are not available yet. Nevertheless first results estimating the total number of frail people in nursing homes at about half a million [Schneekloth (1995)] support the dimensions indicated by Krug and Reh.

[8] Since it is not possible to predict whether these probabilities will rise or decline with growing life expectancy let alone to which extent [see Robine/Cambois (1996)], it seems reasonable to assume constant rates. Hence the assumption of constant rates is widely used in the literature [see e.g. Dinkel (1993), 39; Felderer (1992), 12; Pfaff (1995), 728 or Prognos (1995), 173]. In further research, however, variations of this assumption should be calculated in order to check how sensitive results are.

[9] Crucial for the accuracy of this projection is the way in which long-term care funds make use of their competence to classify the claims of frail people. Since there is only little experience on the evaluating process any projection suffers from a considerable amount of uncertainty in this respect. This is particularly relevant for the estimation of the initial number of beneficiaries. The development of this number rather depends on the constancy of judgement standards.

[10] Since those persons who are voluntary members of statutory sickness funds may either join statutory or private long-term care insurance the exact percentage is unknown yet. The 90% estimate is based on the share of the population covered by statutory sickness funds and used by the Ministry of Social Affairs (BMA) [Jung (1993b), 621]. To guarantee comparativeness this figure is also used in our simulations. In a more recent publication Jung (1994), 5 assumes a coverage of 92%. However, no official calculations based on this estimation are available.

[11] Assuming that benefits are adjusted by a general price index the figures given in section 3 can also be interpreted as real expenditure deflated by the same price index.

[12] Hence, according to our projection the total share of frail persons in nursing homes grows from 27.7% in 1995 to 30.4% in 2030. In keeping constant age-specific utilisation patterns our approach differs from Prognos (1995), 173, who assume a constant ratio of beneficiaries in nursing homes to all beneficiaries amounting to 27.3%.

[13] Actually an increase in contribution rate of 0.2-0.3% is calculated [Prognos (1995), 174]. With a contribution rate climbing from 1.7% in 1996 to 2.3%-2.6% (depending on the chosen scenario) in 2040 (ibid.: 175) this amounts to a cost increase of about 10%.

[14] The average costs of pension benefits for non-professional caregivers are estimated at DM 100 per month, DM 200 per month, and DM 300 per month for each frail person in grade I, II or III, respectively (see section 3. 2. 3 for details). For simplicity, no distinction is made whether professional or family care was chosen.

[15] In saying so we have to keep in mind the basic difference between overall costs of care and expenditure of LTCI funds. Since LTCI benefits are limited the ranking of real costs of certain types of care may greatly differ from the ranking of respective LTCI expenditure, which depends on the legally fixed amounts of payment alone (see Table 1).

[16] In Table 2 monthly payments for nursing home care of DM 2,800 are assumed. However, on average DM 2,500 must not be exceeded (§ 43 sec. 2 SGB XI). Therefore, it would have been necessary to reduce the numbers in all cells of Table 2 by DM 300 if the comparison of spending patterns between home and nursing home care was based on this average figure.

[17] Respective figures for the period from 1990 to 2030 are 33.3% (home care), 53.9% (nursing homes), and 39.0% (overall growth).

[18] Since children are insured free of charge, persons below the age of 16 do not contribute to public long-term care insurance. Pensioners on the other hand do contribute. Therefore the population aged 16 or older can be used as a crude estimate of potential contributors to long-term care insurance [Schmähl (1993a); in reply to Dinkel (1993)].

[19] All of those may apply to be regraded to grade III. It is officially expected that about half a million will try and about 200,000 may succeed [Petrich (1994), 23f.; Jung (1993b), 621].

[20] Due to their construction all scenarios show an identical growth rate. Smaller growth rates for higher dependence grades, however, lead to an expenditure increase even a bit smaller than the respective rate for the total number of frail persons in home care shown in Figure 2.

[21] The respective figure for East Germany is DM 2,868 per month [Schneekloth (1995)].

[22] The Prognos (1995), 171 projection is also based on an average spending of DM 2,500 per month and case.

[23] For a detailed analysis concerning coverage of caregivers in the statutory pension insurance see Petersen (1994).

[24] Since there are pensioners of an age below 65 this estimate can rather be considered as a ceiling.

[25] This figure results from $0.68 \cdot 0.90 - 0.32 \cdot 0.1 = 0.58$ assuming that of 100 non-professional main caregivers none are pensioners in full-time employment, 10 are non-pensioners in full-time employment, 32 are pensioners not in full-time employment and 58 are non-pensioners not in full-time employment.

[26] The Federal Ministry of Labour and Social Affairs assumes a 75% rate of non-professional caregivers and an 80% rate of carers who are not yet pensioners. No allowance is made for carers in full-time employment, who will not benefit from pension arrangements. Thus, the Ministry assumes some 60% (= 75% · 80%) of all frail persons in home care to have a non-professional caregiver possessing a principle legal claim to LTCI funds concerning contributions to pension funds.

[27] Controls show the difference to be small. If West and East German figures are used respectively the overall expenditure for contributions to pension funds for non-professional caregivers are about DM 200 milions per year below the scenario we chose.

[28] Frail persons in grade III who choose transfers in kind receive identical payments whether or not they are in short-term nursing home care.

[29] Originally, the act should have taken effect on January, 1st 1994, with the exception of nursing home care payments, which should start on January, 1st 1996. That is why the official expenditure data and the number of frail persons on which this expenditure is based on relate to 1994.

[30] In a recent internal BMA document a net figure of DM 0.35 billion for April to December 1995 is given, amounting to a fictitious DM 0.467 billion for a twelve-month period.

[31] The maximum amount was increased during the legislative process. However, given the minor financial importance of this type of expenditure no provision for increased expenditure is made in our calculation.

[32] The 'BMA scenario' is based on a 80% rate of people in home care choosing cash transfers. 'Minimal expenditure' differs from that by the assumption of 100% cash transfers chosen in home care, while the 'maximal expenditure' scenario assumes only transfers in kind (100%) to be chosen. Additionally, all three scenarios include expenses on nursing home care, on pension benefits and miscellaneous expenditures as shown in Figure 4, 5, and 6 respectively.

[33] Since spending data are given on an annual basis, time is conceptualized as a discrete variable.

[34] $e = E_1/E_0 - 1 = (D_1 \cdot B_1)/(D_0 \cdot B_0) - 1 = (D_1/D_0) \cdot (B_1/B_0) - 1 = (d+1) \cdot (b+1) - 1 = d + b + d \cdot b$. In the model used before (see section 3) we have kept B constant, i.e. $b = 0$, thus E developed proportionally to D ($e = d$). In equation (3) we no longer base our calculations upon this assumption.

[35] Other contributions include those of unemployed and self-employed members of public LCTI. See Schulte (in this volume) for details on institutional arrangements for the distribution of the resulting financial burden, which are central for all questions connected with income distribution [see Fachinger/Rothgang (1995) on these issues] but not for the overall amount of contributions collected by the LTCI funds.

[36] $c = C_1/C_0 - 1 = (R_1 \cdot Y_1) / (R_0 \cdot Y_0) - 1 = (R_1/R_0) \cdot (Y_1/Y_0) - 1 = (r+1) \cdot (y+1) - 1$
$= r + y + r \cdot y$.

[37] $y_i = Y_{i1} / Y_{i0} - 1 = (M_{i1} \cdot \overline{Y}_{i1}) / (M_{i0} \cdot \overline{Y}_{i0}) - 1 = (M_{i1} / M_{i0}) \cdot (\overline{Y}_{i1} / \overline{Y}_{i0}) - 1$
$= (m_i + 1) \cdot (\overline{y}_i + 1) - 1 = m_i + \overline{y}_i + m_i \cdot \overline{y}_i$.

[38] This assumption is also made by Prognos (1995), 174.

[39] $x = X_1 / X_0 - 1 = (B_1 / P_1) / (B_0 / P_0) - 1 = (B_1 / B_0) / (P_1 / P_0) - 1 = (1+b)/(1+p) - 1$
$= (1+b)/(1+p) - (1+p)/(1+p) = [(1+b) - (1+p)]/(1+p) = (b-p)/(1+p)$.

[40] This follows from equation (14): $x = (b-p)/(1+p) = 0 \Leftrightarrow b - p = 0 \Leftrightarrow b = p$.

[41] The 'general formulae' are taken from equation (3), (12), and (14). The cells result if the 'b' in the general formulae are substituted by the four scenarios, equations (15) to (18), given in the first column and discussed in the previous section.

[42] Since the whole calculation is based on growth rates we also use the growth rate of the price index for deflation: If z_{nom} denotes the growth rate of the nominal value of the parameter under consideration, z_{real} the respective growth rate in real terms, and i the growth rate of the deflationer $z_{real} = z_{nom} - i - i \cdot z_{nom}$ follows as the formula to use.

[43] Prognos (1995), 73 only refers to this deflator for very large periods of time (average inflation rates for 1992-2010 and for 2010 to 2040). However, more detailed data are given for private consumption in monetary *and* real terms. Using a modified version of equation (14) the growth rate of this price index (i) can therefore be calculated as $i = (z_{nom} - z_{real}) / (1 + z_{nom})$ with z_{nom} denoting

the growth rate of private consumption in nominal, and z_{real} the growth rate of private consumption in real terms. Since the growth rates are only rounded to the nearest tenth [Prognos (1995): O-21, O-30, U-21 and U30] we calculated them anew from the absolute figures [Prognos (1995): O-19, O-28, U-19 and U28].

[44] All figures have been calculated with SPSS-PC, version 4.0.1. For a better overview data in Table 7 only contain figures rounded to the nearest ten thousand.

[45] Since detailed contributions in former years are not given this share relates to the estimated figure in the year 2000 [Prognos (1995): U-74, U-83; O-74; O-83].

[46] The contributory income of the employed is equal to their gross labour earnings up to an income threshold (Beitragsbemessungsgrenze). This threshold is automatically adjusted with the growth rate of the average earnings in the preceeding two years (§ 55 sec. 2 SGB XI together with § 159 SGB VI). With a time lag of two years the growth rate of the income threshold therefore follows the growth rate of average earnings. Hence the latter can be used as a good estimator for the growth rate of average contributory income ($\bar{y}_e$) and is used in this way in Table 8.

[47] In nursing homes labour costs amount to more than 70%. However, LTCI will not cover costs for room and board and investment. Therefore, the share of labour costs of direct care costs is even higher approaching almost 100%.

[48] From this follows that neither profits nor losses are assumed. This is clearly what the LTCI is aiming at. So § 84 sec. 2 clause 3 and § 89 sec. 1 clause 3 SGB XI explicitly demand payments sufficient to cover the costs of any efficient working supplier, thus prohibiting both profits and losses.

[49] This assumption is sharper than the respective statement by Baumol/Oates, but nevertheless seems to be quite reasonable. To the contrary, newly introduced quality controls might even lead to a higher staff ratio per service.

[50] In doing so we are a bit pessimistic about productivity gains which are assumed to be zero and quite optimistic about wage development in the care industry not exceeding average. All in all we probably underestimate rather than overestimate the dynamics of price-development for care goods and services.

[51] In scenario 2 benefits are adjusted with the growth rate of the total contributory income (y). In this interpretation Prognos adjusts benefits with the contributory income of all employees y_e. As Table 8 shows both growth rates are closely correlated.

[52] Since we assume that $p = \bar{y}_e$ scenario 3 and the Prognos assumption fall together.

[53] According to Prognos (1995), O-83, U-83 the contribution rate will even decline until 2000 and only reach 1.7% by 2010. Since Prognos also assumes a growing number of frail persons and an adjustment path depending on economic growth it is difficult to see how they reach this result.

[54] Original calculations have actually been based on a 50-50 utilisation rate concerning cash and in-kind benefits. This was shifted towards the 80-20-relation when during the legislative process the amount of benefits was increased and calculations should show this increase to be possible with a given contribution rate.

[55] Figures in brackets have been estimated in order to fit to the ones given.

References

Alber, J. (1990): Pflegebedürftigkeit im Spiegel der öffentlichen Meinung. Ergebnisse einer repräsentativen Umfrage des Jahres 1989, in *Sozialer Fortschritt 39*, 211-216.

Allemeyer, J. (1994): Die Pflegeversicherung. Eine Analyse der Leistungsstrukturen und ihrer Auswirkungen auf die Pflegebedürftigen, in *Altenpflege 2*, 315-320.

Baumol, W. J. (1967): Macroeconomics of Unbalanced Growth: The Anatomy of Urban Crisis, in *American Economic Review 57*, 415-426.

Baumol, W. J./Oates, W. E. (1972): The Cost Disease of the Personal Services and the Quality of Life, in *Skandinaviska Enskilda Banken Quarterly Review 2*, 44-54.

Boese, J./Heuser, M. R.(1986): Pflegeversicherung – ein Konzept zur Lösung der Versorgungsprobleme im geriatrischen Sektor, in *Sozialer Fortschritt 35*, 155-159.

Bretz, M. (1986): Bevölkerungsvorausberechnungen: Statistische Grundlagen und Probleme, in *Wirtschaft und Statistik 66*, 233-260.

Bundesinstitut für Bevölkerungsforschung (1993): *Die Alten der Zukunft – Bevölkerungsstatistische Datenanalyse*. Forschungsbericht im Auftrag des Bundesministeriums für Familie und Senioren. Wiesbaden: Eigenverlag.

Cambois, E./Robine, J.-M. (1996): An International Comparison of Trends in Disability-Free Life Expectancy. *In this volume*.

Deutscher Bundestag (1993): *Gesetzentwurf der Fraktionen der CDU/CSU und der F.D.P.- Entwurf eines Gesetzes zur sozialen Absicherung des Risikos der Pflegebedürftigkeit (Pflegeversicherungsgesetz-PflegeVG)*. Bundestagsdrucksache 12/5262, Bonn.

Dinkel, R. H. (1993): Die Pflegeversicherung: Ein finanzieller Sprengsatz für die Zukunft? in *Sozialer Fortschritt 42*, 39-42.

Engels, W. (1991): Editorial, in *Wirtschafts-Woche, Nr. 42* vom 11.10.1991.

Fachinger, U./Rothgang, H. (1995): *Die Wirkungen des Pflege-Versicherungsgesetzes auf die personelle Einkommensverteilung. Eine Modellanalyse auf der Basis des Pflege-Versicherungsgesetzes*. ZeS-Arbeitspapier Nr. 6/95, Bremen: Zentrum für Sozialpolitik.

Fachinger, U./Rothgang, H./Schneekloth, U. (1995): Resümee und Ausblick, in U. Fachinger/H. Rothgang (eds.): *Die Wirkungen des Pflege-Versicherungsgesetzes*. Berlin: Duncker & Humblot. S. 297-320.

Felderer B. (1992): *Die langfristige Entwicklung einer gesetzlichen Pflegeversicherung. Ökonomische und demographische Perspektiven für die Bundesrepublik Deutschland*. München: Bayerische Rückversicherung.

Götting, U./Haug, K./Hinrichs, K. (1995): The Long Road to Long-Term Care Insurance in Germany: A Case Study in Welfare State Expansion, in *Journal of Public Policy 15*, 285-309.

Götting, U./Hinrichs, K. (1993): Probleme der politischen Kompromißbildung bei der gesetzlichen Absicherung des Pflegefallrisikos – Eine vorläufige Bilanz, in *Politische Vierteljahresschrift 34*, 47-71.

Grönert, J. (1981): Kostenschätzung statt politischer Diskussion? in *Sozialer Fortschritt 30*, 107-109.

Grönert, J. (1982): Die Lücke im System der sozialen Sicherung: Ungenügende Absicherung bei Pflegebedürftigkeit, in *Sozialer Fortschritt 31*, 186-188.

Halsig, N./Zimmermann, P. (1995): Die Situation der Hauptpflegeperson, in E. Olbricht/ A. Kruse/D. Roether/K. Pöhlmann/N. Halsig (eds.): *Möglichkeiten und Grenzen der selbständigen Lebensführung im Alter. Hilfe- und Pflegebedarf in Deutschland.* Endbericht. Manuskript.

Haug, K./Rothgang, H. (1994): Das Ringen um die Pflegeversicherung – ein vorläufiger sozialpolitischer Rückblick, in *Beiträge zum Recht der sozialen Dienste und Einrichtungen (Heft 24)*, Köln: Heymanns, 1-30.

Infratest Sozialforschung/Infratest Epidemiologie und Gesundheitsforschung (1992): *Hilfe- und Pflegebedarf in Deutschland.* Schnellbericht zur Repräsentativerhebung im Rahmen des Forschungsprojekts Möglichkeiten und Grenzen selbständiger Lebensführung im Auftrag des Bundesministeriums für Familie und Senioren. München: Eigenverlag.

Infratest Sozialforschung/Infratest Epidemiologie und Gesundheitsforschung (1993): *Hilfe- und Pflegebedarf in Deutschland.* Endbericht zur Repräsentativerhebung im Rahmen des Forschungsprojekts Möglichkeiten und Grenzen selbständiger Lebensführung im Auftrag des Bundesministeriums für Familie und Senioren München: Eigenverlag.

Jung, K. (1993a): Pflegeversicherung: Auf dem Weg zur fünften Säule der Sozialversicherung, in *Zeitschrift für Sozialhilfe und Sozialgesetzbuch 32*, 505-513.

Jung, K. (1993b): Pflegeversicherung: Auf dem Weg zur fünften Säule der Sozialversicherung, in *Zeitschrift für Sozialhilfe und Sozialgesetzbuch 32*, 618-632.

Jung, K. (1994): Durchgesetzt gegen alle Widerstände, in *Bundesarbeitsblatt 45*, 5-16.

Prognos (1995): *Perspektiven der gesetzlichen Rentenversicherung für Gesamtdeutschland vor dem Hintergrund veränderter politischer und ökonomischer Rahmenbedingungen für den Verband Deutscher Rentenversicherungsträger.* Basel: Prognos Eigendruck.

Krauthausen, H./Schmidt, M. (1994): Rentenrechtliche Situation von Pflegepersonen heute und morgen: Pflegezeitenregelung im Rentenreformgesetz 1992 und Verbesserungen durch das Pflege-Versicherungsgesetz, in *Deutsche Rentenversicherung 6*, 379-392.

Krug, W./Reh, G. (1992): *Pflegebdürftige in Heimen.* Statistische Erhebungen und Ergebnisse. Studie im Auftrag des Bundesministeriums für Familie und Senioren. Band 4 der Schriftenreihe des Bundesministeriums für Familie und Senioren, Stuttgart/ Berlin/Köln: W. Kohlhammer.

Mager, H.-C. (1995): Moral Hazard-Effekte in der (Sozialen) Pflegeversicherung? in U. Fachinger/H. Rothgang (eds.): *Die Auswirkungen des Pflege-Versicherungsgesetzes.* Berlin: Duncker & Humblot, 115-135.

Nöldecke, J. (1985): Wie wirkt sich eine Pflegeversicherung auf die häusliche, ambulante, teilstationäre und stationäre Pflege aus? in *Nachrichtendienst des Deutschen Vereins 65*, 6-10.
Oberender, P. (1986): Ökonomische Aspekte des Pflegefallrisikos – Eine ordnungpolitische Alternative, in W. Gitter/P. Oberender (eds.): *Pflegefallrisiko*. Bayreuth: P.C.O., 27-37.
Petersen, U. (1994): Die soziale Sicherung der Pflegeperson in der gesetzlichen Rentenversicherung, in *Die Angestelltenversicherung 41*, 260-267.
Petrich, C. (1994): Soziale Pflegeversicherung: Die Leistungsberechtigten, in *Bundesarbeitsblatt 45*, 21-24.
Pfaff, A. B. (1995): Häusliche Pflegebedürftige nach dem Pflege-Versicherungsgesetz: Kosten der ambulanten Pflegeleistungen. Auswirkungen der demographischen Entwicklung, in *Die Ortskrankenkasse 22*, 723-731.
Prognos/Dornier (1990): *Angebot und Bedarf an Krankenpflegepersonen bis zum Jahr 2010*. Vorstudie für den Bundesminister für Arbeit und Sozialordnung. (Gesundheitsforschung Band 188), Bonn: Der Bundesminister für Arbeit und Sozialordnung.
Rothgang, H. (1994): Die Einführung der Pflegeversicherung. Ist das Sozialversicherungsprinzip am Ende? in B. Riedmüller/T. Olk (eds.): *Grenzen des Sozialversicherungsstaates*. Leviathan Sonderband 14, 163-187.
Rothgang, H. (1996): Vom Bedarfs- zum Budgetprinzip? Die Einführung der Pflegeversicherung und ihre Rückwirkung auf die Gesetzliche Krankenversicherung, in L. Clausen (ed.): *Gesellschaften im Umbruch*. Verhandlungen des 27. Kongreß der Deutschen Gesellschaft für Soziologie in Halle an der Saale 1995. Frankfurt: Campus, 930-946.
Rückert, W. (1992): *Bevölkerungsentwicklung und Altenhilfe. Folgen der Bevölkerungsentwicklung für die Altenhilfe – von der Kaiserzeit über das Jahr 2000 hinaus*. Köln: Kuratorium Deutsche Altershilfe.
Ruf, T. (1992): Umlage- oder Kapitaldeckungsverfahren bei der Pflegeversicherung. Ökonomen melden sich zu Wort, in *Arbeit und Sozialpolitik 46*, 29-33.
Schmähl, W. (1989): Demographischer Wandel und Finanzierung der Gesetzlichen Krankenversicherung – Auswirkungen und Finanzierungsalternativen, in C. von Ferber et al. (eds.): *Die demographische Herausforderung: Das Gesundheitssystem angesichts einer veränderten Bevölkerungsstruktur*. Beiträge zur Gesundheitsökonomie Band 23, Gerlingen: Bleicher, 281-333.
Schmähl, W. (1992): *Zum Vergleich von Umlageverfahren und kapitalfundierten Verfahren zur Finanzierung einer Pflegeversicherung in der Bundesrepublik Deutschland*. Studie im Auftrag des Bundesministeriums für Familie und Senioren. Schriftenreihe des Bundesministeriums für Familie und Senioren Band 10, Stuttgart/Berlin/ Köln: Kohlhammer.
Schmähl, W. (1993a): Demographische Entwicklung und Pflegeausgaben. Anmerkungen zu einem Beitrag von Reiner Hans Dinkel, in *Sozialer Fortschritt 42*, 233-235.
Schmähl, W. (1993b): The 1992 Reform of Public Pensions in Germany: Main Elements and Some Effects, in *Journal of European Social Policy 1*, 39-51.

Schneekloth, U. (1995): *Möglichkeiten und Grenzen selbständiger Lebensführung in Einrichtungen – erste vorläufige Ergebnisse der Repräsentativerhebung*. Vortrag auf dem Symposium Möglichkeiten und Grenzen selbständiger Lebensführung in Einrichtungen des Bundesministeriums für Familie, Senioren, Frauen und Jugend am 24.3.1995 in Berlin.

Schulz-Nieswandt, F. (1989): Kritik der 'moral hazard'- und 'Sog'-Erwartungen bei Einführung einer Pflege-Sozialversicherung, in *Sozialer Fortschritt 38*, 181-184.

Schulz-Nieswandt, F. (1995): Löst die Pflegeversicherung einen Heimsogeffekt aus? in U. Fachinger/H. Rothgang (eds.): *Die Auswirkungen des Pflege-Versicherungsgesetzes*. Berlin: Duncker & Humblot, 103-114.

Sinha, M. (1993): Umsetzung des Pflegegesetzes. Zur Nutzung empirischer Analysen, in *Arbeit und Sozialpolitik 47*, 60-67.

Sommer, B. (1992): Entwicklung der Bevölkerung bis 2030, in *Wirtschaft und Statistik 72*, 217-222.

Sozialpolitische Umschau 290/93 and 291/3.

Wasem, J. (1986): *Sozialpolitische und ökonomische Analyse von Organisationsproblemen in der Gesundheitssicherung älterer Menschen*. Frankfurt a.M./Bern/New York: Peter Lang.

Wasem, J. (1995): Realisierung und Finanzierung verschiedener home care-Modelle, in *Zentralblatt für Hygiene und Umweltmedizin 197*, 95-110.

von Zameck, W. (1995): Zur Wahl zwischen Geld- und Sachleistungen: Der Einfluß der gesetzlichen Pflegeversicherung auf die Entwicklung des familialen Pflegepotentials und das Erwerbsverhalten von Frauen, in U. Fachinger/H. Rothgang (eds.): *Die Wirkungen des Pflege-Versicherungsgesetzes*. Berlin: Duncker & Humblot, 71-101.

PART FOUR:
THEORETICAL ISSUES AND POLICY RECOMMENDATIONS

11 LONG-TERM CARE INSURANCE AND TRUST SAVING IN A TWO-GENERATION MODEL

Peter Zweifel and Wolfram Strüwe

1 Introduction

In the process of demographic ageing, there is a new risk facing the population of industrialized countries: The risk of needing long-term care (LTC). For example, the number of individuals aged eighty and older (who are believed to be most exposed to this risk) is predicted to grow from 6.3 mn. (1992) to 17.7 mn. by the year 2040 in the U.S.A. and from 1.65 mn. (1991) to 2.3 mn. by the year 2030 in Germany, [see Eisen (1992) and Bundesministerium der Finanzen (1990)].

One response to the problem is to introduce compulsory LTC insurance, as recently decided by the German parliament. This solution has the severe drawback of imposing something for which there is no private demand. As argued by Pauly (1990), a parent's demand for LTC insurance is undermined by a moral hazard effect because the child may decide to reduce his caregiving in favor of care provided by third parties, the cost of which is lowered by compulsory LTC insurance tends to aggravate rather than relieve this problem.

Moreover, alternatives for financing LTC exist that are less susceptible to moral hazard effects. In particular, banks may provide for a trust saving contract tailored to the needs of individuals facing the risk of LTC, using their real property as collateral. Under a variant also known as reversed mortgage [Jacobs/Weissert (1986)], the homeowner is required pay back the major part of his mortgage such that the net value of his real property attains a minimum value. In the event that the LTC risk materializes, the bank obtains title of ownership of the real property. In return, the elderly person receives a contribution towards covering the cost of LTC, retaining the right to live in his home as long as he chooses. Through such a contract, the bank in fact assumes the risk of longevity very much like an insurer does [see e.g. Mayer/Simons (1994) for the different variants of reversed mortgage contracts].

Against this backdrop, the objective of this contribution is to examine and evaluate the relative merits of LTC insurance and trust saving as two instruments for meeting the risk of LTC, using a model of parent-child interaction.

The literature on parent-child interaction is characterized by a curious asymmetry. Typically, altruistic parents try to influence egoistic children, as e.g. in the model by Becker (1974). His "rotten kid theorem" posits that altruistic parents do not need to impose their will on their egoistic children because they can use transfer payments to induce the behavior they desire. However, in that model the child will never increase his wealth to the point of reducing total wealth jointly available to the two generations. It is this assumption that in fact limits the egoism on the part of the child and permits the parent to prevail. Bernheim et al. (1985) in their turn assume that the child values LTC activities positively at first but negatively beyond a value that the parent knows ex ante. Moreover they do not consider the possibility of LTC being provided by a third party, thus failing to recognize the incentive effects emanating from the different instruments used for financing LTC.

In this contribution, both parent and child are modeled as self-interested actors in a principal-agent setting. However, the parent as the principal is viewed as being unable to sanction shirking on the part of the child when the LTC risk materializes. The model serves to examine the question of whether moral hazard effects are indeed strong enough as to annihilate demand for private LTC insurance, as predicted by Pauly (1990)[1]. Moreover, it permits assessment of moral hazard effects in an alternative instrument such as trust saving for LTC[2].

The plan of this paper is as follows. The next section is devoted to expounding a two-generation model in which a parent has the option of buying LTC insurance or a trust saving contract in his attempt to deal with the financial risks of LTC. Both parent and child pursue their own interests differing only with respect to their position in the life cycle. In the third and fourth sections, the child's optimization problem is analyzed in order to determine the effects of the purchase of LTC insurance and trust saving by the parent on his behavior. The fifth section builds on these results to predict the parent's optimal decision with regard to LTC insurance and trust saving, anticipating the child's opportunistic response to the incentives created. The final section is devoted to a comparative evaluation of the two instruments for dealing with the financial risk of LTC.

2   The model

In most formulations of interaction between parent and child, child behavior is modeled differently from parental behavior. In particular, the parent is typically assumed to act in an altruistic manner when the interests of the child are involved. However, when it comes to decide about LTC, the parent deals with a mature offspring rather than a helpless baby, while the child may himself be a parent as well. These considerations call for a symmetric treatment of the two generations. One way to achieve this is to extend the model to cover three periods, in the guise of Hansson/Stuart (1989). During a previous period ($t = -1$), the current parent was affected by the grandparent's risk of LTC (see upper part of Figure 1). At that time, he had to take certain decisions with regard to LTC to be given to the grandparent, which however are considered irreversible at time $t = 0$, the period of interest. For one, the grandparent may have died already; moreover, dispositions made previously (such as referral to a home) can often be modified at exceedingly high cost only. To be sure, the parent's endowed wealth depends importantly on whether or not the grandparent's LTC risk materialized. However, the amount of wealth $\overline{W}^P$ will be considered predetermined at time $t = 0$ when the parent is about to make his decisions.

At $t = 0$ the parent has three decision variables at his disposal (see Table 1). Having terminated his working life, work hours are assumed to be zero. This leaves consumption (C^P), the amount of LTC insurance purchased (reflected by the premium R^P), and the amount of trust saving for financing LTC (B^P) to be decided upon.

LTC insurance provides for partial coverage of the net cost of LTC, which is the difference between H time units of institutional care and A_L^K time units contributed by the child, valued at price p. The part of this visible cost $(H - A_L^K)p$ falling on the parent is determined by a rate of coinsurance c, which in its turn depends negatively on the premium R^P.

Trust saving for LTC amounts to specifying an amount B^P that has to be paid in at $t = 0$ and will be returned at $t = 1$. Since all quantities of the model are in present value for simplicity, there is no (net) interest on this asset in the no-LTC case. In the event of LTC however, the bank takes over title of ownership of the real asset financed by B^P [the house with mortgage reduced by the amount of B^P in the case of the 'reversed mortgage' proposed by Jacobs/Weissert (1986)]. Being a specialized market maker, the bank faces lower transaction cost when selling the asset than would its owner. Competitive pressure will ensure that this advantage must be shared with the contract partner, causing the bank to offer a rate of return in excess of the risk-free rate of interest in the event that the LTC risk materializes. This excess rate of return on B^P is denoted by r (see upper part of Figure 1 and Table 1).

At $t = 1$, the parent may be in need of LTC or continue healthy to the end of his life. In the first event, his utility depends on the amount of care received from his child A_L^K and final wealth W_L^P [3]. Consumption is considered unimportant in this situation, its cost being simply subsumed in pH, the gross cost of LTC provided by third parties. By assumption, the LTC policy stipulates premium payments both at $t = 0$ and $t = 1$, causing R^P to be paid two times[4].

With probability $(1 - \pi)$, the parent does not need LTC, causing his utility of the period to depend on consumption C_N^P along with final wealth W_N^P. Final wealth again is the balance of initial wealth $\overline{W}^P$, consumption in the two periods (C^P, C_N^P), premium payments R^P, with trust savings B^P netting out.

The lower part of Figure 1 shows the optimization problem of the child. In fact, at $t = 0$ the child is in the same situation as his parent at time $t = -1$, who had to determine the amount of LTC and to plan final wealth. By giving care, the child sacrifices time available for work, which is thus given by $(T - A_L^K)$; on the other hand, he may count on receiving a higher bequest W_L^P. In principle, the child's planning horizon should extend beyond $t = 2$; however, for simplicity, it is assumed that (as in the case of the parent at the time) only the decision concerning A_L^K has to be made, whereas the decisions with regard to consumption in a later phase of active life, the purchase of LTC insurance, and the accumulation of trust banking assets are deferred to a later period.

In the event of the parent needing LTC, the utility function of the child comprises consumption C^K, LTC provided A_L^K, and final wealth W_L^K. While consumption and wealth are considered to be normal goods ($\partial U_L^K / \partial C^K > 0$, $\partial U_L^K / \partial W_L^K > 0$), the sign of $\partial U_L^K / \partial A_L^K$ remains open. It will turn out that the implications of the model do not depend on this sign, which adds to its generality. Optimization proceeds under the wealth constraint stating that savings out of labor income plus inherited wealth W_L^P make up disposable wealth of the child W_L^K. On the one hand, a greater amount of LTC activity requires working time to be reduced, causing labor income and hence disposable wealth to be smaller, ceteris paribus (see Figure 1 again). On the other hand, the child can count on a larger bequest W_L^P if he contributes to LTC, which serves to add to disposable wealth.

Finally, in the event that the parent's LTC risk does not materialize no LTC has to be provided, causing the labor income of the child to be larger. Moreover, the child receives bequest W_N^P.

Conclusion 1: LTC activity may be modeled using a principal-agent representation of the relationship between child and parent without assuming anything but self-interest on both sides. In particular, caring activity on the part of the child need not be defined as a good or a bad; rather, it is characterized by its impact on consumption and final wealth.

3 Optimization by the Child

In keeping with the sequence of decisions shown in Figure 1, the child first fixes consumption, i. e. a certain standard of living for the rest of his working life. It is only later, at the time when the LTC risk materializes, that the decision with regard to LTC will be made. Given that the consumption decision is made under risk, the optimization problem reads, assuming maximization of expected utility,

$$\max_{C^K} \quad EU^K = p U_L^K(A_L^K, C^K, W_L^K) + (1-\pi) U_N^K(C^K, W_N^K) \tag{1}$$

with first-order condition

$$\frac{\partial EU^K}{\partial C^K} = 0 = \pi \left[\frac{\partial U_L^K}{\partial C^K} + \frac{\partial U_L^K}{\partial W_L^K} \frac{\partial W_L^K}{\partial C^K} \right] + (1-\pi) \left[\frac{\partial U_N^K}{\partial C^K} + \frac{\partial U_N^K}{\partial W_N^K} \frac{\partial W_N^K}{\partial C^K} \right] \tag{2}$$

$$= \pi \left[\frac{\partial U_L^K}{\partial C^K} - \frac{\partial U_L^K}{\partial W_L^K} \right] + (1-\pi) \left[\frac{\partial U_N^K}{\partial C^K} - \frac{\partial U_N^K}{\partial W_N^K} \right]$$

in view of the wealth constraints shown in Figure 1 and detailed in equations (A.1) and (A.3) of Appendix A.

At time $t = 1$, consumption is therefore predetermined, leaving only the extent of LTC provided (A_L^K) as a decision variable. The necessary condition for an optimum takes into account that also A_L^K has an indirect impact on the child's utility through its effect on final wealth [see Figure 1 and equation (A.1) again]:

$$\frac{dU_L^K}{dA_L^K} = \frac{\partial U_L^K}{\partial A_L^K} + \frac{\partial U_L^K}{\partial W_L^K}\left[\frac{\partial W_L^K}{\partial A_L^K} + \frac{\partial W_L^K}{\partial W_L^P}\frac{\partial W_L^P}{\partial A_L^K}\right] \qquad (3)$$

$$= \underbrace{\frac{\partial U_L^K}{\partial A_L^K}}_{(+/-)} - \underbrace{\frac{\partial U_L^K}{\partial W_L^K}}_{(+)} \cdot \underbrace{[w - c(R^P)p]}_{(+/-)} = 0$$

In the following, it is assumed that $w \neq cp$, implying that the marginal opportunity cost of providing LTC differs from its marginal return in the guise of cost sharing avoided. Since LTC insurance is contracted by the parent and not the child, this inequality will be the rule rather than the exception. Moreover, even in the well-developed market for private health insurance, policies tend to be rather standardized with regard to the rate of coinsurance. The amount of product differentiation is likely to be even less in a market for LTC insurance which is about to develop, implying that the equality $w = cp$ will be satisfied only in exceptional cases.

The solutions to equation (3) may be characterized as follows. If $w < cp$, the child earns a rather low wage rate on the labor market, causing him to have an interest in providing LTC. Should caregiving be positively valued regardless of its extent, ($\partial U_L^K / \partial A_L^K > 0$ for all values of A_L^K), expression (3) has a positive value, precluding an interior solution. Thus, complete specialization in LTC is predicted in this case ($A_L^K = T$). If on the other hand caregiving is a bad or becomes one with increasing value of A_L^K ($\partial U_L^K / \partial A_L^K < 0$), condition (3) has an interior solution ($0 < A_L^K < T$). In the case $w > cp$, the reverse result obtains: In combination with $\partial U_L^K / \partial A_L^K < 0$, the extreme solution $A_L^K = 0$ follows, while in combination with $\partial U_L^K / \partial A_L^K > 0$, an interior solution $0 < A_L^K < T$ is possible. Evidently, it is by leaving the sign of $\partial U_L^K / \partial A_L^K$ open that the solution set is not restricted to corner solutions. Conversely, focusing on interior solutions in the following is justified because it means refraining from imposing a restriction on the sign of $\partial U_L^K / \partial A_L^K$, and thus adding to the generality of the analysis.

4 Comparative Statics of Child Behavior

4.1 Response to Parent's Purchase of LTC Insurance

This subsection is devoted to the analysis of the child's response to the purchase of (additional) LTC insurance by his parent. The predicted response is of great importance to the parent, who values care given by his child in the event that he should have to rely on LTC (see section 5 below).

The purchase of LTC insurance serves to disturb the optimality conditions of the child, who will adjust his decision variables A_L^K and C^K in a way as to neutralize the impacts of this disturbance. In keeping with the argument advanced at the end of the previous section, comparative static analysis will be confined to the neighborhood of an interior solution for A_L^K, where the sign of $\partial U_L^K / \partial A_L^K$ may be left undetermined. In view of condition (3) adjustment of A_L^K to a change dR^P must satisfy

$$\frac{\partial^2 U_L^K}{(\partial A_L^K)^2} dA_L^K + \frac{\partial^2 U_L^K}{\partial A_L^K \partial R^P} dR^P = 0 \tag{4}$$

$$\frac{dA_L^K}{dR^P} = - \frac{\partial^2 U_L^K / \partial A_L^K \partial R^P}{\partial^2 U_L^K / (\partial A_L^K)^2}.$$

Since the denominator of equation (4) must be negative for a maximum, dA_L^K / dR^P has the same sign as $\partial^2 U_L^K / \partial A_L^K \partial R^P$. Using equation (3), one obtains

$$\frac{\partial^2 U_L^K}{\partial A_L^K \partial R^P} = \frac{\partial}{\partial R^P}\left[\frac{\partial U_L^K}{\partial A_L^K}\right] - \frac{\partial}{\partial R^P}\left[\frac{\partial U_L^K}{\partial W_L^K}[w - c(R^P)p]\right] \tag{5}$$

$$= \frac{\partial^2 U_L^K}{\partial A_L^K \partial W_L^K} \frac{\partial W_L^K}{\partial W_L^P} \frac{\partial W_L^P}{\partial R^P} - \frac{\partial^2 U_L^K}{(\partial W_L^K)^2} \frac{\partial W_L^K}{\partial W_L^P} \frac{\partial W_L^P}{\partial R^P}[w - cp] - \frac{\partial U_L^K}{\partial W_L^K}\left[-\frac{\partial c}{\partial R^P} \cdot p\right]$$

$$= \frac{\partial^2 U_L^K}{\partial A_L^K \partial W_L^K} \cdot \underbrace{\left[-\frac{\partial c}{\partial R^P}(H - A_L^K)p - 2\right]}_{(+)}$$
$$\underset{(-)}{(-)}$$

$$-\underset{(-)}{\frac{\partial^2 U_L^K}{(\partial W_L^K)^2}} \underbrace{\left[-\frac{\partial c}{\partial R^P}(H - A_L^K)p - 2\right]}_{(+)} \underset{(+/-)}{[w - cp]} + \underset{(+)}{\frac{\partial U_L^K}{\partial W_L^K}} \underbrace{\left[\frac{\partial c}{\partial R^P} p\right]}_{(-)}$$

$$< 0 \quad \text{if } \pi < \pi_0 \quad \text{and} \quad w < cp$$

$$\gtrless 0 \quad \text{if } \pi < \pi_0 \quad \text{and} \quad w > cp$$

The negative sign of the first term can be justified with reference to a more general model of household production [Becker (1965)]. While additional final wealth W_L^K entails greater utility, its marginal utility declines when time for utilization of this wealth becomes scarce due to time spent on LTC.

The sign of the expression in the bracket is positive as long as the probability π of occurrence of LTC does not exceed a certain limit value π_0. Generally, the relationship between additional benefits (X) and additional premium (R^P) is given by $dX/dR^P = 1/\pi$ if the premium is marginally fair, implying $dX/dR^P > 1$ because of $0 \leq \pi \leq 1$. Especially in the case of LTC insurance, however, the insurer will charge a loading g for administrative expenses and risk, causing the relationship between benefits and premium to become $dX/dR^P = 1/\pi(1+g)$ [5]. Therefore, if π exceeds the limit value $\pi_0 = 1/(1+g)$, the insured will obtain less than a dollar's worth of benefits for his premium. It is under these circumstances that the bracketed expression of equation (5) would be negative. Since a policy that offers less than the premium in exchange for benefits will not find a market, the case $\pi > \pi_0$ will not be pursued further.

Therefore, equations (4) and (5) together imply

$$\frac{dA_L^K}{dR^P} < 0 \quad \text{if } w < cp \quad (6)$$

$$\gtrless 0 \quad \text{if } w > cp.$$

Conclusion 2: The child's predicted response to LTC insurance purchased by the parent depends importantly on the wage rate that the child earns or could earn on the labor market. If this wage rate is below the net price of LTC provided by a third party (after deduction of insurance benefits), improved coverage against the risk of LTC causes the amount of his own caregiving to decrease. If however this wage rate exceeds the net price of LTC, additional coverage has an ambigous impact.

Intuitively, this conclusion hinges on the fact that the child can afford to reduce his own caring activity thanks to increased LTC insurance coverage, being less constrained to spare his wealth by giving care himself. This holds true quite independently of whether the child likes or dislikes giving care. In the process of adjustment, the marginal utility of wealth decreases; this effect may possibly cause the child to provide more care, but only if this has greater influence on his final wealth than does the change of LTC insurance coverage, i.e. only if the attainable wage rate exceeds the net money price of care.

For future use, the sign of dC^K / dR^P is also established. In analogy to equation (4), it corresponds to that of $\partial^2 EU / \partial C^K \partial R^P$, which is given by

$$\frac{\partial^2 EU^K}{\partial C^K \partial R^P} = \frac{\partial}{\partial R^P}\left[\pi\left(\frac{\partial U_L^K}{\partial C^K} - \frac{\partial U_L^K}{\partial W_L^K}\right) + (1-\pi)\left(\frac{\partial U_N^K}{\partial C^K} - \frac{\partial U_N^K}{\partial W_N^K}\right)\right]$$

$$= \pi\left[\frac{\partial^2 U_L^K}{\partial C^K \partial W_L^K}\frac{\partial W_L^K}{\partial W_L^P}\frac{\partial W_L^P}{\partial R^P} - \frac{\partial^2 U_L^K}{(\partial W_L^K)^2}\frac{\partial W_L^K}{\partial W_L^P}\frac{\partial W_L^P}{\partial R^P}\right]$$

$$+ (1-\pi)\left[\frac{\partial^2 U_N^K}{\partial C^K \partial W_N^K}\frac{\partial W_N^K}{\partial W_N^P}\frac{\partial W_N^P}{\partial R^P} - \frac{\partial^2 U_N^K}{(\partial W_N^K)^2}\frac{\partial W_N^K}{\partial W_N^P}\frac{\partial W_N^P}{\partial R^P}\right] \quad (7)$$

$$= \pi\underbrace{\left[\frac{\partial^2 U_L^K}{\partial C^K \partial W_L^K} - \frac{\partial^2 U_L^K}{(\partial W_L^K)^2}\right]}_{(+)}\underbrace{\left(\frac{-\partial c}{\partial R^P}(H - A_L^K)p - 2\right)}_{(-)}$$

$$- 2(1-\pi)\underbrace{\left[\frac{\partial^2 U_N^K}{\partial C^K \partial W_N^K} - \frac{\partial^2 U_N^K}{(\partial W_N^K)^2}\right]}_{(+)}.$$

< 0 if π small.

Since π must be small for LTC insurance to be economically viable [see the discussion below equation (5)], one is led to conclude

$$\frac{dC^K}{dR^P} < 0. \tag{8}$$

4.2 Response to Parent's Trust Saving for LTC

In full analogy to equation (4), the child's optimal reaction to trust saving for LTC by the parent is given by

$$\frac{dA_L^K}{dB^P} = -\frac{\partial^2 U_L^K / \partial A_L^K \partial B^P}{\partial^2 U_L^K / (\partial A_L^K)^2}. \tag{9}$$

Again, the sign of this expression hinges on the sign of the numerator, whose structure is similar to equation (5):

$$\frac{\partial^2 U_L^K}{\partial A_L^K \partial B^P} = \frac{\partial}{\partial B^P}\left[\frac{\partial U_L^K}{\partial A_L^K}\right] - \frac{\partial}{\partial B^P}\left[\frac{\partial U_L^K}{\partial W_L^K}[w - c(R^P)p]\right]$$

$$= \frac{\partial^2 U_L^K}{\partial A_L^K \partial W_L^K} \frac{\partial W_L^K}{\partial W_L^P} \frac{\partial W_L^P}{\partial B^P} - \frac{\partial^2 U_L^K}{(\partial W_L^K)^2} \frac{\partial W_L^K}{\partial W_L^P} \frac{\partial W_L^P}{\partial B^P}[w - cp] \tag{10}$$

$$= \underbrace{\frac{\partial^2 U_L^K}{\partial A_L^K \partial W_L^K}}_{(-)} \cdot r - \underbrace{\frac{\partial^2 U_L^K}{(\partial W_L^K)^2}}_{(-)} \underbrace{[w - cp]}_{(+/-)} \cdot r$$

$$< 0 \quad \text{if } w < cp$$
$$\gtrless 0 \quad \text{if } w > cp.$$

However, given $w < cp$, the value of equation (10) is in all likelihood closer to zero than that of equation (5), since

$$r < -\frac{\partial c}{\partial R^P}(H - A_L^K)p - 2 = \frac{-\partial c / c}{\partial R^P}(H - A_L^K) \cdot cp - 2. \tag{11}$$

The left-hand side, being an interest rate differential, may assume a value of 0.02 (say). With the annual net cost of LTC amounting to some $(H - A_L^K)cp = 20$ (in thousands of USD), the reduction of coinsurance purchased for 1 (thousand) USD worth of annual premium would have to be less than roughly 0.1 or 10 percent, such as from c = 0.30 to c = 0.27 to violate inequality (11). However, even in health insurance with its much higher probability of loss, 1,000 USD of annual premiums is associated with a more marked reduction of coinsurance rates. Given inequality (11), the sum of the first two terms of equation (10) is closer to zero than their counterparts of equation (5) if amounting to a negative quantity. Moreover, equation (10) lacks a negative term present in equation (5). If w > cp, the ambiguity of equations (5) and (10) precludes a ranking of the two values. Thus, one obtains

$$\frac{dA_L^K}{dB^P} < 0 \quad \text{but} \quad \frac{dA_L^K}{dR^P} \gtrless 0 \quad \text{if } w < cp \tag{12}$$

$$\gtrless 0 \quad \text{if } w > cp.$$

Conclusion 3: The child's predicted response to trust saving for LTC by the parent depends on his wage rate in the same way as in the case of LTC insurance (see Conclusion 2). However, it is less likely to be negative than in the case of LTC insurance in the sense that a lower value of the wage rate suffices to make it indeterminate.

For future reference, the sign of dC^K / dB^P also needs to be determined. In analogy to equation (9), it is identical with the sign of $\partial^2 EU_L^K / \partial C^K \partial B^P$,

$$\frac{\partial^2 EU^K}{\partial C^K \partial B^P} = \frac{\partial}{\partial B^P} \left\{ \pi \left[\frac{\partial U_L^K}{\partial C^K} - \frac{\partial U_L^K}{\partial W_L^K} \right] + (1-\pi) \left[\frac{\partial U_N^K}{\partial C^K} - \frac{\partial U_N^K}{\partial W_N^K} \right] \right\}$$

$$= \pi \left[\frac{\partial^2 U_L^K}{\partial C^K \partial W_L^K} \frac{\partial W_L^K}{\partial W_L^P} - \frac{\partial^2 U_L^K}{(\partial W_L^K)^2} \frac{\partial W_L^K}{\partial W_L^P} \right] \frac{\partial W_L^P}{\partial B^P}$$

$$+ (1-\pi) \left[\frac{\partial^2 U_N^K}{\partial C^K \partial W_N^K} \frac{\partial W_N^K}{\partial W_N^P} - \frac{\partial^2 U_N^K}{(\partial W_N^K)^2} \frac{\partial W_N^K}{\partial W_N^P} \right] \frac{\partial W_L^P}{\partial B^P}$$

$$= \pi \cdot \underbrace{\left[\frac{\partial^2 U_L^K}{\partial C^K \partial W_L^K} - \frac{\partial^2 U_L^K}{(\partial W_L^K)^2} \right]}_{(+)} \cdot r > 0, \quad \text{since} \quad \frac{\partial W_N^P}{\partial B^P} = 0. \tag{13}$$

Therefore,
$$\frac{dC^K}{dB^P} > 0. \qquad (14)$$

5 Optimization by the Parent

5.1 The Child as an Agent

The objective function of the parent is assumed to read

$$\max_{C^P, R^P, B^P, C_N^P} EU^P = U^P(C^P) + \pi U_L^P(A_L^K, W_L^P) + (1-\pi)U_N^P(C_N^P, W_N^P) \qquad (15)$$

The particularity of the parent's situation can be seen in that he cannot control the decisions of his child, symbolized by the child's choices $\{C^K, A_L^K\}$, at the time the LTC risk is about to materialize. For one, observability with regard to consumption C^K may frequently be lacking; moreover and more importantly, the cost of sanctioning the child for deviating with his caring activity A_L^K from the value deemed optimal by the parent may well be excessive for a parent in need of LTC. For these reasons, the parent is assumed to treat his child like an agent whose optimal decisions must be accepted as given. In order to ensure incentive compatibility, the child's necessary conditions for an optimum enter the parent's optimization problem in the guise of constraints [see equations (2) and (3)],

$$\frac{\partial U_L^K}{\partial A_L^K} - \frac{\partial U_L^K}{\partial W_L^K}[w - cp] = 0 \qquad (\lambda) \quad (16)$$

$$\pi\left[\frac{\partial U_L^K}{\partial C^K} - \frac{\partial U_L^K}{\partial W_L^K}\right] + (1-\pi)\left[\frac{\partial U_N^K}{\partial C^K} - \frac{\partial U_N^K}{\partial W_N^K}\right] = 0 \qquad (\mu) \quad (17)$$

$\left.\begin{array}{l}\\ \\ \\ \\ \end{array}\right\}$ incentive compatibility

Since the child may always renege on the implicit contract with the parent by breaking the family ties, which would be associated with expected utility $\overline{EU}^K$, the parent must also observe the following participation constraint:

$$\pi U_L^K(A_L^K, C^K, W_L^K) + (1-\pi)U_N^K(C^K, W_N^K) \geq \overline{EU}^K \qquad (\nu) \quad (18) \quad \text{participation constraint}$$

LTC INSURANCE AND TRUST SAVING

This constraint is entered as an equality in the Lagrangean representing the parent's optimization problem,

$$\max_{C^P, R^P, B^P, C_N^P} L = U^P(C^P) + \pi\, U_L^P(A_L^K, W_L^P) + (1-\pi)\, U_N^P(C_N^P, W_N^P)$$

$$-\lambda \left(\frac{\partial U_L^K}{\partial A_L^K} - \frac{\partial U_L^K}{\partial W_L^K}[w - cp] \right) \qquad (19)$$

$$-\mu \left(\left[\frac{\partial U_L^K}{\partial C^K} - \frac{\partial U_L^K}{\partial W_L^K} \right] + (1-\pi) \left[\frac{\partial U_N^K}{\partial C^K} - \frac{\partial U_N^K}{\partial W_N^K} \right] \right)$$

$$-\nu \left\{ \pi U_L^K(A_L^K, C^K, W_L^K) + (1-\pi) U_N^K(C^K, W_N^K) - \overline{EU}^K \right\}.$$

Out of the four decision variables, only two, LTC insurance and trust saving for LTC, shall be considered.

5.2 Optimal Purchase of LTC Insurance from the Parent's Point of View

When deciding about LTC insurance, the parent must take the child's likely responses into account, which in their turn modify his own expected utility as well as the incentive compatibility and participation constraints incorporated in equation (19). For this reason, the total differentials dA_L^K / dR^P and dC^K / dR^P are present in the differentiation of equation (19) w. r. t. R^P. Using the signs derived in appendix A, one has

$$\frac{\partial L}{\partial R^P} = \frac{\partial U^P}{\partial C^P} \underbrace{\left[\pi \frac{\partial C^P}{\partial R^P} \bigg|_L + (1-\pi) \frac{\partial C^P}{\partial R^P} \bigg|_N \right]}_{(+/-)} + \pi \cdot \underbrace{\left[\frac{\partial U_L^P}{\partial A_L^K} \frac{dA_L^K}{dR^P} + \frac{\partial U_L^P}{\partial W_L^P} \frac{\partial W_L^P}{\partial R^P} \right]}_{(+/-)}$$

$$+ (1-\pi) \cdot \underbrace{\left[\frac{\partial U_N^P}{\partial C_N^P} \frac{\partial C_N^P}{\partial R^P} + \frac{\partial U_N^P}{\partial W_N^P} \frac{\partial W_N^P}{\partial R^P} \right]}_{(-)} - \lambda \cdot \underbrace{\frac{\partial}{\partial R^P} \left[\frac{\partial U_L^K}{\partial A_L^K} - \frac{\partial U_L^K}{\partial W_L^K}[w - cp] \right]}_{(+/-)}$$

$$-\mu\pi \cdot \underbrace{\frac{\partial}{\partial R^P}\left[\frac{\partial U_L^K}{\partial C^K} - \frac{\partial U_L^K}{\partial W_L^K}\right]}_{(+)} - \mu(1-\pi) \cdot \underbrace{\frac{\partial}{\partial R^P}\left[\frac{\partial U_N^K}{\partial C^K} - \frac{\partial U_N^K}{\partial W_N^K}\right]}_{(-)} \quad (20)$$

$$-\nu\pi \cdot \underbrace{\left(\frac{\partial U_L^K}{\partial A_L^K}\frac{dA_L^K}{dR^P} + \frac{\partial U_L^K}{\partial C^K}\frac{dC^K}{dR^P} + \frac{\partial U_L^K}{\partial W_L^K}\frac{\partial W_L^K}{\partial W_L^P}\frac{\partial W_L^P}{\partial R^P}\right)}_{(+/-)}$$

$$-\nu(1-\pi) \cdot \underbrace{\left[\frac{\partial U_N^K}{\partial C^K}\frac{dC^K}{dR^P} + \frac{\partial U_N^K}{\partial W_N^K}\frac{\partial W_N^K}{\partial W_N^P}\frac{\partial W_N^P}{\partial R^P}\right]}_{(-)} \leq 0.$$

Since R^P must necessarily be nonnegative whereas the parent might prefer a negative value, it is appropriate to check for a negative value of condition (20). In this case, the corner solution $R^P* = 0$ prevails.

In discussing condition (20), terms in μ will be disregarded throughout. A violation of incentive compatibility with regard to the consumption of the child [condition (17)] does not have an immediate effect on the parent's welfare but only an indirect one by entailing an adjustment of caring activity A_L^K. This argument speaks in favor of a low value of μ.

The first three terms of condition (20) mirror the effect of purchasing LTC insurance on the parent himself. Given a marginally fair premium $(dX/dR^P = 1/\pi)$, a change in insurance coverage would have no wealth effect, causing the first term to be zero. If on the other hand LTC insurance had only a wealth effect $(dA_L^K/dR^P = 0)$, the sum of the second and third terms would have to be positive in the neighborhood of $R^P = 0$, since risk aversion implies $\partial U_L^P/\partial W_L^P > \partial U_N^P/\partial W_N^P$. However, this sum may turn negative for the single reason that the child reduces his caring activity [$dA_L^K/dR^P < 0$ if $w < cp$, see equation (6)].

In the case of a marginally unfair premium, the first term of condition (20) is already negative, and the sum of the second and third term tends towards a negative value as well. Evidently, if parents did not have to take the incentive compatibility and participation constraints imposed on them into account, many would refrain from purchasing LTC insurance ($R^P* = 0$).

However, there are additional influences emanating from the agency relationship (terms in λ, μ and ν). Their total effect is ambiguous, even if terms in μ (relating to incentive compatibility w.r.t. child's consumption) are disregarded. On the one hand, given that $w < cp$, the term in λ is positive [see (A.5) of Appendix A], indicating the parent's reduced dependence on incentive compatibility on the part of his child due to improved LTC insurance coverage. On the other hand, $w < cp$ induces the response $dA_L^K / dR^P < 0$. Now if LTC is bad for the child ($\partial U_L^K / \partial A_L^K < 0$), while the welfare of the parent strongly depends on keeping in touch with the child ($\nu > 0$), then the term in $\nu\pi$ may become so strongly negative as to render expression (20) negative and hence $R^P *$ optimal.

However, if the child can count on earning a high wage rate ($w > cp$), the sign of dA_L^K / dR^P is indeterminate, and the sum of the three first terms may assume a positive value, indicating personal interest of the parent in LTC insurance. In addition, the participation constraint (term in $\nu\pi$) need not militate against its purchase in this case, permitting an interior optimum with $\partial L / \partial R^P = 0$ and $R^P * > 0$.

Conclusion 4: If the child curtails his caring activity in response to the parent's purchase of LTC insurance (a response that has to be expected in case of a low wage rate) the purchase of LTC insurance would run counter to the parent's personal interest in many cases. If however the child can count on earning a high wage rate, LTC insurance may be in the parent's interest.

In order to obtain more definite results, the limiting cases ($\pi \to 0$, $\pi \to 1$) may be analyzed. However, $\pi \to 1$ would cause π to exceed the limiting value π_0 which precludes the purchase of LTC insurance, as shown in the context of equation (5). Therefore, it remains to be seen whether with $\pi \to 0$, LTC insurance would be contracted. In this case, condition (20) reduces approximately to

$$\frac{\partial L}{\partial R^P} = \underbrace{\frac{\partial U^P}{\partial C^P} \frac{\partial C^P}{\partial R^P}\bigg|_N}_{(-)} + \underbrace{\left[\frac{\partial U_N^P}{\partial C_N^P} \frac{\partial C_N^P}{\partial R^P} + \frac{\partial U_N^P}{\partial W_N^P} \frac{\partial W_N^P}{\partial R^P}\right]}_{(-)}$$

$$- \lambda \cdot \underbrace{\frac{\partial}{\partial R^P}\left[\frac{\partial U_L^K}{\partial A_L^K} - \frac{\partial U_L^K}{\partial W_L^K}[w-cp]\right]}_{(+/-)} - \mu \cdot \underbrace{\frac{\partial}{\partial R^P}\left[\frac{\partial U_N^K}{\partial C^K} - \frac{\partial U_N^K}{\partial W_N^K}\right]}_{(-)} \quad (21)$$

$$-v \cdot \underbrace{\left[\frac{\partial U_N^K}{\partial C^K} \frac{dC^K}{dR^P} + \frac{\partial U_N^K}{\partial W_N^K} \frac{\partial W_N^P}{\partial R^P} \right]}_{(-)}.$$

For a parent constituting a good risk, the direct effect of LTC insurance indicated by the leading two terms) is negative, calling for $R^{P*} = 0$. A positive value of R^{P*} would be a possibility if [given $w < cp$, see equation (5)] incentive compatibility is very decisive ($\lambda > 0$) or if the participation constraint is crucial ($v > 0$).

Conclusion 5: For a parent constituting a good risk, the purchase of LTC insurance would run counter his personal interest. However he may decide otherwise in view of the necessity to respect the incentive compatibility and participation constraints imposed by the child.

5.3 Optimal Trust Saving from the Parent's Point of View

Differentiating the objective function given in (19) w.r.t. B^P this time and using the sign restrictions derived in appendix B, one has

$$\frac{\partial L}{\partial B^P} = \frac{\partial U^P}{\partial C^P} \underbrace{\left[\pi \frac{\partial C^P}{\partial B^P} \bigg|_L + (1-\pi) \frac{\partial C^P}{\partial B^P} \bigg|_N \right]}_{(+) \quad (=0)} + \pi \cdot \underbrace{\left[\frac{\partial U_L^P}{\partial A_L^K} \frac{dA_L^K}{dB^P} + \frac{\partial U_L^P}{\partial W_L^P} \frac{\partial W_L^P}{\partial B^P} \right]}_{(+/-)}$$

$$+ (1-\pi) \cdot \underbrace{\left[\frac{\partial U_N^P}{\partial C_N^P} \frac{\partial C_N^P}{\partial B^P} + \frac{\partial U_N^P}{\partial W_N^P} \frac{\partial W_N^P}{\partial B^P} \right]}_{(=0)} - \lambda \cdot \underbrace{\frac{\partial}{\partial B^P} \left[\frac{\partial U_L^K}{\partial A_L^K} - \frac{\partial U_L^K}{\partial W_L^K} [w - cp] \right]}_{(+/-)}$$

$$- \mu\pi \cdot \underbrace{\frac{\partial}{\partial B^P} \left[\frac{\partial U_L^K}{\partial C^K} - \frac{\partial U_L^K}{\partial W_L^K} \right]}_{(+)} - \mu(1-\pi) \cdot \underbrace{\frac{\partial}{\partial B^P} \left[\frac{\partial U_N^K}{\partial C^K} - \frac{\partial U_N^K}{\partial W_N^K} \right]}_{(=0)} \quad (22)$$

$$- v\pi \cdot \underbrace{\left[\frac{\partial U_L^K}{\partial A_L^K} \frac{dA_L^K}{dB^P} + \frac{\partial U_L^K}{\partial C^K} \frac{dC^K}{dB^P} + \frac{\partial U_L^K}{\partial W_L^K} \frac{\partial W_L^K}{\partial W_L^P} \frac{\partial W_L^P}{\partial B^P} \right]}_{(+/-)}$$

$$-v(1-\pi) \cdot \left[\underbrace{\frac{\partial U_N^K}{\partial C^K} \frac{dC^K}{dB^P}}_{(+)} + \underbrace{\frac{\partial U_N^K}{\partial W_N^K} \frac{\partial W_N^K}{\partial W_N^P} \frac{\partial W_N^P}{\partial B^P}}_{(=0)} \right] \leq 0.$$

In view of the similarity with condition (20), it is clear that many a parent will refrain from trust saving for LTC as well. At the same time, the set of parameter values resulting in a negative sum of the first three terms is smaller here than in the case of LTC because the first term of condition (22) is always positive; moreover, dA_L^K / dB^P has a smaller absolute value if negative ($w < cp$) in the second term (in π) than dA_L^K / dR^P in (20). In fact, the excess rate of return r may even be high enough as to compensate the negative effect of [see equation (B.1) of appendix B].

The comparison with condition (20) leads to ambiguous results with regard to the participation constraint. While the smaller value of dA_L^K / dB^P (given $w < cp$) serves to weaken its adverse effect in comparison with the corresponding term in $v\pi$ of condition (20), the child's consumption response dC^K / dB^P [which is unambiguously positive rather than negative, see equations (14) and (8)], reinforces it.

Conclusion 6: Providing for LTC through trust saving tends to be more in the parent's personal interest than the purchase of LTC insurance. However, the participation constraint imposed by the child may nevertheless annihilate private demand for trust saving for LTC.

Finally, the limiting case $\pi \to 0$ needs to be considered. Condition (22) then reduces to

$$\frac{\partial L}{\partial B^P} = -\lambda \cdot \frac{\partial}{\partial B^P} \underbrace{\left[\frac{\partial U_L^K}{\partial A_L^K} - \frac{\partial U_L^K}{\partial W_L^K} [w - cp] \right]}_{(+/-)} - v \left[\underbrace{\frac{\partial U_N^K}{\partial C^K}}_{(+)} \underbrace{\frac{dC^K}{dB^P}}_{(+)} \right] \quad (23)$$

For a parent constituting a good risk, the direct effect of trust saving for LTC becomes identically zero, indicating neutrality at $B^{P*} = 0$. A positive value of B^{P*} would be a possibility if [given $w < cp$, see equation (10)] incentive compatibility is very decisive ($\lambda > 0$) while the participation constraint is of little importance (v small).

Conclusion 7: For a parent constituting a good risk, trust saving for LTC does not affect his personal interest. He may decide in favor of this instrument however if incentive compatibility considerations outweigh participation considerations with regard to his child.

6 Comparative Evaluation and Conclusions

These concluding remarks are based on a model that does not posit altruism between generations. When deciding about providing for his long-term care (LTC) risk, the parent nevertheless cannot regard his own interests in the narrow sense but has to take the likely responses on the part of the child into account. In particular, buying LTC insurance often is not in the parent's personal interest because it is exactly in the case of the child having a comparatively low wage rate ($w < cp$), a situation basically encourageing caregiving, that he has to count on a reduction of LTC activity on the part of the child (see Table 2). The moral hazard effect discussed by Pauly (1990) thus strikes precisely where its impact is greatest. As long as most care is given by daughters that are not in the labor market, this likely response undermines a parent's possible interest in LTC insurance in many cases. Pressure to purchase LTC insurance seems to originate mainly from the necessity of keeping generational relationships compatible with the child's pursuing his own objectives as a self-interested agent.[6]

The moral hazard effects of trust saving are less pronounced and may even be neutralized by its positive wealth effect. Still, the need to make the child participate can be of overriding importance, causing parent's interest in an instrument of the 'reversed mortgage' type to vanish as well [as documented empirically by e.g. Venti/Wise (1991) or Mayer/Simons (1994)]. Generally, the agency role of the child serves to reinforce the parent's interest in trust saving only under rather restrictive conditions. In particular, the parent's welfare must not depend strongly on the participation decisions of his child (see Table 2 again).

In sum, trust saving for LTC seems to be less affected by problems of the moral hazard type than is LTC insurance because it gives less incentives to those who have traditionally provided much of informal caregiving to diminish their efforts. The additional question that should be addressed in the future is whether possibly a combined use of both instruments might serve to avoid their drawbacks while profiting from possible synergies.

Appendix A

In this appendix, the signs entered in condition (20) are justified. Optimization w.r.t. R^P proceeds given conditional budget constraints. With probability π, the restriction holds (see Figure 1)

$$C^P = \overline{W}^P - R^P - B^P - c(R^P) \cdot (H - A_L^K)p - R^P + (1+r)B^P - W_L^P, \quad (A.1)$$

implying

$$\left.\frac{\partial C^P}{\partial R^P}\right|_L = \frac{\partial W_L^P}{\partial R^P} = \left[-\frac{\partial c(R^P)}{\partial R^P}(H - A_L^K)p - 2\right] > 0, \text{ if } \pi < \pi_0. \quad (A.2)$$

This sign of expression (A.2) follows from the discussion below equation (5). With probability $(1-\pi)$, the wealth constraint states

$$C^P = \overline{W}^P - R^P - B^P - C_N^P - R^P + B^P - W_N^P, \quad (A.3)$$

implying

$$\left.\frac{\partial C^P}{\partial R^P}\right|_N = \frac{\partial W_N^P}{\partial R^P} = -2 < 0. \quad (A.4)$$

This means that the sign of the first term in condition (20) is uncertain. The sign of the second term (in π derives from (A.2) and depends on (6) in the text. The sign of the third term [in $(1-\pi)$] follows from (A.3) and (A.4). The sign of the fourth term depends on [w - cp], as shown in equation (5):

$$\lambda \frac{\partial}{\partial R^P}\left[\frac{\partial U_L^K}{\partial A_L^K} - \frac{\partial U_L^K}{\partial W_L^K}[w-cp]\right] \begin{array}{l} < 0 \text{ if } w < cp \\ \gtrless 0 \text{ if } w > cp \end{array} \quad (A.5)$$

The fifth term (in $\mu\pi$) of condition (20) refers again to the situation where LTC risk materializes. It corresponds to the first term of equation (7):

$$\mu\pi \frac{\partial}{\partial R^P}\left[\frac{\partial U_L^K}{\partial C^K} - \frac{\partial U_L^K}{\partial W_L^K}\right]$$

$$= \mu\pi \underbrace{\left[\frac{\partial^2 U_L^K}{\partial C^K \partial W_L^K} - \frac{\partial^2 U_L^K}{(\partial W_L^K)^2}\right]}_{(+)} \cdot \underbrace{\left[-\frac{\partial c}{\partial R^P}(H - A_L^K)p - 2\right]}_{(+)} > 0. \quad (A.6)$$

Moreover, the sixth term can be signed using the analogy to the second term of equation (7),

$$\mu(1-\pi)\frac{\partial}{\partial R^P}\left[\frac{\partial U_N^K}{\partial C^K} - \frac{\partial U_N^K}{\partial W_N^K}\right]$$

$$= \mu(1-\pi)(-2)\cdot\underbrace{\left[\frac{\partial^2 U_N^K}{\partial C^K \partial W_N^K} - \frac{\partial^2 U_N^K}{(\partial W_N^K)^2}\right]}_{(+)} < 0. \tag{A.7}$$

With regard to the seventh term of (20), one obtains from (6) and (7) in the text as well as (A.2):

$$\nu\pi\left[\frac{\partial U_L^K}{\partial A_L^K}\frac{dA_L^K}{dR^P} + \frac{\partial U_L^K}{\partial C^K}\frac{dC^K}{dR^P} + \frac{\partial U_L^K}{\partial W_L^K}\frac{\partial W_L^P}{\partial R^P}\right] \gtrless 0. \tag{A.8}$$
$$\quad\;\;(+/-)\;(+/-)\quad\;\;(+)\;\;(-)\quad\;\;(+)\;\;(+)$$

With probability $(1-\pi)$, the parent does not need LTC, and the eighth and final term of condition (20) reads due, to (7) and (A.4)

$$\nu(1-\pi)\left[\frac{\partial U_N^K}{\partial C^K}\frac{dC^K}{dR^P} + \frac{\partial U_N^K}{\partial W_N^K}\frac{\partial W_N^P}{\partial R^P}\right] < 0. \tag{A.9}$$
$$\quad\quad\;\;(+)\quad(-)\quad\;\;(+)\quad(-)$$

Appendix B

This appendix is devoted to the derivation of the signs entered in condition (22). Optimization w.r.t. B^P proceeds with conditional budget constraints. With probability π, the restriction (A.1) holds (see also Figure 1). Thus,

$$\left.\frac{\partial C^P}{\partial B^P}\right|_L = \frac{\partial W_L^P}{\partial B^P} = -1 + (1+r) = r > 0. \tag{B.1}$$

With probability $(1-\pi)$, the wealth constraint (A.3) holds. Therefore,

LTC INSURANCE AND TRUST SAVING

$$\left.\frac{\partial C^P}{\partial B^P}\right|_N = \frac{\partial W_N^P}{\partial B^P} = -1 + 1 = 0. \tag{B.2}$$

This means that the sign of the first term of condition (22) is positive. The sign of the second term (in π) derives from (B.1) and (12) in the text. The zero value of the third term [in $(1-\pi)$] is the consequence of (B.2). The sign of the fourth term (in λ) depends on $[w-cp]$, as shown in equation (10):

$$\lambda \cdot \frac{\partial}{\partial B^P}\left[\frac{\partial U_L^K}{\partial A_L^K} - \frac{\partial U_L^K}{\partial W_L^K}[w-cp]\right] \quad \begin{array}{l} < 0 \text{ if } w < cp \\ \gtrless 0 \text{ if } w > cp \end{array} \tag{B.3}$$

The fifth term of condition (22) refers again to the situation where LTC risk materializes. It corresponds to the first term of equation (13):

$$\mu\pi \cdot \frac{\partial}{\partial B^P}\left[\frac{\partial U_L^K}{\partial C^K} - \frac{\partial U_L^K}{\partial W_L^K}\right] = \mu\pi \cdot \underbrace{\left[\frac{\partial^2 U_L^K}{\partial C^K \partial W_L^K} - \frac{\partial^2 U_L^K}{(\partial W_L^K)^2}\right]}_{(+)} \cdot r > 0. \tag{B.4}$$

Moreover, the sixth term can be signed using the analogy to the second term of equation (13),

$$\mu(1-\pi)\frac{\partial}{\partial B^P}\left[\frac{\partial U_N^K}{\partial C^K} - \frac{\partial U_N^K}{\partial W_N^K}\right] = 0. \tag{B.5}$$

With regard to the seventh term of (22), one obtains from (12) and (13) in the text as well as (B.1),

$$\pi\left[\underbrace{\frac{\partial U_L^K}{\partial A_L^K}}_{(+/-)}\underbrace{\frac{dA_L^K}{dB^P}}_{(+/-)} + \underbrace{\frac{\partial U_L^K}{\partial C^K}}_{(+)}\underbrace{\frac{dC^K}{dB^P}}_{(+)} + \underbrace{\frac{\partial U_L^K}{\partial W_L^K}}_{(+)}\underbrace{\frac{\partial W_L^P}{\partial B^P}}_{(+)}\right] \gtrless 0. \tag{B.6}$$

With probability $(1-\pi)$, the parent does not need LTC, and the eighth and final term of condition (22) reads, due to (13) and (B.2),

$$v(1-\pi)\left[\underbrace{\frac{\partial U_N^K}{\partial C^K}}_{(+)}\underbrace{\frac{dC^K}{dB^P}}_{(+)} + \underbrace{\frac{\partial U_N^K}{\partial W_N^K}}_{(+)}\underbrace{\frac{\partial W_N^P}{\partial B^P}}_{(=0)}\right] > 0. \tag{B.7}$$

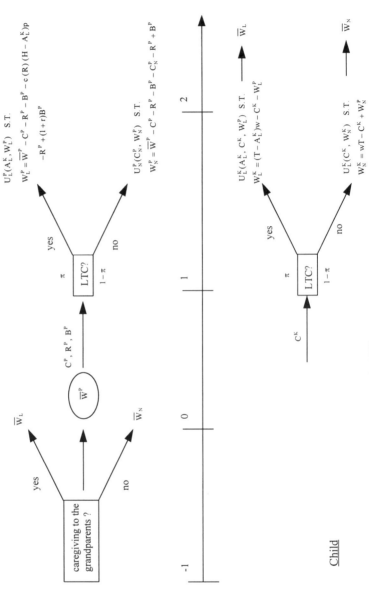

Figure 1: Interactions between generations in LTC

LTC INSURANCE AND TRUST SAVING

Table 1: List of Variables in the Model

Decision variables:

A_L^K	: Care given by the child (in time units)
B^P	: Trust saving through a bank with $r > 0$
C^K	: Child's consumption
C^P	: Parent's consumption during the time without LTC risk (not examined)
C_N^P	: Consumption of the parent in the normal state without LTC (not examined)
R^P	: Premium for LTC insurance

Exogenous variables:

g	: Loading for administrative cost and risk of the insurer
H	: Time used for LTC
p	: Price of LTC provided by a third party (per time unit)
r	: excess rate of return on trust saving
T	: Total time available to the child
w	: wage rate of the child (per time unit)
$\overline{W}^P$	: Initial wealth of the parent
π	: Probability of LTC risk materializing

Derived decision variables:

$c(R^P)$	: Rate of coinsurance of the parent in the case of LTC (c' < 0)
W_L^K	: Final wealth of the child in the case of LTC
W_N^K	: Final wealth of the child in the case of no LTC
W_L^P	: Final wealth of the parent in the case of LTC
W_N^P	: Final wealth of the parent in the case of no LTC

Table 2: Overview of results

	Personal interest of parent				Interest due to the agency relationship		
	Given generally?	Reinforcement/ attenuation by the child's response (dA_L^K)?	Limiting case $\pi \to 0$		General case	Limiting case $\pi \to 0$	General conditions for use of the instrument $(R^{P*} > 0, B^{P*} > 0)$
Instrument used to deal with LTC risk							
LTC insurance	no (Conclusion 4)	(additional) attenuation, if $w < cp$ uncertain, if $w > cp$ (Conclusion 2)	negative (Conclusion 5)		uncertain (Conclusion 4)	conditionally positive (Conclusion 5)	strong dependency of the parent on the decision taken by the child
Trust saving for LTC	conditionally yes (Conclusion 6)	attenuation less likely than with LTC insurance (Conclusion 3)	neutral (Conclusion 7)		uncertain (Conclusion 6)	conditionally positive (Conclusion 7)	considerable autonomy on the part of the parent

Notes

1 Demand for private LTC insurance is also undermined by the existence of public welfare, as pointed out by Buchholz/Wiegard (1992). This problem is not considered here for simplicity.

2 Distributional issues are entirely abstracted from. The reader interested in them is referred to Breyer (1991).

3 The inclusion of final wealth in the parent's utility function is not meant to reflect an (altruistic) bequest motive but the uncertainty about time of death (which however is not modeled formally here).

4 Alternatively, payment of premium could be waived in the event of loss. This would cause π_0, the probability of LTC at which the premium of the policy exceeds benefits, to be lower [see equation (5)].

5 See Friedmann/Warshawsky (1990) for the consequences of such loadings.

6 For a more detailed discussion of the pros and cons of compulsory Long-Term Care insurance, see Zweifel/Strüwe (1994).

References

Becker, G. S. (1965): A Theory of the Allocation of Time, in *Economic Journal 75*, 493-517.
Becker, G. S. (1974): Theory of Social Interactions, in *Journal of Political Economy 82*, 1063-1093.
Bernheim, B./Shleifer, A./Summers, L. (1985): The Strategic Bequest Motive, in *Journal of Political Economy 93*, 1045-1076.
Breyer, F. (1991): Verteilungswirkungen unterschiedlicher Formen der Pflegevorsorge (Distributional Impacts of Alternative Forms of Provision for Long-term Care), in *Finanzarchiv N.F. 49*, 84-103.
Buchholz, W./Wiegard, W. (1992): Allokative Ueberlegungen zur Reform der Pflegevorsorge (Allocative Considerations Concerning the Reform of Provision for Long-term Care), in *Jahrbücher für Nationalökonomie und Statistik 209*, 441-457.
Bundesministerium der Finanzen (1990) (ed.): *Stellungnahme des Wissenschaftlichen Beirates beim Bundesministerium der Finanzen zur Finanzierung von Pflegekosten* (Report of the Scientific Advisory Body to the Federal Ministry of Finance Concerning the Financing of Long-Term Care Costs). Bonn.
Eisen, R. (1992): Alternative Sicherungsmöglichkeiten bei Pflegebedürftigkeit, (Alternatives for Dealing with Long-Term Care Risk), in *Sozialer Fortschritt 41*, 236-241.
Friedman, B. M./Warshawsky, M.J. (1990): The Cost of Annuities: Implications for Saving Behavior and Bequests, in *Quarterly Journal of Economics 105*, 135-154.
Hansson, I. /Stuart, Ch. (1989): Social Security as Trade Among Living Generations, in *American Economic Review 79*, 1182-1195.
Jacobs, B./Weissert, W.G. (1986): Catastrophic Costs of Long-Term Care, in *Journal of Policy Analysis and Management 5*, 378-383.

Mayer, C.J./Simons, K.V. (1994): Reverse Mortgages and the Liquidity of Housing Wealth, in *Journal of the American Real Estate and Urban Economics Association 22*, 235-255.

Pauly, M. V. (1990): The Rational Nonpurchase of Long-Term-Care Insurance, in *Journal of Political Economy 95*, 153-168.

Richter, W. F. (1993): *Bequeathing Like a Principal*, Discussion Paper of the University of Dortmund, Nr. 93-01.

Venti, S.F./Wise, B.A. (1991): Ageing and the Income Value of Housing Wealth, in *Journal of Public Economics 44*, 371-397.

Zweifel, P./Strüwe, W. (1994): Pflegeleistung und Pflegeversicherung in einem Zwei-Generationen-Modell (Long-term Care Services and Insurance in a Two-Generation Model), in *Finanzarchiv N.F. 51*, 28-48.

12 LONG-TERM CARE – AN INTER- AND INTRAGENERATIONAL DECISION MODEL

Roland Eisen and Hans-Christian Mager

1 Introduction: Prospects and Problems

Two observations make it worthwhile to understand how family decisions are made concerning care for an elderly parent. First, we see, over the last generation, a trend from having children care for an elderly parent to having the elderly parent live alone or live in an institution such as a nursing home. Second, more and more governments are concerned by the rising costs of public assistance programs especially designed to pay for the elderly and disabled elderly. This is partly due to the rising costs in institutionalized care; therefore, more and more elderly – including the wealthy – cannot afford to pay or have spent down their wealth, and become dependent on welfare. In Germany, two thirds of all disabled persons (receiving long-term care) living in nursing homes receive services (or payments) after an income test.[1]

In the near future, this pattern is expected to change for the worse. First, because the changing age structure of most (industrialized) countries lead one to expect a growing demand for services for long-term care (see Figure 1).

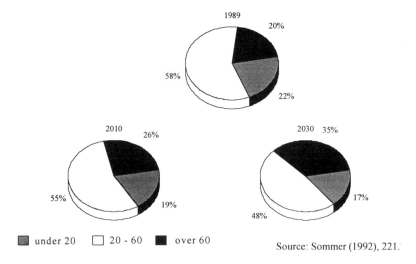

Figure 1: Age structure of German population in percentage 1989, 2010 and 2030

Second, because the supply of home or informal care will diminish. There are two reasons for the latter expectation: (1), there are smaller families, i.e. less children who can take care of their parents; (2), the labor force participation rate of women is growing, so that daughters or daughters-in-law are no longer willing or able to provide their parents with care. Presently, three fourths of all long-term care receivers get care privatly in their home from their daughters or daughters-in-law.[2]

These trends in turn, increase the burden because the transition from home or informal long-term care to institutionalized care raise costs. As a result, there are significant social and financial implications associated with these trends and projections. The sociological literature has extensively examined which factors affect the family decision underlying these trends.[3] However, there is little work on this subject in the economic literature besides the mere descriptions of the problem (see Figure 2).

It is obvious that most of the factors taken into account to explain the household decisions relating to care are themselves results of economic decisions of the past. "In particular, while it is reasonable to assume that greater geographic distance[4] and the labor force participation of a child[5] will reduce the probability of the child caring for a parent, it is unreasonable to assume that these two characteristics are exogenous. A child who intends to care for a parent may move

LTC – AN INTER- AND INTRAGENERATIONAL DECISION MODEL

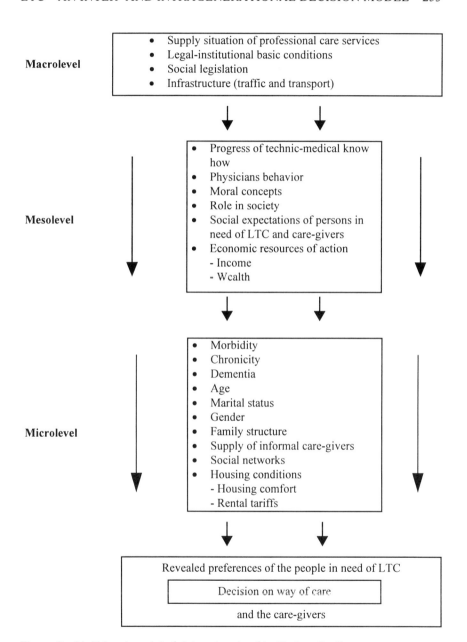

Figure 2: Multi-level model of determinants of institutionalization

closer to the parent or have the parent move closer to her, and she may leave her job (or take a part-time job) to care for the parent.[6] Thus, causality possibly runs both ways."[7]

A recent survey done by Infratest (1992) shows, e.g. that 20% of the persons in need of care live alone, 34% live in two-person and 22% in three-person households, whereas 24% live in households with four or more persons. These results strongly contradict the average household structure in Germany.[8] Hence, there are good reasons for assuming that the disabled elderly live in households that are hitherto not influenced by the processes of individualization and singularization.

One has, in particular, to take it a step further: The choice of living arrangements – as an independent household, with adult children or other related or unrelated persons, or in an institution – has many implications for the well-being of the elderly, and it is accompanied by many external effects. Living alone or living together with other family members makes a difference with regard to illness and long-term care. Thus, the choice of living arrangements – including the deliberate choice of whether to have own children – influences the decision regarding long-term care. Furthermore, living arrangements affect the eligibility of elderly persons for certain types of government assistance programs. They induce demand of certain social support services such as district nursing or meals-on-wheels etc..[9] Therefore, it is important to observe changes in living arrangements as well as to understand the determinants which make up decision on living arrangements. Thus, at least some of the family characteristics and characteristics of living arrangements depend on prior family decisions and must be treated as endogenous variables. The family decisions concerning care for the elderly must be viewed as a continuous process in the life cycle of the family.

To develop a model for this intricate and dynamic decision, two possibilities are in principal open: First, the problem can be incorporated into a principal-agent model where the parent(s) are the principal and the children the agents in the sense that the agents do things or expand efforts to serve both the principal's interest and their own. Second, a game-theoretic model can be constructed that considers the family as a "joint production unit" in which a conflict might exist on how the joint outcome is distributed.

The remainder of the essay is organized as follows: In section two, the family is defined as a "production unit". In the third section a principal-agent model of the family is discussed, but in families with more than one child, the decision between the children has to be described as a subgame. Hence, in the fourth section a game theoretic two-stage decision model is constructed. In the second stage the children decide which of them will care for the parent (or none), depending on the results of the first stage where the parents have decided upon their "living conditions". In the fifth section some comparative statics results are derived, especially with regard to insurance and costs of long-term care. Some remarks concerning future research conclude the essay.

2 Families and Households as Production and Insurance Units

Families or households[10] are regarded as exchange organizations where the members cooperate and produce (household) specific commodities, especially personal services. A basic characteristic of these personal commodities or services is that they cannot be acquired in external markets or aquired in the desired quality or only at high prices. A distinctive feature of families is the low (transaction) costs of the intrafamily welfare production.[11] The family as a "production unit" can exploit comparative economies in production by different members specializing in various activities: market work, home or care activities. Through joint consumption of non-divisible, household specific (club) goods as well as through increasing returns to scale, the family can realize efficiency gains. Another characteristic of the intra-household production process is that the produced personal services have material as well as immaterial characteristics. In a certain sense, there are joint production processes where several outputs are produced simultaneously: The value of the service "family care" stems not only from the direct utility of the physical care but there are also indirect benefits, e.g. affection, safety and so on. However, these benefits might also be examples of unseparable production.

Based on the above arguments, problems with activities of daily living (ADL) and/or instrumental activities of daily living (IADL) can be specified as losses in household productivity. Persons facing such problems have to counterbalance them. This may be done with the use of various strategies. The disabled person could try to support him or herself for instance through intensive and extensive use of adequate household technologies.[12] But if the household productivity remains on a critical low level, informal or formal care is of pressing necessity. Thus, care giving (by children) for those in need of care (parents) can be viewed as a specific service, that can be provided cheaper within the family for two reasons. First, there are internal restrictions in the sense of budget constraints or non-optimal demand for long-term care insurance in earlier periods. Second, there are also external restrictions in the sense of market supply restrictions caused by insufficient production capacity.

The affective relationship that characterizes a family plays a special role in that it can generate altruistic behavior necessary for the delivery of informal care. Under certain circumstances, families receive cooperation gains. The family is, in a certain sense, also an insurance community for the risk of (long-term) care.[13] To secure the needs in case of care by the family only implicit contracts are available. These implicit contracts differ in important respects from standard insurance contracts. First, there is no unique relationship between the delivered quantity of care and the compensation, and usually there are no contributions. However, in the German civil code there exists an obligation of maintenance (e.g. alimony) for family members. Second, the unexhausted wealth of parents due to family care can be seen – in the case of inheritance – as a "final" compensation. Family transfers *inter vivos* play a similar role. As in the case of normal insurance contracts, implicit contracts also are subject to the dangers of "free riding" and "moral hazard": If one child is caring for the parent, the other children are able to neglect their duties. Also, there is a strong incentive to breach the contract in the case of informal care: By breaching the explicit or implicit arrangements to deliver care, the offender can obtain unintended benefits. If Long-Term Care insurance existed, this tendency could be intensified.

3 The Family as a Principal-Agent Relationship

The starting point of most principal-agent-problems is the incentive compatibility of contracts. Usually, the task is finding a (linear) payment schedule, in our case consisting of a payment in case of care and a certain "inheritance" or legacy, to induce the child to give care level a if there is a "loss" D due to disability. The parent takes into account that her/his decision will influence the behavior of the child or the children. Assuming all children behaving identically we can proceed as if there were just one agent.

Usually, the problem is dealt with in two steps:[14] In the first step the decision of the child is formalized given a certain probability that the parent will become dependent or frail, and given a payment schedule. In the second step the decision of the parent is considered: One must find a (linear) division between paying the child inter vivos and/or through a bequest to induce it to provide care in the required (or desired) quantity and quality, given the child's incentive constraint and its reservation utility.

In a model with one "retirement period" (and, therefore, one expected "care period") the optimal payment schedule for the P-A-model reflects the trade-off between the inefficient, unobservable efforts taken by the child against the inefficient risk sharing. There is no "uncertainty" with regard to death and, therefore, there are no "unexpected bequests". It would be more appropriate to consider a model with more than one period, i.e. at least two retirement periods with different probabilities to become disabled. Then the optimal payment scheme also depends on time. Consider the case – as mentioned by Richter (1993) – that the cost of caring correlates positively across time: "With advancing time, the optimal payment schedule will put increasing weight on the risk component" (in our example: on the bequest part)! "If bequests and gifts inter vivos are interpreted as more and less uncertain payments, respectively, for services by the heir, then the view gains support that the observed prevalence of transfers at death results from the testator's objective to provide his (or her) heir with correct incentives"[15]

Admittedly, up until now, many decisions have not been considered, especially the decision to take out long-term care (LTC) insurance. As Mark Pauly has shown, it may not be in the interest of the parent(s) to aquire LTC insurance, because it is the heir "who would scoop the pool".[16] Furthermore, even if LTC insurance is purchased, full insurance of the expected costs is neither available nor efficient because of the inherent moral hazard. Therefore, the elderly person has to bear a certain (residual) risk, and self-insurance, through precautionary savings, is a plausible argument.[17] Given, the (conditional) probability of frailty is increasing with age, the necessity of self-insurance for elderly people is higher. However, the duration of care is shorter the later in life one is subject to the risk of long-term care, therefore, the "income equivalent loss" tends to diminish. As a result, the optimal time profile of "precautionary savings" is unclear a priori. Furthermore, as shown by Kimball (1990), given the possibility of insurance and "self-insurance", the result depends not only on the risk aversion coefficient but rather on the change of this coefficient or the "coefficient of prudence".

Other, more interesting problems not dealt with until now in the literature are that of many agents (or children) and that of specifying the way in which multiple agents (the children) choose their actions given their strategic interdependence. As formulated by Rees (1990), 87, "(...) the principal-agent model now contains a subgame to be played out among agents". Different possibilities exist to model this subgame: Either we assume that the chosen actions constitute a Nash equilibrium, i.e. each agent (child) chooses his optimal action treating all others' actions as given, or there is cooperative behavior among the children. Furthermore, the principal (the parent) can be "(...) seen as a kind of Stackelberg leader: he chooses the contract to maximize his utility given the reaction function of the agent as defined by his maximization condition".[18]

Myerson (1991) has generalized this as a *Bayesian game* model with incomplete information: Suppose there are n players, indexed i ∈ {1,..., n}, with A_i the set of possible actions for player i. Each player may be one of a number of possible 'types', t_i, and T_i is the set of all possible types i could be. A type i is a complete description of i's information and beliefs about anything relevant to the game. Each player also possesses a probability distribution on the set of possible types of each other player, where this distribution may also depend on his or her own type. Finally each player has a utility function that specifies a utility for each possible set of actions of all players, and each possible set of types of all players, including him or herself. A Bayesian game of incomplete information is then a specification of each players' decision set, type set, probability distribution or others' type sets, and utility function.

4 The Family Decision Concerning Long-Term Care: A Game-theoretic Analysis

4.1 Setting the Ground: Cooperative vs. Non-Cooperative Behavior

In a certain sense it seems inadequate to model the family decision process in terms of a household utility function with neo-classical properties. Even if we consider the household (family) as a community of individuals, combining their efforts to gain an extra rent through joint "production", this approach seems no longer appropriate. Different views may exist within the family regarding the distribution of the joint outcome or regarding the decision concerning care for an elderly parent. The questions are: which child cares for the parent? Should the parent stay alone or move to a nursing home when needed? Each of these decisions allocates costs and benefits in quite a different way between the family members. The literature is full of famous novels telling family stories of love and struggle. It seems, therefore, adequate (if not necessary) to proceed to game-theoretic bargaining models to analyze the intra-family decision processes.[19]

In these game-theoretic approaches, every family member maximizes his/her own individual utility, and they allow for modelling of both cooperative and non-cooperative behavior within the family. One might argue whether a cooperative solution concept is more plausible than a noncooperative concept, especially in this family decision context. Producing a surplus in the family normally requires communication and long-term contracts, and this is tantamount to cooperative behavior. Furthermore, noncooperative equilibrium points are in general

LTC – AN INTER- AND INTRAGENERATIONAL DECISION MODEL

not Pareto-optimal, and every member can gain by some agreement[20]. Cooperative games result in Pareto-optimal solutions where the internal allocation of goods and services is determined by the respective bargaining power of the family members. Nevertheless, it is true that this assumption does not hold for all cases and especially for the problem with which we are dealing. Many of the family related welfare gains depend on past investments. When there are differences in these investments, e.g. sunk costs, then a moral hazard or "hold up" problem may arise: all members of the family can derive greater profit by breach of contract. Despite the altruism within a family, the parents should be aware of not having the "last word" in this decision process and should therefore behave strategically.[21] To deal with this possibility, dynamic strategic cooperative models had to be developed. The modelling of family decisions as a dynamic strategic cooperative game makes it possible to analyze the endogenous changes of the possibility space and the distribution of the outcomes.

Before proceeding we want to fix the time structure and content of the decisions made. The decisions concerning long-term care for the elderly parents must be viewed as an ongoing process between different generations and within generations. To keep the model tractable we do not analyze all inter- and intragenerational decisions and their interconnectedness. Rather we take the following decision and time structure (see Figure 3): We take into account only the parent's decisions in point $t = 0$ concerning savings or wealth accumulation (as an approximation for the "living arrangements") and purchasing of LTC insurance. We disregard the decision of the children at this time, knowing that these decisions (e.g. relating to leaving the parents' home, marrying, having children, working or not) influence the children's decisions beyond $t = 1$.

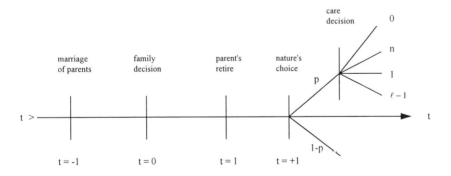

Figure 3: Time structure of family decision process

In order to take account of the possibility that parent(s) can act as a "strategic testator (testatrix)", and the children can "breach contracts" (i.e. the "generational contracts" in the sense of "I care for you when you're young, you care for me when I'm old"), we model the family decision in point $t = 1$ as a bargaining game. Here we stress two extremes: either the family cooperates ("large coalition") or else every member acts on his own. Formally, there are $1 + n$ members denoted by $k = 0, 1, ..., n$, where $k = 0$ represents the parent(s), and $k, j = 1, ..., n$, the n children, then

$$\mathcal{V}(n+1) = u_0 + ... + u_n \text{ and } u_k \geq \mathcal{V}(\{k\}) \text{ or}$$

$$u_k < \mathcal{V}(\{k\}) \quad \text{for } k = 1, ..., n$$

where $\mathcal{V}(\{k\})$ is the value of the singleton, $\mathcal{V}(n+1)$ the value of the "great coalition", and u_k the utility of the outcome.

For the model we use the idea of a cooperative game[22] where the intrafamily allocation of commodities and services is determined by the bargaining power of the players. The bargaining power in turn is determined by the individual utility levels in case of a conflict, i.e. external alternatives are of decisive importance. It seems adequate, therefore, to use the Nash solution concept that gives a family utility function based upon assumptions of rational negotiation.

The conflict point plays a crucial role in the bargaining process: First, it determines the outcomes in case of conflict, and second, according to the rules of the game, the distribution of the outcome between the "players". We have to abandon only the assumption of a fixed "conflict point". The conflict point cannot be treated as fixed and exogenously given for two reasons: First, there are changes in the environment that have consequences for the individual "status quo" outcomes, e.g. changes in public transfers or old-age care systems. Second, the conflict point depends on past family decisions because savings, insurance, labor force participation and other "living conditions" influence the conflict options.

LTC – AN INTER- AND INTRAGENERATIONAL DECISION MODEL

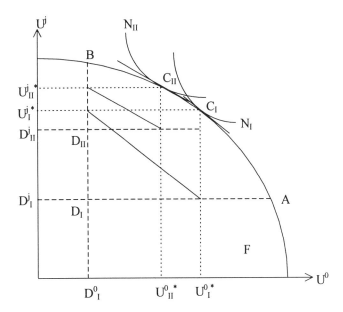

Agenda: U^0 and U^j are utility levels; F is the utility frontier or upper right boundary of the feasible set; if cooperative gains exist, the 'conflict point' D_I lies inside the utility frontier; the negotiation set is the part between A and B; C_I is the Nash solution for $N = \Pi\,(U^k - D^k) = $ const.; a change in the conflict point (to D_{II}) shows the change in the "marginal rate of utility transfer" within the family, which is equivalent to a change in the bargaining position.

Figure 4: Nash solution concept with two different conflict points

4.2 The Formal Model and First Results

It is assumed that the utility functions are intertemporarily additive:

$$U^k = U_1^k + U_2^k \qquad \text{for } k = 0,1..., n, \text{ and } t = 1,2 \text{ the two periods.}$$

Since changes in time discounts are not discussed, U_2^k can be interpreted as the discounted value of the utility of person k in period 2.

Given our time structure, the bargaining takes place in t = 2. Thus, the Nash solution is characterized by a division of the cooperative gain so that the product of the individual gains is maximized:

$$\max N = \Pi\,(U_2^k - D_2^k)^n \quad \text{for } k = 0,1,\ldots, n$$

$$\text{s.t. } (U_2^k) \in P,\ U_2^k \geq D_2^k$$

where P describes the payoff space, i.e. all feasible utilities, U_2^k the payoff (utility level) of individual k if an agreement is reached, and D_2^k is the conflict payoff of individual k (utility level of the outside option).

Therefore, the family or inter- and intragenerational decision process can be written as follows:

$$\max EU^0 = \max\,(U_1^0 + EU_2^0) \tag{1}$$

$$\max N = \max \Pi(U_2^k - D_2^k)^n \quad \text{for all } k = 0,1,\ldots, n, \tag{2}$$

subject to the following constraints:

$$W_1^0 = \overline{Y} + w_1^0 T_1^0 - pX_1^0 - MK - P(\alpha) \tag{a}$$

for the first period, and for the second period

$$W_N^0 = (W_1^0 + rW_1^0) - pX_2^0 - MK - P(\alpha) \tag{b}$$

when the parents are healthy, and

$$W_L^0 = (W_1^0 + rW_1^0) - pX_2^0 - P(\alpha) - \varepsilon MK - (1-\varepsilon)HK$$
$$- p_H\left[(1-a)H + \sum H^j\right] \quad \Rightarrow (\lambda_2^0) \tag{c}$$

when the parents are disabled, and need LTC services; where $\varepsilon = 1$ if the dwelling is adequate for a disabled person or $\varepsilon = 0$ if not; and for the children

$$W_N^j = Y^j + \frac{W_N^0}{n} - pX^j + \delta^j w^j M^j \tag{d}$$

$$W_L^j = Y^j + \frac{W_L^0}{n} - pX^j + \delta^j w^j M^j + p_H H^j \quad \Rightarrow (\lambda_2^j) \tag{e}$$

and the "production function" of care services

$$C = Z\left(\sum_j a^j H^j; H\right) \quad \Rightarrow (\mu) \tag{f}$$

where a^j is the "personal" productivity including "feelings"; and

$$U^k = U^k(W_L^k, C) \tag{g}$$

$$T^j = H^j + L^j + \delta^j M^j \quad \Rightarrow (v^j) \tag{h}$$

where $\quad \delta^j = 0$ for $j = 1, ..., \ell$ and $\delta^j = 1$ for $j = \ell+1, ..., n$

describing the possibilities of the children to work in the market[23], and the Conflict points[24]

$$D_2^k = \overline{U}^k(\overline{W}, C)$$

are given for the parents by:

$$\max U_2^0(\overline{W}, C)$$

s.t. $\overline{W} = (W_1^0 + r\, W_1^0) - P(\alpha) - pX_2^0 - \varepsilon MK - (1-\varepsilon) HK - (1-\alpha) p_H H$,

and $\quad\quad\quad\quad\quad\quad C = Z(H)$;

for the children by:

$$\max U^k(\overline{W}^j)$$

s.t. $\overline{W}^j = \delta^j w^j M^j + Y^j - pX^j$ and $T^j = L^j + \delta^j M^j$.

Notation: U = utility, W = wealth, Y = non-labor income, $P(\alpha)$ = premium for LTC insurance, α = coverage, pX = consumption expenditures, MK = rental cost of housing, HK = "hotel cost" of nursing homes, p_H = price of formal care, W_N^0/n or W_L^0/n = bequest of the children, a^j = "productivity" of child j in rendering services to the parents, T^j = time, H^j = hours of informal care, M^j = market labor hours, w^j = market wage, L^j = leisure, H = formal care delivered through the market.[25]

The Optimum Solutions in Period 2

We solve this model recursively. First, the maximization problem in period 2 is solved, taking into account that some of the variables are choice variables determined "strategically" in the first period (i.e. prior to "nature's choice").

Therefore, the following Lagrangian can be formed:

$$\mathcal{L}_2 = \prod_k (U_2^k - D_2^k)^\eta \qquad (3)$$

$$+ \lambda_2^0 \{W_1^0 + rW_1^0 - P(a) - pX_2^0 - \varepsilon MK - (1-\varepsilon)HK - p_H[(1-\alpha)H + \sum H^j] - W_L^0\}$$

$$+ \sum_j \lambda_2^j \left\{ Y^j + \frac{W_L^0}{n} - pX^j + p_H H^j + \delta^{\,j} w^j M^j - W_L^j \right\}$$

$$+ \mu \left\{ Z\left(\sum_j a^j H^j; H \right) - C \right\}$$

$$+ \sum_j \nu^j [T^j - H^j - \delta M^j - L^j]$$

$$+ \sum_j \sigma^j M^j + \sum_j \rho^j H^j .$$

The following first-order conditions can be derived:

$$\frac{\partial \mathcal{L}_2}{\partial W_L^0} = \sum_k \left[\eta (U^k - D^k)^{\eta-1} \frac{\partial U^k}{\partial W_L^0} \prod_{j \ne k}(U^j - D^j)^\eta \right] - \lambda_2^0 + \frac{1}{n}\sum_j \lambda_2^j = 0$$

$$= \eta \prod_j (U^k - D^k)^\eta \sum_k \frac{\partial U^k / \partial W_L^0}{(U^k - D^k)} - \lambda_2^0 + \frac{1}{n}\sum_j \lambda_2^j = 0$$

$$= \eta \prod_j (U^k - D^k)^\eta u*(W_L^0) - \lambda_2^0 + \frac{1}{n}\sum_j \lambda_2^j = 0$$

where
$$u*(W_L^0) = \sum_k \frac{\partial U^k / \partial W_L^0}{(U^k - D^k)}$$

$$\frac{\partial \mathcal{L}_2}{\partial W_L^j} = \sum_k \left[\eta (U^k - D^k)^{\eta-1} \frac{\partial U^k}{\partial W_L^j} \prod_{k \ne j}(U^j - D^j)^\eta \right] - \lambda_2^j = 0$$

$$= \eta \prod_k (U^k - D^k)^\eta u*(W_L^j) - \lambda_2^j = 0$$

where
$$u*(W_L^j) = \sum_k \frac{\partial U^k / \partial W_L^j}{(U^k - D^k)}$$

LTC – AN INTER- AND INTRAGENERATIONAL DECISION MODEL

$$\frac{\partial \mathcal{L}_2}{\partial C} = \sum_k \left[\eta (U^k - D^k)^{n-1} \frac{\partial U^k}{\partial C} \prod_{j \neq k}(U^j - D^j)^n \right] - \mu = 0$$

$$= \eta \prod_k (U^k - D^k)^n u^*(C) - \mu = 0$$

where
$$u^*(C) = \sum_k \frac{\partial U^k / \partial C}{(U^k - D^k)}$$

$$\frac{\partial \mathcal{L}_2}{\partial H} = -\lambda_2^0 p_H (1-\alpha) + \mu Z_H = 0$$

$$= \lambda_2^0 = \frac{\mu Z_H}{p_H(1-\alpha)} \quad \text{for} \quad \frac{\partial Z}{\partial H} = Z_H$$

$$\frac{\partial \mathcal{L}_2}{\partial L^j} = \eta \prod_k (U^k - D^k) u^*(L^j) - \upsilon^j = 0$$

(for all j, using a similar definition for $u^*(L^j)$)

$$\frac{\partial \mathcal{L}_2}{\partial H^j} = -\lambda_2^0 p_H + \lambda_2^j p_H + \mu Z_{\tilde{H}} a^j - v^j + \rho^j = 0$$

$$= \rho^j = v^j + p_H(\lambda_2^0 - \lambda_2^j) - \mu Z_{\tilde{H}} a^j, \text{ where } Z_{\tilde{H}} = \frac{\partial Z}{\partial \tilde{H}} \text{ with } \tilde{H} = \sum a^j H^j,$$

for all j,

$$\frac{\partial \mathcal{L}_2}{\partial M^j} = \lambda_2^j \delta w^j - v^j \delta + \sigma^j \delta = 0$$

for $\quad \delta^j = 0 \Rightarrow M^j = 0$

for $\quad \delta^j = 1 \Rightarrow \sigma^j = v^j - \lambda_2^j w^j$

and

$\partial \mathcal{L}_2 / \partial \lambda_2^0 = 0; \; \partial \mathcal{L}_2 / \partial \lambda_2^j = 0; \; \partial \mathcal{L}_2 / \partial \mu = 0; \; \partial \mathcal{L}_2 / \partial v^j = 0; \; \sigma^j M^j = 0; \; \rho^j H^j = 0.$

From these conditions the following relationship showing the "rate of substitution between leisure and care" results (see Appendix I):

$$\frac{\rho^j}{\eta\prod_{k}(U^k - D^k)^n u*(C)} + \frac{Z_H}{1-\alpha} + p_H \cdot \frac{u*(W_L^j)}{u*(C)} + Z_{\tilde{H}} a^j = \frac{u*(L^j)}{u*(C)} =$$

$$= w^j \frac{u*(W_L^j)}{u*(C)} + \frac{\sigma^j}{\eta\prod_{k}(U^k - D^k)^n u*(C)}. \quad (4)$$

Considering the family as a "production unit" producing a "club good"[26], the surplus is realized by efficient allocation of the members' time resources. For the optimal division of work then the following results must hold.

Result 1:

If any child j allocates time to the market as well as to the caring for parents, then

$$M^j > 0, H^j > 0 \Rightarrow \delta^j = 1, \sigma^j = 0, \rho^j = 0$$

$$\Rightarrow \frac{Z_H}{1-\alpha} + Z_{\tilde{H}} a^j = \frac{u*(L^j)}{u*(C)} = \frac{u*(W_L^j)}{u*(C)}(w^j - p_H).$$

In this case, the marginal product of an additional hour of care is equal to the marginal rate of substitution between leisure and "consumption of care" (as evaluated by the total family), and this is equal to the marginal return of work in the market and at home, deflated by the value of "consumption of care" •

At the beginning, we differentiated two types of children, those for whom $\delta^j = 0$, and those for whom $\delta^j = 1$, consequently $M^i = 0$ for $\delta^j = 0$ and $M^j > 0$ for $\delta^j = 1$. If we further assume, because of the former decision, it is true that $a^i > a^j$, i.e. those not working in the market are more "productive" in caring for the parents, and $w^j > p_H$, we derive:

Result 2:
Either

$$\frac{Z_H}{1-\alpha} + Z_{\tilde{H}} a^j < \frac{Z_H}{1-\alpha} + Z_{\tilde{H}} a^i = -p_H \frac{u*(W_L^j)}{u*(C)} < \frac{u*(W_L^j)}{u*(C)}(w^i - p_H)$$

or

$$\frac{Z_H}{1-\alpha} + Z_{\tilde{H}} a^j > \frac{Z_H}{1-\alpha} + Z_{\tilde{H}} a^i = \frac{u*(W_L^j)}{u*(C)}(w^j - p_H) > -p_H \frac{u*(W_L^j)}{u*(C)}.$$

LTC – AN INTER- AND INTRAGENERATIONAL DECISION MODEL

In both cases, i cares for the parents while j works in the market, but an exclusive specialization of j does not necessarily follow; whether j also cares, depends upon the "care technology", i.e. the "production function" of C •

If, on the contrary $a^j > a^i$, i.e. "the worker" is also more productive in caring, then we have

Result 3:

Depending on whether

$$\frac{p_H(u*(W_L^j)/u*(C))}{Z_{\tilde{H}}a^j} < \frac{(w^j - p_H)(u*(W_L^j)/u*(C))}{Z_{\tilde{H}}a^i}$$

or

$$\frac{p_{II}(u*(W_L^j)/u*(C))}{Z_{\tilde{H}}a^j} > \frac{(w^i - p_{II})(u*(W_L^j)/u*(C))}{Z_{\tilde{H}}a^i}$$

the child with the higher ratio works only in the market. But j spends time in both activities, if

$$\frac{(w^j - p_H)u*(W^j)/u*(C)}{Z_{\tilde{H}}a^j} > 1 \bullet$$

The Optimum Decision in Period 1

To solve the parents' problem of period 1, we introduce the indirect expected utility function $\tilde{V}^{0*}$ giving the maximum value of the second period subgame:

$$\max EU^0 = \max(U_1^0 + \tilde{V}^{0*}) \quad \text{with respect to } W_1^0, \alpha \quad (5)$$

$$\text{s.t. } W_1^0 = \bar{Y} - pX_1^0 + w_1^0 T_1^0 - P(\alpha)$$

where
$$\tilde{V}^{0*} = (1-\pi)U_2^0 + \pi U_2^{0*}(U^{j*}),$$

i.e. U_2^{0*} is a function of all the optimal values of the children U^{j*} resulting from the subgame in period 2, and U_2^0 is the discounted value.

From the Lagrangian

$$\mathcal{L}_1 = U_1^0(W_1^0) + \tilde{V}^{0*}(H^j, M^j, w^j, p_H, \alpha, W_L^0, W_L^j, W_N^0, W_N^j)$$
$$+ \lambda_1^0[\overline{Y} - pX_1^0 + w_1^0 T_1^0 - P(\alpha) - W_1^0]$$

the following first-order conditions result:

$$\frac{\partial \mathcal{L}_1}{\partial W_1^0} = \frac{\partial U_1^0}{\partial W_1^0} + (1-\pi)\frac{\partial U_2^0}{\partial W_1^0} + \pi \sum_j \frac{\partial U_2^{0*}}{\partial U^{j*}} \cdot \frac{\partial U^{j*}}{\partial W_1^0} - \lambda_1^0 = 0$$

$$\Rightarrow \lambda_1^0 = \frac{\partial U_1^0}{\partial W_1^0} + (1-\pi)\frac{\partial U_2^0}{\partial W_1^0} + \pi \upsilon^*(W_1^0)$$

where

$$\upsilon^*(W_1^0) = \sum_j \frac{\partial U_2^{0*}}{\partial U^{j*}} \cdot \frac{\partial U^{j*}}{\partial W_1^0}$$

$$\frac{\partial \mathcal{L}_1}{\partial \alpha} = \pi \sum_j \frac{\partial U_2^{0*}}{\partial U^{j*}} \cdot \frac{\partial U^{j*}}{\partial \alpha} - \lambda_1^0 \frac{\partial P}{\partial \alpha} = 0$$

$$\Rightarrow \pi \upsilon^*(\alpha) = \lambda_0^1 \cdot \frac{\partial P}{\partial \alpha}$$

where

$$\upsilon^*(\alpha) = \sum_j \frac{\partial U^{0*}}{\partial U^{j*}} \cdot \frac{\partial U^{j*}}{\partial \alpha}.$$

This last equation deserves one comment: Given the fact that most insurance premiums are marginally unfair, there is a maximum probability of frailty π_0 beyond which no rational individual would buy this insurance[27].

These first-order conditions are used to transform the total differential of problem (5):

$$dEU^0 = \frac{\partial U_1^0}{\partial W_1^0} dW_1^0 + dU_2^{0*} \quad \text{and}$$

$$dU_2^{0*} = (1-\pi) dU_2^0 + \pi \sum_j \frac{\partial U_2^{0*}}{\partial U^{j*}} dU^{j*}.$$

LTC – AN INTER- AND INTRAGENERATIONAL DECISION MODEL

Inserting the first-order condition for W_1^0 yields:

$$dEU^0 = \left[\lambda_1^0 - (1-\pi)\frac{\partial U_2^0}{\partial W_1^0} - \pi\upsilon^*(W_1^0)\right]dW_1^0 + (1-\pi)dU_2^0 + \pi\sum_j \frac{\partial U_2^{0*}}{\partial U^{j*}}\cdot dU^{j*}.$$

For the total differential of the Nash-function for the second period results:

$$dN = \eta\prod_k(U^k - D^k)^n \cdot \sum_{j\neq k}(U^k - D^k)^{-1}(dU_2^j - dD_2^j)$$

$$= \eta\frac{\prod(U^k - D^k)^n}{(U^k - D^k)}\left[\sum_{j\neq k}\frac{\partial U_2^j}{\partial W_L}dW_L + \sum\frac{\partial U_2^j}{\partial C}dC + \sum\frac{\partial U_2^j}{\partial L^j}dL^j - \sum dD_2^j\right].$$

Inserting the first-order conditions of problem (4) yields:

$$dN = \eta\prod(U^k - D^k)^n\left[u^*(W_L^j)dW_L + u^*(C)dC + u^*(L^j)dL^j \quad \sum_{j\neq k}\frac{dD_2^k}{(U^k - D^k)}\right]$$

or – after some manipulations –

$$= \frac{\eta\prod(U^k - D^k)^n}{(U^k - D^k)}\sum dU^k$$

$$= \prod(U^k - D^k)^n\left[u^*(W_L^j)dW_L + u^*(C)dC + u^*(L^j)dL^j\right] =$$

$$= \left(\lambda_2^0 + \sum\lambda_2^j\left(1-\frac{1}{n}\right)\right)dW_L + \mu dC$$

$$-(\rho^j - p_H(\lambda_2^0 - \lambda_2^j) + \mu Z_{\tilde{H}}a^j)dH^j - (\delta\sigma^j + \lambda_2^j\delta w^j)dM^j.$$

Using both parts, the total differential can be written as

$$dEU^0 = \left[\lambda_1^0 - (1-\pi)\frac{\partial U_2^0}{\partial W_1^0} - \pi\upsilon^*(W_1^0)\right]dW_1^0 + (1-\pi)dU_2^0$$

$$+\pi\left[\left(\lambda_2^0 + \sum\lambda_2^j\left(1-\frac{1}{n}\right)\right)dW_L + \mu dC - (\rho^j - p_H(\lambda_2^0 - \lambda_2^j) + \mu Z_{\tilde{H}}a^j)dH^j - (\delta\sigma^j + \lambda_2^j\delta w^j)dM^j\right]$$

where the difference to the "normal" situation is called forth by the bargaining effect.

4.3 Comparative Statics Analysis: Changes in wealth, wages, prices and insurance coverage

We are especially interested in the effects of changes of the following parameters on the previous results: wealth (W_1^0) of parents, price of formal care (p_H), wage rates of the children (w^j), and insurance coverage (α). In order to evaluate these changes, we use the total differential of problem (5), and analyze the "bargaining effect" as well as the "welfare effect", i.e. the change of the bargaining power and total utility resulting from these changes.

Wealth of Parent(s) (W_1^0)

The *bargaining effect* is given by the differentiation of the conflict points (see problem (1)) $D^k = U^k(...)$:

$$\max U^0(C, \overline{W}) \tag{6}$$

$$\text{s.t. } \overline{W} = W_1^0 + rW_1^0 - P(\alpha) - pX_2^0 - \varepsilon\, MK - (1-\varepsilon)HK - (1-\alpha)p_H \cdot H$$

and
$$C = Z(H).$$

The Lagrangian is now:

$$\mathcal{L} = U^0(C, \overline{W}) + \lambda_1[W_1^0 + rW_1^0 - P(\alpha) - pX_2^0 - \varepsilon MK - (1-\varepsilon)HK - (1-\alpha)p_H H]$$
$$+ \lambda_2[Z(H) - C]. \tag{7}$$

First-order conditions are:

$$\frac{\partial U^0}{\partial \overline{W}} = \lambda_1 \Rightarrow \overline{U}_W^0 = \lambda_1$$

$$\frac{\partial U^0}{\partial C} = \lambda_2 \Rightarrow \overline{U}_C^0 = \lambda_2.$$

Differentiation of the conflict function in the optimum with respect to $\overline{W}$ yields:

$$\frac{dD^0}{d\overline{W}} = \frac{\partial U^0}{\partial C} \cdot \frac{dC}{d\overline{W}} + \frac{\partial U^0}{\partial \overline{W}} \cdot d\overline{W}$$

$$\frac{dC}{d\overline{W}} = Z_H \cdot \frac{dH}{d\overline{W}}.$$

Using the first-order conditions, the marginal change in the conflict outcome results:

$$\frac{dD^0}{d\overline{W}} = \lambda_1 d\overline{W} + \lambda_2 Z_H \frac{dH}{d\overline{W}} > 0.$$

The conflict point of the children does not change.

Given this, the reaction of the cooperative outcome on a change of the conflict points is derived. The cooperative surplus will be divided according to the (marginal) rate of substitution, i.e.

$$\frac{\sum(U^j - D^j)}{(U^0 - D^0)} = -\sum_j \frac{\partial U^j}{\partial U^0}.$$

Therefore (see Appendix II),

$$\frac{dU^0}{dD^0} = \frac{1}{2 - \frac{(U^0 - D^0)^2}{\sum_j(U^j - D^j)} \sum_j \frac{d^2 U^j}{dU^{0\,2}}} < 1 \text{ and } > 0, \text{ and}$$

$$\frac{\sum dU^j}{dD^0} = \sum_j \frac{dU^j}{dU^0} \cdot \frac{dU^0}{dD^0} = \frac{\frac{\sum(U^j - D^j)}{(U^0 - D^0)}}{2 - \frac{(U^0 - D^0)^2}{\sum(U^j - D^j)} \cdot \sum_j \frac{d^2 U^j}{dU^{0\,2}}} < 0.$$

Therefore, the *bargaining effect* is:

$$\frac{dU^0}{d\overline{W}} = \frac{dU^0}{dD^0} \cdot \frac{dD^0}{d\overline{W}} = \left[\frac{1}{2 - \frac{(U^0 - D^0)^2}{\sum_j(U^j - D^j)} \cdot \sum_j \frac{d^2 U^j}{dU^{0\,2}}} \right] \cdot \left(\lambda_1 d\overline{W} + \lambda_2 Z_H \frac{dH}{d\overline{W}} \right).$$

The *welfare* or *wealth effect* is derived as follows:

$$\sum_k \frac{dU^k}{d\overline{W}}\bigg|_{D=\text{fix}} = \sum \frac{dU^k}{dN} \cdot \frac{dN}{d\overline{W}}\bigg|_{D=\text{fix}}$$

Fixed interfamily transfers result in:

$$T' = \frac{\prod(U^j - D^j)^\eta}{(U^0 - D^0)^\eta} = k \Rightarrow (U^0 - D^0)^\eta = \frac{\prod(U^j - D^j)^\eta}{k},$$

and therefore:

$$N = \prod(U^j - D^j) \cdot (U^0 - D^0) = \frac{2}{k}\prod_j(U^j - D^j)^\eta.$$

Differentiation, keeping D^j fixed, yields:

$$dN = \frac{2\eta}{k}\prod_j(U^j - D^j)^\eta \sum_j(U^j - D^j)^{-1} \cdot dU^j \quad \text{or}$$

$$\frac{k}{2\eta\prod_j(U^j - D^j)^\eta} = \sum_{j \neq k}(U^j - D^j)^{-1} \cdot \frac{dU^j}{dN} = \frac{1}{2\eta(U^0 - D^0)^\eta}.$$

Furthermore:

$$\left.\frac{dN}{d\overline{W}}\right|_{D=\text{fix}} = \eta\prod_k(U^k - D^k)^\eta \cdot \sum_{j \neq k}(U^j - D^j)^{-1} \cdot \frac{dU^j}{d\overline{W}} = (\lambda_2^0 - \frac{1}{n}\sum\lambda_2^j)$$

using the first-order condition of the Langrangian (3). Combining both equations yields the wealth effect of a change of parent's wealth:

$$\sum \frac{1}{(U^j - D^j)} \cdot \frac{dU^j}{dN} \cdot \frac{dN}{d\overline{W}} = (\lambda_2^0 - \frac{1}{n}\sum\lambda_2^j) \cdot \frac{1}{2\eta(U^0 - D^0)^\eta}$$

Therefore, we can formulate the following

Result 4:
Increased wealth strengthens the parents' bargaining position, and the wealth effect increases the demand for formal care (if this is a normal good) •

Change of the Price of Formal Care (p_H)

With similar reasoning we derive for a change of the price of formal care (see Appendix III):

$$\frac{dD^0}{dp_H} = \left\{\lambda_1 d\overline{W} + \lambda_2 Z_H \frac{dH}{d\overline{W}}\right\} H[\alpha\varepsilon - (1 - \alpha)].$$

LTC – AN INTER- AND INTRAGENERATIONAL DECISION MODEL

The *bargaining effect* is, therefore, given by:

$$\frac{dU^0}{dp_H} = \frac{dU^0}{dD^0} \cdot \frac{dD^0}{dp_H} =$$

$$\left[\frac{1}{2 - \frac{(U^0 - D^0)^2}{\sum(U^j - D^j)} \cdot \sum \frac{d^2 U^j}{dU^{02}}} \right] \left\{ \lambda_1 d\overline{W} + \lambda_2 Z_H \frac{dH}{d\overline{W}} \right\} H \left[\alpha \varepsilon - (1-\alpha) \right]$$

The *wealth effect* of a change of the price of formal care, is derived as before:

$$\sum(U^j - D^j)^{-1} \cdot \left. \frac{dU^k}{dp_H} \right|_{D=fix} = \sum(U^j - D^j)^{-1} \cdot \frac{dU^j}{dN} \cdot \left. \frac{dN}{dp_H} \right|_{D=fix}.$$

The first part is identical to the problem above; the second part yields:

$$\left. \frac{dN}{dp_H} \right|_{D=fix} = \eta \prod (U^k - D^k)^\eta \cdot \sum(U^j - D^j)^{-1} \cdot \frac{dU^j}{dC} \cdot \frac{dC}{dp_H}.$$

Using the appropriate first-order conditions of the Lagrangian (3) yields:

$$\left. \frac{dN}{dp_H} \right|_{D=fix} = \mu Z_H \cdot \frac{dH}{dp_H}.$$

Combining both parts, we arrive at:

$$\sum(U^j - D^j)^{-1} \cdot \left. \frac{dU^k}{dp_H} \right|_{D=fix} = \frac{1}{2\eta(U^0 - D^0)^\eta} \cdot \mu Z_H \frac{dH}{dp_H}.$$

Therefore we can formulate the following

Result 5:
An increase in the price of "formal care" decreases the bargaining power of the parents (because the last term is negative for $\alpha < 1$) and decreases the amount of formal care (because dH/dp_H is negative) •

Changes of the Wage Rates (w^j):

Changes in the wage rates w^j (in comparison to p_H) have the following effects:

$$\frac{dD^0}{dw^j} = \frac{dD^0}{dW^j}\frac{dW^j}{dw^j} \Rightarrow \frac{dD^0}{dw^j} = 0;$$

i.e. the conflict point of the parents does not change. But the conflict points of the children are changed:

$$\max U^j(\overline{W}^j, L^j)$$

s.t. $\overline{W}^j = \delta^j w^j M^j + Y^j - pX^j$ and $T^j = L^j + \delta^j M^j$.

Forming the Lagrangian

$$\mathcal{L}^j = U^j(...) - \lambda\,(\delta^j w^j M^j + Y^j - pX^j - \overline{W}^j) - \mu\,(L^j + \delta^j M^j - T^j)$$

the following first-order conditions hold:

$$\frac{\partial \mathcal{L}^j}{\partial \overline{W}^j} = \frac{\partial U^j}{\partial \overline{W}^j} - \lambda = 0 \;\Rightarrow\; \frac{\partial U^j}{\partial \overline{W}^j} = \lambda \;\text{ or }\; U^j_W = \lambda$$

$$\frac{\partial \mathcal{L}^j}{\partial L^j} = \frac{\partial U^j}{\partial L^j} - \mu = 0 \;\Rightarrow\; \frac{\partial U^j}{\partial L^j} = \mu \;\text{ or }\; U^j_L = \mu$$

$$\frac{\partial \mathcal{L}^j}{\partial M^j} = \lambda\delta^j w^j - \mu\delta^j = 0 \;\Rightarrow\; \lambda\delta^j w^j = \mu\delta^j$$

$$\Rightarrow U^j_L \delta^j = U^j_W \delta^j w^j \;\text{ or }\; \frac{U^j_L}{U^j_W} = w^j.$$

Differentiation of the conflict function yields:

$$\frac{dD^j}{dw^j} = \frac{dU^j}{dW^j}\cdot\frac{dW^j}{dw^j} + \frac{dU^j}{dL^j}\cdot\frac{dL^j}{dw^j}$$

$$\frac{dW^j}{dw^j} = \delta^j \cdot w^j \frac{dM^j}{dw^j} + \delta^j \cdot M^j$$

$$0 = \frac{dL^j}{dw^j} + \frac{dM^j}{dw^j} \;\Rightarrow\; \frac{dM^j}{dw^j} = -\frac{dL^j}{dw^j}.$$

LTC – AN INTER- AND INTRAGENERATIONAL DECISION MODEL

Using the first-order conditions results in:

$$\frac{dD^j}{dw^j} = \frac{dL^j}{dw^j}(U_L^j - \lambda\delta^j w^j) + \lambda\delta^j M^j$$

and, therefore, since $U_L^j - \lambda\delta^j w^j = 0$ in the optimum:

$$\frac{dD^j}{dw^j} = 0 \text{ for } j = 1,\ldots,\ell \quad \text{but} \quad \frac{dD^j}{dw^j} = \lambda\delta^j M^j \text{ for } j = \ell+1,\ldots,n.$$

The *bargaining effect* of an increase in the wage rate w^j is given by (see Appendix II):

$$\sum \frac{dU^j}{dw^j} = \sum \frac{dU^j}{dD^j} \cdot \frac{dD^j}{dw^j} = \left[\frac{1}{2 - \frac{(U^0 - D^0)^2}{\sum(U^j - D^j)} \sum \frac{d^2 U^j}{dU^{j2}}}\right] \sum_j \lambda M^j.$$

For the *welfare effect* we proceed as before:

$$\sum_{k \neq j}(U^j - D^j)^{-1} \frac{dU^k}{dw^k}\bigg|_{D=\text{fix}} = \sum (U^j - D^j)^{-1} \frac{dU^k}{dN} \cdot \frac{dN}{dw^j}\bigg|_{D=\text{fix}}, \quad \text{and}$$

$$\frac{dN}{dw^j} = \eta \prod (U^k - D^k)^\eta \sum (U^j - D^j)^{-1} \cdot \frac{dU^j}{dM^j} \cdot \frac{dM^j}{dw^j}.$$

Using the appropriate first-order conditions of the Langrangian (3) and noting that $dM^j = -dL^j$, yields

$$\frac{dN}{dw^j}\bigg|_{D=\text{fix}} = 0 \text{ for } j = 1,\ldots,\ell \quad \text{and} \quad \frac{dN}{dw^j}\bigg|_{D=\text{fix}} = -\upsilon^j \frac{dU^j}{dw^j} \quad \text{for } j = \ell+1,\ldots,n.$$

Combining the equations results in:

$$\sum(U^j - D^j)^{-1} \frac{dU^k}{dw^j}\bigg|_{D=\text{fix}} = \frac{1}{2\eta(U^0 - D^0)^\eta} \cdot \sum(\upsilon^j \frac{dM^j}{dw^j}) \quad \text{for } j = \ell+1,\ldots,n.$$

We can summarize this in the following

Result 6:

An increase in the wage rate increases the "bargaining power" of every child (who works in the market; $\delta = 1$), and for all children together; this effect lowers (through Result 2) informal care. But there may be a substitution between children providing care, because an increase in w^j increases total wealth •

Change in Insurance Coverage

Finally, we analyze a change in the insurance coverage. From the maximization of the constraint utility function, we get as before: $(\partial U^0 / \partial \overline{W})^0 = \lambda_1$ and $\partial U^0 / \partial C = \lambda_2$. The differentiation of the conflict function gives

$$\frac{dD^0}{d\alpha} = \frac{dD^0}{d\overline{W}} \cdot \frac{d\overline{W}}{d\alpha} \Rightarrow \frac{dD^0}{d\overline{W}} = U_C^0 \cdot \frac{dC}{d\overline{W}} + U_W^0 \cdot d\overline{W} = \left(\lambda_1 \cdot d\overline{W} + \lambda_2 \cdot \frac{dC}{d\overline{W}}\right)$$

$$\frac{dC}{d\overline{W}} = Z_H \cdot \frac{dH}{d\overline{W}}$$

$$\frac{d\overline{W}}{d\alpha} = p_H \cdot H - \frac{dP}{d\alpha} > p_H H \quad \text{for} \quad \pi < \pi^0$$

$$\Rightarrow \frac{dD^0}{d\alpha} = \left[\lambda_1 d\overline{W} + \lambda_2 Z_H \frac{dH}{d\overline{W}}\right]\left(p_H H - \frac{dP}{d\alpha}\right).$$

The *bargaining effect*, therefore, is given by:

$$\frac{dU^0}{d\alpha} = \frac{dU^0}{dD^0} \cdot \frac{dD^0}{d\alpha}$$

$$= \left[\frac{1}{2 - \frac{(U^0 - D^0)^2}{\sum(U^j - D^j)} \cdot \sum \frac{d^2 U^2}{dU^{02}}}\right]\left(\lambda_1 d\overline{W} + \lambda_2 Z_H \frac{dH}{d\overline{W}}\right)\left(p_H H - \frac{dP}{d\alpha}\right) > 0.$$

For the *welfare effect* of a change in insurance coverage, we proceed as before:

$$\sum(U^j - D^j)^{-1} \cdot \frac{dU^k}{d\alpha}\bigg|_{D=fix} = \sum(U^j - D^j)^{-1} \frac{dU^k}{dN} \cdot \frac{dN}{d\alpha}\bigg|_{D=fix}$$

LTC – AN INTER- AND INTRAGENERATIONAL DECISION MODEL

and – the first part is identical –

$$\left.\frac{dN}{d\alpha}\right|_{D=fix} = \eta\prod(U^k - D^k)^\eta \sum(U^j - D^j)^{-1} \frac{dU^j}{dW} \cdot \frac{dW}{d\alpha}.$$

Using the first-order conditions of the Lagrangian (3) yields:

$$\left.\frac{dN}{d\alpha}\right|_{D=fix} = \left[\lambda_1 - \frac{1}{n}\sum\lambda_2^j\right]\left(p_H \cdot H - \frac{dP}{d\alpha}\right) > 0.$$

Combining both parts results in:

$$\sum(U^j - D^j)^{-1}\left.\frac{dU^k}{d\alpha}\right|_{D=fix} = \frac{1}{2\eta(U^0 - D^0)^\eta}\left(\lambda_1 - \frac{1}{n}\sum\lambda_2^j\right)\left(p_H H - \frac{dP}{d\alpha}\right).$$

Therefore, we can formulate the following

Result 7:
An increase in coverage strengthens the bargaining power of the parents considerably (as compared to a wealth increase). Because of the wealth effect, formal care increases. The result regarding informal care is unclear •

5 Conclusions and Caveats:

German figures, on who cares for the disabled elderly, show a very clear pattern: 20% of the elderly in need of care live alone, 34% in two-person households, whereas 46% live in households with three or more persons. Furthermore, the primary caregivers are the spouse (37%), the daughter (26%) or daughter-in-law (9%), mother (16%), other relatives and friends (11%).[28]

The basic findings of our model, which treats the family as a "production and insurance unit" playing a cooperative game, are confirmed by this data. Furthermore, the seven results of our model agree with empirical evidence. However, since the available data set is not as detailed as our model requires, we have not tested our (theoretically) derived results. Nevertheless, it remains a desideratum to do so.

As typical in any new analysis, there are several caveats. Although, the model used in this analysis does extend the standard decision model in several important ways, it still is limited by the exclusion of several important points.

First, we have not included the problem of moral hazard. It is considered only to the extent that the parents cannot be sure, in the first period, that in the second period, the children uphold the "implicit contract". As we can see from principal-agent models the parents can act strategically when deciding on the bequests. We simply have assumed that – whichever of the children provides the care – the wealth is divided equally between the children.

Second, the substitution between money and in-kind benefits was not modelled. However, the insurance mechanism is such that the disabled can choose freely on the open market and the insurer will pay the bill, where the price may be the result of the "market" or of a negotiation between producers and insurers (or sickness funds).

Third, the issue of substitution between caring at home versus staying in a nursing home, a real possibility, is only touched on. We argue that going to a nursing home is only the last choice if the living accomodations are not suitable.

Fourth, it would be an interesting task to extend the model to allow for – not only strategic behavior of the parent(s), but also – the children to form different coalitions. The assumption of cooperative behavior within the family is not always adequate.

Appendix I (see page 266, equation 4)

From the first-order conditions we get:

$$\rho = v^j + p_H(\lambda_2^0 - \lambda_2^j) - \mu Z_{\tilde{H}} \alpha^j.$$

Inserting for
$$v^j = \eta \prod_j (U^j - D^j)^n u^*(L^j)$$

$$\mu^j = \eta \prod_j (U^j - D^j)^n u^*(C)$$

$$\lambda_2^0 = -\frac{\mu Z_H}{p_H(1-\alpha)}$$

$$\lambda_2^j = \eta \prod_j (U^j - D^j)^n u^*(W_L^j)$$

we get

$$\rho^j = \eta \prod_j (U^j - D^j)^\eta u*(L^j)$$

$$+ p_H \left[\frac{Z_H}{p_H(1-\alpha)} \cdot \eta \prod_j (U^j - D^j)^\eta u*(C) - \eta \prod_j (U^j - D^j)^\eta u*(W_L^j) \right]$$

$$- Z_{\tilde{H}} \alpha^j \eta \prod_j (U^j - D^j)^\eta u*(C)$$

$$= \eta \prod_j (U^j - D^j)^\eta \left[u*(L^j) - \frac{Z_H}{(1-\alpha)} \cdot u*(C) - u*(W_L^j) \cdot p_H - Z_{\tilde{H}} \alpha^j u*(C) \right]$$

$$\frac{\rho^j}{\eta \prod_j (U^j - D^j)^\eta} = u*(C) \left[\frac{u*(L^j)}{u*(C)} - Z_H / (1-\alpha) - \frac{u*(W_L^j)}{u*(C)} \cdot p_H - Z_{\tilde{H}} \alpha^j \right]$$

Second:

$$\sigma^j = v^j - \lambda_2^j w^j = \eta \prod_j (U^j - D^j)^\eta u*(L^j) - \eta \prod_j (U^j - D^j)^\eta u*(W_L^j) \cdot w^j$$

$$\frac{\sigma^j}{\eta \prod_j (U^j - D^j)^\eta} = u*(C) \left[\frac{u*(L^j)}{u*(C)} - \frac{w^j u*(W_L^j)}{u*(C)} \right]$$

$$\frac{\sigma^j}{\eta \prod_j (U^j - D^j)^\eta u*(C)} = \frac{u*(L^j)}{u*(C)} - \frac{w^j u*(W_L^j)}{u*(C)}$$

$$\frac{\rho^j}{\eta \prod_j (U^j - D^j)^\eta u*(C)} = \frac{u*(L^j)}{u*(C)} - Z_H / (1-\alpha) - \frac{u*(W_L^j)}{u*(C)} \cdot p_H - Z_{\tilde{H}} \alpha^j.$$

$$\frac{u*(L^j)}{u*(C)} = \frac{w^j u*(W_L^j)}{u*(C)} + \frac{\sigma^j}{\eta \prod_j (U^j - D^j)^\eta u*(C)}$$

$$\frac{u*(L^j)}{u*(C)} = p_H \frac{u*(W_L^j)}{u*(C)} + Z_{\tilde{H}} \alpha^j + Z_H / (1-\alpha) + \frac{\sigma^j}{\eta \prod_j (U^j - D^j)^\eta u*(C)}$$

$$\Rightarrow \frac{\sigma^j}{\eta \prod_j (U^j - D^j)^n u*(C)} + Z_{\tilde{H}} \alpha^j + \frac{Z_H}{(1-\alpha)} + p_H \frac{u*(W_L^j)}{u*(C)} = \frac{u*(L^j)}{u*(C)}$$

$$= w^j \frac{u*(W_L^j)}{u*(C)} + \frac{\sigma^j}{\eta \prod_j (U^j - D^j)^n \cdot u*(C)}.$$

Appendix II (see page 271 and 275)

The division of the surplus follows the (marginal) rate of substitution between the family members, i.e. for $k = 0, 1, ..., n$ and $j = 1, ..., n$

$$\frac{\sum_j (U^j - D^j)}{U^0 - D^0} = -\sum_j \frac{dU^j}{dU^0} \quad \text{or} \quad \sum_j (U^j - D^j) = -\sum_j \frac{dU^j}{dU^0} (U^0 - D^0).$$

Differentiation with respect to D^0 gives

$$\sum_j \frac{dU^j}{dU^0} \cdot \frac{dU^0}{dD^0} = -\sum_j \frac{dU^j}{dU^0} \left[\frac{dU^0}{dD^0} - 1 \right] - (U^0 - D^0) \cdot -\sum \frac{d^2 U^j}{dU^{02}} \cdot \frac{dU^0}{dD^0}$$

$$\Rightarrow \sum \frac{dU^j}{dU^0} \cdot \frac{dU^0}{dD^0} = -\sum \frac{dU^j}{dU^0} \cdot \frac{dU^0}{dD^0} + \sum \frac{dU^j}{dU^0} - (U^0 - D^0) \sum \frac{d^2 U^j}{dU^{02}} \cdot \frac{dU^0}{dD^0}.$$

Rearranging yields

$$\sum \frac{dU^j}{dU^0} \cdot \frac{dU^0}{dD^0} + \sum \frac{dU^j}{dU^2} \cdot \frac{dU^2}{dD^2} + (U^0 - D^0) \sum \frac{d^2 U^j}{dU^{02}} \cdot \frac{dU^0}{dD^0} = \sum \frac{dU^j}{dU^0},$$

$$\frac{dU^0}{dD^0} \left[2 \sum \frac{dU^j}{dU^0} + (U^0 - D^0) \sum \frac{d^2 U^j}{dU^{02}} \right] = \sum \frac{dU^j}{dU^0} = -\frac{\sum (U^j - D^j)}{(U^0 - D^0)}$$

LTC – AN INTER- AND INTRAGENERATIONAL DECISION MODEL

$$\Rightarrow \frac{dU^0}{dD^0} = \frac{-\frac{\sum(U^j - D^j)}{U^0 - D^0}}{-2\frac{\sum(U^j - D^j)}{U^0 - D^0} + (U^0 - D^0)\sum\frac{d^2U^j}{dU^{02}}}$$

$$\Rightarrow \frac{dU^0}{dD^0} = \frac{1}{2 - \frac{(U^0 - D^0)^2}{\sum(U^j - D^j)} \cdot \sum\frac{d^2U^j}{dU^{02}}}$$

$$\Rightarrow \sum\frac{dU^j}{dD^0} = \sum\frac{dU^j}{dU^0} \cdot \frac{dU^0}{dD^0} = \frac{-\frac{\sum(U^j - D^j)}{(U^0 - D^0)}}{2 - \frac{(U^0 - D^0)^2}{\sum(U^j - D^j)} \sum\frac{d^2U^j}{dU^{02}}}$$

$$\Rightarrow \sum\frac{dU^j}{dD^j} = \frac{1}{2 - \frac{(U^0 - D^0)^2}{\sum(U^j - D^j)} \sum\frac{d^2U^j}{dU^{02}}}$$

Appendix III (change in the price of formal care; see page 272)

The starting point is equation (6) and the Lagrangian in (7), now evaluated with respect to changes in the price of formal care. Differentiating the conflict function in the optimum with respect to p_H yields

$$\frac{dD^0}{dp_H} = \frac{dD^0}{d\overline{W}} \cdot \frac{d\overline{W}}{dp_H} \quad \text{and}$$

$$\frac{dD^0}{d\overline{W}} = \frac{\partial U}{\partial C} \cdot \frac{dC}{d\overline{W}} + \frac{\partial U}{\partial W} \cdot d\overline{W}, \quad \text{where}$$

$$\frac{dC}{d\overline{W}} = Z_H \cdot \frac{\partial H}{\partial W} \quad \text{and}$$

$$\frac{d\overline{W}}{dp_H} = -(1-\alpha)H + p_H \cdot H \frac{\partial \alpha}{\partial p_H} = H\left[p_H \frac{\partial \alpha}{\partial p_H} - (1-\alpha)\right] = H[\alpha \varepsilon - (1-\alpha)]$$

where ε = demand elasticity of insurance coverage $= \frac{\partial \alpha}{\alpha} \cdot \frac{p_H}{\partial p_H}$.

Using the first-order conditions, the marginal change in the conflict outcome results:

$$\frac{dD^0}{dp_H} = \left[\lambda_1 d\overline{W} + \lambda_2 Z_H \frac{dH}{\overline{W}}\right] \cdot H\{\alpha \varepsilon - (1-\alpha)\}.$$

Acknowledgment

The authors thank Matthias F. Maneth, Peter Ockenfels and Dr. Notburga Ott (all University of Frankfurt) for valuable comments and assistance. Hans-Christian Mager gratefully acknowledges the financial support of the Volkswagen-Foundation.

Notes

1 See Krug/Reh (1992).
2 See Infratest (1992).
3 See Horowitz (1985) for a survey.
4 See, for example, Ikels (1983) or Litwak/Kulis (1987) for some evidence.
5 See, for example, Wolf/Soldo (1988).
6 See, for example, Cantor (1983) or Stone/Short (1990).
7 Stern (1993), 1-2.
8 The german average household structure in 1991 was as follows: 33.6% of all households were one-person households, 30.8% were two-persons, 17.1% were three-persons households and 18.5% were four and more persons households.
9 See e.g. Börsch-Supan/Mc Fadden/Schnabel (1993).
10 In the following analysis the notion of family and household are treated as perfect substitutes.
11 See Pollak (1985) and Ben-Porath (1980).
12 See Hampel (1992).
13 See for instance, Kotlikoff/Spivak (1981), 373.

14 For an elaborate version in this direction see Zweifel/Strüwe (1996) in this volume.
15 Richter (1993), 4-5.
16 See Pauly (1996) in this volume.
17 See Zweifel/Strüwe (1996) in this volume.
18 Rees (1990), 88.
19 See Ott (1993) for details.
20 See Shubik (1984), 172.
21 See Becker (1981).
22 A behavior is called cooperative if (a) the interests are homogenous or (b) may be conflicting, but the players are able to make binding arrangements.
23 Since we do not explicitly formulate the decision of the children in the first period, we have to take as given that, e.g. some children are married and have own children, and, therefore, are not going to work in the market. These children may especially be able to deliver services for the disabled parents because they can realize "advantages of joint production" in caring for the parents and their own children.
24 We see the problem that, by caring for the parents, one of the children can secure the wealth for all children, so it is – at the outset – unclear what is the conflict point for the children. Side payments or equivalent utility transfers are (implicitly) paid. In other words, the LTC services are „club goods" for the family.
25 The parameters η or η^j (in equation 2) describe different types of the children, specifying the rôle to be filled. The numbers η^k may be interpreted as the "bargaining power" of players $k = 0, 1,..., n$; cf. Binmore/Dasgupta (1987), 156/7.
26 As in Samuelson (1954), equation (4) shows that the sum of all marginal utilities is equal to the marginal product.
27 Zweifel/Strüwe (1996) in this volume demonstrate this.
28 See Infratest (1992).

References

Becker, G. S. (1981): *A Treatise on the Family*, Cambridge: Harvard University Press.
Ben-Porath, Y. (1980): The F-Connection: Families, Friends and Firms and the Organisation of Exchange, in *Population and Development Review 6*, 1-30.
Binmore, K./Dasgupta, P. (1987) (eds.): *The Economics of Bargaining*, Oxford: University Press.
Börsch-Supan, A./Mc Fadden, D./Schnabel, R. (1993): *Living Arrangements: Health and Wealth Effects*. National Bureau of Economic Research (NBER) Working Paper 4398: Cambridge, MA.
Cantor, M. (1983): Strain Among Caregivers: A Study of Experience in the United States, in *The Gerontologist 23*, 597-604.

Hampel, J. (1992): *Technische Hilfsmittel statt Betreuung? Erhaltung und Unterstützung einer selbständigen Lebensführung im Alter* ("Technical aids vs. care"), WZB working paper P92-106, Berlin.
Horowitz, A. (1985): Family Caregiving to the Frail Elderly, in *Annual Review of Gerontology and Geriatrics 6*, 194-246.
Ikels, C. (1983): The Process of Caretaker Selection, in *Research on Aging 5*, 491-509.
Infratest (1992): *Hilfe- und Pflegebedürftige in privaten Haushalten*, Endbericht ("Care Receivers in Private Households"), München.
Kimball, M. S. (1990): Precautionary Saving in the Small and in the Large, in *Econometrica 58*, 53-73.
Kotlikoff, L. J./Spivak, A. (1981): The Family as an Incomplete Annuities Market, in *Journal of Political Economy 89*, 372-391.
Krug, W./Reh, G. (1992): *Pflegebedürftige in Heimen Statistische Erhebungen und Ergebnisse.* ("Care Receivers in Nursing Homes"). Studie im Auftrag des Bundesministeriums für Familie und Senioren. Stuttgart et al.: Kohlhammer.
Litwak, E./Kulis, S. (1987): Technology, Proximity, and Measures of Kin Support, in *Journal of Marriage and the Family 49*, 649-661.
Myerson, G. (1991): Game Theory. Analysis of Conflict. Cambridge: Harvard University Press.
Ott, N. (1992): *Intrafamily Bargaining and Household Decisions*, Berlin et al.: Springer.
Pauly, M. V. (1996): Almost Optimal Insurance for Long-Term Care, in this volume.
Pollack, R. A. (1985): A Transaction Cost Approach to Families and Households, in *Journal of Economic Literature XXIII*, 581-608.
Rees, R. (1987): *The Theory of Principal and Agent: Part II*, in J.D. Hey and P.J. Lambert (eds.): Surveys in the Economics of Uncertainty, New York: Blackwell, 70-91.
Richter, W. F. (1993): *Bequething Like A Principal*, Discussion Paper Nr. 93-01, University of Dortmund/Germany.
Samuelson, P. A. (1954): The Pure Theory of Public Expenditure, in *Review of Economics and Statistics 36*, 387-389.
Selten, R./Güth, W. (1981): Game Theoretic Analysis of Wage Bargaining in a Simple Business Cycle Model, in *Journal of Mathematical Economics 10*, 177-195.
Shubik, M. (1984): A Game Theoretic Approach to Political Economy, in *Interational Journal of Game Theory 4*, 25-55.
Sommer, B. (1992): Entwicklung der Bevölkerung bis 2030 (Demographic Development in Germany), in *Wirtschaft und Statistik 72*, 217-222.
Stern, S. (1993): *Estimating Family Long-Term Care Decisions in the Presence of Endogenous Child Characteristics*, Working Paper, University of Virginia.
Stone, R. J./Short, P. F. (1990): The Competing Demand of Employment and Informal Caregiving to Disabled Elders, in *Medical Care 28*, 513-526.
Wolf, D./Soldo, B. (1988): Household Composition Choices of Older Unmarried Women, in *Demography 25*, 387-403.
Zweifel, P./Strüwe, W. (1996): Long-Term Care Insurance and Trust Saving in a Two-Generation Model, in this volume.

13 THE ASSESSMENT AND THE REGULATION OF QUALITY IN LONG-TERM CARE

Gabriele Johne

1 Introduction

When faced with the problem of expanding the availability of long-term care services to meet the needs of a growing elderly and disabled population while simultaneously containing costs, the quality of care becomes a major area of conflict. This is also apparant in the context of the implementation of the Statutory Social Long-Term Care Insurance in Germany. While the political debate about coverage for long-term care needs has been dominated by financing issues during the formation of the new insurance law [Eisen (1992), 236], it is the the material aspects, such as the quality of care, which have become an issue of growing public interest with the passing of the bill on the new long-term care insurance scheme.

As new demands concerning professional care standards and goals of care provision are emerging in the course of recent research developments in the field of gerontology and geriatrics, fears are being voiced – especially from interest and professional groups – that the cost containment elements inbuilt in the new long-term care insurance could lead to standards of care lower than those which are professionally recognized. On the other hand, there is also a concern that providing what from a professional perspective would be considered an appropriate level of quality, might cause a significant rise in expenditure for care services, with correspondingly higher burdens for the economically active population.

The aim of this paper is to provide some clarifications that seem essential in the light of these conflicting perspectives. It deals with the central question as of whether the regulatory mechanisms under the new long-term care insurance can achieve the provision of an appropriate level of service quality. In this context, the determination of an appropriate quality level is crucial. There is, however, a clear lack of consensus on what would be an 'appropriate' level of quality in long-term care provision. While the attainment of high-quality care is often considered a noncompromising aspect of the provision of long-term care, it is obvious that an appropriate level of service quality does not mean 'maximum quality' from an economic perspective, but rather the amount which members of society really prefer and are willing to pay for.

2 The concept of quality in nursing home care

Quality of care is probably one of the most complex and least understood concepts in the current debate on health and long-term care. Research on the issue has not yet yielded a consensus on the definition of quality, let alone its measurement. While there is a widespread notion that measures aimed at increasing efficiency in long-term care provision deteriorate the quality of services, it is surprisingly rarely asked how the putative decline in quality will manifest itself exactly. Some of the existing, rather tentative approaches to an objective identification of distinct dimensions of long-term care quality will be outlined below.

2.1 Dimensions of nursing home care quality

The quality of nursing home care is multidimensional. This stems from the fact that in nursing homes, care provision is really a mixture of health services, housing, and other services in an institutional living arrangement [Zedlewski et al. 1990, 122]. Two principal dimensions are typically distinguished: the quality of care and the quality of life. Quality of care includes the 'technical' aspects of nursing home services, for instance how well does a nursing home assess the care needs of its residents, develop a care plan and implement that plan? To what extent is the goal of care provision actually being achieved? Quality of life issues include the degree to which the residents have privacy and independence as well as the social and psychological components of service provision and the amenities of care [Feldstein (1989), 580].

Long-term care differs from health care because of the nature of the need it meets. Rather than treating acute health problems, it encompasses personal and nursing care to compensate for chronic functional disabilities and involves helping with actitivities that individuals normally perform by themselves. Because a nursing home is a total living situation for a long-term care patient, including not only the care itself but also the environment in which this care is provided, quality of life issues constitute an important dimension of the quality of nursing home care.

Professionals often regard technical aspects of care, such as rehabilitative efforts and the provision of 'activating care' as the essential aspect of nursing home care. They argue that since disability is not a static state, for a number of nursing home residents the degree of impairment depends heavily on the kind of services provided and on rehabilitative efforts. From their perspective, the view about long-term care being mostly compensatory and custodial tends to discount the importance of intervention into the restorative needs of persons in nursing homes.

Overall, there are grounds for the assumption that the critical service sought by most nursing home patients themselves is assistance with basic activities of daily living as well as a pleasant, supportive living environment: "The criteria for a satisfactory meal differ from those of a satisfactory diet, and both are relevant to the quality of long-term care" [Kane/Kane 1988, 136]. Goals concerning the provision of long-term care can therefore be conflicting and trade-offs may occur, as when comfort is sacrificed in the interest of safety.

2.2 Who should evaluate the quality of nursing home care?

At this point, it becomes obvious that the notion of quality is complicated further by the question of who defines it and who should decide on the value of the services provided. A basic premise underlying economics is that consumers, individually, are capable of assessing the quality of the commodities they purchase and that, collectively, they are capable of assuring desired levels of quality. Professional judgement of experts may serve as an additional source of information, but should by no means take the place of individual judgement.

The current emphasis on quality assessment by professionals and other experts reflects the widely held notion that consumers of nursing home care generally lack the competence to assess quality of care and to ensure compliance with desired standards of care. A number of reasons are brought forward in support of this assumption: People seeking nursing home admission suffer from cognitive impairments that make it difficult for them to consider alternatives or to choose among different nursing homes. In addition, long-term care services are typical 'experience goods', of which consumers are in general unable to judge the quality prior to the act of consumption. It is often argued that after placement in an institution, a nursing home resident will not easily be able to switch to another nursing home [Bishop (1988), 124]. However, there is also evidence that consumers of nursing home care are in fact able to choose among many attributes of the nursing home service and to make their own decisions concerning the desired quality and quantity of care services. Generally, most of the care provided in nursing homes is not technically very sophisticated, and can be judged as pleasant or unpleasant by the patients. Nyman (1989), 227 found that private nursing home patients respond reasonably to differences in prices and quality across nursing homes and concluded that his findings "contrast with the widely held view that nursing home consumers are economically irrational".

The assumption that persons with disability-related needs lack the ability to adequately assess the quality of nursing home care might be attributed to the professional bias in favour of providing all persons in need of long-term care with the best care available and their bias in favour of the more sophisticated services such as rehabilitative and activating care. While the general ability of consumers to judge quality of care in nursing homes is often questioned, it seems that "professionals too are only beginning to understand its technical attributes" [Bishop (1988), 123]. Moreover, the assessment of quality is inherently subjective and consumer preferences with respect to the amount and type of care provided are by no means homogenous. From the search of the literature one may conclude that we know next to nothing about how professional judgement on the quality of nursing home care would compare with the judgement of those who receive the care. It seems very unlikely, however, that supplier and consumer preferences with respect to the desired quality of care are similar.

Hence, it is questionable whether prescriptive standards of acceptable care and external quality evaluation would automatically be welfare enhancing. There are reasons for the assumption that in the nursing home market, the present lack of consumer information and market transparency is the result of an excess demand and a lack of competition between alternative suppliers of nursing homes: in this situation, few incentives exist for consumers to actively seek additional information or for suppliers to provide this information. Thus, a clear distinction needs to be made between the intrinsic characteristics of the services themselves and characteristics resulting from the incentives which are induced by inappropriate regulatory measures in the market for nursing home care. In order to detect such inappropriate regulation, the main elements of the organizational structure of the care provision under the new insurance need to be examined in order to determine their impact on the quality of care that is produced. Prior to this, an overview will be given in the following section of the quality control devices available in the area of long-term care.

2.3 Approaches to the assessment of nursing home care quality

Given the consensus that, in the area of long-term care, evaluating service quality and ensuring an appropriate level of care should not be left to the consumers themselves, substitutes for quality assessment are needed. The evaluation of quality by an external agency would be such a substitute. To be used as a basis for quality assessment, the components of quality need to be specified in such a way that they can be effectively employed in control processes, i.e. a translation into specific criteria and standards is necessary.

Measures of quality of nursing home care have been built on the techniques developed in the acute care sector. The objectives associated with the quality of care can be classified according to the structure, process, or outcome of care (see table 1).

Table 1: Elements of Structure, Process, and Outcome Quality of Care

Structural indicators	Process indicators	Outcome indicators
Qualification of staff	Diagnostic testing	Client satisfaction
Number of nurses per resident	Therapeutic interventions	General well-being
Equipment and physical facilities	Compliance with professional standards	Average length of stay of residents in the various categories
Organizational structure	Documentation	Improvement of functional status of the residents
Patient care expenditures per day	Rehabilitation therapy	
	Availability of services	

Source: Based on Donabedian (1982).

The structure domain refers to the nature of the inputs used in the production of services. It encompasses the tools and resources that providers of care have at their disposal, and the physical and organizational settings within which they work. Generally, the concept includes all conditions under which the provider-client-relationship occurs. The process domain focuses on the care provision itself, i.e. on the activities that go on between the practitioner and the client and includes all the activities, pursuits, and behaviours of the care providers. The third domain, outcome, refers to the effectiveness in meeting the stated objectives of the service provision, i.e. to the measured change in consumer behaviour as well as the impact of care on the functional status and the well-being of the residents [Donabedian (1980)]. Changes in the physical, functional, and psychosocial status of the patient are often suggested as appropriate for the development of outcome measures in long-term care [Kurowski/Shaughnessy (1990), 105].

Most quality assessment methods and regulatory standards applied to the provision of long-term care services are based on structural and process variables. In the nursing home care sector in Germany, minimum structural standards are fixed in the 'Heimmindestbauverordnung' (HeimMindBauV) as well as in the recently implemented 'Heimpersonalverordnung'. The 'Heimmindestbauverordnung' contains minimum building standards concerning for example the size of the rooms, the number of persons per room, the temperature etc. The 'Heimpersonalverordnung' specifies requirements for the staffing of nursing homes as well as for educational standards. Adherence to these standards is assured by the local authorities. While these local authorities have a significant amount of freedom of choice concerning the specific contents of their quality controls, in practice, it is mainly compliance with building standards that is checked [Spieß/Wagner (1994), 5]. Process measures are very rarely used, even though in the discussion about adequate quality assurance methods in long-term care, demands concerning the improvement of care planning and documentation are often raised.

Outcome measures for nursing home quality, such as comfort, dignity of the care received as well as improvement of the status of the residents are hardly used at all. This neglect stems from the fact that outcome is the most difficult aspect from a criteria measurement viewpoint. This is due to the fact that reliable and valid methods for measuring outcomes are only being developed slowly. The relationship between the improvement of health or functional status and the receipt of care is very difficult to establish due to great difficulties in controlling intervening factors which confound the process-outcome relationship. Since the care recipients contribute to the outcome as well, it can never be assumed that measured change is the direct result of the care provision [Kurowski/Shaughnessy (1990)].

However, several problems pertain to the use of structure and process variables as indicators for quality as well: the validity of these factors rests on a presumed causal link in the sense that an increase in the quality of structural factors would lead to a corresponding increase in the quality of process factors, which in turn leads to a high quality of outcomes. Studies that have investigated the relationship of structural and process measures of quality to the outcome of care, however, found few significant associations between structural indicators and the process or outcome of care provision.[1] Consequently, the existing methods of using mostly structural indicators as measures for service quality are of limited usefulness [Nyman (1990), 239]. Despite the difficulties related to the measurement of outcomes, only outcomes are really meaningful for quality assessment, since they can provide a summary of the net effect of the nursing home services provided on the health and well-being of the residents. Hence, outcome evaluation of nursing home care is receiving a lot of attention recently as the most adequate way to approach the concept of quality.[2]

In summary, quality assessment of nursing home care is impeded by problems of definition, measurement, and understanding of causality. Moreover, the goals of long-term care provision themselves often seem to be unclear. However, the lack of measures for evaluating the degree of goal attainment of long-term care provision should not lead us to the assumption that "quality is what providers are doing" [Rebscher (1990), 24] or to fall into the argumentation trap that characterized the quality-evaluation discussion in the US health-care sector 20 years ago: more services, more staff and better equipment mean "better quality". Such an assumption would only feed the escalation of costs and utilization of services, without necessarily enhancing the overall quality of long-term care provision.

3 Assuring the quality of nursing home care: the organization of the German Social Long-Term Care Insurance

Since 1995, the risk of long-term care need is covered within the Statutory Social Long-Term Care Insurance ('Soziale Pflegeversicherung'). The insurance scheme provides cash benefits and benefits in kind for home care and also covers part time institutional care as well as institutional care when home care cannot be adequately guaranteed. Persons are eligible for benefits under the social long-term care insurance if they require help in performing their regular activities of daily living. Benefits are graded according to the severity of the need for long-term care. The care services are provided not by the care insurance funds, but by third-party suppliers which the care insurance funds enter into contract with.

With the implementation of the new insurance, a new institutional framework is established for quality assurance in long-term care.[3] The institutional arrangements and the mechanisms for payment under the insurance also influence the quality of care by the incentives they create.

3.1 Competition between various suppliers of care

The most obvious mechanism for assuring adherence to desirable levels of quality is free market competition between alternative suppliers and free expression of consumer preferences. If consumers can express differences in tastes by selecting from amongst differentiated products, they tend to consider the two characteristics 'price' and 'quality' simultaneously. This way, competition leads to an efficient resource allocation by providing services at quality levels which consumers judge to be worth paying for.

The prevailing excess demand in the market for nursing home care makes it unnecessary for providers to compete for patients by providing high-quality care. This excess demand stems largely from entry barriers to the market for nursing homes as a result of current regulations.[4] Generally, these regulations work in favour of nursing homes which belong to the voluntary sector or the public sector. However, since nonprofit suppliers have not been able to adapt to the increasing demand for nursing home care [Spieß/Wagner 1994], waiting lists for nursing home places have resulted. In this situation, nursing homes have no incentive to improve quality (and, in many instances incur additional expenses).

It is expected that, with the partial removal of entry barriers under the new long-term care insurance, competition between alternative suppliers of nursing home care will be enhanced. When consumers are able to choose between different institutions, they will consider mainly the quality of the service provided, which, in turn, will foster competition on the basis of quality. On the other hand, the fact that the prices a nursing home can charge for accomodation and meals (the 'hotel costs' of nursing home care) as well as the prices for the care itself are negotiated between the care insurance funds, the communes and the service providers is often assumed to have a negative effect on the quality of care. There is concern that financial interests might be the dominant force in the negotiations, leading to a low reimbursement level which constrains the quality of care provided [Deutsche Gesellschaft für Gerontologie (1993), Kuratorium Deutsche Altershilfe (1994)].

ASSESSMENT AND REGULATION OF QUALITY IN LTC

Obviously, there is no reason to assume that prices for social services that are determined in such negotiations approximate an optimal price, i.e. the price that would be set in competitive markets. However, it has never actually been proven that the services provided, for instance in the health care sector, would not have been available in the same quality and quantity if the payers had bargained for lower prices per unit of service delivered. Therefore, the assumption which is often supported by the service suppliers themselves, i.e. that a decrease in the amount of monetary resources flowing into the long-term care sector would automatically decrease quantity and quality of the services provided, should be critically examined.

3.2 Reimbursement of Nursing Home Care Costs

The reimbursement of nursing homes has traditionally been based on costs incurred. As a consequence, incentives for nursing homes to keep expenditures low were almost nonexistent. With the implementation of the new long-term care insurance, the prevailing cost-reimbursement system is replaced by prospectively determined, case-based payments reflecting the costs of providing care to different types of residents. This will have several advantages: 1. Fixed reimbursement levels per resident based on the type of case rather than on the costs of the resources actually used for care provision give nursing homes a strong incentive to minimize expenditures per case and to curb inefficiencies. 2. Since the reimbursement level is detached from the costs actually incurred, a nursing home does not have an incentive to generate cost. 3. Since the reimbursement depends on the value of services provided, this type of payment also contributes to greater equity in reimbursement. 4. Also, payments based on the degree of incapacity of a resident (reflecting the expected resource requirements for care provision) encourage facilities not to discriminate against heavy-care residents and they ensure that residents receive adequate amounts of care once admitted [Breyer (1994), 23].

However, this type of prospective reimbursement reflects a reliance on the status quo situation of the residents and fails to link incentives to high quality of care. The improvement of resident status results in a regrouping of the resident into a lower category and thus leads to lower reimbursement for the nursing home. Thus, rehabilitative efforts and the provision of activating care is punished instead of rewarded, resulting in disincentives for nursing homes to improve a residents' functioning level. Under this type of payment system, it will be difficult to induce service providers to undertake efforts aimed at improving the status of the residents. Some kind of outcome-based payment would be needed by which nursing homes whose resident care results in better-than-expected outcomes are rewarded and homes whose residents fare worse than expected are penalized. Unfortunately, the outcome dimension of quality is very difficult to monitor, since, as mentioned before, reliable methods of assessing meaningful outcomes are still insufficient. In order to be able to base payments on outcomes, the care insurance funds would need to be able to obtain evidence of change in clients status and on departures from expected outcomes of care. In this sense, since the improvement of the functional status of the residents is an important public policy goal[5], refinement of outcome measurement is essential.[6] Major information gaps still exist which obstruct the refinement of policies to ensure the quality of long-term care.

3.3 Quality assessment and quality control

With the implementation of the new long-term care insurance, the responsibility for quality control of nursing homes has been placed on the care insurance funds. External quality assurance is part of the care insurance funds' legal obligation to safeguard the provision of long-term care (§ 69 SGB XI). They are required to assure that the care provided by the suppliers corresponds to generally accepted standards of care provision (§ 28 Abs. 3 SGB XI). Specifically, their task will be to develop standards for quality of care and quality assurance as well as methods for the control of care quality (§ 80 Abs. 1 SGB XI). The carriers of long-term care facilities that enter into a supply contract with a care insurance fund will be subject to binding quality assurance requirements.[7] Noncompliance to these requirements will lead to the end of the supply contract. Presently, the 'Heimaufsichtsbehörde' is the regulatory agency in charge of quality assurance in the nursing home care industry. This agency is also part of the municipal administration in charge of Social Assistance. It is often assumed that this agency is interested primarily in limiting its expenditures, and therefore follows the easiest path – accepting lower quality standards instead of enforcing high quality standards to the financial detriment of the municipalities [Spieß/Wagner (1993)].

There is reason to assume that the care insurance funds – in comparison with the municipalities – are less interested in keeping expenditures for long-term care services low, since they are under less budgetary pressure. Nevertheless, it is questionable whether they can be expected to pursue quality control very rigorously, since they are not subject to any market competition, and even if they were, these quality assurance activities cannot be expected to contribute very much to the provision of a level of quality that is socially desirable. This will be demonstrated in the next section, in which an analysis of quality assurance methods will be applied to the system of long-term care provision.

4   Limitations of quality standards and quality assurance of nursing home care under the Social Long-Term Care Insurance

The parameters used in assessing acceptable quality of care may differ, based upon preferences and ideologies [Tancredi (1989), 92]). Because of its slippery and highly relativistic definition, 'quality' all too easily lends itself to use by providers in order to achieve their own objectives, for instance the avoidance of undesired competition or the justification of a higher reimbursement level.[8] From this perspective, it is not very surprising that adherence to professional standards so often comes at the request of the providers of care themselves (rather than at the request of consumers of care or their relatives, i.e. those who benefit from the quality of services).

In addition, quality assessment measures tend to focus on the micro-quality of care. Hence some important aspects of the overall quality of the system of long-term care provision are neglected [Burger/Johne (1994)]. In the ongoing discussion on the quality of long-term care the assumption prevails that the enhancement of the quality of individual treatments or of the care provided in single institutions will automatically enhance the quality of the system of long-term care provision as a whole. This idea, which is well entrenched among many professionals and providers of care, implies that the quality of the entire system of nursing home care provision could be assessed by examing the quality of single nursing homes. It ignores the existence of a tradeoff between 'micro-quality' and 'macro-quality' of care in the face of an overall resource constraint.[9]

Micro-quality is observed at the nexus between individual providers of care and the recipients of this care. It encompasses the effectiveness of a single treatment or the quality of the performance of an individual supplier of care services. Macro-quality, in contrast, refers to the impact of the entire long-term care system on the well-being of those it is intended to serve (i.e. also includes aspects such as access to care). In the discussion on the quality of long-term care, this distinction is often neglected.

The relationship between micro- and macro-quality of care is depicted in a diagramm (see figure 1).[10] In the face of constrained resources for the production of nursing home care, rising micro-quality of care implies access to nursing home care for fewer persons (a move from point B to D or A). The proposition of maximizing micro-quality in the sense of providing every person in need of long-term care with the highest level of care quality (a move to point H in the diagramm) would only be valid in the absence of a resource constraint. For a system that operates under a resource constraint, a decision has to be made on the trade-off between those two dimensions of quality.

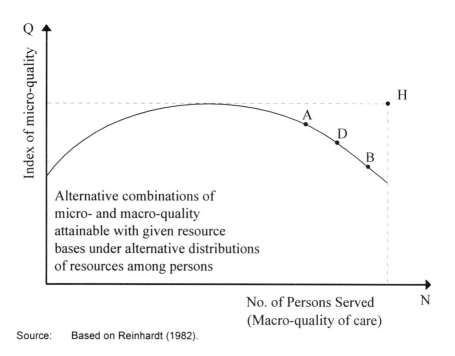

Source: Based on Reinhardt (1982).

Figure 1: Relationship between Micro- and Macro-Quality of Nursing Home Care

The respective weights given to micro- and macro-quality of care can only be established through a political consensus [Reinhardt (1982), 168], since there does not seem to exist any clearcut agreement on the threshold level of quality of care or of the acceptable cost of attaining it: Professionals attach greater value to long-term care services as opposed to other services; however, they do not bear the costs of their decision.[11] Consumers of long-term care under a social insurance do not bear the entire costs of their consumption, either. In the case of third-party-payment, the trade-off between rising quality of services and the related rise in costs for the economy does not enter their purchasing decision. Thus, from the perspective of the consumers, rising quality of care is generally desirable [Meyer (1994), 155]. The insured population who ultimately bears the costs has little opportunity of limiting their payment under a social insurance. In the absence of demand distortions introduced by third-party-payment, consumers generally do not wish a maximum quality level of the commodities they purchase, but prefer to sacrifice bits of quality in order to obtain savings. In the area of long-term care as well, decisions to economize by forgoing some arguable quality would not be irrational on the face of it.[12]

The fact that individuals differ in their preferences concerning the dimensions of the quality of long-term care services leads to a third difficulty: Ultimately, quality standards defined by some external agency (other than some minimum safety or technical standards) would need to define something unknown: If standard norms are set, these cannot account for individual, heterogenous preferences. In most instances, the standards defined are close to maximum quality of care. Presently, the quality discussion in the long-term care sector is guided by the implicit assumption that more resources devoted to the provision of long-term care services would automatically enhance service quality, which, in turn, would automatically enhance overall welfare. However, an appropriate level of quality obviously does not mean the highest level of quality that is technically attainable, but rather an 'optimal' level of quality in the sense that the relationship between the value of care outcomes (considering both individual and social benefits) and the resource expenditures necessary to produce them need to be considered [Vuori (1980), 976]. Just as is the case with any other commodity, in the area of long-term care the achievement of an optimal level of quality requires the sacrifice of services that are principally useful. Uniform standards will not be able to guarantee such an optimal level in service quantity and quality.

Another potential pitfall of quality assurance in nursing home care is that an efficient resource allocation between alternative forms of long-term care provision is not achieved. The setting of high quality standards in nursing home care may cause resources to be drawn away from the provision of alternative types of long-term care provision unless the quality of the placement process is assured as well. It has to be kept in mind that nursing homes are but one input in the production of long-term care services: Institutional care is only one of several alternative living arrangements for the elderly disabled. They may also live with family members who provide informal assistance or may seek paid home care services.

Any combination of micro- and macro-quality on the depicted production possibility curve implies an efficient use of the resources available for long-term care, so that with a given resource base, the micro quality could not be increased without reducing the number of persons served or vice versa (see figure 2). Points below the curve, e.g. point C, represent economically inefficient provider systems. A system of long-term care provision would be considered inefficient if for instance some consumers were overserved – to their own detriment – while others lacked adequate services. In the German system of long-term care provision there is reason to assume that due to inadequate financing[13] and a lack of access to home care services, some persons are unnecessarily placed in nursing homes, while at the same time a number of persons being cared for in private households lack sufficient professional assistance. In Germany, like in most of the other OECD countries, "the absence of sufficient and affordable alternatives

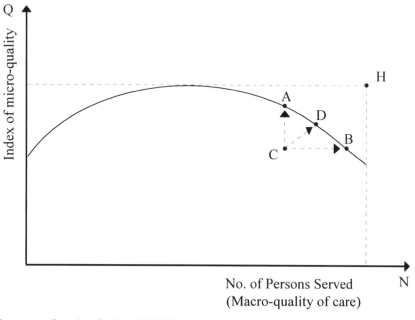

Source: Based on Reinhardt (1982).

Figure 2: Relationship between Micro- and Macro-Quality and Efficiency of LTC

has made the institutional solutions the only one on offer for many families" [OECD (1994), 38]. Overall efficiency and overall quality of care would be enhanced if lower-cost substitutes, such as home care services, were used whenever it was medically and socially possible.[14] This way, a mere reallocation of resources could move society from point C to points A or D or B. The development of different forms of care provision as alternatives to institutional care would in this sense contribute to an enhancement in the efficiency of the system of long-term care as well as to a higher overall quality of long-term care.

Hence, an inefficient situation may be perpetuated unless, in the process of care planning and care placement, quality is also assured. Specifically, persons in need of long-term care should not be placed in institutional care unless home care does not seem feasible. In order to achieve this, the criteria that determine eligibility for nursing home care have yet to be developed. In addition, there is a need for better coordination between the different services and the groups providing these services. It would seem that in the area of care placement, quality assurance has hardly begun.[15]

In summary, there are many reasons to doubt the effectiveness of professional standards and assurance of adherence to those standards by government agencies as mechanisms for resolving medical-economic issues. The main objection is that such standards affect the allocation of society's limited resources and are therefore of immense public importance. If they cannot reasonably be expected to reflect sensible priorities with respect to resource use, then they deserve substantially less credibility than they currently appear to enjoy. When the quality of an entire system is to be evaluated, there are other aspects besides micro-quality which need to be considered, for instance efficiency and resource allocation.[16] Therefore, a case could be made instead for examining more crucially the mechanism by which the quantity and quality of services provided are determined. From this perspective, the focus of interest might be shifted away from the evaluation of single services, special technologies or the monitoring of care delivery in single institutions, to which economics has little to contribute, to the question of how a system for financing long-term care would need to be organized in order to achieve the kind of service provision in volume, structure, and quality levels which corresponds to the preferences of the population.

5 Alternative Options and Some Concluding Thoughts

What can be concluded from these reflections? It is certainly conceivable that under the new social long-term care insurance, competitive forces and changes in the regulatory constraints can move the nursing home sector towards better quantity, cost and quality outcomes. In this sense, several measures have been proposed, such as improving information concerning the quality of services provided by different suppliers, the relaxation of supply constraints by eliminating subsidization for nursing homes (Spieß/Wagner 1993), changed reimbursement methods that better reflect product differences and are based ideally on outcomes of care [Kane (1986), Norton (1992)] or, alternatively the provision of benefits-in-money to persons in need of long-term care [Oberender (1986), 34]. However, both the provision of information to consumers as well as the implementation of reimbursement methods that better reflect outcomes of care would require salient indicators on the quality of care. Such indicators are still elusive. Consequently, more empirical research and data would be needed especially on outcome measurement. Approaches to the development of such measures of quality exist [Kane et al. (1983); Kane (1986)]; their refinement remains an important issue on the long-term care services agenda. It would permit the regulation of nursing homes to rescind most of the arbitrary regulations based on structure and process criteria that miss many of the elements of care quality that are most critical and most difficult to capture.[17]

Thus, the refinement of approaches to quality measurement and assurance is, without doubt, an essential task from the perspective of an efficient and effective long-term care delivery system. However, improving the quality of the nursing home care sector by itself will not address overall resource concerns. Problems will remain under the statutory social long-term care insurance which is often said to be the optimal arrangement with respect to the social protection of the disabled and dependent elderly, since it fits best into the existing system of social security in Germany. The politically determined level of benefits under the social long-term care insurance and the prescriptive standards of acceptable care and appropriate spending under which the long-term care system must operate are rather arbitrary and cannot be expected to reflect the wishes of the population about how their resources are employed. In addition, changes in consumer tastes and preferences or advances in technology may cause a discrepancy between the 'optimal' level of service volume and quality and the administratively determined level. These pitfalls, however, are the inevitable consequence of two rather widely accepted assumptions: 1. Individuals cannot be expected to make their own, informed decisions with respect to the desired level of care services and the desired type of insurance. 2. Equivalent standards of care for all citizens need to be centrally determined.

A challenge to such prevalent notions would allow for a consideration of alternative delivery modes and financing mechanisms for long-term care with greater reliance on consumer choice and competition.[18] It would have been feasible, for instance, to establish an obligation for minimum insurance, leaving the choices under which conditions and with which company to ensure to the individuals themselves. There are several arguments in favour of this idea. In a heterogenous society individuals have different preferences with respect to the quantity and quality of a commodity they consume. Also, long-term care is different from acute medical care in the sense that it involves many basic choices about lifestyle [Merill/Somers (1989)]. In addition, freedom of choice with respect to the type and condidition of insurance for all individuals would have fostered competition between various insurers, so that cost-effective types of insurance which are matched to the preferences of the individuals would have developped. Precisely because it is so difficult to specify comprehensively and exhaustively the attributes of long-term care quality, adequate incentives for providers and financing institutions to enforce processes of internal quality assurance might have been more effective.

While this approach is incompatible with the notion of equivalent standards for all citizens, it lessens the need to implement such undesirable strategies as restricting eligibility for benefits, reducing benefits for eligible recipients and putting price controls on service providers that might lead to a reduction in services. It would also provide the basis for a strong presumption that the allocation of resources at any point fairly reflects consumer desires with respect to the quality and quantity of services provided. If various types of insurance were allowed to be developed, it is likely that suppliers would attempt to work towards reducing informational deficits on the side of the consumers and provide valid quality indicators. Thus, approaches directed more towards the enhancement of competition between insurance types and towards a strengthening of the consumer role would also have been desirable from the perspective of quality assurance.

Notes

[1] An overview of empirical studies using structure, process, and outcome measures of quality to assess quality of nursing home care is given by Kurowski/Shaughnessy (1990).

[2] Developing indicators for outcome evaluation specifically for nursing home care has long been regarded as essential, and pioneering work has been done. One example of an attempt to develop such outcome indicators is the study conducted by the Rand Corporation in Los Angeles [Kane et al. (1983a)].

[3] The improvement of long-term care quality has been one of the explicit goals in the implementation of the social long-term care insurance [Blüm (1993), 7].

⁴ Spieß (1993), 66-71 provides a detailed analysis of these main regulatory elements, namely entry barriers for commercial suppliers, subsidization of public and nonprofit suppliers as well as price controls.

⁵ The legislator explicitly demands that 'activating care' is provided to persons in need of long-term care (§ 28 SGB XI).

⁶ In the United States, several research projects have investigated the possibility of employing alternative reimbursement methods for nursing homes which tie increased payments to improved resident outcomes. A demonstration project in the San Diego area was conducted in 1980 to test the effectiveness of monetary incentives in improving the health of nursing home residents. Nursing homes were given three kinds of financial incentives: payments tied to admission in order to encourage them to admit patients with severe disabilities, payments tied to outcomes in order to encourage nursing homes to improve the functional status of the residents, and payments tied to discharge in order to foster the discharge of those residents for whom home care would be feasible. The incentive regulation was found to have caused better access, quality and to have lowered overall cost of care. For the results see Norton (1992), 105-128. For an overview of initiatives in the area of incentive-based approaches to quality assurance see Willemain (1983).

⁷ Note that quality assurance in nursing home care also encompasses those services which are not funded by the care insurance funds, i.e. the 'hotel costs' and additional services.

⁸ The setting of minimum quality standards involves the creation of entry barriers to the market, see Leland (1979).

⁹ Donabedian emphasizes the importance of distinguishing different levels of aggregation of the quality of health care: "When one evaluates the performance of a practitioner case by case it is easy to slip into the assumption that his time, attention, and other resources are unlimited, and to expect that, in each case, the maximum attainable benefit is realized...". When a target population is examined, the appropriate criterion of quality becomes the net aggregate benefit. See Donabedian (1980), 18-19.

¹⁰ Note that the index of micro-quality, which refers to the care received by each recipient, is a hypothetical one, since there does not exist a consensus on a meaningful operationalization of the quality of long-term care.

¹¹ The interest of suppliers in a high level of service supply at maximum quality can be explained from an ethical perspective as well as from self-interest: While recipients of services should be provided with 'the best care available', this also enables suppliers to justify higher costs and prices and thus increases their income. See Knappe (1993), 117.

¹² Therefore, it is not obvious that the level of quality provided under the statutory social long-term care insurance generally is 'too low'.

¹³ Under the current financing system the costs for nursing home care are covered but not the costs for alternatives to such care, creating a distortion in prices facing the elderly person which favors institutional care.

¹⁴ It has to be kept in mind though, that home care is generally more costly than nursing home care for elderly or incapacitated people with severe needs [see Rieben (1982), Blackwell et al. (1992)]. Hence, whether the provision of community care services always induces a reduction of institutional care remains questionable, see Schulz-Nieswandt (1990), 45. On the other hand, the idea behind a policy which favours community care is not only to unburden public budgets, but to enable people to remain independent and live in their preferred environment as long as possible.

¹⁵ Although some improvement could be expected in the improvement of the co-ordination and managment of care through the development of case management, see OECD (1994), 45. In Ger-

many, the demand for improved 'care planning' on the basis of an assessment of care needs is currently raised.

[16] Brook, R.H./Lohr, K.N. (1986) state for the U.S. health care sector that "tomorrow's important issues require that information from all these areas be integrated into a 'macro' model that will address continuing problems in the medical system" (1986, 710).

[17] It has to be noted, though, that reimbursement systems of this type are complex and involve significant administrative costs. See Cotteril (1990), 660.

[18] One of the options that have been proposed prior to the implementation of the statutory social long-term care insurance is the implementation of an obligation for insurance against nursing risk, in which the insured persons are free to decide with which company and under which conditions to insure themselves. See Knappe (1994).

References

Bishop, Chr. E. (1988): Competition in the Market for Nursing Home Care, in W. Greenberg (ed.): *Competition in the Health Care Sector: Ten Years Later*, Durham/London: Duke University Press, 199-138.

Blackwell, J./O'Shea, E./Moane, G./Murray, P. (1992): *Care Provision and Cost Measurement: Dependent Elderly People at Home and in Geriatric Hospitals*. Dublin: Economic and Social Research Institute.

Blüm, N. (1993): Politik der Nähe, in *Bundesarbeitsblatt 7-8*, 5-9.

Breyer, F. (1994): Entgeltverfahren und Wirtschaftlichkeitsanreize bei sozialen Diensten, in E. Knappe/S. Burger, (eds.): *Wirtschaftlichkeit und Qualitätssicherung in sozialen Diensten*. Frankfurt/New York: Campus, 13-29.

Brook, R.H./Lohr, K.N. (1986): Efficacy, Effectiveness, Variations, and Quality, in *Medical Care 24*, 710-722.

Burger, S./Johne, G. (1994): Die Qualität sozialer Dienste im Spannungsfeld zwischen sozialpolitischem Anspruch und ökonomischer Rationalität, in E. Knappe/S. Burger, (eds.): *Wirtschaftlichkeit und Qualitätssicherung in sozialen Diensten*. Frankfurt/New York: Campus, 111-139.

Cotteril, P.G. (1990): Provider Incentives Under Alternative Reimbursement Systems, in R.J. Vogel/H.C.Palmer (eds.): *Long-Term Care. Perspectives from Research and Demonstrations*. Rockville/MD: Aspen, 625-664.

Deutsche Gesellschaft für Gerontologie und Geriatrie, Institut für Gerontologie, Forschungsstelle für Sozialrecht und Sozialpolitik am Fachbereich Rechtswissenschaft II der Universität Hamburg (1993): *Memorandum zur Qualitätssicherung bei Pflegebedürftigkeit*. Hamburg: mimeograph.

Donabedian, A. (1980): *Explorations in Quality Assessment and Monitoring*, Vol. I: The Definition of Quality and Approaches to its Assessment. Michigan: Ann Arbor

Eisen, R. (1992): Alternative Sicherungsmöglichkeiten bei Pflegebedürftigkeit, in *Sozialer Fortschritt 41*, 236-241.

Feldstein, P. J. (1989): *Health Care Economics*, 3rd ed. New York et. al.: Delmar.

Kane, R.L. et. al. (1983): *Outcome-based Reimbursement for Nursing Home Care.* Santa Monica: Rand Cooperation.
Kane, R.L. (1986): Outcome-based Payment: A New Beginning?, in *Health Progress, April*, 36-70.
Kane, R. A./Kane, R. C. (1988): Long-Term Care: Variations on a Quality Assurance Theme, in *Inquiry 3*, 132-146.
Knappe, E. (1993): Der Konflikt zwischen Gruppeninteressen und Kostenreduzierung, in H.R. Vogel/M. Gerharz/K. Hässner (eds.): *Illusionen der Gesundheitspolitik.* Stuttgart/New York: Gustav Fischer, 115-125.
Knappe, E. (1994): Eine Pflegeversicherung für die soziale Marktwirtschaft, in *Volkswirtschaftliche Korrespondenz der Adolf-Weber-Stiftung 33*.
Kuratorium Deutsche Altershilfe (1994): *Thesen zu Auswirkungen des Pflegeversicherungsgesetzes auf die Qualität der Pflege.* Köln: mimeograph.
Kurowski, B.D./Shaughnessy, P.W. (1990): The Measurement and Assurance of Quality, in R.J. Vogel/H.C. Palmer (eds.): *Long-Term Care. Perspectives from Research and Demonstrations.* Rockville/MD: Aspen, 103-132.
Lehmkuhl, D. et al. (1986): Alte Menschen in Heimen, in *Zeitschrift für Gerontologie 19*, 56-64.
Leland, H. (1979): Quacks, Lemons, and Licensing: A Theory of Minimum Quality Standards, in *Journal of Political Economy 87*, 1328-1346.
Merill, J.C./Somers, S.A. (1989): Long-Term Care: The Great Debate on the Wrong Issue, in *Inquiry 32*, 317-320.
Meyer, D. (1994): Gesundheitspolitik und Steuerung des medizinisch-technischen Fortschritts, in *Jahrbücher für Nationalökonomie und Statistik*, 148-165.
Norton, E.C. (1992): Incentive Regulation of Nursing Homes, in *Journal of Health Economics 11*, 105-128.
Nyman, J.A. (1989): The Private Demand for Nursing Home Care, in *Journal of Health Economics 8*, 209-231.
Nyman, J.A. (1990): The Future of Nursing Home Policy: Should Policy be Based on an Excess Demand Paradigm?, in *Advances in Health Economics and Health Services Research 11*, 229-250.
Oberender, P. (1986): Ökonomische Aspekte des Pflegefallrisikos – Eine ordnungspolitische Alternative, in W. Gitter/P. Oberender (eds.): *Pflegefallrisiko*, Bayreuth: P.C.O., 27-37.
OECD (1994): *Caring For Frail Elderly People – New Directions in Care.* Paris: OECD Social Policy Studies No. 14.
Rebscher, H. (1990): Der Ordnungsrahmen von Qualitätssicherungskonzepten in der GKV – Ziele, Bedingungen, Möglichkeiten und Grenzen, in P. Oberender (ed.): *Umbruch und Neuorientierungen im Gesundheitswesen.* Bayreuth: P.C.O., 19-51.
Reinhardt, U.E. (1982): Quality Assessment of Medical Care: An Economist's Perspective, in H.K. Selbmann/K.K. Überla (eds.): *Quality Assessment of Medical Care.* Gerlingen: Bleicher, 165-174.

Schulz-Nieswandt, F. (1990): *Stationäre Altenpflege und "Pflegenotstand" in der Bundesrepublik Deutschland.* Frankfurt am Main et al.: Peter Lang.

Spieß, K. (1993): Angebot und Nachfrage stationärer Altenhilfeeinrichtungen: Analyse eines regulierten Marktes, in *Reihe "thema" des Kuratoriums Deutsche Altershilfe (84).* Köln.

Spieß, K./Wagner, G. (1993): Re-Regulierung des Marktes für Altenpflege erforderlich, in *DIW Wochenbericht 60,* 419-422.

Spieß, K./Wagner, G.: (1994): In-Patient Long Term Care in Germany – Selected Problems of Insurance and Services. *Diskussionspapier Nr. 94-07 aus der Fakultät für Sozialwissenschaft der Ruhr-Universität Bochum.*

Tancredi, Laurence R. (1988): Defining, Measuring, and Evaluating Quality of Care, in Frank A. Sloan et. al. (eds.): *Cost, Quality, and Access in Health Care.* San Francisco/London: Jossey Bass, 90-126.

Vuori, H. (1980): Optimal and Logical Quality: Two Neglected Aspects of the Quality of Health Services, in *Medical Care 10,* 975-985.

Willemain, T.R. (1983): Survey-based Indices for Nursing Home Quality Incentive Reimbursement, in *Health Care Financing Review 5,* 83-90.

Zedlewski, S.R. et al. (1990): *The Needs of the Elderly in the 21st Century.* Washington D.C.: Urban Institute Press.

14 ALMOST OPTIMAL SOCIAL INSURANCE FOR LONG-TERM CARE

Mark V. Pauly

1 Introduction

Most people spend most of their lives in good health. Sometimes these periods are interrupted by relatively brief but severe illnesses for which medical services are effective. If the services are not effective, death follows, but if they do work, the person soon returns to normal life. In such cases, the main adverse consequence of the period of illness is its cost – in terms of medical care cost, lost income, and lost social interaction – all losses which can be, and are, to some extent, offset by conventional insurances.

An occurrence which is less common but still possible is that the period of illness – that is, the period of high medical need and impaired social function – continues over a long period of time with neither death nor recovery as an outcome. Services provided in such cases constitute "long term care." Conventional insurances have been (for good reason, I will argue) incapable of covering such chronic illness events. Likewise, permitting individuals and families to deal as well as they can with periods of prolonged misery seems both unfair – because of the uneven incidence of such events – and inefficient – because such events so distort the opportunities available to people.

Dealing in some fashion with the financing of long term care has therefore become part of many health reform proposals. In addition, the notion that government ought to be able to "give" us better long term care coverage appeals to those in the population at high risk or fear of needing such care. Finally, the empirical fact that private insurance coverage designed to cover the cost of long term care is minuscule has lead analysts and planners to view this "gap" as something much in need of closing in the process of reform.

In this paper I will argue that, to the contrary, the absence of private coverage against long term care expenses is probably both individual and socially rational. Long term care coverage for the elderly population, which has been most vociferous in seeking additional coverage as a way of obtaining a share of the benefit from health reform, is paradoxically least socially valuable, relative to its value for other age groups.

I want to be clear, however, that I am not arguing that it is impossible in theory for social efficiency to be improved by publicly provided coverage against long term care. There are some potential gains from such coverage, compared to the current situation, but I will argue that they are likely to be very small, even under the most efficiently managed government program, and very likely to turn negative under the usual ultimately inefficient process of public administration and political choice. Compared to the other problems in the health care system, the problem of changing or reforming the financing of long term care is of minor importance. Were there sufficient wisdom and political energy to deal appropriately with all possible problems, some improvements in public policy toward long term care might be undertaken; I will indicate what those improvements are. But the most fundamental message, in the current era of ambition to do something about health care combined with political turmoil about how to do it, will probably be to leave well enough in long term care financing alone for the present.

When economists offer advice on public policy questions, such as the pricing of care for long term chronic illness, they often use welfare economics as the basis for their advice about desirability. The assumption that actual governments either can or wish to achieve economic efficiency is, however, highly dubious. Indeed, two economists from different political perspectives (Kenneth Arrow and James Buchanan) won the Nobel Prize in economics in part for proving that government cannot be relied upon to do the efficient thing.

Slightly more formally, an idealized, omniscient government financed by individualized lump sum taxes can always replicate the competitive equilibrium in private goods, and deal as well with any externalities or market failures that might arise. It is precisely because of skepticism about the existence of such an ideal government, however, that many economists favor the use of competitive markets for resource allocation purposes. But when economists analyze insurance arrangements, often the skepticism seems to evaporate and governments are endowed with powers to raise revenues efficiently, decide what it is efficient to do, and carry out those tasks in an ideal fashion for each person – often helped (analytically speaking) by the simplifying assumption of identical preferences.

In this paper I want to take what is perhaps a more realistic approach to analyzing social insurance arrangements, with a specific application to insurance to cover the cost of long term care for the frail chronically ill. The best way to approach this problem would be to model the government imperfections explicitly – to incorporate the excess burden of tax finance, the distortion of uniform provision despite diverse preferences, and the probable deviation of political equilibria from the social optimum directly in the model. Unfortunately, the empirical information needed to quantify these costs of "government failure," and to trade them off against estimates of the cost of market failure, do not exist. I therefore take the more manageable task of specifying a model of social insurance with minimal government intervention – a "Jeffersonian" model in the American tradition – that is constructed to deal with what I regard to be the most serious aspects of market failure in efficient resource allocation. This approach explicitly leaves some efficiency stones unturned, with the hope that, once the (hypothesized) more serious deficiencies in market efficiency have been remedied, one can ask whether real world goverments are up to the task of dealing with whatever inefficiencies remain.

2 Criteria for Judgement

The objectives that I postulate for financing of long term care are the same as the objectives used in other discussions of health reform. We want a system that achieves equity, in the sense of being fair across individuals of different circumstances and in the sense of treating individuals in the same fundamental circumstances in the same fashion. We also want the system to be efficient, which fundamentally means not only that costs are minimized for whatever program is enacted, but that the choice of program depends on a comparison of the benefits with the costs.

In what follows, I will deal with the issue of efficiency by breaking questions of financing into three major parts: (1) appropriate insurance coverage for risk averse people; (2) appropriate quantity of long term care used by the population; (3) appropriate quality for the care that is consumed. In each case, the word "appropriate" does not mean the highest possible or the largest amount. Instead, it reflects a balancing of costs and benefits. For example, long term care should not be of the highest possible quality, or available to everyone who can get positive benefit from it, because in each case there will be some users whose benefit, from additional quantity or quality, though positive, is less than its cost.

In considering benefits from long term care, however, we ought not to limit our consideration to benefits to the individual receiving the care, or even to that person's family. Instead, we ought to think of benefits as potentially being obtained by others in the community who are concerned about the well-being of the particular individual. This "altruistic externality" characterizes care for people with long term illnesses just as it characterizes care for acute illnesses or preventive care, but the difficulty of obtaining objective measures of how much people really do value others' use of care makes application of the concept difficult and debatable. Nevertheless, it is important to keep in mind that ultimately the definition of appropriateness is resting on nothing more, and nothing less, than the values that citizens place, and that those values, fundamentally, can be represented by the amount of income that they are willing to sacrifice in order to see the outcome in question achieved. In this discussion, I reject the notion of a separate public interest or social good, above and beyond the values held by individuals. One difficulty raised by taking this point of view is that the interests of minor children or unborn heirs are taken into account only insofar as they are represented by the desires of parents and grandparents. While I will argue that this difficulty can be solved, it will cause some complications in the analysis.

We also need a definition of "long term care." I will generally define such care as having two characteristics: (1) it is care provided to people with chronic illnesses; (2) those people will generally have some deficiency in their ability to perform the usual functions of work, housekeeping, or social interaction. Thus, long term care would not be represented by coverage of a drug for a fully functioning person with a chronic illness, and it would also not be represented by assistance for a person, of whatever age, who is still capable of performing the functions of daily life. That is, long term care is more than housing for the elderly, more than servants' services, and more than medical services to manage people with chronic illnesses.

On the other hand, I do not limit long term care solely to the provision and insurance coverage of nursing home services. Care in a nursing home is one common way of improving the well-being of people who have chronic and incapacitating illnesses, but almost always there is an alternative to nursing home care, defined broadly to include all types of formal and informal care provided outside of a standard nursing home setting. It may be that the person receives non-institutional formal care, which I will define to mean care provided by a health professional in return for payment, in their own home. Alternatively, informal care may be provided by family members or friends in the community, for which monetary payment might not be paid, or might be paid for services that would not ordinarily be defined as medical, such as housecleaning.

3 How we Currently Provide and Pay for Long-Term Care

There are, by all measures, relatively few Americans who need long term care and receive none of it. Although there are occasional tragic stories of a frail, usually elderly, person who dies from neglect, in most cases, a person unable to perform their normal functions because of illness is able to obtain some help somewhere. The reason is that persons truly in need are usually easy to detect, and the connection between provision of care and improvement in the person's health or well-being is immediate and obvious. There is no analog to the underuse of services with a preventive dimension, or services for a serious or hidden symptom, that characterizes acute care. In addition, in contrast to medical care for acute illnesses, it appears to be relatively easier to substitute services provided by nonprofessionals in the care of people with long term chronic illnesses, even in the provision of some services which might be labeled medical. Consequently, the problem of access to needed care, especially on the part of the uninsured, which correctly characterizes the debate over insurance coverage for acute care, does not really fit the circumstances of long term care. Instead, the issue here is not whether a person has access to some services in the event of an illness; rather, it is whether a person is able to obtain appropriate amounts and types of those services.

Slightly more than half of nursing home care in the U.S. is provided by the Medicaid programs administered by different states. Although there is partial federal funding and some federal oversight of this program, it is for the most part structured by the government of each state as that government sees fit. Since all states have democratically elected governments, it follows that the quantity and quality of long term care provided by state Medicaid programs reflect the desires of citizens of those states.

There is substantial variation across states in the form of Medicaid benefits for the chronically ill and in the quality or generosity of coverage for those persons. In most states, people become eligible for Medicaid benefits in one of two ways: either they are of such low income and assets when they first get sick that they are already covered by the state Medicaid program, or they "spend down" their assets in the early treatment of chronic illness and then become eligible for Medicaid. A minority of states do not permit people to become eligible for Medicaid by spending down; in such states, at least in principle, a person who starts off with income and wealth above the poverty line may receive no or minimal public long term care benefits, whereas a person who is initially below the poverty line does become eligible. In practice, however, this inequity tends to be mitigated by state-level administrative adjustments to their eligibility rules.

States determine how much they will pay for nursing home benefits. Ordinarily, payment is made on a per day basis, with the state essentially administering the price that is to be paid to nursing homes and the state certifying nursing homes as eligible for Medicaid payments. In addition to controlling the price that will be paid, states control the number of long term care beds in nursing homes in many states via their certificate of need laws. It is generally believed that states use such laws to hold down the number of nursing home beds in order to contain state expenditures for nursing home care. They use certificate-of-need laws to limit the access of the chronically ill to long term institutional care. Scanlon (1988) argues that certificate of need limits, rather than incomplete insurance coverage, are primarily responsible for underservice.

While I will discuss this matter in more detail below, it is worth noting at this point that any alleged deficiencies in state Medicaid programs, either in terms of eligibility or in terms of the quality of care that can be provided with per-day payment the state makes available to nursing homes, are fundamentally the "fault" of citizens of the state; that is, they are largely representative of the decisions of taxpayers in the state. If states are not generous in providing Medicaid nursing home benefits, is it presumably because their citizens do not wish them to be generous – since there is no external influence that forbids the state from paying more for more humane treatment. This means that potential reforms in the financing of long term care need fundamentally to deal with the likelihood that proposals for more generous public benefits will go counter to the desires (already expressed in state Medicaid programs) of many non-elderly, non-ill citizens, for low taxes rather than high quality of care for the chronically ill.

While almost all public coverage of nursing home care is provided via the Medicaid program, much of the public coverage of formal care for chronic illness for the elderly rendered outside of nursing homes is paid for by Medicare. Medicare's payments for home care are, however, limited to payments for nursing care provided by health professionals; Medicare does not pay for housekeeping or other services that may be as if not more essential to maintaining the quality of life for a chronically ill person in the home. However, Medicare payments for home health nursing are one of the most rapidly rising components of the Medicare program; their costs have grown many times faster than the costs of hospital or physician care. Medicare is now much more explicit in informing beneficiaries that it does not cover nursing home care.

The second source of funds for nursing home care is private long term care insurance. This also is growing fairly rapidly, but still represents only 3% of total nursing home spending [CBO (1991)], up from 2% ten years ago. In addition, it appears that the rate of growth in this type of insurance, while rapid, is not high enough to make it an important influence for the foreseeable future.

Finally, nearly half of nursing home expenses are paid privately out of pocket. Individuals pay such expenses either by using their social security, pension benefits or other income to cover the cost of nursing home care, or by drawing down assets in order to pay for nursing home or chronic care. On average, the amount of assets drawn down in connection with admissions and longer stays in nursing homes is relatively minimal, because the most common users of long term care, the elderly, do not have high assets on average – but there are a few who consume substantial amounts of assets. The typical source of out-of-pocket payments is public or private pension income, often paid simultaneously with the receipt of Medicaid benefits.

This brief description of financing for nursing home care indicates that, at least for nursing home care, the market is already dominated by a kind of social insurance that will pay for that care. Medicaid, after all, is tax financed insurance available to everyone. This insurance has a deductible, which depends on the person's wealth. In fact, the Medicaid eligibility rules do not usually require complete exhaustion of a person's assets or income in order to qualify for payment. A portion of assets may be reserved if there is a spouse or other family member in the household. In addition, even a single or widowed person can retain assets in the form of an owned home, and protect a small amount of other assets (about $2000) and income (about $600) for personal needs. In return, however, Medicaid will confiscate social security and private pension payments except for the small amount for personal expenses. (The amount people are permitted to retain varies across states, so that this implicit "copayment" varies.)

The net effect of this policy is that, at least for persons with no dependents, Medicaid provides a kind of social insurance for nursing home care with a deductible approximately equal to one's wealth and copayments approximately equal to one's income less personal expenses. A person need not fear being unable to pay for nursing home care (at least at the level of quality that taxpayers have chosen for Medicaid), so that it is correct to say that all are insured. A person does need to fear exhausting their assets or losing the ability to make discretionary expenditures out of income. The question of whether there should be *additional* coverage (in excess of Medicaid's coverage) in a reformed medical care system for nursing home care then comes down to the question of whether a deductible equal to one's wealth or copayments nearly equal to one's income are too large to be efficient. That is, should there be coverage to protect a larger share of assets or income? It also comes down to the question of whether the level of quality that can be purchased with what tax payers are willing to put into the Medicaid program is, in some sense, inefficiently or inequitably low.

Medicaid insurance coverage is considerably more generous – in terms of what it pays – if the person enters a nursing home than if the person stays at home. (However, it is probably more generous – in terms of what it allows the family to retain – if the person stays at home.) There has been considerable outcry and journalistic expose of situations in which a frail ill person preferred to stay at home, could be cared for more cheaply at home, and yet was forced to enter a nursing home in order to qualify for Medicaid benefits. I will discuss in more detail the substitution of care at home for institutional care below, but for the present it is worthwhile to note that the reason for this seemingly unreasonable policy is as a device to hold down spending. The government's fear, whether justified or not, is that if coverage was made available for care for persons in their own homes, the demand for such care would expand substantially. There would be moral hazard associated with home care insurance. So even if coverage for home care is cheaper per person, if it were covered by insurance, it might be demanded by so many more people that total expenses would rise. Most obviously, use of the certificate of need device as a method of holding down Medicaid spending would cease to be effective once every private home was a potential nursing home. All of this discussion is highly speculative, however, and the cost saving potential of alternatives to nursing home care depends critically on empirical magnitudes – fundamentally on the cross-elasticity and own-elasticity of demand for nursing home and home care.

4 Optimal Insurance against Costs Associated with Chronic Disabling Illness

What kind of insurance against the costs of long term care ought to be provided by a society that values equity and efficiency? I will argue that ideal social insurance roughly approximates the form Medicaid takes. However, there can be some modifications to Medicaid that would significantly improve it. Those modifications deal with coverage for the non-elderly, for persons who do return to normal life, and perhaps, with the reduction of cross-state variation in Medicaid generosity. The ideal form of social insurance is what I would term (with more regard to accuracy than to marketing) "Reformed Medicaid" (RM). Modifications in social policy, much more modest than would be entailed in full incorporation of long term care into National Health Insurance, would be sufficient to produce this "Reformed Medicaid."

In order to illustrate what RM would be like, and why it would be efficient and equitable, I first note a very important proposition: If the only type of long term care available were care in a nursing home, *the current form of the Medicaid program, which protects some wealth but which effectively has a wealth related deductible, would appear to be close to ideal.* However, this wealth related deductible can be defined *independently* of a person's pre-illness wealth. This would be accomplished by a policy that need only specify how much of a family's assets will be protected, not how much need be spent before protection becomes effective. A Reformed Medicaid plan would guarantee to protect up to some (probably modest) amount of assets for all. Protecting up to $X thousand in assets obviously implies that the deductible is (initial assets − X), which is wealth related. This approach differs both from that of the Pepper commission, which proposed to cover the first part of a stay, or that of the Norton/Newhouse (1994) and ACP-AGS proposal of a month or dollar deductible [Weiner (1994)].

If the expenditure on long term care is independent of the level of coverage for it – which I will argue below, appears to be roughly the case for nursing home care – a RM policy obviously protects $X thousand in assets but puts at risk all assets in excess of $X thousand. Ordinarily it is inefficient to put risk averse people in danger of losing large chunks of their wealth, and many analysts have used this proposition to argue that insurance against long term care expenses, like insurance against other costly risks, ought to be much more extensive than it is.

The argument does not apply, however, because the risk that would be covered by long term care insurance is, for the greatest part, different from the risk against which other insurance (including acute care health insurance) protection is demanded. Specifically, approximately 80 percent of long term care spending (primarily nursing home spending) goes to provide care to people who will never return to a normal life with normal functioning. However long the stay in a nursing home, they will be discharged only when dead or when being transferred to a hospital in which death is imminent. This means that, for the greatest part of total expense, long term insurance protects assets that would become part of the estate of the patient. Long term care insurance protects bequests, and those bequests are primarily received by heirs who are not dependent, who are not poor, and who (from a social point of view) are not particularly deserving of transfers. In effect, Medicaid provides coverage sufficient to guarantee access to decent quality care for persons who need it, but does not use public funds to protect bequests to adult heirs. To argue for more generous coverage, one would have to argue that it is equitable or efficient to make transfers to these heirs. I do not believe there is an equity argument, and an efficiency argument, while possible, is very weak.

The primary question for reform might be, however, whether such a program with a mean deductible equal to bequests leaves – for the very small minority of people who do recover to some approximation of normal life – an adequate amount of assets protected. It may well be that protecting only owner-occupied housing value and some small amount of other assets would be regarded by most persons who do recover as insufficient. One possibility for obtaining more appropriate protection and yet limiting the cost of the program would be to condition the amount of asset value that can be retained on whether or not the person resumes normal life. That is, a person might receive more generous coverage, with a much smaller claim against wealth, if the person does indeed recover. One way – though not the only way– to achieve this objective would be to continue the Medicaid spend down rule as at present, but rebate some portion of the amount spent down for people who recover.

The problem with such a solution is that current Medicaid rules do not require documentation of the wealth level the person started with, but only that they eventually achieve sufficiently low wealth and income to meet the spend down rules. A solution would be to permit individuals to alert the Medicaid program when they have been in a nursing home as a private patient for a defined period of time and when their assets hit some lower bound. For example, a person in a nursing home whose assets fall to the value of housing plus, a small amount, say, $25,000 might alert the Medicaid program. The program would not begin to pay for the nursing home expenses until the person's assets fell further but the notification would be sufficient to trigger a payment, should the person recover, that would bring their assets back up to $25,000, or any other targeted amount.

A simpler approach, and perhaps a more equitable one, would simply be to make the level of payment for nursing home care for persons whose total nursing home stay exceeds that covered by Medicaid larger if they recover. For instance, a person who was in a nursing home for six months and then met the Medicaid spend down rule would have the nursing home cost from that point on were covered by Medicaid and, in addition, if the person recovered, Medicaid might pay for two or three months of the six month initial stay. In effect this would relieve the person of the obligation of paying that bill and return the value to the person. The payment for the "extra" nursing home days could be made directly to the individual. In contrast to the previous case, all persons would be eligible for a uniform benefit; the benefit would not be greater for those with more initial wealth. This is preferable to the Norton-Newhouse proposal to make deductibles depend on *anticipated* return home. Instead, we only require that we wait and see.

How much more would such a revised Medicaid system cost, as compared to the current system? To answer this question, one would first have to specify the additional amount of wealth to be protected. Roughly, however, only 10 to 20 percent of persons who receive Medicaid nursing home benefits ever return home. Since the amount of privately-paid nursing home care is approximately equal to the amount of Medicaid-paid care, it seems obvious that the additional cost to the Medicaid program could not, in any circumstances, exceed 10 to 20 percent more – and very likely would be much less. Providing government paid nursing home benefits to those who do recover, with the amount of benefit set in advance to be a certain number of days or dollars, would seem to be good way, at relatively modest costs, to guarantee all elderly some nursing home coverage when they need it, without either creating distortive incentives or inequities. Indeed, the only additional incentive offered by such a program would be an incentive to recover, in order to collect one's insurance benefits, which seems to be a beneficial incentive. Two well-designed studies show that the availability of subsidized formal community care did not result in a reduction in informal care giving [Kemper (1988), Edelman/Hughes (1990)]. This is not quite the same thing as saying that the demand for formal care will not increase when it is insured – even if the formal services complement (rather than substitute for) family provided services.

5 Nursing Home Coverage for People with Dependents

As already noted, the primary function of long term care insurance that covers the cost of nursing home care is to protect the bequest to heirs. Whether there is social benefit from such protection would appear to depend largely on whether or not the heirs were dependents of the user of the nursing home. The most obvious circumstance in which such a dependent would be of considerable importance would be in the case of a parent of minor children who is forced to use a nursing home. In such a case, the cost of nursing home care could substantially reduce the income and assets a family can make available for its minor children, with adverse consequences in terms of their standard of living and in terms of the well being or peace of mind of both parents, the incapacitated one and the healthy one. Thus, a very strong case can be made for the provision of coverage against the cost of nursing home care for parents with minor children. A reformed Medicaid program would provide such coverage, or would subsidize private insurance to provide such coverage. Although it is too complex a topic to discuss here, the various rules states now use to limit long term care benefits to the non-elderly (principally requirements that they be disabled for several years) could usefully be reexamined.

Of course, the likelihood that a person young enough to have minor children will need to go into a nursing home is much lower than the likelihood of nursing home care for widows or widowers or elderly persons whose children are grown. However, precisely for that reason, such insurance coverage would be relatively inexpensive, and yet it would be highly valuable in the rare but possible circumstance in which nursing home care is needed.

It appears, somewhat surprisingly, that purchase of private insurance coverage against the cost of nursing home care for people with minor dependents is currently relatively rare. Loss-of-income coverage or disability coverage is typically obtained by workers, but this coverage usually only replaces a portion of lost wages and does not take into account additional expenses that might be associated with nursing home use. It is in fact a puzzle as to why the private market has not been more aggressive in marketing such coverage, although it is interesting that when employers have made such coverage available, the highest rate of purchase does seem to be among young parents rather than among middle aged workers with grown children.

Even in this case, however, one possible explanation for the absence of coverage is the fact that, once the person in the nursing home dies, their claim on family consumption will cease. The fact that young parents are likely also to be workers, either in the market or in the household, probably means that the net impact on net family consumption opportunities from the death of either parent is likely to be highly negative. Therefore, coverage against the cost of nursing home care would seem to make sense.

Things are somewhat more complicated in the case of elderly persons with no dependent children, but with a spouse. That spouse is not usually a dependent of the elderly person in any physical sense (although there are exceptions). If the pension income shared by both spouses is lost on the death of one spouse, then there can be severly adverse financial consequences. But often the type of pension arrangement is one that was chosen by the family, not imposed on them. Still the combination of large nursing home bills with the potential loss of some or all of one's pension income can be a serious risk to the surviving spouse. The Medicaid program does protect some of the assets for the surviving spouse, and the fact that extended nursing home stays for such persons are more typically followed by death means that the family's remaining assets can be conserved for the survivor because the death of one of the partners, roughly speaking, cuts the family's consumption expenditures nearly in half.

Another consideration is that the person with a spouse may be less likely to use formal care (either institutional or non-institutional) than an otherwise similar uninsured person, because the spouse can provide assistance. Norton and Newhouse (1994) have argued that the ability of a spouse to provide care offsets the greater need to protect assets or income for such a spouse. If the family is impoverished by chronic illness, the spouse may not be able to continue to provide care. If there is no effect of insurance coverage on the propensity of family members to provide care – a common assertion in the literature – the Norton/ Newhouse argument is incorrect in competitive private insurance markets. Nursing home coverage when a spouse is present would be less likely to provide benefits to persons with a spouse, but it should carry a lower premium than similar insurance sold to someone with no spouse. The value of asset protection, which is what ideal insurance provides, should be greater for the household with a surviving spouse.

Norton and Newhouse raise another consideration: should "family situations" be taken into account in determining the socially optimal level of insurance coverage? They reject such considerations on grounds of "practical difficulties," but I think this rejection is both too sweeping and unnecessary. Some family situations should be considered. The presence of surviving dependents with need for asset protection is a family situation that should be taken into account. Beyond this, they are right: whether non-dependent relatives are near or distant, caring or uncaring, is not relevant as long as the presence of nursing home insurance does not affect what these relatives will do. I will come back to the question of what happens if there is moral hazard below.

From a social point of view, the question really is whether the level of asset protection Medicaid currently furnishes for the surviving spouse is socially adequate or not. Since non-housing wealth of the elderly represents a fairly small portion of the resources that fund their consumption, in general it would be hard to argue for much more generous public coverage or a higher level of protected assets for the surviving spouse. There still might be a private demand, on the part high-wealth families, to protect wealth for the surviving spouse, and (as usual) the fact that private benefits must be offset the Medicaid spend down may discourage private insurance coverage. The bottom line here seems to be, as elsewhere in this discussion, that there may some market failure in the development of insurances intended to protect the assets of relatively high wealth families. However, the practical question is whether correcting that market failure – inadequate insurance coverage for well-off heirs – really is important enough to justify a public long term care insurance program.

6 Moral Hazard and Nursing Home Care

If nursing home care were the only kind of formal care whose cost might be covered by public or private insurance, the literature appears to suggest that the problem of moral hazard need not be large, and therefore that deductibles or cost sharing are unnecessary in public or private insurances. The argument about moral hazard is based in part on introspection – no one, it is argued, would want to go to a nursing home until they needed to, and the presence of insurance would not make them more likely to want to go. In part it is based on empirical studies. While there is a wide range of estimated price elasticities, most of them are fairly small. For instance, a recent study by Reschovsky (1994) found no significant price elasticity for private pay patients, and significant but small (-0.3) elasticity for Medicaid eligibles. Assets and income have neither insignificant or small effects, a result similar to that of Sloan/Hoerger/Picone (1992).

On balance, moral hazard appears to be a minor problem for nursing home care, and therefore no tie of eligibility to ADLs or other measures of health state should really be necessary. However, as will be shown below, things are likely to be quite different for formal non-institutional care.

Some proposals for nursing home financing envision a kind of copayment, in part to make sure that the resident pays for the housing component of the stay. The Pepper commission proposed a 20% coinsurance, and Norton-Newhouse proposed cost sharing equal to an estimate of the housing cost. The "protected assets" Reformed Medicaid strategy need have no cost-sharing; the person spends their full income on the full cost of care if assets are above the limit.

7 Home Care vs. Nursing Home Care

One of the most frequently discussed issues in long term care policy is what type of insurance coverage should be provided for formal non-institutional care. People would generally prefer, studies show, to be cared for in their own homes rather than in a nursing home, and in some circumstances home care may be cheaper. This truly lower cost is not necessarily achievable, however, especially if the person needs more or less continuous care from a professional. The reason is that, in a nursing home, one health professional can care for a large number of frail people simultaneously, whereas, in the home, one professional can only care for one person. Thus, for a frail person who needs a full time care giver, there are relatively few ways in which home care actually reduces the amount of inputs provided to that person – relative to nursing home care.

Of course, the fact that household-provided inputs are typically not paid for, even under insurance coverage that pays for home care, makes the apparent cost of home care look lower than the cost of nursing home care. Care provided by family members or friends is treated, from an insurance perspective, as if it were free – but that care has a truly lower cost, compared to nursing home care, only if the family members have lower opportunity costs than nursing home employees. To the extent that the care taker is retired, the opportunity cost is in terms of the value of her lost leisure time, rather than lost wages, but still can be substantial. In addition, the space in a home may be made available at zero opportunity cost, since the family is unlikely to purchase a smaller home or apartment just because one member is in a nursing home – but even this may change over the long term. In any case, the portion of nursing home cost that represents the pure accommodation cost is relatively small.

The conclusion is that home care is generally more costly than nursing home care for elderly or incapacitated people with severe needs. It may be less costly for people with chronic illnesses who are able to be alone at night or for long periods of time, and it certainly may be less costly than an inefficiently run or overly lavish nursing home.

For an individual who would otherwise have been willing to use a nursing home, home care *may* be cheaper. It would then seem sensible that insurers, both public and private, should be willing to pay for such lower cost services which family members and the patient may prefer when there is a cost advantage. The problem, as noted above, is that making benefits available without the requirement to leave one's private home and enter a nursing home may open the flood gates to demands for assistance with activities of living on the part of much a large number of people than the number that would have been users of nursing homes. This "moral hazard" or "woodwork effect" in theory may cause the total cost of providing such coverage to a given population to be higher than the cost of paying for nursing home care alone. Indeed, studies of experiments in which both types of care were covered, in one circumstance, or in which home care was available but not covered, and the other found that the more generous coverage did not save money. More people did use home care, and quality of life was generally rated higher, but costs were either not reduced or were increased slightly. [Kemper (1988)]

A potential solution to this moral hazard dilemma is to try to limit access to home care to those who need it. One technique for doing so, which seems to hold considerable promise, is to tie eligibility for home care to a person's performance in terms of functional scales, such as the well known "Activities of Daily Living" (ADL). The hope is that it will be possible to measure the need or suitability of assistance precisely enough so that payments will only be made for whom they are suitable. There is some evidence that such devices can be effective, at least to the extent to ensuring the total costs do not rise, but the jury is still out on the definitive answer to the question. Moreover, we have no notion of whether using an administrative tool like the ADL scale might cause some people to be improperly denied benefits, and therefore to suffer a utility loss which is not directly measured. Presumably, however, since such a person would always have the option of using a nursing home, the problem is not too serious.

The most fundamental issue here is that the techniques for controlling moral hazard in the case of people with chronic illness who are incapacitated are not well evaluated. It therefore seems undesirable, at this point, to specify a particular technique as worthy of support. One alternative is to rely on vouchers or market-like choices to let people decide what sort of options they would be offered and to allow experimentation with alternatives. For instance, one approach would be to allow people to opt out of Medicaid, receive the expected value of the payments that would be made on their behalf, and use those payments to purchase insurance which does offer home care option under various restrictions [Pauly (1990)]. Information about the quality of care and the outcomes obtained would be crucial to avoid underprovision of care in this arrangement, but it probably could be done. Moreover, techniques for measuring the quality of nursing home care are reasonably well developed, and, in any case, people who have chronic illness have plenty of time for themselves or their families to asses the quality of care they are receiving – if any one is concerned about the welfare of the sick frail person.

What is also unknown is what happens if there is no coverage for non-institutional formal care. The person may go to a nursing home sooner than anticipated or desired, although this substitution is not sufficiently frequent to increase costs. The alternative, presumably, is that family and friends provide care, or that the person receives no care. The effect of payments for formal non-institutional care on wealth – the problem to which true insurance is directed – appears to be relatively small. The problem of optimal subsidies for such care (which just happens to be labelled "insurance" because the demand for care varies unpredictably) is more difficult, and obviously must be resolved politically. Here again, however, failure in private insurance markets seems much less important then getting the level, type, and conditions of eligibility for formal non-institutional care right in a reformed Medicaid program.

The crusade for benefits outside the nursing home has been the centerpiece of much of the debate on inclusion of long term care benefits in health reform. The Clinton plan in fact limited itself to proposing to add some modest home care benefits to Medicare as its contribution to this issue. However, it would seem that the decision on where to render care to the chronically ill is a relatively minor administrative matter, and would best be handled after the decisions on coverage of a given type and on the costliness of that coverage was made.

8   Insurance Coverage for Heirs

As already noted, the primary function of nursing home and other long term care insurance coverage is to protect or reduce the risk associated with bequests to heirs. If the heirs are risk averse, or if the patient has preferences as to the certainty of the estate to bequeathed, there is some efficiency gain available from insuring against the cost of nursing home care. People would rather give and receive certain bequests than risky ones. However, in a private market this insurance would probably be purchased, not by the nursing home patient, but by the heirs, since they are the ones who will benefit from it. As I have observed elsewhere, intra family dynamics may make it difficult for children to buy nursing home insurance coverage on a parent, but there is some evidence that such coverage is attractive in the private market [Pauly (1990)].

Beyond this observation, however, is there any social purpose to be served by insuring the estate available to children or other heirs or by providing public (or mandated) coverage for bequests? At one level, the answer would seem to be largely negative. It is not obvious that there is any substantial social advantage to protecting bequests given to non-dependent, non-poor heirs of elderly persons. Those individuals should, if they wish, be allowed to insure their bequests, but the modest amount of utility lost by potential market failure in the emergence of that insurance market hardly seems sufficient to justify inclusion of such benefits in a health reform package – especially since the protection of bequests to heirs has virtually nothing to do with health. Widespread private insurance would potentially alter the distribution of wealth across generations (as would alternative ways of funding public insurance) [Breyer (1991)]. If there was a social consensus on intergenerational redistribution – something that appears unlikely in the United States but might exist in Germany – a case for public insurance might exist.

However, there is a more fundamental issue that may be of some social concern, and that may be affected to some extent by the protection insurance coverage offers to heirs. It is well known that a large portion of the non-institutional care provided to people who have chronic illness and are incapacitated, especially to the frail elderly, is provided by family members. In and of itself, this fact does not suggest any necessary alteration in policy since private payment for formal versions of such care would have to come from the same family members who provide the informal care themselves. Presumably, the reason they choose to provide the care themselves, rather than hire outsiders or strangers to do it, is because, on balance, they think that they can provide better care or care at lower cost than could be available in the market. It is beyond doubt that providing such care can be a substantial burden on the family members who do so, but, in one sense, the burden of such care can be represented by the amount the family would have had to pay to hire a substitute. This is an amount which can be large, but is less than infinite.

However, there are two potential defects in the way family members are currently involved in the care of the frail elderly that might benefit from improvement. The first one is related to the fact that the need for family members to provide care is not distributed uniformly over the non-patient population. In any given family, a parent may or may not need care at some point during their lives. Those families whose parents contract illnesses which are lengthy and debilitating will generally suffer more than those families whose parents' illnesses are brief and painless before death occurs. Moreover, the number of children affects the burden per child for caring for a frail parent. If equally acceptable caregivers could be hired, the family members could spread that cost. Or the estate could be adjusted to offset divergent effort.

The second issue is that parents and children alike may prefer that the parent be cared for by a family member, rather than by a hired stranger. But the family care giver would like some respite from the continuing burden of caring for a frail elderly person. Here again, however, it seems that the cost of such assistance could be quantified, and then it would be up to the family to decide whether it is willing to pay the cost or not. The notion that a family member is being worn out by caring for a frail elderly person, when the family member could have purchased a substitute, is not an argument for government payment.

One potential solution to this problem goes back to the question of defining the elderly person's need for care, touched on earlier. If it were possible, by observing an ADL score, to judge which persons were in need of help and which not, one form an insurance could take is simply to pay a fixed dollar amount per time period, conditional on the ADL score, which a family could then use however it wished. It could use it to purchase nursing home care for the elderly person, it could use it to provide professional care at home, or it could use family members to provide the care at home and spend the money on other items of consumption which would help alleviate the burden on family members. Such an approach would also seem to be a good way to smooth the risk of parental need across families of the same size, although the question of dealing with small versus large families is a much more difficult one to answer.

9 Medicaid Incentives and the Private Purchase of Long Term Care Insurance

One potential reason for the failure of private insurance markets, of the type just discussed, to emerge in practice may be the existence of the Medicaid program. The fact that the Medicaid spend down includes private insurance benefits, when available, presumably discourages people from purchasing such private insurance. Is there any way to avoid this distorted incentive? One way to do so, which I have described elsewhere, involves permitting individuals to "voucher out" their Medicaid expenditures as a subsidy to purchase private long term care insurance of whatever type they find most pleasing, subject to some regulatory constraints on adequacy relative to Medicaid. The idea is simple: imagine that at age 64 a set of people about to become eligible for the Medicaid long term care benefits were offered a choice. They could either choose to go on Medicaid, should they need nursing home care, or they could choose to receive the current discounted value of the Medicaid payments that would have been made on their behalf as a payment to them in the form of a voucher or subsidy for purchase of private nursing home insurance. This choice would have to be made by individuals currently not suffering from chronic illness.

10 Conclusion

The precise design of an ideal social long term care insurance, I have taken pains to emphasize, must depend on a political judgment. I have no special expertise to make these choices. However, I can outline a prototype form for the ideal insurance.

This Reformed Medicaid is described by a single parameter – the maximum amount of assets that society feels must be protected. Once a person applies for Reformed Medicaid insurance coverage, he knows that his wealth will not fall below that level. There is no social purpose served by subsidizing additional insurance coverage.

An example – and it is only that – may help to illustrate these concepts. Imagine that the monthly cost of nursing home care is $4,000, of which $1,500 is room and board and the remainder represents either medical services or support services. Suppose the amount of assets that can be retained is $20,000, and consider a person who initially has $40,000 in assets and a monthly income of $2,900. Finally, assume that the amount of monthly income to be retained for incidentals is $400. If this person entered a nursing home, she would initially pay the full cost herself, using $2,500 of income and $1,500 of assets per month. After approximately 13 months, the person's assets would have been drawn down to $20,000. From that point onwards, $2,500 of the nursing home cost would be covered by the person's income. She would be guaranteed $400 of spending money each month and an estate of $20,000. (If she recovered from her illness, her asset portfolio could be increased, if the "wait and see" option is added to the plan.)

Contrast this scheme with the alternatives. If she had to pay for room and board, as under the Norton-Newhouse or ACP-AGS proposals,[1] she would retain $1,400 per month, but have to pay 20% coinsurance ($500) on the $2,500 per month "medical services" portion of the nursing home cost, or a net of $900. If her monthly income were higher, she would retain more of it under either of these proposals, but not under the Reformed Medicaid Proposal.[2] For instance, if her monthly income were $3,900, she would retain $1,900 under Norton-Newhouse or ACP-AGS, in contrast to the $900 retained under Reformed Medicaid. It is unclear what social objective is served by spending public funds so that non-poor nursing home residents can have more spending money. It will, however, be necessary to permit persons receiving home or community based care to retain some income for room and board . So some judgments will have to be made as to what constitutes an adequate exclusion.

The design features of Reformed Medicaid might need to be modified if either nursing home care or the use of home and community services are highly responsive to the presence of insurance. As already noted in the discussion of home care, basing the public payment – any payment – on ADLs or some other clear indicator of need is one way to control inappropriate use. The question is whether such an eligibility standard is flexible and enforceable enough to control such additional use as is regarded as undesirable. After all, for those who believe that some chronically ill persons are going without home and community services that they ought to have because they are unwilling to pay their cost out of pocket, some increase in use – some moral hazard – is positively desirable (and not immoral).

If it happens that basing eligibility on ADLs or other forms of case management is incapable of restraining excessive use, then some copayment might be added. In order to make the copayment function as an effective deterrent, one might argue for allowing people to retain excess assets or income. That is, since care becomes free when a person spends down, it might in theory be desirable to allow people to retain some assets to make it less likely they will hit this free care level. However, our knowledge of whether this elaboration would be effective is so minimal that it seems undesirable to start with it. Should Reformed Medicaid trigger an explosion in the use of home and community services, despite the presence of care management, copayment combined with high asset limits could be added.

The overall design of an ideal program can be based on a rationalized and reformed version of the Medicaid program. I realize that the Medicaid program, across the board, has a bad reputation. Part of this bad reputation arises from the stinginess of many state programs. However, since the same stingy taxpayers would have to support a federal program, there is no design feature to make the stinginess go away (short of abolishing democracy, or, perhaps, taking the dangerous step of fully public insurance with no means test). It also acquired a bad reputation because of poor administration, and scandals, which imply that a federal program, also unlikely to be inoculated against defects in our fallen natures, should at least be held to minimum intervention and maximum scrutiny.

The main point of this paper is to argue that there is a case for the public provision of long term care insurance, but that most of that provision could be accommodated by a broadening and rationalization of the Medicaid program. Fundamentally, I believe that the Medicaid program represents the soundest structure for subsidizing nursing home care and other care needs of the long term chronically ill. It needs to be improved in the case of chronically ill people with dependents, especially for people below age 65 who are parents, and there are some modifications that could be made to the asset test – as a function of recovery – that could improve matters.

What is definitely not needed is a broad-scale general new entitlement for long term care coverage, especially if such coverage is made available to the widowed or single elderly with no dependents. Paying for coverage for these individuals would only help to smooth out the estates that they leave to heirs, but would do little good for the beneficiaries themselves or for society.

A case can be made, I believe, that the quality of care available under current Medicaid levels of reimbursement is too low, and I have offered some reasons why it may be difficult for persons who might want to supplement or "top out" Medicaid payments in order to achieve higher quality will find it difficult to do so. Fundamentally, I believe, however, the main guard against excessively low quality under Medicaid is the political process itself. It is not at all obvious to me that the level of quality provided by the Medicaid program represents a level below the minimum adequate amount society would want to make available to all its members. It is difficult to think of a reason why the political process would choose levels of quality below that which voters really prefer – and are willing to pay for. Perhaps permitting individuals to use more of their own assets and wealth to purchase long term care coverage might help them improve quality and do no harm, but it may also lead to invidious comparisons of quality levels achieved and distorted incentives.

Most fundamentally, the long term care system is the least in need of repair of all the nation's health care systems. There are some relatively modest steps that can be taken to improve it, but much of the dissatisfaction we all feel with that system is related not to things that government, or any creation of human imagination, can improve, but instead is related to the universal disquiet we all feel at the inevitability of old age and the frailty which often accompanies it. We cannot expect the government to repeal the aging process, and perhaps it is too much to expect it to make improvements in the financing of the inevitable without doing more harm than good. For those who are optimistic about the capability of government to manage the system and itself, there are some small improvements that could be considered. For those more skeptical of the ability of government to do anything but solve the most serious problems, it might be better to leave well enough alone.

Notes

[1] The ACP-AGS proposal would also include a 3-month deductible, and the cost-sharing would only apply to home and community based non-residential services.

[2] The ACP-AGS discussion is not clear on this matter. In that proposal, residents of nursing homes "would pay, *at a minimum*, an amount equal to the average living costs in the state or area (one-bedroom apartment, food, and basic necessities)" (emphasis added). It is unclear from this whether residents who have high incomes would be required to pay more than this minimum. An obscure discussion of the role of "market forces" in setting the rate is not illuminating.

References

Breyer, F. (1991): Verteilungswirkungen unterschiedlicher Formen der Pflegevorsorge, in *Finanzarchiv N.F. 49*, 84-103.

CBO (1991): *Policy Choices for Long-Term Care*. Washington, DC: US Congress.

Edelman, P./Hughes, S. (1990): The Impact of Community Care on Provision of Informal Care to Homebound Elderly Persons, in *Journal of Gerontology 45*, 74-584.

Kemper, P. (1988): The Evaluation of the National Long Term Care Demonstration: Overview of Findings, in *Health Services Research 23*, 161-174.

Norton, E.C./Newhouse, J.P. (1994): Policy Options for Public Long Term Care Insurance, in *Journal of the American Medical Association 271*, 1520-1524.

Pauly, M.V. (1990): The Rational Nonpurchase of Long Term Care Insurance, in *Journal of Political Economy 98*, 153-168.

Reschovsky, J. (1994): *The Role of Medicaid and Economic Factors in Nursing Home Markets*. Working paper presented at Annual Health Economics Conference: University of Pennsylvania.

Scalon, W. (1988): A perspecitive on Long-term Care for the Elderly, in *Health Care Financing Review 10*, Annual Supplement, 7-15.

Short, P.F./Kemper, P./Cornelius, L.S./Walden, D.C. (1992): Public and Private Responsibility for Financing Nursing Home Care: The Effect of Medicaid Asset Spend-down, in *Milbank Memorial Fund Quarterly 10*, 277-298.

Sloan, F.A./Hoerger, J.J./Picone, G. (1992): Effects of Strategic Behavior and Public Subsidies on Families' Savings and Long Term Care Provision. Working paper: Vanderbilt University, forthcoming in: *Journal of Health Economics*.

Wiener, J. (1994): Financing of Long-Term Care: A Proposal by the American College of Physicians and the American Geriatrics Society, in *Journal of the American Medical Association 271*, 1525-1529.

Subject Index

4 % Fallacy **5**, 103
Accomodation costs **8**, 163
Activities of Daily Living (ADL) **2**, 26; **3**, 55; **6**, 117; **7**, 128; **9**, 172; **12**, 255; **14**, 320
Affective relationship **12**, 256
Age structure **12**, 251
Altruism **3**, 45; **11**, 242; **12**, 259
Altruistic externality **14**, 310
Ambulant social services **9**, 178
Asset
   accumulation **3**, 46; **11**, 228
   protection **14**, 314
Asymmetry in preferences **3**, 47
Bargaining models **12**, 258
Bargaining power **3**, 51; **12**, 259
Benefits
   in cash **2**, 29; **6**, 117; **8**, 158; **10**, 190; **13**, 291
   in kind **2**, 29; **6**, 121; **8**, 158; **10**, 190; **13**, 291
Bequest
   motive **3**, 47
   unexpected **12**, 257
Beveridgian model **8**,157
Bismarckian approach **8**, 157
Care
   community **3**, 50; **6**, 117; **8**, 152; **14**, 317
   formal **2**, 29; **3**, 46; **7**, 126; **12**, 252; **14**, 311
   informal **2**, 29; **3**, 46; **4**, 92; **6**, 115; **7**, 126; **11**, 242; **12**, 252; **14**, 310
   institutional **2**, 34; **6**, 117; **8**, 150; **11**, 227; **13**, 291; **14**, 312
   home **2**, 29; **6**, 119; **7**, 125; **8**, 160; **10**, 183; **12**, 252; **13**, 291;

14, 312
  plan **6**,118; **7**, 126; **13**, 286
  probabilities **10**, 183
  quality **6**, 122; **8**, 164; **9**, 178; **13**, 285; **14**, 309
  services (and related goods) **7**, 127; **10**, 202; **12**, 253; **13**, 285
  stationary **9**, 180; **10**, 187
Case managed care **7**, 126
Case management **7**, 126; **14**, 327
Categorial approach **8**, 156
Channeling experiment **7**, 125
Club goods **12**, 255
Cognitive disabilities **6**, 117; **9**, 175
Cognitively unaware persons **3**, 60
Community
  Long-Term Care Insurance (CLTCI) **6**, 115
  service **6**, 120; **7**, 127; **8**, 152; **14**, 326
Compulsory health insurance **6**, 116
Contributions (to LTCI) **10**, 201
Cooperation gains **12**, 256
Cooperative behavior **12**, 257
"Cost explosion" **4**, 79; **10**, 181
Costs of LTC **10**, 181; **12**, 255; **14**, 308
Decision model(s) **12**, 251
Decisions
  Family **3**, 45; **12**, 251
  Household **12**, 252
  Intra-family **3**, 45; **12**, 258
Degree of
  disability **2**, 26; **9**, 172
  dependency **6**, 118
Dementia **9**, 177; **12**, 253
Demographic ageing **11**, 225

Demographic development **8**, 149; **9**, 180; **10**, 182
Dependence on care **8**, 151; **9**, 172
Disability ratios **2**, 32
Diseases
  chronic **1**, 12; **5**, 106; **9**, 172
Displacement **7**, 130
Dynamic equilibrium **1**, 12
Dynamic strategic cooperative games **12**, 259
Eligibility standard(s) **3**, 50; **14**, 326
Eligibility criteria **6**, 117; **7**, 128
Entry barriers **13**, 292
Environment
  living **13**, 287
Event history analysis **5**, 104
Expenditure for care services **13**, 286
Financing LTC **6**, 118; **13**, 299; **14**, 308
Goal attainment **13**, 291
Goods
  experience **13**, 288
Government failure **14**, 309
Grade of dependence **10**, 185
Health
  care **4**, 79; **7**, 127; **13**, 287; **14**, 308
  expectancy **1**, 11
  insurance **3**, 48; **6**, 116; **8**, 151; **10**, 184; **11**, 230; **14**, 315
  status **1**, 12; **5**, 108; **13**, 290
Health shock **3**, 46
Hours
  of formal care **3**, 59; **7**, 130
  of informal care **3**, 59; **7**, 130; **12**, 263

SUBJECT INDEX

Household
  equivalent APW income **2**, 37
  productivity **12**, 255
  production **4**, 81; **7**, 130; **11**, 232; **12**, 255
  utility function **12**, 258
Implicit contract **11**, 236; **12**, 256
Incentive compatibility **11**, 236; **12**, 256
Infratest Care-Interval-Model **9**, 172
Institutionalization
  determinants of **5**, 103; **12**, 253
  probability (life-time) **3**, 51; **5**, 105
  rate of **5**, 104; **6**, 115
  risk of **5**, 106; **7**, 133
Instrumental Activities of Daily Living (IADL) **2**, 26; **3**, 55; **7**, 128, **9**, 172; **12**, 255
Insurance
  arrangements **14**, 309
  coverage **6**, 119; **14**, 308
  principle **6**, 117
  private **3**, 46; **6**, 123; **8**, 153; **14**, 308
  public **10**, 181; **14**, 320
  social **13**, 285; **14**, 307
  statutory LTC **13**, 285
Insurance systems
  Bismarckian **8**, 157
  Jeffersonian **14**, 309
  tax financed **2**, 29; **14**, 313
Israel
  LTC-system **6**, 115
  social security administration **6**, 116;
Jeffersonian model **14**, 309
Joint production **12**, 255

Labo(u)r
  force participation **4**, 85; **8**, 153; **10**, 190; **12**, 252
  equivalent average production worker **2**, 36
Life
  cycle **12**, 254
  expectancy **1**, 11; **2**, 35; **5**, 104; **8**, 149; **10**, 182
  increment-decrement life table **1**, 14
  table **1**, 13; **5**, 106
Life expectancy
  disability free **1**, 12; **2**, 35
Living arrangements **7**, 125; **12**, 254; **13**, 297
LTC
  classification of **2**, 26
  compulsory **11**, 225
  costs **7**, 126; **8**, 160; **10**, 181; **12**, 255; **14**, 314
  demand for **13**, 292; **14**, 314
  expenditure **2**, 31; **6**, 115; **10**, 182; **13**, 294; **14**, 315
  institutional **4**, 79
  optimal purchase **11**, 237
  systems **2**, 25
Market failure **14**, 308
Market transparence **13**, 288
Markov chain **7**, 131
Medicaid **3**, 46; **7**, 125; **14**, 311
Medical service of health insurance (MDK) **10**, 185
Medicare **3**, 56; **7**, 128; **14**, 312
Moral hazard **11**, 225; **12**, 256, **14**, 314
Morbidity
  compression of **1**, 12

Mortality
  decline in **1**, 11
Multinomial logit model **7**, 132
Nash equilibrium **3**, 51; **12**, 257
National Insurance Institute (NII) **6**, 116
National Long-Term Care Survey (NLTCS) **3**, 46
National Nursing Home Survey (NNHS) **3**, 56
Non-professional carers **10**, 186
Non-Cooperative behaviour **12**, 258
Nonpurchase (of LTC insurance) **3**, 48
Number of frail people **10**, 182
Nursing home care **2**, 29; **3**, 48; **7**, 125; **10**, 184; **13**, 286; **14**, 310
Nursing homes **3**, 55; **5**, 112; **6**, 116; **7**, 125; **8**, 151; **10**, 184; **13**, 288; **14**, 310
Old age homes **6**, 116; **8**, 159
OLS **4**, 89
Optimal choice of
  nursing home care **3**, 47
  formal care **3**, 47
  informal care **3**, 47
Optimal response functions **3**, 47
Organizational structure **13**, 289
Panel data **2**, 32; **5**, 104
Pareto principle **12**, 259
Pension insurance **8**, 154; **10**, 193
Performance indicators **2**, 26
Personal care **6**, 116; **7**, 127; **8**, 150; **13**, 287
PflEG-Project **2**, 25
Preferences of
  parent **3**, 47
  child **3**, 47
  consumer **13**, 288
Prices of formal care **3**, 49; **12**, 263
Principal agent
  relationships **11**, 226; **12**, 256
Principle of the provision of
  services in kind **8**, 158
Private insurance **2**, 29; **3**, 46, **6**, 123; **8**, 153; **11**, 226; **14**, 308
Probability
  of entering a nursing home **3**, 46; **5**, 105; **7**, 134
  of entry **3**, 46
  of receipt of Medicaid **3**, 55
Professional caregivers **10**, 193
Provider client relationships **13**, 290
Provision of Long-Term Care
  women's role **4**, 79
Public insurance **2**, 29; **10**, 184; **14**, 320
Quality
  appropriate level of **13**, 286
  assessment **13**, 287
  assurance **13**, 290
  concept **13**, 291
  control **13**, 289
  dimensions **13**, 286
  evaluation **13**, 288
  macro **13**, 295
  micro **13**, 295
  of care **6**, 122; **8**, 164; **9**, 178; **13**, 285; **14**, 309
  of life **7**, 126; **13**, 286
  standards **8**, 164; **9**, 179
  structure **13**, 189
Rectangularization **1**, 12
Reformed Medicaid **14**, 315

SUBJECT INDEX 335

Regression model
  log-linear **5**, 104; **7**, 132
Regulatory standards **13**, 290
Reimbursement
  prospective **13**, 293
Residential care **8**, 152
Retirement
  age of **4**, 86; **5**, 112; **8**, 154
Reversed mortgage **11**, 226
Rotten kid theorem **11**, 226
Reservation wage
  for caregiving **4**, 79
  gender specific **4**, 80
Savings **3**, 45; **10**, 185
Savings, precautionary **12**, 257
Sheltered housing **5**, 112; **6**, 116
Sick funds **4**, 84; **6**, 116; **8**, 158; **10**, 189; **12**, 278
Social assistance **2**, 30; **5**, 107; **8**, 154; **10**, 192; **13**, 294
Social equalization system **8**, 154
Social insurance **8**, 152; **10**, 181; **13**, 296; **14**, 307
Social maintenance system **8**, 154
Social services
  ambulant **9**, 178
Socio-Economic Panel (SOEP) **2**, 32; **5**, 104
Stackelberg leader **12**, 257
Standardized model cases **2**, 26
Strategic bequest model **3**, 46
Sullivan's value method **1**, 13
Supplemental security income **7**, 127
Transaction costs **4**, 82; **11**, 228; **12**, 255
Transfer payments **11**, 226
Transfers
  in kind **3**, 45; **10**, 184
  in cash **3**, 45; **10**, 184
  inter vivos **12**, 256
Trust Saving **11**, 225
Unemployment insurance **8**, 154
Universal approach **6**, 118; **8**, 156
Voucher **4**, 80; **14**, 322
Wage rate **3**, 49; **11**, 130; **12**, 274
Welfare economics **14**, 308

Developments in Health Economics and Public Policy

1. P. Zweifel and H.E. Frech III (eds.):
   Health Economics Worldwide. 1992   ISBN 0-7923-1219-8
2. P. Zweifel:
   Bonus Options in Health Insurance. 1992   ISBN 0-7923-1722-X
3. J.R.G. Butler:
   Hospital Cost Analysis. 1995   ISBN 0-7923-3247-4
4. M. Johannesson:
   *Theory and Methods of Economic Evaluation
   of Health Care.* 1996   ISBN 0-7923-4037-X
5. R. Eisen and F.A. Sloan:
   *Long-Term Care: Economic Issues and
   Policy Solutions.* 1996   ISBN 0-7923-9824-6

KLUWER ACADEMIC PUBLISHERS — BOSTON / DORDRECHT / LONDON